Software Engineering: Principles and Applications

Software Engineering: Principles and Applications

Edited by **Tom Halt**

New York

Published by NY Research Press,
23 West, 55th Street, Suite 816,
New York, NY 10019, USA
www.nyresearchpress.com

Software Engineering: Principles and Applications
Edited by Tom Halt

International Standard Book Number: 978-1-63238-493-5 (Hardback)

Printed in the United States of America.

Contents

Preface VII

Chapter 1   **The Establishment of Three-Dimensional Model of Human Knee Joint** 1
Ziyue Liu, Fuzhong Wang

Chapter 2   **E-Learning Optimization using Supervised Artificial Neural-Network** 6
Mohamed Sayed, Faris Baker

Chapter 3   **Formalization of Federated Schema Architectural Style Variability** 15
Wilhelm Hasselbring

Chapter 4   **Automatic Accompaniment to Arab Vocal Improvisation: From Technical to Commercial Perspectives** 36
Fadi M. Al-Ghawanmeh, Zaid R. Shannak

Chapter 5   **The *IRIS* Development Platform and Proposed Object-Oriented Data Base** 46
Mihai-Octavian Dima

Chapter 6   **Enhancing ERS-A Algorithm for Pattern Matching (EERS-A)** 54
Dima Suleiman, Mariam Itriq, Aseel Al-Anani, Rola Al-Khalid, Amjad Hudaib

Chapter 7   **A MATLAB-Based Numerical and GUI Implementation of Cross-Gradients Joint Inversion of Gravity and Magnetic Data** 65
Junjie Zhou, Xingdong Zhang, Chunxiao Xiu

Chapter 8   **Automatic and Manual Proliferation Rate Estimation from Digital Pathology Images** 74
Lama Rajab, Heba Z. Al-Lahham, Raja S. Alomari, Fatima Obaidat, Vipin Chaudhary

Chapter 9   **Quantifying Reusability of Object Oriented Design: A Testability Perspective** 81
Mahfuzul Huda, Yagya Dutt Sharma Arya, Mahmoodul Hasan Khan

Chapter 10   **Four Sliding Windows Pattern Matching Algorithm (FSW)** 90
Amjad Hudaib, Rola Al-Khalid, Aseel Al-Anani, Mariam Itriq, Dima Suleiman

Chapter 11   **Semantic Enrichment of XML Schema to Transform Association Relationships in ODL Schema** 102
Doha Malki, Mohamed Bahaj

Chapter 12   **E-Government Strategy and Plans in Jordan** 112
Yousef Kh. Majdalawi, Tamara Almarabeh, Hiba Mohammad, Wala Quteshate

Chapter 13   **Automatic Synchronization of Common Parameters in Configuration Files** 125
Moupojou Matango Emmanuel, Moukouop Nguena Ibrahim

Chapter 14   **Reusable Function Discovery by Call-Graph Analysis**   134
              Dan Zhao, Li Miao, Dafang Zhang

Chapter 15   **ADTEM-Architecture Design Testability Evaluation Model to Assess Software
              Architecture Based on Testability Metrics**   142
              Amjad Hudaib, Fawaz Al-Zaghoul, Maha Saadeh, Huda Saadeh

Chapter 16   **The Research of Event Detection and Characterization Technology of Ticket Gate
              in the Urban Rapid Rail Transit**   152
              Yunfeng Hou, Chaoli Wang, Yunfeng Ji

Chapter 17   **Towards Designing an Intelligent Educational Assessment Tool**   162
              Tháir Hamtini, Shahd Albasha, Marwa Varoca

Chapter 18   **Content-Based Image Retrieval Using SOM and DWT**   170
              Ammar Huneiti, Maisa Daoud

Chapter 19   **Comparative Analysis of Operating System of Different Smart Phones**   181
              Naseer Ahmad, Muhammad Waqas Boota, Abdul Hye Masoom

Chapter 20   **Timed-Automata Based Model-Checking of a Multi-Agent System: A Case Study**   194
              Nadeem Akhtar, Muhammad Nauman

Chapter 21   **Analyzing the Impact of Different Factors on Software Cost Estimation in
              Today's Scenario**   202
              Deepa Gangwani, Saurabh Mukherjee

Chapter 22   **A Blind DWT-SCHUR Based Digital Video Watermarking Technique**   209
              Lama Rajab, Tahani Al-Khatib, Ali Al-Haj

Chapter 23   **Optimizing Software Effort Estimation Models using Firefly Algorithm**   219
              Nazeeh Ghatasheh, Hossam Faris, Ibrahim Aljarah, Rizik M. H. Al-Sayyed

Chapter 24   **Multimedia Internet-Based Platform Project for Saudi Students' English
              Language Learning**   229
              Basim H. Alahmadi

Chapter 25   **Toward Developing a Syllabus-Oriented Computer-Based Question-Banks
              Software to Support Partially Computerized Exams**   235
              Sulieman Bani-Ahmad

Chapter 26   **Metric Based Testability Estimation Model for Object Oriented Design:
              Quality Perspective**   252
              Mahfuzul Huda, Yagya Dutt Sharma Arya, Mahmoodul Hasan Khan

Chapter 27   **Distributed C-Means Algorithm for Big Data Image Segmentation on a Massively
              Parallel and Distributed Virtual Machine Based on Cooperative Mobile Agents**   262
              Fatéma Zahra Benchara, Mohamed Youssfi, Omar Bouattane, Hassan Ouajji,
              Mohammed Ouadi Bensalah

              Permissions

              List of Contributors

Preface

Software engineering deals with designing codes and programs for universal audience or customized application for a small organization. Softwares are designed with the help of programming languages such as java, C++, and COBOL. This book primarily deals with the core subjects of software engineering such as knowledge acquisition, automated software design and synthesis, automated software specification, software design methods, software domain modeling and meta-modeling, software engineering decision support, etc. The various advancements in this field are glanced at and their applications as well as ramifications are looked at in detail. This book elucidates the principles, concepts and innovative models around prospective developments with respect to this discipline. Students, researchers, experts and all associated with software engineering will benefit alike from this book.

After months of intensive research and writing, this book is the end result of all who devoted their time and efforts in the initiation and progress of this book. It will surely be a source of reference in enhancing the required knowledge of the new developments in the area. During the course of developing this book, certain measures such as accuracy, authenticity and research focused analytical studies were given preference in order to produce a comprehensive book in the area of study.

This book would not have been possible without the efforts of the authors and the publisher. I extend my sincere thanks to them. Secondly, I express my gratitude to my family and well-wishers. And most importantly, I thank my students for constantly expressing their willingness and curiosity in enhancing their knowledge in the field, which encourages me to take up further research projects for the advancement of the area.

Editor

The Establishment of Three-Dimensional Model of Human Knee Joint

Ziyue Liu, Fuzhong Wang

Department of Physics, Tianjin Polytechnic University, Tianjin, China
Email: liufred@live.cn

Abstract

Objective: To discuss a method to establish a three-dimensional model of healthy human knee joint, which can be used for further knee joint biomechanics analysis and simulation. Methods: CT scan and medical image three-dimensional reconstruction software (Mimics) were used to obtain the knee joint three-dimensional finite element model (FEM) according to reverse engineering theory. Results: FEM of knee joint with complete bone structure was established by Mimics. Conclusion: Three-dimensional FEM was established according to CT images exports as IGES file. The model can be used for knee joint biomechanics finite element analysis to provide references and proposals for the clinical diagnoses of knee joint illness, and the design of artificial knee joint prosthesis.

Keywords

Knee Joint, Mimics, Three-Dimensional Model

1. Introduction

With the weight-bearing and motor function, knee joint is the most complex joint in human body. It is easily hurt or caught various diseases due to the mechanical environment and movement condition it is located. With the fastest-ageing society on earth, osteoarthritis and other diseases related will be a hot spot and it will affect people's life standard. Reinforcing the research capacity has a magnificent meaning for improving elder people's living quality. Current studies consider that the mechanism of osteoarthritis no matter caused by sports injuries or cartilage failure is the improper stress distribution in the joint [1]-[4]. It is hard to explain the mechanism of stress transfer and distribution by traditional biomechanics research. With the assistance of finite element analysis, we can stimulate movement of joint in various conditions, and by this way we can acknowledge the stress distribution in different parts. To establish a relatively complete finite element model of the health human knee joint with proper mechanical properties and anatomy structure is the basis for further research and provides a digital experiment platform for repeated stimulation. In this paper, we introduce a method to establish three-dimensional finite element model of human knee joint based on CT images and conduct a simple analysis on the model to verify its accuracy. The main procedure of our research is shown in **Figure 1**. This process is somewhat like 3-D printing technology that both are the procedure of 3-D model reestablishment. While 3-D printing is to rebuild a real object according to the digital data, the model established in this essay is stored as electronic document available for knee joint finite element analysis.

2. Materials and Methods

2.1. Devices and Software

Computer (CPU: Intel® Core™ i5-2430 2.40 GHz*2, RAM: 8.00 GB, GPU: GT-540M, OS: win7), CT images, Mimics medical image three-dimensional rebuilding software, Ansys 11.0 finite element analysis software. The CT images come from the database of visible human project of the US national library of medicine. 800 1 mm scanned healthy woman lower limbs CT images were downloaded as Dicom format. Mimics was programmed in 1992 and widely used in digital medical field. The initial propose was to apply CT scan images in rapid prototyping manufacturing. With the growing improvement, it is now widely used in Computer-Aided Mechanical Engineering, including medical three-dimensional modeling based on medical images, computer-aided design, finite element and hydromechanics analysis, rapid prototyping manufacturing, visual operation planning, anthropotomy measurement analysis, etc. Ansys is a powerful engineering stimulation software widely used in many fields including structural mechanics, multiphysics, fluid dynamics, explicit dynamics, electromagnetics, and hydrodynamics.

2.2. Experiment Method

1) Input the data of the model: import the 800 Dicom CT images to Mimics. Original axial view, coronal plane and vertical plane from the scanned data was observed as **Figure 2**.

2) Rebuild the three-dimensional model: image thresholding segmentation was the first step of the modeling procedure and mask was obtained. Since it is the knee joint that need modeling, we selected the object region by "region growing" in the toolbar, shown as **Figure 3**, distal femur, patella, tibial plateau of the right leg was selected. The default gray value of the bone is only reference, the auto generated mask may not cover all the bone in the region. There would be a lot of small cracks, bumps and pits, shown as **Figure 4**. We need to modify the mask until all the area is covered completely. At last "smooth object" option was used to optimize the model produced, the knee joint model is shown as **Figure 5**.

3) Preliminary treatment of the finite element analysis: before the analysis, the model needed to be meshed to finite element grid model, this was obtained by FEA module in Mimics. The grid was optimized by remesh module. The finite element model (**Figure 6**) was obtained for further research.

4) Apply material properties to the model:

The parameters in **Table 1** were preferred from previous literature [5].

5) Loads and boundary conditions: approximately 40% of the body weight is applied to each knee when standing. In this paper, we consume the total weight is 60 Kg, so 235 N was applied on the mechanical axis of

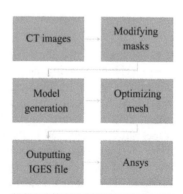

Figure 1. Research procedure.

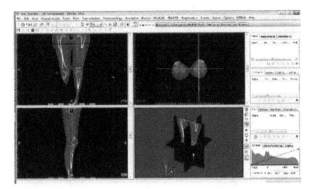

Figure 2. Lower limbs tomoscan.

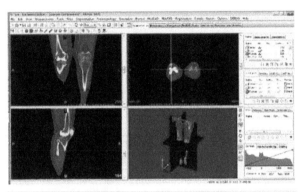

Figure 3. Region selected.

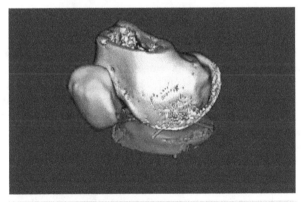

Figure 4. Flaw of the original model.

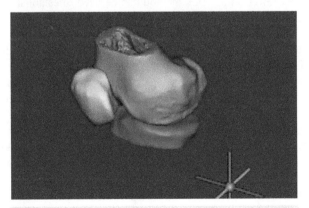

Figure 5. Model after optimization.

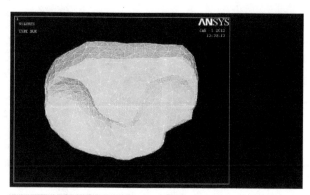

Figure 6. The gridded tibial plateau.

Table 1. Material properties of the components of the knee joint model.

Material	Young's modulus (MPa)	Poisson's radio (µ)
Femur	12,000	0.3
Tibia	6900	0.49
Patella	12,000	0.3

the top femur. The boundary condition was set that tibia and femur were kept fixed in all direction. The model was solved by Ansys 11.0.

3. Results

In this paper, we established the model of a healthy human knee joint, and conducted biomechanics analysis to it. **Figure 7** shows the Von Mises stress distribution of the tibial plateau.

Von Mises stress was chosen to evaluate the stress index in this analysis. It is a combined stress defined according to the 4th strength theory reflecting the average stress level each dot inside the material, and one of the most objective indices in finite element analysis [5]. The maximum of the Mises stress locates in the contact region of femoral condyle and tibial plateau. The maximum stress is 25 MPa at the edge of the tibial plateau. The result is corresponded with clinical cases that injury of inner side meniscus and tibial plateau is more common and the maximum of the Von Mises stress accord with other researches [6]. This means that the model established can be used to present the authentic status of human knee joint.

4. Discussion

In this research, we built the knee joint model including distal femur, patella, and tibial plateau precisely based on the CT images of human lower limbs. This method can be used to establish knee joint model fast and accurately, and the file is suitable to directly transfer to finite element analysis software (Ansys) for biomechanics simulation.

However, the soft tissue of the knee joint (ligament, joint capsule, synovial fluid, etc.) was not obtained. This is due to the fact that CT image cannot provide the soft tissue outline as clear as the bone tissue [7]. To accomplish this part, one way is to depict the soft tissue according to the anatomy structure of knee joint on the CT-conducted model which may contribute to the untruthfulness of the model because of the lack of accuracy. Another method is to use MRI image which can show soft tissue clearly [8]. We will integrate our present work with MRI image in the future.

Model with intact knee joint structure can be used in the further finite element analysis to simulate knee joint under certain conditions and the information obtained is beneficial to knee arthropathy diagnosis and knee prosthesis design [9]. The advantages of finite element analysis are evident that the model can be tested constantly, the cost is lower than traditional research, and most importantly it can reveal the inner interaction of knee joint such as the stress distribution of the surface of the tibial plateau in different gaits. These are all problems that

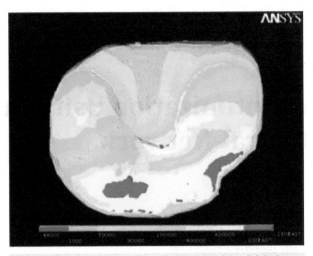

Figure 7. The Von Mises stress distribution of the tibial plateau.

traditional specimen test and clinical research cannot solve. Since 1960s, finite element method has widely applied in biomechanics analysis. It had successfully utilized in hip joint, knee joint, spine, shoulder, etc. [10]. The finite element analysis is a strong addition and useful tool in the study of biomechanics and it will become the development trend in the future.

References

[1]   Zhang, S.N. and Lu, A.Y. (2005) Animal Model of Musculoskeletal Motion Injury Research. *Chinese Journal of Sports Medicine*, **31**, 185-188.

[2]   Zhang, H.P. and Song, J.R. (2010) Establishment and Application of Animal Experimental Models of Acute Skeletal Muscle Injury. *Journal of Clinical Rehabilitative Tissue Engineering Research*, **11**, 458-463.

[3]   Zhao, T., Weng, L., You, Y.-H., *et al.* (2013) The Appearance of X-Ray and MR Imaging in Osteochondral Fracture of Knee Joint after Acute Injury. *Chinese Journal of Radiology*, **37**, 985-988.

[4]   Teng, Y., Wang, Z., Li, D.C., *et al.* (2008) Fabrication of Custom-Made Artificial Semi-Knee Joint Based on Rapid Prototyping Technique: Three-Dimensional Reconstruction of Femoral Condyle. *Chinese Journal of Reparative and Reconstructive Surgery*, **41**, 257-260.

[5]   Niu, Y.F. (2012) The Impact of Cartilage Hardening of the Knee Articular Cartilage to the Stress Distribution of Knee Joint. M.Sc. Thesis, Tianjin Polytechnic University, Tianjin.

[6]   Chantarapanich, N., Nanakorn, P., Chernchujit, B., *et al.* (2009) A Finite Element Study of Stress Distributions in Normal and Osteoarthritic Knee Joints. *Journal of the Medical Association of Thailand*, **17**, 223-226.

[7]   Gíslason, M.K., Stansfield, B. and Nash, D.H. (2010) Finite Element Model Creation and Stability Considerations of Complex Biological Articulation: The Human Wrist Joint. *Medical Engineering and Physics*, **34**, 246-249.

[8]   Luring, C., Hufner, T., Perlick, L., *et al.* (2006) The Effectiveness of Sequential Medial Soft Tissue Release on Coronal Alignment in Total Knee Arthroplasty: Using a Computer Navigation Model. *Journal of Arthroplasty*, **21**, 428-434. http://dx.doi.org/10.1016/j.arth.2005.05.031

[9]   Manda, K., Ryd, L. and Eriksson, A. (2011) Finite Element Simulations of a Focal Knee Resurfacing Implant Applied to Localized Cartilage Defects in a Sheep Model. *Journal of Biomechanics*, **44**, 794-801. http://dx.doi.org/10.1016/j.jbiomech.2010.12.026

[10] Hopkins, A.R., New, A.M., Rodriguez-y-Baena, F., *et al.* (2010) Finite Element Analysis of Unicompartmental Knee Arthroplasty. *Medical Engineering and Physics*, **15**, 347-351.

E-Learning Optimization Using Supervised Artificial Neural-Network

Mohamed Sayed[1,2], Faris Baker[1]

[1]Faculty of Computer Studies, Arab Open University, Kuwait City, Kuwait
[2]On Leave from Faculty of Engineering, Alexandria University, Alexandria, Egypt
Email: msayed@aou.edu.kw, fbaker@aou.edu.kw

Abstract

Improving learning outcome has always been an important motivating factor in educational inquiry. In a blended learning environment where e-learning and traditional face to face class tutoring are combined, there are opportunities to explore the role of technology in improving student's grades. A student's performance is impacted by many factors such as engagement, self-regulation, peer interaction, tutor's experience and tutors' time involvement with students. Furthermore, e-course design factors such as providing personalized learning are an urgent requirement for improved learning process. In this paper, an artificial neural network model is introduced as a type of supervised learning, meaning that the network is provided with example input parameters of learning and the desired optimized and correct output for that input. We also describe, by utilizing e-learning interactions and social analytics how to use artificial neural network to produce a converging mathematical model. Then students' performance can be efficiently predicted and so the danger of failing in an enrolled e-course should be reduced.

Keywords

Artificial Neural Networks, E-Learning, Prediction Models, Supervised Learning

1. Introduction

Education is imperative for every nation for it improves the life of individuals by training them with skills and knowledge that let them cope with life challenges. Technological developments today influence every aspect of life including education. Technology provides speed and convenience for people and hence becomes a vital instrument in the educational process [1]. In blended learning model [2] where face to face learning is combined with technology, students and tutors as well as other stakeholders use computers and internet to communicate and collaborate. The widespread of social networks has inspired some educational institutions to investigate the impact of this paradigm on the learning outcome. The use of internet provides opportunities to analyze the electronic activities performed for capturing patterns, trends and intelligence. In blended learning students watch interactive lectures, take quizzes through a learning management system (LMS) and hence prepare themselves for the coming face to face class with their tutors. In this way, tutors spare their time for discussion and solving student's difficulties. The LMS provides not only e-courses for students, but also a platform to communicate with peers and tutors. Anytime a student or a tutor login into the LMS, a digital record is stored representing the activities performed. In the end of each semester, a large amount of data will be generated regarding every course offered in the university. The data generated illustrate the successes, and the difficulties encountered in the learning process.

Educational theorists [3]-[5] have identified some parameters that contribute to the learning successes. These factors include student engagement, student self-regulation, student interaction with his/her peers, tutors total experience and tutors time involvement with their students. In addition, the support of the university administration contributes to a higher achievement of students as well as tutors. Moreover, a meaningful engagement which includes a high quality of discourse is imperative in learning and gives an impetus for sharing information. All these parameters have to be investigated in the large data generated during the semester and analyzed to improve and correct the process of learning [6] [7].

Inspired by advances in social networks analytics, the document analysis concept is carried out through the study of engagement in the e-learning during a semester identifying several variables that describe the student engagement. The network of co-occurrences between different variables, collected on a specific set, allows the quantitative study of the structure of contents, in terms of the nature and intensity level of correlations or interconnections. The sub-domains are placed using the structural equivalence techniques by grouping variables at different stages. A scientific field is characterized by a group of variables, which signify its concepts, operations and methodologies. The structure described by the frequency of co-occurrences of conceptual variables exposes the important relationships across these variables. These analyses of co-occurrences of variables give us the authority to comprehend the static and dynamic sides of the room in which we can relate and place their work in a hierarchy of scientific research concepts. This technique assorted as co-variable analysis, provides a direct quantitative manner of linking the conceptual contents.

According to Edelstein [8], there are five prevalent kinds of information: sequences, association, classifications, clusters and prediction. Likewise, the general purpose of neural networks is to provide powerful solutions to associations, classifications, clusters and predictions problems. Moreover, neural networks possess the destiny to impart from experience in order to change for the better by improving their performance and adapting themselves. The neural networks are also able to transact with deprecatory information (incomplete or noisy data) and can be very efficient, in particular where it is not possible to designate the patterns or steps that take part to the resolution of a problem. In many cases neural network techniques tend to be difficult to understand and there is no clear advantage over more conventional techniques. However, there are features of neural networks which distinguish them from other techniques. The fact that the network can be trained to perform a task, and the ability of the network to generalize from the training data enables it to carry out successfully when presented with a previously unseen problem.

In the present research, a normalized co-variable matrix from 56 most-used categorized variables (features or predictors) is used to study the contribution to learning process. This matrix is split using its mean density to conclude the correlation matrix and build the network map. In order to achieve higher levels of computational capacity, an exceedingly complex structure of neural networks is required. We use a multilayer perceptron neural network which maps a set of input variables onto a set of output data. It consists of multiple layers of nodes in a directed graph at which each layer is connected to the next one. It is one of the most popular and successful techniques for many subjects such as content analysis, pattern recognition and document image analysis. It is also a potent technique to solve many real world problems such as predicting time-series in monetary world, identifying clusters of valuable customers, and diagnosing medical conditions and fraud detections, (see for instance [9]-[12]).

The multilayer perceptron neural network has not been applied comprehensively, to the best of our knowledge, to e-learning optimization using supervised and unsupervised learning. The questions which arise then are whether the neural network technique is indeed appropriate to such problem, whether the architecture used to implement the technique reduces its effectiveness or complements it, and whether the technique produces a particular system that attaches to the problem.

2. Theoretical Framework and Neural Network

The aim of regression methods is to provide a definite model which can be helpful in deriving a specific group that one of the database objects belongs to based on its features. One of the usual functions of regression methods includes determining future activities of student engagement so that the institute could alter the e-learning strategy [13].

Data mining is an automatic analysis technique in large data sets whose purpose is to extract unobserved correlations (or dependencies) between the data stored in data ware houses or other relational database schemes. The end-user may even not be aware of these data correlations and dependencies, although the knowledge derived from extracting them may turn out to be exceedingly beneficial. Data mining techniques [14] may be divided into several basic groups, each sharing with specific purposes and complications. The k-nearest neighbors (k-NN) algorithm is one of the most popular and non-parametric method used in classification and regression. Its purpose is to find k-nearest neighbors of the discipline (using some predefined metrics) and ascribe it to a certain class that is predominant in all successfully found subjects. A drawback of skewed class distribution renders this method of classification less acceptable. Another commonly used technique which accepts the vantage of being comparatively unsophisticated and efficient is the naïve (or simple) discriminate analysis. There are other techniques that require a learning set form a numerous groups such as artificial neural networks, simple and oblique decision trees, and support vector machines (SVM) methods. All of these techniques are founded on a similar principle that consists of choosing a structure (for example: multi layered perception for neural networks, leaves representing class labels and branches representing conjunction of features for decision tree, and core function for the SVM method). Some of these methods consist of putting the best parameters that permit to minimize erroneous classifications on the given learning set (for instance: using the error back propagation method or optimization methods).

The artificial neural network (ANN) is a parallel and iterative method made up of simple processing units called neutrons. While a multilayer neural network is a web of simple neurons called perceptron. The principle concept of a single perceptron was introduced by Frank Rosenblatt in 1958. A multilayer perceptron neural network (MLP) is a perceptron-type network which distinguishes itself from the single-layer network by having one or more intermediate layers. Backward propagation of errors (or simply back propagation), which has been used since the 1980s to adjust the weights, is a widespread process of training artificial neural networks. It is usually used in conjunction with an optimization method such as gradient descent. In an attempt to minimize the loss function; on each of training iteration, the current gradient of a loss function with respects to all the calculated weights in the network is evaluated and then the gradient is fed to the optimization method which employs it to update the weights. In this study we selected the standard Levenber-Marquardt Algorithm (LMA) [15], a curve-fitting algorithm that minimizes the sum of the squares of errors between the data points and the parameterized loss function. In some few cases, the process of training (or learning) could lead to over (or under) training phenomena and hence one may prove that it is time-consuming.

3. Data Set Description

In order to study the variables that contribute to the learning process and to the educational outcome we propose to consider specific variables during the semester of engagement relevant to students, to the peers, to the tutor and to the university administration. The 56 variables, see **Table 1**, are categorized according to its characteristics and ownerships. Moreover, we have to decide the most suitable machine learning algorithm for the selected features regression.

Data is contextual, the sequences and the environment of the data has also to be accounted for. For example, an activity performed by a student who has a limited background is not the same as the one who has the entire necessary prerequisite. After data acquisition from the online activities performed by all participants, filtering has to be applied in order to remove irrelevant data. Once all the data are clean and relevant, a second stage of features extraction, clustering and classifications is applied in order to extract knowledge from the data. As mentioned above, there are many methods for features extraction and regression such as artificial neural network, decision tree, Markov model, Bayesian probability, principle component analysis, support vector machine, and regression analysis [16]. In this paper, the explored variables are configured in a back propagation neural network

Table 1. Categorized data set description.

Class	Variable	Full name	Class	Variable	Full name
Student online engagement	Var. 1	Login into the e-class.	Student content analysis	Var. 30	Course keywords used.
	Var. 2	Participate in the e-learning forums.		Var. 31	Question context.
	Var. 3	Starts a new thread in the forums.		Var. 32	Answer context.
	Var. 4	Reads a thread from a classmate.		Var. 33	Comment context.
	Var. 5	Votes on a post reply as "LIKE".		Var. 34	Disputation comment.
	Var. 6	Votes on a post reply as "DISLIKE".		Var. 35	Cumulative comment.
	Var. 7	Receivesa "LIKE" reply.		Var. 36	Exploratory comment.
	Var. 8	Receives a "DISLIKE" reply.		Var. 37	Effective interaction.
	Var. 9	Starts a thread that a classmate votes up.		Var. 38	Ineffective interaction.
	Var. 10	Starts a thread that a classmate votes down.	Tutors online engagement	Var. 39	Answer a question.
	Var. 11	Enters the online quizzes.		Var. 40	Give a comment.
	Var. 12	Solves the online questions.		Var. 41	Start a thread.
	Var. 13	Answers the online question at first instance.	E-course design	Var. 42	Number of questions provided.
Student self-regulation	Var. 14	Enjoyment.		Var. 43	Number of hours per week required from a student.
	Var. 15	Anxiety.		Var. 44	Personalized (relevant to student background).
	Var. 16	Boredom.	University support	Var. 45	System downtime.
	Var. 17	Hopelessness.		Var. 46	Low participated student identification.
	Var. 18	Self-efficacy.		Var. 47	High participated student identification.
	Var. 19	Effort.		Var. 48	System bandwidth.
	Var. 20	Ambition.		Var. 49	Emails send to the student.
	Var. 21	Goal oriented.		Var. 50	Emails send to the tutor.
	Var. 22	Self-organized.	Student information	Var. 51	Year of admission.
Student background	Var. 23	GPA before the e-course.		Var. 52	Semester of admission.
	Var. 24	Average grades of prerequisite courses for the e-course.		Var. 53	Total credit hours.
	Var. 25	High School GPA.		Var. 54	Number of warnings.
	Var. 26	Family education.		Var. 55	Student status.
	Var. 27	Number of family members.		Var. 56	Over all GPA.
	Var. 28	Family income.			
	Var. 29	Residency location.			

algorithm that will investigate their impact on the educational outcome.

The identified values of the variables will be used to train the neural network. For more information about the variables the reader is referred to [3] [11] [17]-[20].

4. Backward Propagation Algorithm

Multilayer neural network is a particular type of network which consists of a group of sensory units. These units are observed as cascading layers; an input layer, one (or more) intermediate-hidden layers and an output layer of neurons. The neural network is completely connected such that all neurons of each layer are connected to all neurons in the preceding layer. At the beginning of the backward propagation process we should consider how many hidden layers are required. The computational complexity can be seen by the number of single-layer networks combined into this multilayer network. In this multilayer structure, the input nodes pass the information into the units in the first hidden layer then the outputs from the first hidden layer are passed into the next layer, and so on. It is worth noting that the network is a supervised learning, *i.e.*, both the inputs and the outputs should be provided. The network processes the inputs and compares its resulting outputs against the desired corresponding outputs. Errors are then calculated, giving rise to the system to regularize the weights and control the network. This process takes place over and over as the weights are continually adjusted.

The back propagation algorithm of multilayer neural network is summarized in forward and backward stages. In the forward stage, the signal that transfers out of the network (through the network layers) is calculated as follows:

$$s_j^l = \sum_{i=0}^{n^{l-1}} w_{ji}^l \, y_i^{l-1}$$

where $l = 0, 1, \cdots, L$ are network layers indexes, $l = 0$ and $l = L$ represent the input and output layers respectively, n^l corresponds to the number of neurons in the layer l and $j = 0, 1, \cdots, n^{l-1}$. Here y_i^{l-1} is the output function corresponding to the neuron i in the previous layer $l-1$ and w_{ji}^l is the weight of the neuron j to the neuron i in the layer l. In addition to the variable weight values, an extra input that represents bias is added, *i.e.*, for $i = 0$, $y_0^{l-1} = 1$ and w_{j0}^l depict the bias that is applied to neuron j in the layer l. The output of neuron j in the layer l is given by the neuron activation function of j:

$$y_j^l = f_j\left(s_j^l\right).$$

The error at the output layer is

$$e_j^l = y_j^l - O.$$

It represents the difference between the target output for an input pattern and the network response. It is used to calculate the errors at the intermediate layers. This is done sequentially until the error at the very first hidden layer is computed. After computing the error for each unit, whether it is at a hidden unit or at an output unit, the network then fine-tunes its connection weights by performing the backward. The general idea is to use the gradient descent to update the weights so that the square error between network output values and the target output values are reduced. The backward can be performed as follows:

$$z_j^{l-1} = f'\left(s_j^{l-1}\right) \sum_{i=0}^{n^l} w_{ji}^l z_i^l$$

where $l = L, L-1, \cdots, 2$, $j = 0, 1, \cdots, n^{l-1}$ and

$$z_j^L = f'\left(s_j^L\right) e_j^L.$$

The learning rate which is a typically a small value between 0 and 1 controls the size of weight modulations. Here the derivative $f'(x)$ governs the weight adjustments, depending on the actual output $f(x)$.

The major problem in training a neural network is deciding when to stop the training. The algorithm brings to an end when the network reaches minimum errors which can be calculated by the mean square errors (MSE) between the network output values and the desired output values. The number of training and testing iterations can also be used as stopping criteria.

5. Training the Network and Discussion

Training the neural network to emerge the right output for a given input is a computational iterative procedure. The evaluated root mean square error of the neural network output (on each training iteration) and the way which the error changes with training iteration are utilized to determine the convergence of the training. The challenge is to determine which indicators and input data could be practiced, and to amass enough training data to improve the network appropriately. Many factors interact with each other to generate the observed data. These factors are organized into multiple layers, representing multiple abstractions, weights and biases. By using various numbers of layers and neurons, different levels of abstractions spawn with different features. It is possible to train a neural network to perform a particular function by adjusting the weights of the connections between the neurons. Errors are propagated backward through the network to control weight adjustments. Network layers are trained when errors fall below a threshold.

The process of training the neural network is summarized as follows: input data is continuously applied, actual outputs are calculated, and weights are adjusted such that the application of inputs produce desired outputs (as close as possible). Weights should converge to some value after many rounds of training and differences between desired and actual outputs are minimized.

In our experiment, we observed 1879 students (in one semester) using student information criteria, mentioned **Table 1**, as a sample for our educational inquiry. We used 70% of the data (1315 samples) for training, 15% of the data (282 samples) for validation, and 15% of the data (282 samples) for testing. The training data were represented to neural network, and the network was adjusted according to its error. The validation was used to measure network generalization, and to halt training when generalization stops improving as indicated by an increase in the mean square error of the validation samples. The testing data have no effect on the training; they only provide performance measurement during and after training.

The first run of the algorithm using 50 hidden neurons produced the result in **Table 2**. The Mean Square Error measured the average squared differences between outputs and targets while regression values R calculated the correlation between outputs and targets. An R value of 1 means a close relationship between the calculated output and the target while a value of 0 means no relationship. Plotting the histogram of error values, as presented in **Figure 1**, showed the majority of the points fall between −0.6 and +0.7 and mostly around 0.04 values. This indicates that the training algorithm has only few outliers and generally of a good prediction outcome. Examining the regression values R (**Figure 2**), demonstrated the validation scatter diagram, which plots the actual data from validation portion against the neural network estimate, gave a straight-line graph (independent and objective validation metric) with a slope extremely close to one and an intercept close to zero. The validation is comprehensive as the data is picked out at random over all the available data set. The training data were represented to the neural network algorithm, and the network was adjusted to minimize its error, the validation measured network generalization, and halted training when generalization stopped improving. The mean square errors stopped decreasing after iteration (epoch) 12 (**Figure 3**). During the training of the algorithm, an increase in the mean square error will stop the training of the validation samples. Bearing in mind training multiple times will

Table 2. Results of the algorithm with 50 hidden neurons.

	Samples	MSE	R
Training	1315	1.81246e−1	9.20899e−1
Validation	282	3.33569e−1	8.64064e−1
Testing	282	2.21908e−1	9.09618e−1

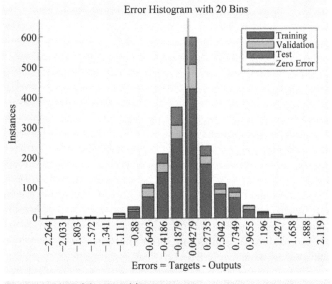

Figure 1. Plot of the error histogram.

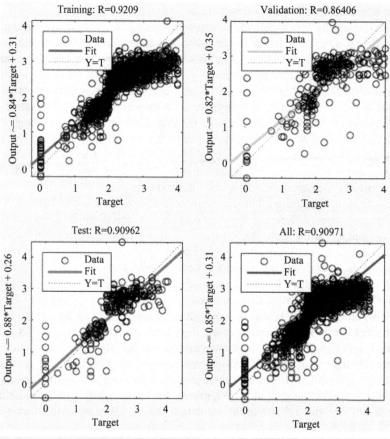

Figure 2. Plot of the regression values (R).

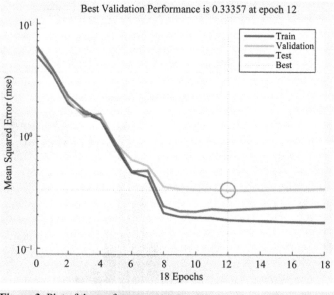

Figure 3. Plot of the performance.

generate different results due to different initial conditions and sampling.

After iteration 12, the gradient decent calculated by back propagation algorithm was not increasing and in a further 6 validation iterations, hence stopped at epoch 18 with value 0.035909 (**Figure 4**). At iteration 12, the validation stopped after 6 trails because the error between the outputs and the target values was not decreasing

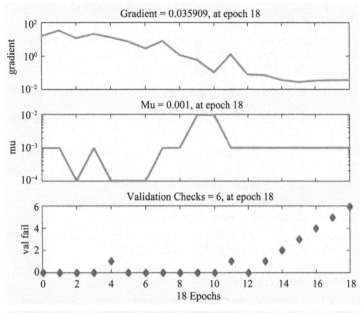

Figure 4. Plot of the training state.

further as well as Mu values. The neural network became ready and trained to perform the desired function which is to predict the Grade Point Average (GPA) for future students, provided predictors are available.

6. Conclusions

Neural networks learn from examples and capture functional relationships between variables in the data even if the underlying relationships are nonlinear or unknown. Even though neural networks are not perspicuous in their expectation, they can outperform all other methods of association, classifications, clusters and prediction of supervised and unsupervised learning as proved with their high performance prediction for non-linear systems. Furthermore, the training algorithm may change depending on the neural network structure, unless the nearly common training algorithm used when designing networks is the back-propagation algorithm. The major problem in training a neural network is deciding when to finish operations as well as the overtraining phenomena which occur when the system memorizes patterns and thus lacks the power to extrapolate.

Due to our research constraint in our experiment, we selected only subset predictors in our training algorithm for students GPA; however, in future research it can be extended to all other variables that have not been selected and hence improve the performance outcome. The nature and the causes of the correlations between the predictors have to be explored. Furthermore, there are opportunities to experiment with other learning algorithms and contrast with neural network.

References

[1] Soller, A. and Lesgold, A. (2003) A Computational Approach to Analyzing Online Knowledge Sharing Interaction. *Proceedings of Artificial Intelligence in Education*, Sydney, 20-24 July 2003, 253-260.

[2] Sayed, M. and Baker, F. (2014) Blended Learning Barriers: An Investigation, Exposition and Solutions. *Journal of Education and Practice*, **5**, 81-85.

[3] Vohs, K.D. and Baumeister, R.F. (2011) Handbook of Self-Regulation: Research, Theory, and Applications. 2nd Edition, Guilford Press, New York.

[4] Zhao, C.M. and Kuh, G.D. (2004) Adding Value: Learning Communities and Student Engagement. *Research in Higher Education*, **45**, 115-138. http://dx.doi.org/10.1023/B:RIHE.0000015692.88534.de

[5] Zimmerman, B.J. (2008) Investigating Self-Regulation and Motivation: Historical Background Methodological Developments, and Future Prospects. *American Educational Research Journal*, **45**, 166-183. http://dx.doi.org/10.3102/0002831207312909

[6] Ferguson, R. and Shum, S.B. (2012) Social Learning Analytics: Five Approaches. *Proceedings of the 2nd International*

Conference on Learning Analytics and Knowledge, Vancouver, 29 April-2 May 2012, ACM Press, New York. http://dx.doi.org/10.1145/2330601.2330616

[7]   Yoo, J. and Kim, J. (2014) Can Online Discussion Participation Predict Group Project Performance? Investigating the Roles of Linguistic Features and Participation Patterns. *International Journal of Artificial Intelligence in Education*, **24**, 8-32. http://dx.doi.org/10.1007/s40593-013-0010-8

[8]   Edelstein, H.A. (1999) Introduction to Data Mining and Knowledge Discovery. 3rd Edition, Crows Corporation, Potomac.

[9]   Chang, C.Y., Wang, H.J. and Li, C.F. (2010) Image Content Analysis Using Modular RBF Neural Network. *Journal of Computers*, **21**, 39-52.

[10] Haykin, S. (1998) Neural Network: A Comprehensive Foundation. 2nd Edition, Prentice Hall, New York.

[11] Srimani, P.K. and Kamath, A.S. (2012) Neural Networks Approach for the Performance Analysis of Learning Model—A Case Study. *International Journal of Current Research*, **4**, 236-239.

[12] Srimani, P.K. and Kamath, A.S. (2012) Data Mining Techniques for the Performance Analysis of a Learning Model—A Case Study. *International Journal of Computer Applications*, **53**, 36-42.

[13] Romero, C. and Ventura, S. (2007) Educational Data Mining: A Survey from 1995 to 2005. *Expert Systems with Applications*, **33**, 135-146. http://dx.doi.org/10.1016/j.eswa.2006.04.005

[14] Bigus, J.P. (1996) Data Mining with Neural Networks: Solving Business Problems from Application Development to Decision Support. McGraw Hill, New York.

[15] Liu, H. (2010) On the Levenberg-Marquardt Training Method for Feed-Forward Neural Networks. *Proceedings of the 6th International Conference on Natural Computation*, Yantai, 456-460.

[16] Guyon, I. and Elisseff, A. (2003) An Introduction to Variable and Feature Selection. *The Journal of Machine Learning Research*, **3**, 1157-1182.

[17] Mercer, N. (2004) Sociocultural Discourse Analysis: Analyzing Classroom Talk as a Social Mode of Thinking. *Journal of Applied Linguistics*, **1**, 137-168. http://dx.doi.org/10.1558/japl.2004.1.2.137

[18] Sayed, M. (2013) Blended Learning Environment: The Effectiveness in Developing Concepts and Thinking Skills. *Journal of Education and Practice*, **4**, 12-17.

[19] Tempelaar, D.T., Niculescu, A., Rienties, B., Gijselaers, W.H. and Giesbers, B. (2012) How Achievement Emotions Impact Students' Decisions for Online Learning, and What Precedes Those Emotions. *The Internet and Higher Education*, **15**, 161-169. http://dx.doi.org/10.1016/j.iheduc.2011.10.003

[20] Winne, P.H. and Baker, R.S. (2013) The Potentials of Educational Data Mining for Researching Metacognition, Motivation and Self-Regulated Learning. *Journal of Educational Data Mining*, **5**, 1-8.

3

Formalization of Federated Schema Architectural Style Variability

Wilhelm Hasselbring

Software Engineering Group, Department of Computer Science, Kiel University, Kiel, Germany
Email: hasselbring@email.uni-kiel.de

Abstract

Data integration requires managing heterogeneous schema information. A federated database system integrates heterogeneous, autonomous database systems on the schema level, whereby both local applications and global applications accessing multiple component database systems are supported. Such a federated database system is a complex system of systems which requires a well-designed organization at the system and software architecture level. A specific challenge that federated database systems face is the organization of schemas into a schema architecture. This paper provides a detailed, formal investigation of variability in the family of schema architectures, which are central components in the architecture of federated database systems. It is shown how the variability of specific architectures can be compared to the reference architecture and to each other. To achieve this, we combine the semi-formal object-oriented modeling language UML with the formal object-oriented specification language Object-Z. Appropriate use of inheritance in the formal specification, as enabled by Object-Z, greatly supports specifying and analyzing the variability among the studied schema architectures. The investigation also serves to illustrate the employed specification techniques for analyzing and comparing software architecture specifications.

Keywords

Federated Database Systems, Software Architecture, Formal Specification, Software Product Families, Software Variability

1. Introduction

A software product family consists of software systems that have some common functionality and some variable functionality [1]. The interest in software product families and software product lines emerged from the field of software reuse when developers and managers realized that they could obtain much greater reuse benefits by reusing software architectures instead of only reusing individual software components. The basic philosophy of software product families is reuse through the explicitly planned exploitation of commonalities of related products [2] and proper management of *variability* in software systems [3] [4].

Product development in software product families is organized into two stages: domain engineering and application engineering [5]. The idea behind this approach to product engineering is that the investments require to develop the reusable artifacts during domain engineering are outweighed by the benefits of deriving the individual products during application engineering.

For large, complex software systems, the design of the overall system structure (the software architecture) is a central problem. The *architecture* of a software system defines that system in terms of components and connections among those components [6] [7]. It is not the *design* of that system which is more detailed. The architecture shows the correspondence between the requirements and the constructed system, thereby providing some rationale for the design decisions. This level of design has been addressed in a number of ways including informal diagrams and descriptive terms, module interconnection languages, and frameworks for systems that serve the needs of specific application domains. An architecture embodies decisions about quality properties. It represents the earliest opportunity for evaluating those decisions. Furthermore, reusability of components and services depends on how strongly coupled they are with other components in the system architecture. Performance, for instance, depends largely upon the complexity of the required coordination, in particular when the components are distributed via some network.

Similar to civil engineering where the engineer knows that a house includes a roof at the top and a cellar at the bottom etc., with compiler construction the software engineer should know that a compiler contains a pipeline including lexical analysis, parsing, semantic analysis, and code generation. As yet, this is not the case for all areas of software development. In the present paper, we investigate the schema architecture of federated database systems to make some progress in this domain enabling formal analysis and comparison of specific federated schema architectures. The schema architecture is a central part in the architecture of federated database systems. We study the family of federated schema architectural styles in this paper.

Constructing a formal specification requires some effort that should be justified. The primary motivation for formalizing federated schema architecture styles is to enable analysis and comparison of specific schema architectures for evaluating and selecting appropriate architectural variations. Usually, formal specifications consist of interleaved passages of formal, mathematical text and informal prose explanation. We propose a three-level interleaving of formality in the specification:

- Informal prose explanation (illustrated with examples);
- Semi-formal object-oriented modeling (we use the UML for this purpose);
- Rigorous formal specification (we use Object-Z for this purpose).

An important goal is to obtain a well structured formal specification. Formal specifications are often criticized by practitioners, because it is hard to comprehend them. To some extent, the problems are due to missing (visual) structure in the specification. With our approach, the object-oriented diagrams provide an overview of the formal specification, and a first level of (semi) formalization. In our view, graphical specifications are appropriate for providing an overview, while textual specifications are appropriate for providing details.

Our contribution is a detailed, formal investigation of variability in the family of some representative schema architectures. These schema architectures are central components in the architecture of their federated database systems. It is shown how the variability of specific architectures can be compared to the reference architecture and to each other. The investigation also serves to illustrate the employed specification techniques for analyzing and comparing software architecture specifications.

In Section 2, we discuss software product families and their architectures, as far as relevant for the present paper. Section 3 gives an overview of federated database systems in general and the reference schema architecture in particular, before the reference schema architecture is formalized in Section 4. This formalization allows for a precise comparison with specific architectures in Section 5. Sections 6 and 7 discuss related work and draw some conclusions.

2. Software Product Families and Their Architectures

The study of software architecture has evolved from the seminal work of Perry & Wolf [8], Garlan & Shaw [6], and others. Architecture Description Languages (ADLs) have emerged to lend formal rigor to architecture representation [9]. Despite more than two decades of research on architecture description languages [9], in industrial practice software architectures are usually described informally or semi-formally with diagrams using boxes, circles and lines together with accompanying prose. The prose explains the diagrams and provides some rationale for the chosen architecture. Typical examples are the above-mentioned *pipeline* architecture for the various phases of a compiler or a *client-server* architecture for distributed information systems. Such figures often give an intuitive picture of the system's construction, but the semantics of the components and their connections/interactions may be interpreted by different people in different ways (due to the informality). Some specific advantages of formality in software architecture description may be summarized as follows:

- Software architectures become amenable to analysis and evaluation [10]. This helps to evaluate architectures and to guide in the selection of architectural variations as solutions to specific problems.
- Software architectures can be a basis for *design reuse* [11] [12], provided that the individual elements of the architectural descriptions are defined independently and in a precise way. Re-usable architectures give designers a *blueprint* in development by helping them avoid typical design errors.
- Software architectures support improved program understanding as a basis for system evolution if its specification is well understood: retaining the designer's intention about a system organization should help maintainers preserve the system's design integrity [13] [14].
- Formality can allow prototyping for early design evaluation [15].
- Testing may be supported by deriving test plans from formal architectural descriptions [16] [17].
- Proper tool support for designing and analyzing software architectures becomes possible [18].

Reference architectures play an important role in domain engineering. *Domain engineering* is an activity for building reusable components, whereby the systematic creation of domain models and architectures is addressed. Domain engineering aims at supporting *application engineering* which uses the domain models and architectures to build concrete systems. The emphasis is on reuse and product lines. The Domain-Specific Software Architecture (DSSA) engineering process was introduced to promote a clear distinction between domain and application requirements [19]. A Domain-Specific Software Architecture consists of a domain model and a reference architecture. The DSSA process consists of domain analysis, architecture modeling, design and implementation stages as illustrated in **Figure 1** [5]. The DSSA process concentrates on gathering architectural information about specific application domains. Reference architectures are the basic structures used to build systems in a product line. The domain model characterizes the *problem space*, while the *reference architecture* addresses the *solution space* in domain engineering.

Software architectures address the attributes indicated above for single systems. DSSA capture architectural commonality of multiple, related systems, *i.e.*, systems within the same domain. DSSA are central to domain-specific reuse, in that they provide a framework for creating assets and constructing systems within a domain. Domain engineering also allows for product-line development, which seeks to achieve reuse across a family of systems [20] [21]. Federated database management systems can be regarded as such a family of systems.

3. Federated Database Systems

A *database system* consists of a database management system and one or more databases that it manages. In many application areas, data is distributed over a multitude of heterogeneous, autonomous database systems.

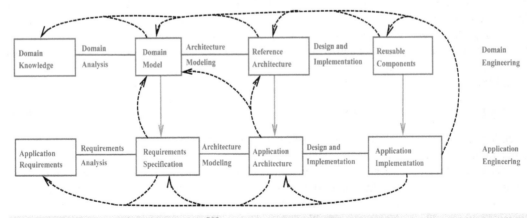

Figure 1. The DSSA engineering process [5].

These systems are often isolated and an exchange of data among them is not easy. On the other hand, support for dynamic exchange of data is required to improve the business processes. Global access to several local systems and consistently replicating/moving data among systems are typical requirements.

A federated database system is an integration of such autonomous database systems, where both local applications and global applications accessing multiple database systems are supported [22]. A federated database system is a complex *system of systems* which requires a well designed organization at the software architecture level. The work on federated database systems centers around three issues: autonomy, heterogeneity, and distribution.

- Federated database systems are characterized by a controlled and sometimes limited integration of **autonomous** database systems. Often, there are conflicts between requirements of integration and autonomy.
- **Heterogeneity** is caused by different database management and operating systems, as well as the design autonomy among component database systems.
- In the case of federated database systems, much of the **distribution** is due to the existence of individual database systems *before* a federated database system is built (legacy systems).

Federated database systems may be distinguished as being *tightly* and *loosely* coupled [22]. In the case of loosely coupled federated database systems, each component site builds its own federated schema by integrating its local schema with the export schemas of some other component sites. Loose coupling promotes integration and interoperability via *multidatabase query languages* which allow uniform access to all component database systems [23]. It does not require the existence of integrated schemas, leaving many responsibilities, such as dealing with multiple representations of data and resolving semantic mismatch, to the programmer of component database systems. Tight coupling requires schema integration. The present paper discusses tightly federated database systems with a schema-based integration architecture.

3.1. The System Architecture of Federated Database Systems

Let us start with a look at the typical overall system architecture of federated database systems, which is displayed in **Figure 2**. In a federated database system, both global applications and local applications are supported. The local applications remain autonomous to a great extent, but must restrict their autonomy to some extent to participate in the federation. Global applications can access multiple local database systems through the federation layer. The federation layer can also control global integrity constraints such as data value dependencies across multiple component database systems. The dependencies among the schemas in the component database systems are specified on the federation layer within a *schema architecture*, which is a kind of *metadata* describing the local systems, their correspondences, and what is offered to global applications.

To achieve a division of labor between system components, database *wrappers* should be connected to the component database systems to simplify the kernel. The database wrappers transform the data between the local data models and the canonical data model of the federation layer (see below). **Figure 2** illustrates this division of labor between federation layer kernel and wrappers. The local database management systems of the component databases see the wrappers as local applications. This approach allows for a "separation of concerns" between the federation kernel and the component wrappers. The responsibility for monitoring and announcing changes in component database systems is delegated from the kernel of the federation layer to the wrappers for the individual component database systems. This way, the kernel of the federation layer may see the component database systems as active database systems [24]. An active database system is an extended conventional database system which has the capability to monitor predefined situations (situations of interest) and to react with defined actions. "Separation of concerns" is an important principle to manage complexity in software engineering [25].

3.2. The Five-Level Reference Schema Architecture for Federated Database Systems

As mentioned in the previous subsection, the schema architecture is a central component of the federation layer. A problem that all federated database system face is the organization of schemas in such a schema architecture. A reference architecture for schemas is useful to clarify the various issues and choices within those complex federated systems. It provides the framework in which to understand, categorize and compare different architectural options for developing specific systems. A reference architecture can be used as a basis for analysis and comparison of such-like architectures, as will be shown later in Section 5.

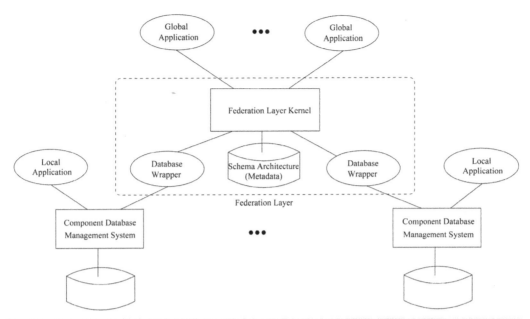

Figure 2. The general system architecture of federated database systems with database wrappers as mediators between component database systems and federation layer kernel.

For federated database systems, the traditional three-level schema architecture [26] must be extended to support the dimensions of distribution, heterogeneity, and autonomy. The generally accepted reference architecture for schemas in federated database systems is presented in [22] and, in the same form, in [27] where approaches to object-orientation in multidatabase systems are surveyed. The diagram in **Figure 3** illustrates this schema architecture which presents, apart from the dots that indicate repetition, a possible configuration of schemas in a federated database system. The different schema types are:

Local Schema: A Local Schema is the conceptual schema of a component database system which is expressed in the (native) data model of that component database system.

Component Schema: A Component Schema is a Local Schema transformed into the (canonical) data model of the federation layer. Object-oriented data models such as ODMG are often employed as canonical data models [28].

Export Schema: An Export Schema is derived from a Component Schema and defines an interface to the local data that is made available to the federation.

Federated Schema: When Exported Schemas are semantically heterogeneous, it is necessary to integrate them using another level. A Federated Schema on this higher level is the result of the integration of multiple Export Schemas; thus, providing an integrated view. Top-down or bottom-up integration strategies may be applied [29] [30].

External Schema: An External Schema is a specific view on a Federated Schema or on a Local Schema. External Schemas may base on a specific data model different to the canonical data model. Basically, External Schemas serve as specific interfaces for applications. External Schemas serve global applications if filtered from a Federated Schema, while serving local applications when filtered from a Local Schema.

This schema architecture, which is managed by the federation layer, specifies the dependencies/correspondences among the individual schemas. The database wrappers in **Figure 2** need to know the corresponding Local and Component Schemas, and the mapping between the native and canonical data models. The upper levels in the canonical data model are managed by the federation kernel, which may offer External Schemas in some native data models to global applications. Two important features of the schema architecture are how autonomy is preserved and how access control is managed [22]. Autonomy is preserved by dividing the administrative control among some component database system administrators and a federation system administrator. The Local, Component and Export Schemas are controlled by the component system administrators. The federation system administrator defines and manages the Federated Schemas and the External Schemas which are related to the Federated Schemas. Note, however, that one person can take on the role of several system administrators.

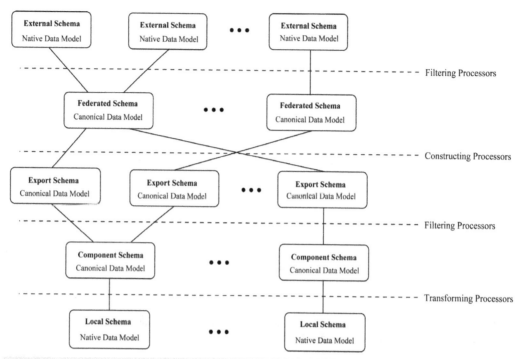

Figure 3. The five-level schema architecture as presented by Sheth & Larson [22]. We indicate the corresponding processor types between the levels my means of dotted lines.

The accompanying text in [22] explains that several options and constraints in the schema architecture are available, some of which are:

- Any number of External Schemas can be defined.
- Any number of Federated Schemas can be defined.

A federated database system with multiple federations allows the tailoring of the use of the federated database system with respect to multiple classes of global federation users with different data access requirements.

- Schemas on all levels, except the Local and Federated Schemas, are optional.

Note that a schema architecture which consists of just one Federated Schema and some Local Schemas still concurs with the five-level schema architecture of [22]. The other levels contain no schemas in this case.

- A component database system can participate in more than one federation and continue the operation of local applications. Thus, Local Schemas may be mapped to several Component, Export, and also External Schemas.

These constraints are not defined formally, particularly not explicit in **Figure 3** which is meant to illustrate the reference architecture. It is necessary to read the informal descriptions in [22] very carefully to comprehend all these options and constraints. In Section 4, a formal specification will be presented which defines these options and constraints with mathematical rigor.

As reported in [31], this reference schema architecture of [22] is generally accepted as the basic structure in federated database systems or at least for comparison with other specific architectures. However, several modifications have been proposed, as shall be discussed in Section 5. However, this reference provides a basic architecture for managing the complexity of resolving data heterogeneity among component systems.

4. Formalization of the Reference Schema Architecture

Software architectures hide many of the implementation details which are not relevant to understanding the important differences among alternate architectures. A formal specification language such as Object-Z [32] [33] is well-suited for concentrating on the essential concerns and neglecting irrelevant details through abstraction. The graphical, semi-formal UML specification will be employed for providing an overview of the specified software architectures, as well as the structure for the formal Object-Z specification itself. As mentioned in the introduction, the specification of the federated schema architecture style is presented in three steps:

Step 0: Informal prose explanation: done in Section 3.2. (with examples);
Step 1: Semi-formal modeling: see Section 4.1. (with the UML);
Step 2: Rigorous formal specification: see Section 4.2. (with Object-Z).

The goal is to obtain a well structured formal specification. With our approach, the object-oriented UML models provide an overview of the formal Object-Z specification and a first level of (semi) formalization.

4.1. First Step: The Semi-Formal UML Specification

The Unified Modeling Language (UML) is a graphical modeling language that has been standardized by the Object Management Group [34]. **Figure 4** displays our first step towards formally specifying the reference schema architecture for federated database systems using the UML notation for class diagrams. In this model, some of the constraints and options for the architecture, which were discussed in Section 3, are defined by means of the *multiplicities* at the associations among classes. The example schema architecture in **Figure 3** can be regarded as an instance of the class model in **Figure 4**, which defines a *metamodel* for schemas and their associations in the reference schema architecture. In **Figure 3**, *multiplicity* of schemas was indicated by means of some dots.

A more detailed account of the model in **Figure 4** is given as follows. Rectangles are the UML symbols for classes. Inheritance for specialization and generalization is shown in UML as a solid-line path from the subclass to the superclass, with a hollow triangle at the end of the path where it meets the superclass. In the UML, multiplicities for associations are specified through numerical ranges at the association links. The default multiplicity is 1. If the multiplicity specification comprises a single asterisk, then it denotes the unlimited non-negative integer range (zero or many). The arrows attached to the association names indicate the direction for reading the names which are annotations to associations. For instance, the association between Local Schema and Component Schema in **Figure 4** specifies that each Component Schema is transformed from exactly one Local Schema, but each Local Schema can be transformed into multiple Component Schemas, when the corresponding component database participates in more than one federation.

Some additional constraints, which are not specified in the UML model, are the following.

- Federated Schemas are required to be integrated from *at least one* Local, Component or Export Schema, *i.e.*, Federated Schemas must be connected to the ground and not levitate.
- Each Export Schema is filtered from at least one Component or Local Schema.
- Each External Schema is derived from either one Federated or one Local Schema. External Schemas which are directly derived from Local Schemas are used for local applications.

Those additional constraints cannot be specified *graphically* within this class diagram. It is necessary to specify them textually by means of additional informal prose and/or the UML Object Constraint Language [34] [35]. The Object Constraint Language allows some predicate logic to be specified. However, the class diagram in **Figure 4** is a *semi-formal* specification as the *semantics* of the UML notation has not been specified formally.

To summarize, this UML diagram has already specified many details of the schema architecture that were not explicitly specified in the illustration of [22] in **Figure 3**. However, still several details are missing in the graphical model. Consider, for instance, the constraint that Federated Schemas are required to be integrated from *at least one* Local, Component or Export Schema. Furthermore, the semantics of the UML notation is not fully formally specified. Therefore, we take the second step to further formalize the schema architecture by means of a formal specification language.

4.2. Second Step: The Formal Object-Z Specification

Object-Z [32] [33] is an extension of the formal specification language Z [36] to facilitate specification in an object-oriented style. It is a conservative extension in the sense that the existing syntax and semantics of Z are retained in Object-Z. Object-Z specifications are strongly typed, what means that all defined elements have to be used within a correct typing context.

The following Object-Z specifications are presented in a bottom-up way, what means that classes are defined before they are used by other classes. Similar to Z, Object-Z obeys the principle of *definition before use*. Such bottom-up development is typical for object-oriented techniques [37]. Similarly, federated database systems themselves can be developed bottom-up starting with the integration of existing component database systems, but also top-down starting with the development of a global federation layer and the subsequent integration of

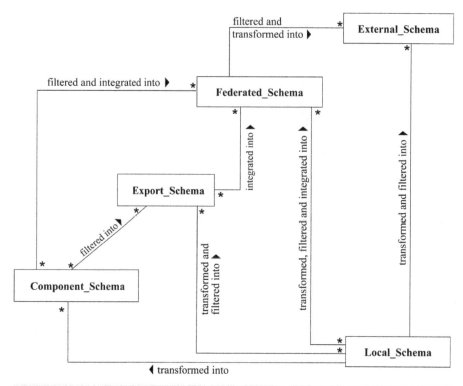

Figure 4. Modeling the five-level reference schema architecture for tightly coupled federated database systems as a UML class diagram.

(possibly new) component database systems [29], and even with a combination of both strategies [30].

Specifying the schema architecture of federated database systems, data models for describing schemas are basic.

[DATA_MODEL]

Basic type definitions introduce new types in Z and Object-Z, whose internal structure is not relevant for the specification. In our specification, we abstract from the details of data models since these details are not relevant on the schema *architecture* level.

The different data models used in the schema architecture are then defined in an axiomatic definition.

$Native\_Data\_Model, Canonical\_Data\_Model : DATA\_MODEL$

It is important to find the right level of abstraction for describing software architectures. On the architectural level of the schema architecture, there is nothing more to be said about the data models. This would be a concern of detailed design. Let the Object-Z class.

DB_Schema
$dm : DATA\_MODEL$

denote possible database schemas without specifying the concrete data models. Because we are—at the architecture level—not interested in the detailed content of a database schema, the class *DB_Schema* has no additional attributes or operations.

The class *DB_Schema* is an *abstract* or *deferred* class [37] which will be specialized through inheritance into *concrete* classes for the different schema types later on. Object-Z provides no explicit syntactical constructs for distinguishing abstract classes from concrete classes. We assume that object instances of the class

DB_Schema contain all relevant information on schemas in databases in the federation. This assumption is made on the grounds of simplification: we do not want to have to overspecify the Object-Z class at this stage of the architecture specification. The five different schema types are then defined as subclasses of *DB_Schema* as follows.

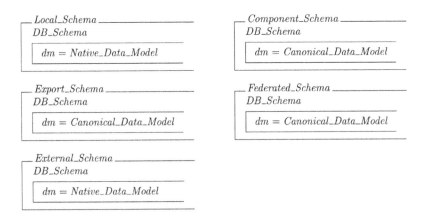

If we had used plain Z [36], *basic type definitions* would have been introduced instead of the above class specification as it has been done above with the basic type *DATA_MODEL*. However, with this Object-Z specification of the abstract class *DB_Schema* we are able to supply additional details later on in the specification through inheritance. Such an undertaking would not be possible with only using plain Z's basic type definitions.

As illustrated in **Figure 3** and **Figure 4**, a schema architecture consists of schemas on the five levels as defined in the class *Schema_Sets*.

```
┌─ Schema_Sets ─────────────────────────────────────────────────────────
│
│  LocS : ℙ Local_Schema
│  ComS : ℙ Component_Schema
│  ExpS : ℙ Export_Schema
│  FedS : ℙ Federated_Schema
│  ExtS : ℙ External_Schema
│
└────────────────────────────────────────────────────────────────────────
```

The class *Schema_Mapping* represents the mappings among those schemas in *Schema_Sets*. It *inherits* the schema sets and adds the mappings (incremental specification by means of object-oriented inheritance).

```
┌─ Schema_Mapping ──────────────────────────────────────────────────────
│  Schema_Sets
│ ┌──────────────────────────────────────────────────────────────────────
│ │  LocStoExpS : Local_Schema ↔ Export_Schema
│ │  LocStoComS : Local_Schema ↔ Component_Schema
│ │  LocStoFedS : Local_Schema ↔ Federated_Schema
│ │  ComStoExpS : Component_Schema ↔ Export_Schema
│ │  ComStoFedS : Component_Schema ↔ Federated_Schema
│ │  ExpStoFedS : Export_Schema ↔ Federated_Schema
│ │  FedStoExtS : Federated_Schema ↔ External_Schema
│ │  LocStoExtS : Local_Schema ↔ External_Schema
│ ├──────────────────────────────────────────────────────────────────────
│ │  Some consistency constraints among the schema sets and their mappings exists. One con-
│ │  straint is the following: The schemas mapped to each other must exist in the schema sets:
│ │
│ │  dom LocStoExpS ⊆ LocS ∧ ran LocStoExpS ⊆ ExpS ∧ dom LocStoComS ⊆ LocS ∧
│ │  ran LocStoComS ⊆ ComS ∧ dom LocStoFedS ⊆ LocS ∧ ran LocStoFedS ⊆ FedS ∧
│ │  dom ComStoExpS ⊆ ComS ∧ ran ComStoExpS ⊆ ExpS ∧ dom ComStoFedS ⊆ ComS ∧
│ │  ran ComStoFedS ⊆ FedS ∧ dom ExpStoFedS ⊆ ExpS ∧ ran ExpStoFedS ⊆ FedS ∧
│ │  dom FedStoExtS ⊆ FedS ∧ ran FedStoExtS ⊆ ExtS ∧ dom LocStoExtS ⊆ LocS ∧
│ │  ran LocStoExtS ⊆ ExtS
│ └──────────────────────────────────────────────────────────────────────
└────────────────────────────────────────────────────────────────────────
```

So far, we defined the components of a schema architecture which are sets of schemas and mappings among the schemas in these sets. Now, the question arises: How to define the schema architecture itself? Particularly, the question is *how* to specify the reference architecture such that it can be compared to the architectures of specific systems. We define the reference architecture as a specialization of *Schema_Sets* that satisfies several constraints.

Reference_Architecture

Schema_Mapping

For a schema architecture to conform with the reference architecture, Local and Federated Schemas are required (the other levels may be empty):

$\#FedS \geq 1 \wedge \#LocS \geq 1$

Each Component Schema is mapped from *exactly one* Local Schema:

$\forall l_1, l_2 : LocS;\ c : ComS \bullet$
$\quad (l_1 \mapsto c) \in LocStoComS \wedge (l_2 \mapsto c) \in LocStoComS \Rightarrow l_1 = l_2$

Each Export Schema must be mapped from *at least one* Component or Local Schema:

$ExpS \subseteq (\mathrm{ran}\ ComStoExpS \cup \mathrm{ran}\ LocStoExpS)$

Each Federated Schema must be mapped from *at least one* Export, Component or Local Schema:

$FedS \subseteq (\mathrm{ran}\ ExpStoFedS \cup \mathrm{ran}\ ComStoFedS \cup \mathrm{ran}\ LocStoFedS)$

Each External Schema must be mapped from *exactly one* Federated or Local Schema (External Schemas that are directly derived from Local Schemas are used for local applications):

$\forall l_1, l_2 : LocS;\ f_1, f_2 : FedS;\ e_1, e_2 : ExtS \bullet$
$\quad ((l_1 \mapsto e_1) \in LocStoExtS \wedge (l_2 \mapsto e_1) \in LocStoExtS \Rightarrow l_1 = l_2) \wedge$
$\quad ((f_1 \mapsto e_1) \in FedStoExtS \wedge (f_2 \mapsto e_1) \in FedStoExtS \Rightarrow f_1 = f_2) \wedge$
$\quad ((l_1 \mapsto e_1) \in LocStoExtS \wedge (f_1 \mapsto e_2) \in FedStoExtS \Rightarrow e_1 \neq e_2)$

As mentioned before, most of these constraints cannot be specified graphically in the UML model of Section 4.1. After formalizing the reference schema architecture of [22], we formalize and compare some specific federated schema architectures to the reference and to each other in the following section.

5. Formalization and Comparison of Some Specific Systems

In this section, we relate the concepts of the reference architecture to those realized in some specific federated database management systems. The purpose is not to survey these systems comprehensively, but to show how the reference schema architecture can be compared to the schema architectures of various federated database systems. Such a representation aims to support the task of studying and comparing these systems.

We will exemplarily formalize and compare the IRO-DB, IBM InfoSphere, FOKIS, and BLOOM schema architectures in the following subsections to wrap up with a comparison in Section 5.5.

5.1. The IRO-DB Schema Architecture

The IRO-DB (Interoperable Relational and Object Databases) [38] project developed a set of tools to achieve interoperability of pre-existing relational databases and new object-oriented databases. One of the main goals of the project was the provision of a path for integrating the relational database technology to object-oriented database technology.

In the IRO-DB architecture, it is emphasized that there may be multiple Federated Schemas and not one global integrated schema. Therefore, Federated Schemas are called *interoperable schemas* in their schema architecture. Component Schemas are not used, instead Local Schemas are always directly transformed into Export Schemas. Also, External Schemas are not used; instead individual interoperable schemas can directly be specified for specific requirements of global applications. **Figure 5** displays the semi-formal UML model for the IRO-DB schema architecture. We intentionally leave the layout in the style of the UML model for the reference schema architecture for easier visual comparison with **Figure 4**.

Essentially, the IRO-DB schema architecture is a subset of the reference architecture. We specify the specific

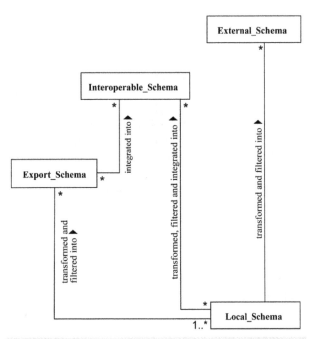

Figure 5. Modeling the IRO-DB schema architecture as a UML class diagram.

architectural constraints of the IRO-DB schema architecture as a specialization of the Object-Z class *Schema_Mapping* in two steps. First, we define a basic schema architecture as follows.

___ *Basic_Architecture* _____
Schema_Mapping
_____

 As in the reference architecture, in the basic schema architecture both Local and Federated
 Schemas are required:

 $\#FedS \geq 1 \wedge \#LocS \geq 1$

 As opposed to the reference architecture, in the basic schema architecture there exist no
 Component Schemas and no mappings from/to them:

 $0 = \#ComS = \#LocStoComS = \#ComStoExpS = \#ComStoFedS$

 Each Export Schema must be mapped from *at least one* Local Schema:

 $ExpS \subseteq \operatorname{ran} LocStoExpS$

 Each Federated Schema must be mapped from *at least one* Export or Local Schema:

 $FedS \subseteq (\operatorname{ran} ExpStoFedS \cup \operatorname{ran} LocStoFedS)$

In the second step, the IRO-DB schema architecture is specified as a specialization of the basic architecture with the following constraints.

___ *IRO_DB_Architecture* _____
FedS is renamed to InteropS while inheriting the Schema_Mapping:

$Basic\_Architecture[InteropS/FedS]$
_____

 As opposed to the reference architecture, in the IRO-DB schema architecture no mappings
 from Federated to External Schemas are supported:

 $0 = \#FedStoExtS$

This two-step specialization allows for reuse of the basic architecture for similar systems, as we will see in the following subsection.

5.2. The IBM InfoSphere Schema Architecture

IBM InfoSphere Federation Server [39] is a commercial federated database system that provides global access to multiple heterogeneous databases, formerly known as IBM DB2 Universal DataJoiner [40]. It provides transparent access to tables at remote databases through user defined aliases (so-called *nicknames*) that can be accessed as if they were local tables. The InfoSphere Federation Server is also a fully functional relational database system, based on IBM DB2. Among other features, the DB2 query optimizer is available at the federation layer and inserts, updates and deletes are redirected to the integrated, local databases.

Schema integration with InfoSphere Federation Server is accomplished via nicknames. As an example, nicknames to external Oracle database and Sybase database tables are defined with InfoSphere as follows.

```
CREATE NICKNAME O_EMP FOR ORACLE.USER_X.EMP

CREATE NICKNAME S_OFFICE FOR SYBASE.USER_Y.OFFICE
```

These nicknames correspond to Export Schemas in the reference architecture. Views over these nicknames can then be defined via standard SQL.

```
CREATE VIEW FEDERATED_SCHEMA
    AS SELECT O_EMP.EMPNAME, S_OFFICE.OFFICENO
       FROM O_EMP, S_OFFICE
       WHERE O_EMP.EMPNO = S_OFFICE.EMPNO
```

This federated view corresponds to the Federated Schemas in the reference architecture. **Figure 6** displays the UML model for the InfoSphere schema architecture.

The specific architectural constraints of the InfoSphere schema architecture are again specified as a specialization of the Object-Z class *Basic_Architecture* as follows.

InfoSphere_Architecture
Export Schemas are Nicknames and Federated Schemas are views:
$Basic\_Architecture[Nicknames/ExpS, FedView/FedS]$

Thus, apart from some renaming, the InfoSphere schema architecture is just a basic architecture.

5.3. The FOKIS Schema Architecture

This section discusses a federated schema architecture which has been designed according to the specific requirements of integrating replicated information among heterogeneous components of hospital information systems [41]. It is rather obvious that the reference schema architecture of [22] has been designed primarily to support global access to the component database systems, only secondarily to support data replication. However, the reference schema architecture is a good framework for resolving the syntactic and semantic conflicts among heterogeneous schemas and for integrating the schemas. Therefore, the reference schema architecture has been extended in FOKIS by Publish, Subscribe and Publish/Subscribe distinction for Export Schemas to adequately support the algorithms for updating replicated information with the FOKIS system. This distinction does not exist in the reference architecture.

Figure 7 displays the class diagram for this extended schema architecture using the UML notation. The distinct specializations of Export Schemas replace the Export Schemas in the reference architecture.

Publish_Schema
Export_Schema

Subscribe_Schema
Export_Schema

PubSub_Schema
Export_Schema

Export Schema becomes an abstract class [37] in this architecture: in actual instances of the schema architec-

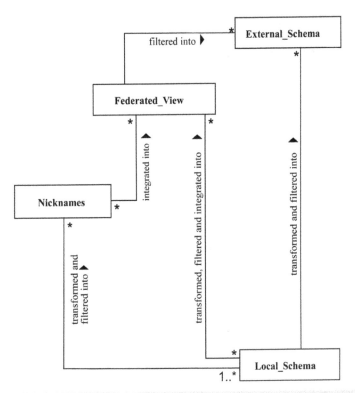

Figure 6. Modeling the InfoSphere schema architecture as a UML class diagram.

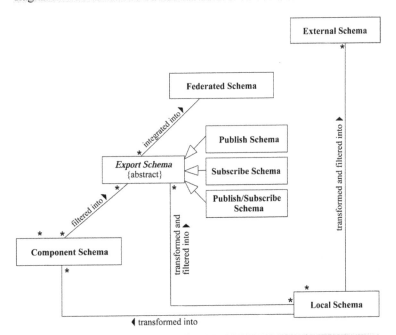

Figure 7. Modeling the FOKIS schema architecture as a UML class diagram.

ture only the subclasses of Export Schema are instantiated. The concrete classes Publish Schema, Subscribe Schema, and Publish/Subscribe Schema inherit all associations from *Export Schema*. There will be no instances (schemas) of the abstract class *Export Schema* in an instantiated schema architecture.

Specifying a Subscribe Schema in this architecture is a subscription to change notifications for the corresponding data. Publish Schemas specify data to be exported to other systems. Publish/Subscribe Schemas define data to be both imported and exported. The schema types determine the change algorithms for integration of replicated information in an event-based interaction architecture as discussed in [41]. The FOKIS schema architecture is then specified in Object-Z as follows.

FOKIS_Architecture
Schema_Mapping

$PublishS : \mathbb{P} \, Publish\_Schema$
$SubscribeS : \mathbb{P} \, Subscribe\_Schema$
$PubSubS : \mathbb{P} \, PubSub\_Schema$

As opposed to the reference architecture, in the FOKIS schema architecture no mappings from Local and Components Schemas directly to the Federated Schemas are allowed:

$LocStoFedS = \varnothing \wedge ComStoFedS = \varnothing$

As in the reference architecture, in the FOKIS schema architecture both Local and Federated Schemas are required. Additionally, Export Schemas are required:

$\#FedS \geq 1 \wedge \#LocS \geq 1 \wedge \#ExpS \geq 1$

As opposed to the reference architecture, in the FOKIS schema architecture there exist no mappings from Federated to External Schemas for global applications:

$\#FedStoExtS = 0$

The (abstract) extension of Export Schemas contains its intensional subclasses (polymorphism) which are disjoint:

$ExtS = PublishS \cup SubscribeS \cup PubSubS \wedge \mathrm{disjoint}\langle PublishS, SubscribeS, PubSubS \rangle$

Each specialization of Export Schema is filtered from at least one Component or Local Schema:

$ExpS \subseteq (\mathrm{ran}\, ComStoExpS \cup \mathrm{ran}\, LocStoExpS)$

Each Export Schema is integrated into exactly one Federated Schema:

$\forall\, e_1, e_2 : ExpS;\ f : FedS \bullet$
$\quad (e_1 \mapsto f) \in ExpStoFedS \wedge (e_2 \mapsto f) \in ExpStoFedS \Rightarrow e_1 = e_2$

Each External Schema is derived from either one Federated or one Local Schema:

$\forall\, l_1, l_2 : LocS;\ f_1, f_2 : FedS;\ e_1, e_2 : ExtS \bullet$
$\quad ((l_1 \mapsto e_1) \in LocStoExtS \wedge (l_2 \mapsto e_1) \in LocStoExtS \Rightarrow l_1 = l_2) \wedge$
$\quad ((f_1 \mapsto e_1) \in FedStoExtS \wedge$
$\qquad (f_2 \mapsto e_1) \in FedStoExtS \Rightarrow f_1 = f_2) \wedge$
$\quad ((l_1 \mapsto e_1) \in LocStoExtS \wedge$
$\qquad (f_1 \mapsto e_2) \in FedStoExtS \Rightarrow e_1 \neq e_2)$

5.4. The BLOOM Schema Architecture

The BLOOM approach to federated database systems consist of a schema architecture with several federated schemas and a functional architecture [42] [43]. The functional architecture in BLOOM includes the components needed to build the federation and the main modules of the execution architecture, see also Section 3.1. The reference schema architecture has been extended in BLOOM to deal with security aspects not well addressed previously. A new seven-level schema architecture framework has been developed in BLOOM. **Figure 8** displays the UML model for this BLOOM schema architecture.

In particular, the authorization schema level with a filter mechanism to federated external schemas has been added to the reference architecture to address security concerns on the schema level.

Authorization_Schema
DB_Schema

$dm = Canonical\_Data\_Model$

FDBS_External_Schema
DB_Schema

$dm = Canonical\_Data\_Model$

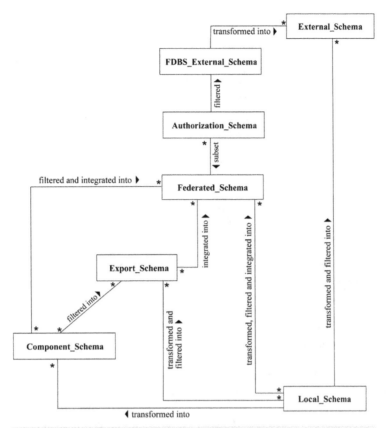

Figure 8. Modeling the BLOOM seven-level schema architecture as a UML class diagram.

With these additional schema levels, we can specify the BLOOM schema architecture.

```
__ BLOOM_Architecture _____
  Reference_Architecture
 _____
  AuthorizationS : ℙ Authorization_Schema
  FDBS_ExtS : ℙ FDBS_External_Schema

  In Object-Z, → specifies total functions and ⤖ bijective functions:

  FedStoAuthS : Federated_Schema → Authorization_Schema
  AuthStoFDBSExtS : Authorization_Schema ⤖ FDBS_External_Schema
  FDBSExtStoExtS : FDBS_External_Schema → External_Schema

  The schemas mapped to each other must exist in the schema sets:

  dom FedStoAuthS ⊆ FedS ∧ ran FedStoAuthS ⊆ AuthS ∧
  dom AuthStoFDBSExtS ⊆ AuthS ∧ ran AuthStoFDBSExtS ⊆ FDBS_ExtS ∧
  dom FDBSExtStoExtS ⊆ FDBS_ExtS ∧ ran FDBSExtStoExtS ⊆ ExtS

  The additional schema levels must not be empty:

  #FDBS_ExtS ≥ 1 ∧ #AuthS ≥ 1

  Each Authorization Schema is mapped from exactly one Federated Schema:

  ∀ a₁, a₂ : AuthS; f : FedS •
      ((a₁ ↦ f) ∈ FedStoAuthS ∧ (a₂ ↦ f) ∈ FedStoAuthS) ⇒ a₁ = a₂
```

5.5. Comparison of the Schema Architectures

Figure 9 illustrates the structure of our Object-Z specifications as a UML class diagram. This model is not part of the specifications for the schema architectures, it documents the structure of these specifications.

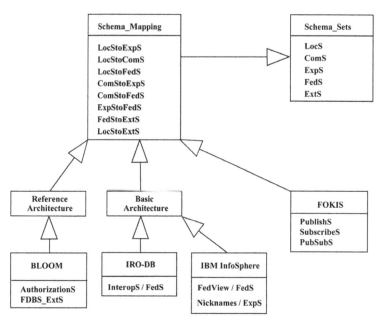

Figure 9. The structure of our Object-Z specification modeled as a UML class diagram.

The super classes *Schema_Sets* and *Schema_Mapping* define the general components of a schema architecture as sets of schemas and mappings among the schemas in these sets. Both the reference architecture and the architectures of the selected systems are direct or indirect specializations of the class *Schema_Mapping*. The different ways of specializing the *Schema_Mapping* serve as one means to compare the specific systems with the reference architecture and with each other on a high level.

The IRO-DB and IBM InfoSphere schema architectures are minimal subsets of the *Schema_Mapping*, they share the *Schema_Mapping*. Some schema types have different names in these architectures. The IRO-DB and IBM's InfoSphere schema architectures can be seen as some kind of minimal approach, which imposes several restrictions, if we compare it to the reference architecture. The FOKIS schema architecture has been designed according to the specific requirements of integrating replicated information among heterogeneous information systems. The mechanisms for publishing and subscribing to specific data items required some extensions to the generic part, while retaining its fundamental structure. The BLOOM schema architecture extends the reference architecture with several structures for security mechanisms.

The different ways of specializing and constraining the super classes serve as a means to compare the specific systems with the reference architecture and with each other. The specialization hierarchy already offers a gross overview of the similarities and differences. The detailed comparison can be done by taking a close look at the formal Object-Z specification. However, there exists an important difference between architectural comparisons on the UML and the Object-Z levels: On the UML level we compare individual class diagrams to each other. On the Object-Z level the comparison is based on the amount of customization of the schema mappings required for constructing the specific schema architectures. This allows for a more detailed comparison.

6. Related Work

6.1. Formalization of Architectural Styles and Design Patterns

Formalization of architectural styles aims to allow formal checks of conformance between architecture and implementation to predict the impact of changes, to formally reason about a system's architectural description, or to make rigorous comparisons among different architectural descriptions [44]. Various approaches to formalizing architectural styles have been proposed [45]-[47]. Within the overall framework of domain engineering, our work presented in this paper addresses the reference and application schema architecture construction. Specific schema architectures for individual federated database systems have been constructed with the reference schema architecture in mind. The formal comparison allows for a detailed analysis of similarities and differences among the architectural variations. Reuse on the design level plays an important role in this context [12]. On the programming level, reuse is usually accomplished by means of high-level programming language constructs, function libraries, or object-oriented class frameworks. On the design level, design patterns and established software architectures are essential. Design patterns [48] are "micro-architectures" while software architectures are more coarse-grained designs. A design pattern describes a family of solutions to a recurring problem. Patterns form larger wholes like pattern languages or handbooks when woven together so as to provide guidance for solving complex problem sets. Patterns express the understanding gained from practice in software design and construction. The patterns community catalogs useful design fragments and the context that guides their use. Approaches to formalizing patterns address pattern detection on source code [49] or supporting the work with patterns in integrated development environments [50] [51]. Our work intends to formalize variability analysis on the architectural level.

6.2. Formalizing the Unified Modeling Language

Because the UML comprises several different notations with no formal semantics attached to the individual diagrams, it is not possible to apply rigorous automated analysis on them. Several approaches introduce mappings between metamodels describing UML and some formal languages [52]. For instance, France *et al.* [53] employ Z, and Snook & Butler [54] employ the B method for formalizing the UML. These approaches enable the construction of rules for transforming UML models into specifications in some formal language. The resulting specifications derived from UML diagrams enable, for instance, execution through simulation or analysis via model checking. The goal of these approaches is to assign formal semantics to UML models. Our approach is to employ the UML for alleviating the comprehension of formal specifications (in Object-Z in our case). Similar to our work, Kim & Carrington [55] propose an integrated framework with UML and Object-Z for developing a precise and understandable specification. This work is motivated by the assessment that formal specification techniques provide a systematic approach to produce a precise and analyzable software specification. However, the notations provided by most formal specification techniques are often difficult to use and understand. Kim & Carrington intend to overcome these limitations by combining graphical specification techniques with formal specification techniques to show that an integrated approach is beneficial for both graphical and formal specification techniques. Representing formal specifications using appropriate diagrams can improve understanding of the formal specifications. So, the work of Kim & Carrington is similar to our approach. We are applying it to product-line variability analysis.

6.3. Software Variability Analysis

Software product families were defined by Parnas [56] as a set of programs to constitute a family whenever it is worthwhile to study programs from the set by first studying the common properties of the set and then determining the special properties of the individual family members. The SCV (Scope, Commonality and Variability) analysis method, for instance, is an approach that provides a systematic way of identifying and organizing a product family to be created [57]. SCV analysis is one approach to defining a family by identifying commonalities, *i.e.* assumptions that are true for all family members, variabilities, *i.e.* assumptions about what can vary among family members, and common terminology for the family. Variability analysis with SCV contains guidelines and requirements to assist in the identification and analysis of variabilities, which may include a cost-benefit analysis. Ramachandran & Allen [58] employ semi-formal data-flow context diagrams and use-case diagrams for variability analysis, while we are combining class diagrams with a formal specification language. Metzger *et al.* [3] formalize the documentation of variability in software product lines. They emphasize the difference between software variability and product-line variability. We formalize product-line variability for the family of federated schema architectures, while Metzger *et al.* formalize feature diagrams that are used for documenting variability. Another formalization of feature models may be found in [59].

7. Conclusions and Future Work

The highest costs in software development is generally in system maintenance and the addition of new features. If it is done early on, architectural evaluation can reduce that cost by revealing a design's implications [10]. This, in turn, can lead to an early detection of errors and to the most predictable and cost-effective modifications to the system over its life cycle. There are several reasons to consider an architectural view.

1) Architecture is often the first design artifact that represents decisions on how requirements of all types are to be achieved. As the manifestation of early design decisions, it represents design decisions that are hardest to change and hence most deserving of careful consideration.

2) An architecture is also the key artifact in successfully engineering a product line. Product-line engineering is the disciplined, structured development of a family of similar systems with less effort, expense, and risk than it would be incurred if each system were developed independently.

3) The architecture is usually the first artifact to be examined when a programmer (particularly a maintenance programmer) who is unfamiliar with the system begins to work on it.

The individual federated database management systems studies in this paper were developed independently, as far as we know. However, the published papers on these systems all refer to the reference architecture of [22]; thus, all systems were inspired by that basic reference. Our comparison investigates the similarities and differences of the realized specific architectures. The formal specifications clarified several aspects of the specific schema architectures that were not explicit in the informal descriptions. Appropriate use of inheritance in the formal specification, as enabled by Object-Z, greatly supports specifying and analyzing the variability among the studied schema architectures. The different ways of specializing the general parts via inheritance in the specification serve as a means to compare the specific systems with the reference architecture and with each other.

However, some training in formal notations is required to understand the formal specification. To address this, our formal specification is accompanied with informal prose explanation and a semi-formal specification employing the established object-oriented modeling notation UML. The object-oriented specification with the combination of the UML and Object-Z allowed for an incremental, well-structured construction of the formal specifications.

A formal model such as the presented one provides a precise, mathematically based description of a family of systems. The model attempts to capture a class of systems that is otherwise understood only idiomatically, and to expose the essential characteristics of that family while hiding unnecessary details. One of the benefits of doing this is that we can analyze various properties of systems designed in this style. Such an analysis could be supported by an animation of the formal specification as presented in [60].

Formal specifications have the advantage of precision and unambiguousness, what is not the case for those object-oriented modeling techniques which are usually used in industrial settings. On the other hand, the textual mathematical notation of formal specifications is only intelligible with a solid mathematical background, while object-oriented models are usually understandable for the average programmer. The combination of a semi-formal object-oriented modeling language with a formal object-oriented specification language aims at exploiting the advantages of both approaches. An important contribution of this paper is the formalization of the schema architecture for federated database systems which can be used as a guide by software engineers who intend to build a specific federated database system. Future work could aim at building a product line for developing similar federated systems.

Federated database management systems are already a research topic for many years, and database systems in general are a well-understood research area with a reasonable formal underpinning. These established fundamentals helped with formalizing and comparing the architectures. In the future, we intend to apply the presented approach to less established areas, such as variability in service-centric integration architectures [61] and in peer-to-peer architectures [62].

References

[1]   Gomaa, H. (2004) Designing Software Product Lines with UML: From Use Cases to Pattern-Based Software Architectures. Addison-Wesley, Boston.

[2]   Deelstra, S., Sinnema, M. and Bosch, J. (2004) Experiences in Software Product Families: Problems and Issues during Product Derivation. In: Nord, R.L., Ed., *Software Product Lines, Lecture Notes in Computer Science Volume* 3154, Springer-Verlag, Berlin, 165-182.

[3]   Metzger, A., Pohl, K., Heymans, P., Schobbens, P. and Saval, G. (2007) Disambiguating the Documentation of Variability in Software Product Lines: A Separation of Concerns, Formalization and Automated Analysis. *Proceedings of the* 15th *IEEE International Requirements Engineering Conference*, Delhi, 15-19 October 2007, 243-253.

[4]   Galster, M., Weyns, D., Tofan, D., Michalik, B. and Avgeriou, P. (2014) Variability in Software Systems—A Syste-

matic Literature Review. *IEEE Transactions on Software Engineering*, **40**, 282-306.
http://dx.doi.org/10.1109/TSE.2013.56

[5]   Hasselbring, W. (2002) Component-Based Software Engineering. In: Chang, S.K., Ed., *Handbook of Software Engineering and Knowledge Engineering*, World Scientific Publishing, Singapore, 289-305.
http://dx.doi.org/10.1142/9789812389701_0013

[6]   Shaw, M. and Garlan, D. (1996) Software Architecture: Perspectives on an Emerging Discipline. Prentice Hall, Englewood Cliff.

[7]   Taylor, R.N., Medvidovic, N. and Dashofy, E.M. (2009) Software Architecture: Foundations, Theory, and Practice. John Wiley and Sons, Hoboken.

[8]   Perry, D. and Wolf, A. (1992) Foundations for the Study of Software Architecture. *ACM SIGSOFT Software Engineering Notes*, **17**, 40-52. http://dx.doi.org/10.1145/141874.141884

[9]   Medvidovic, N. and Taylor, R.N. (2000) A Classification and Comparison Framework for Software Architecture Description Languages. *IEEE Transactions on Software Engineering*, **26**, 70-93. http://dx.doi.org/10.1109/32.825767

[10] Clements, P., Kazman, R. and Klein, M. (2001) Evaluating Software Architectures: Methods and Case Studies. Addison-Wesley, Boston.

[11] Frakes, W.B. and Kang, K. (2005) Software Reuse Research: Status and Future. *IEEE Transactions on Software Engineering*, **31**, 529-536. http://dx.doi.org/10.1109/TSE.2005.85

[12] Shaw, M. (1995) Architectural Issues in Software Reuse: It's Not Just the Functionality, It's the Packaging. *Software Engineering Notes*, **20**, 3-6.

[13] Bennett, K.H. and Rajlich, V.T. (2000) Software Maintenance and Evolution: A Roadmap. *Proceedings of the Conference on the Future of Software Engineering*, Limerick, 4-11 June 2000, 73-87.

[14] Müller, H., Wong, K. and Tilley, S.R. (1995) Dimensions of Software Architecture for Program Understanding. *Proceedings of the International Workshop on Software Architecture*, Dagstuhl, 20-24 February 1995, 1-4.

[15] Luckham, D.C., Kenney, J.J., Augustin, L.M., Vera, J., Bryan, D. and Mann, W. (1995) Specification and Analysis of System Architecture Using Rapide. *IEEE Transactions on Software Engineering*, **21**, 336-355.
http://dx.doi.org/10.1109/32.385971

[16] Muccini, H., Bertolino, A. and Inverardi, P. (2004) Using Software Architecture for Code Testing. *IEEE Transactions on Software Engineering*, **30**, 160-171. http://dx.doi.org/10.1109/TSE.2004.1271170

[17] Bertolino, A., Corradini, F., Inverardi, P. and Muccini, H. (2000) Deriving Test Plans from Architectural Descriptions. *Proceedings of the 22th International Conference on Software Engineering*, Limerick, 4-11 June 2000, 220-229.

[18] Shaw, M., De Line, R., Klein, D.V., Ross, T.L., Young, D.M. and Zelesnik, G. (1995) Abstractions for Software Architecture and Tools to Support Them. *IEEE Transactions on Software Engineering*, **21**, 314-335.
http://dx.doi.org/10.1109/32.385970

[19] Taylor, R.N., Tracz, W.J. and Coglianese, L. (1995) Software Development Using Domain-Specific Software Architectures. *ACM SIGSOFT Software Engineering Notes*, **20**, 27-38. http://dx.doi.org/10.1145/217030.217034

[20] Macala, R., Stuckey, L. and Gross, D. (1996) Managing Domain-Specific, Product-Line Development. *IEEE Software*, **13**, 57-67. http://dx.doi.org/10.1109/52.493021

[21] Dikel, D., Kane, D., Ornburn, S., Loftus, W. and Wilson, J. (1997) Applying Software Product-Line Architecture. *Communications of the ACM*, **30**, 49-55.

[22] Sheth, A. and Larson, J. (1990) Federated Database Systems for Managing Distributed, Heterogeneous, and Autonomous Databases. *ACM Computing Surveys*, **22**, 183-236. http://dx.doi.org/10.1145/96602.96604

[23] Tresch, M. and Scholl, M.H. (1994) A Classification of Multi-Database Languages. *Proceedings of the 3rd International Conference on Parallel and Distributed Information Systems*, Austin, 28-30 September 1994, 195-202.
http://dx.doi.org/10.1109/PDIS.1994.331716

[24] Widom, J. and Ceri, S., Eds. (1996) Active Database Systems—Triggers and Rules for Advanced Database Processing. Morgan Kaufmann, San Francisco.

[25] Ghezzi, C., Jazayeri, M. and Mandrioli, D. (2003) Fundamentals of Software Engineering. 2nd Edition, Prentice Hall, Englewood Cliffs.

[26] Date, C.J. (2004) An Introduction to Database Systems. 8th Edition, Addison-Wesley, Reading.

[27] Pitoura, E., Bukhres, O. and Elmagarmid, A. (1995) Object Orientation in Multidatabase Systems. *ACM Computing Surveys*, **27**, 141-195. http://dx.doi.org/10.1145/210376.210378

[28] Roantree, M., Murphy, J. and Hasselbring, W. (1999) The OASIS Multidatabase Prototype. *ACM SIGMOD Record*, **28**, 97-103. http://dx.doi.org/10.1145/309844.310066

[29] van den Heuvel, W.-J., Hasselbring, W. and Papazoglou, M. (2000) Top-Down Enterprise Application Integration with Reference Models. *Australian Journal of Information Systems*, **8**, 126-136.

[30] Hasselbring, W. (2002) Web Data Integration for E-Commerce Applications. *IEEE Multimedia*, **9**, 16-25. http://dx.doi.org/10.1109/93.978351

[31] Conrad, S., Eaglestone, B., Hasselbring, W., Roantree, M., Saltor, F., Schönhoff, M., Strässler, M. and Vermeer, M.W.W. (1997) Research Issues in Federated Database Systems: Report of EFDBS' 97 Workshop. *SIGMOD Record*, **26**, 54-56. http://dx.doi.org/10.1145/271074.271089

[32] Duke, R., Rose, G. and Smith, G. (1995) Object-Z: A Specification Language Advocated for the Description of Standards. *Computer Standards and Interfaces*, **17**, 511-533. http://dx.doi.org/10.1016/0920-5489(95)00024-O

[33] Smith, G. (1999) The Object-Z Specification Language. Kluwer Academic Publishers, Boston.

[34] OMG Unified Modeling Language Version 2.5, December 2013. http://www.omg.org/spec/UML/

[35] Warmer, J. and Kleppe, A. (2003) The Object Constraint Language: Getting Your Models Ready for MDA. 2nd Edition, Addison-Wesley Professional, Boston.

[36] Spivey, J.M. (1992) The Z Notation: A Reference Manual. 2nd Edition, Prentice-Hall, Englewood Cliff.

[37] Meyer, B. (1997) Object-Oriented Software Construction. 2nd Edition, Prentice-Hall, Englewood Cliff.

[38] Gardarin, G., Finance, B. and Fankhauser, P. (1997) Federating Object-Oriented and Relational Databases: The IRO-DB Experience. *Proceedings of the 2nd IFCIS International Conference on Cooperative Information Systems*, Kiawah Island, 24-27 Jun 1997, 2-13.

[39] IBM Corporation (2013) Data Virtualization: Delivering On-Demand Access to Information throughout the Enterprise. http://ibm.com/software/products/us/en/ibminfofedeserv/

[40] Venkataraman, S. and Zhang, T. (1998) Heterogeneous Database Query Optimization in DB2 Universal Data Joiner. *Proceedings of the 24th International Conference on Very Large Data Bases*, New York, 24-27 August 1998, 685-689.

[41] Hasselbring, W. (1997) Federated Integration of Replicated Information within Hospitals. *International Journal on Digital Libraries*, **1**, 192-208. http://dx.doi.org/10.1007/s007990050016

[42] Rodrguez, E., Oliva, M., Saltor, F. and Campderrich, B. (1997) On Schema and Functional Architectures for Multilevel Secure and Multiuser Model Federated DB Systems. *Proceedings of the International CAiSE'97 Workshop Engineering Federated Database Systems*, Barcelona, 16-17 June 1997, 93-104.

[43] Saltor, F., Campderrich, B., Rodriguez, E. and Rodriguez, L.C. (1996) On Schema Levels for Federated DB Systems. *Proceedings of the Parallel and Distributed Computing Systems*, Reno, 19-21 June 1996, 766-771.

[44] Abowd, G., Allen, R. and Garlan, D. (1995) Formalizing Style to Understand Descriptions of Software Architecture. *ACM Transactions on Software Engineering and Methodology*, **4**, 319-364. http://dx.doi.org/10.1145/226241.226244

[45] Bernardo, M. and Inverardi, P., Eds. (2003) Formal Methods for Software Architectures, Volume 2804 of Lecture Notes in Computer Science. Springer, Berlin.

[46] Pahl, C., Giesecke, S. and Hasselbring, W. (2007) An Ontology-Based Approach for Modelling Architectural Styles. *Proceedings of the 1st European Conference on Software Architecture*, Aranjuez, 24-26 September 2007, 60-75.

[47] Pahl, C., Giesecke, S. and Hasselbring, W. (2009) Ontology-Based Modelling of Architectural Styles. *Information and Software Technology*, **51**, 1739-1749. http://dx.doi.org/10.1016/j.infsof.2009.06.001

[48] Gamma, E., Helm, R., Johnson, R. and Vlissides, J. (1995) Design Patterns—Elements of Reusable Object-Oriented Software. Addison Wesley, Reading.

[49] Albin-Amiot, H., Cointe, P., Guéhéneuc, Y.-G. and Jussien, N. (2001) Instantiating and Detecting Design Patterns: Putting Bits and Pieces Together. *Proceedings of the 16th IEEE International Conference on Automated Software Engineering*, San Diego, 26-29 November 2001, 166-173.

[50] Mak, J.K.H., Choy, C.S.T. and Lun, D.P.K. (2004) Precise Modeling of Design Patterns in UML. *Proceedings of the International Conference on Software Engineering*, Edinburgh, 23-28 May 2004, 252-261.

[51] Guennec, A.L., Sunyé, G. and Jézéquel, J.-M. (2000) Precise Modeling of Design Patterns. In: Evans, A., Kent, S. and Selic, B., Eds., *UML 2000—The Unified Modeling Language, Volume 1939 of Lecture Notes in Computer Science*, Springer, Berlin, 482-496.

[52] Mc Umber, W.E. and Cheng, B.H.C. (2001) A General Framework for Formalizing UML with Formal Languages. *Proceedings of the 23rd International Conference on Software Engineering*, Toronto, 12-19 May 2001, 433-442.

[53] France, R., Evans, A., Lano, K. and Rumpe, B. (1998) The UML as a Formal Modeling Notation. *Computer Standards & Interfaces*, **19**, 325-334. http://dx.doi.org/10.1016/S0920-5489(98)00020-8

[54] Snook, C. and Butler, M. (2006) Uml-B: Formal Modeling and Design Aided by UML. *ACM Transactions on Software Engineering and Methodology*, **15**, 92-122. http://dx.doi.org/10.1145/1125808.1125811

[55] Kim, S.-K. and Carrington, D. (2000) An Integrated Framework with UML and Object-Z for Developing a Precise and Understandable Specification: The Light Control Case Study. *Proceedings of the 7th Asia-Pacific Software Engineering Conference*, Singapore, 5-8 December 2000, 240-248.

[56] Parnas, D. (1976) On the Design and Development of Program Families. *IEEE Transactions on Software Engineering*, **2**, 1-9. http://dx.doi.org/10.1109/TSE.1976.233797

[57] Coplien, J., Hoffman, D. and Weiss, D. (1998) Commonality and Variability in Software Engineering. *IEEE Software*, **15**, 37-45. http://dx.doi.org/10.1109/52.730836

[58] Ramachandran, M. and Allen, P. (2005) Commonality and Variability Analysis in Industrial Practice for Product Line Improvement. *Software Process: Improvement and Practice*, **10**, 31-40. http://dx.doi.org/10.1002/spip.212

[59] Czarnecki, K., Helsen, S. and Eisenecker, U. (2005) Formalizing Cardinality-Based Feature Models and Their Specialization. *Software Process: Improvement and Practice*, **10**, 7-29. http://dx.doi.org/10.1002/spip.213

[60] Hasselbring, W. (1994) Animation of Object-Z Specifications with a Set-Oriented Prototyping Language. *Proceedings of the 8th Z User Meeting*, Cambridge, 29-30 June 1994, 337-356.

[61] Pahl, C., Hasselbring, W. and Voss, M. (2009) Service-Centric Integration Architecture for Enterprise Software Systems. *Journal of Information Science and Engineering*, **25**, 1321-1336.

[62] Bischofs, L., Giesecke, S., Gottschalk, M., Hasselbring, W., Warns, T. and Willer, S. (2006) Comparative Evaluation of Dependability Characteristics for Peer-to-Peer Architectural Styles by Simulation. *Journal of Systems and Software*, **79**, 1419-1432. http://dx.doi.org/10.1016/j.jss.2006.02.063

4

Automatic Accompaniment to Arab Vocal Improvisation: From Technical to Commercial Perspectives

Fadi M. Al-Ghawanmeh[1], Zaid R. Shannak[2]

[1]Music Department, University of Jordan, Amman, Jordan
[2]SRS International, Amman, Jordan
Email: f_ghawanmeh@ju.edu.jo, zaid.shannak@gmail.com

Abstract

In this multidisciplinary study, the main research question was how to improve the value of entrepreneurial initiatives that provide the web service of automatic accompaniment to Arab singing. As an example and case study, we considered the Mawaweel website that offered an automatic accompaniment to Arab vocal improvisation as a main service. After overviewing the website, we conducted a survey examining the satisfaction of its visitors in regard to presentation and quality of service. It was found that the Mawaweel website had potential to achieve success as the majority of the 22 respondents expressed general satisfaction after their first visit to the website, with an average rate of 75%. However, respondents' ratings were strict when discussing specific aspects about the website presentation and service quality, and the means of average rates were 68.32% and 50.23% respectively. The standard deviations of average rates were 15.70% and 19.13%, respectively. This revealed a sense of inhomogeneity in the values of the different aspects of the website presentation, and an expanded sense of inhomogeneity in the quality of the different services delivered by the website. We then compared the Mawaweel website to other websites and proposed specific improvements to the aspects with average rate below 50%.

Keywords

Music Informatics, Entrepreneurial Web Business, Automatic Accompaniment, Arab Music, Survey Research

1. Introduction

The population of the Arab region, occupying most of the Middle East and North Africa, is growing rapidly.

According to [1], this should imperatively be accompanied by a powerful economic growth as the population will double to reach 800 million by 2050. The reference also added that the arrival of new technologies, the opening up of Arab economies, and the capital yielded by oil investments are all factors encouraged the development of small and medium enterprises in the Arab region.

The Arab world internet population is growing much faster. According to [2] and as shown in **Table 1**, the number of internet users grew from 20 million to 77 million in the Middle East and from 34 to 140 million in Africa with growth rates of 285% and 311%, respectively. This far exceeds the worldwide growth rate, which is 96%. These statistics affirm the competence of the web as a promising investment venue for the Arab world.

The growth of the media and entertainment sector in the Arab world is also impressive. According to [3] and as depicted in **Figure 1**, the spending on media and entertainment doubled between 2003 and 2007 to reach $10 billion with a compound annual growth rate of 19%. The figure also shows that the total investment in the Arab region is still far below the numbers reported in different parts of the world such as China or Germany where the total investments are $74 billion and $111 billion, respectively. This means that the Arab region has a huge potential for further growth in this promising industry. All the above-presented statistics affirm the significance of this study as we aim at improving the commercial value of an entrepreneurial web-based entertainment initiative that is targeted at the Arab people.

In this multidisciplinary article, we aimed at increasing the traffic and the commercial significance of the Mawaweelwebsite [4], as an example of sites offering the service of automatic musical accompaniment to Arab singing. As we considered the survey research as an efficient model for measuring costumers' satisfaction and for obtaining their feedback, we overviewed the Mawaweel website, and then we prepared and disseminated a survey to a sample of potential users. The survey assessed the users' level of satisfaction, mainly concerning two

Table 1. Growth of internet users between 2007 and 2012 [2].

Region	2007 (millions)	2012 (millions)	Growth
Africa	34	140	311%
Asia	418	1017	143%
Europe	322	501	56%
Middle East	20	77	285%
North America	233	273	17%
Latin America	110	236	115%
Oceania	19	24	26%
Worldwide	1156	2268	96%

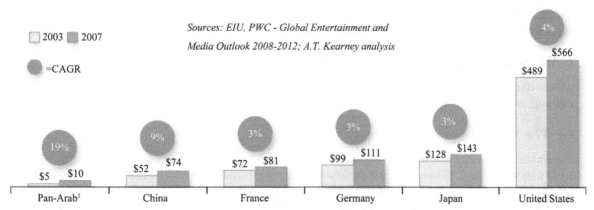

Notes: All monetary amounts in billons of U.S. dollars; CAGR = compound annual growth rate

[1]Algeria, Bahrain, Egypt, Jordan, Kuwait, Lebanon, Libya, Morocco, Oman, Qatar, Syria, Saudi Arabia and the UAE

Figure 1. Spending and growth in media and entertainment [3].

sides: website presentation and quality of service. The results showed that the Mawaweel website has the ability to succeed, especially if specific improvements are applied to the quality of service, and to the presentation of its home page.

The remaining sections of this article are organized as follows. Literature review is discussed in Section 2. The Mawaweel website is overviewed in Section 3. Methodology and work schedule is tackled in Section 4. The survey is demonstrated in Section 5 and is discussed in Section 6. Proposed improvements to the website are explained in Section 7. Finally, in Section 8, we conclude our contribution presented in this article and suggest a future work.

2. Literature Review

In [5], an analytic hierarchy process was applied to examine the influence of website quality on the performance and success of e-business. The authors explored different quality factors and compared their importance in deciding the preference of websites. Results of their study showed that the top business performance is delivered by the websites with the top quality. The commercial scenarios of the web were investigated in [6]; two main classes of websites were identified: traffic control and destination websites. The former class included search engines, incentive websites and malls (websites comprising a pool of online storefronts). The key role of such websites is to guide customers to destination websites, including: content websites, web storefronts and virtual presence websites. The authors claimed that the marketing purpose is to integrate traffic and destination websites to create and secure recurring visits.

In [7], an assessment of the process of developing e-business models was performed with focus on on-line music and news in Europe. Among the two promising models mentioned in their contribution, was the model combining the making, acquisition and virtual dissemination of media content. The influence of language and culture on the usability of commercial websites was studied in [8]. It was found that the observed usability grew with websites originally written in the users' mother tongue.

The use of information and communication technologies (ICT) as a tool to extend the goals of the music education curriculum was discussed in [9]. This reference encouraged instructors as well as students' to benefit of the diverse musical opportunities presented by ICT. In [10], it was statistically found that the time period spent by students on the website of a particular university module correlates with the students' performance in that module. The educational process in the Irish traditional virtual music community (IrTrad) was investigated in [11]. It was found that YouTube videos encouraged heated conversations tackling the different features of the videos, such as: value, authenticity and helpfulness in teaching and learning.

Recently, there have been remarkable efforts in music technology research in Jordan. In [12], music analysis software were utilized effectively to enhance teaching and learning expressive Arab singing. In [13] [14], a computer toolbox was proposed to improve learning and using Arab woodwinds. The toolbox benefited of a melodic music information retrieval model discussed in [15] [16]. In those contributions, as well as in [17], the particularity of Arab music was considered when proposing tools and models for woodwinds. Such customized research can function as basic building blocks for commercial software serving both the educational and the entertainment industries in the Arab world.

3. Mawaweel: The Term and the Website

We clarified the definition of the term Mawaweel in Section 2.1. Then we presented the Mawaweel website and application in Section 2.2.

3.1. The Term

The classical/traditional vocal improvisation of the Arab region is called in Arabic: Mawwāl (plural: Mawaweel). It is a non-metric musical form which is usually related to the narrative poetry. It is usually headed by a brief instrumental improvisation as an introductory stage aimed at developing the feeling of "saltanah", or modal ecstasy. In this musical form, the singer shows her/his expertise and talents whereas the instrumentalists give support to her/him. They achieved this by following the singer's lead throughout every improvised phrase, and by summarizing the phrase upon completion. Besides, the instrumentalists insert their own artistic touches on what they follow and recapitulate [18] [19]. The interactivity and liveliness among the improviser, the instrumentalists and the audience are amongst the main reasons for which the Mawwāl form gets much impact and admire on listeners.

3.2. Website

Mawaweel is a web application that offers an automatic musical accompaniment to Arab sung improvisation, [20]. The website of this application has only one page [4], and it is presented in **Figure 2**. The page has the following layout: a brief guidance on how to use the application is presented on top, just below the title. The Mawaweel application (as a web applet) is in the middle of the page. And finally, a hyperlink to examples of automatically accompanied improvisations using the Mawaweel application is shown at the bottom of the page, with a brief description of its content.

Using the Mawaweel application, the user may record her/his vocal improvisation before listening to its playback with five different ways of accompaniment. The accompaniment ways provided by the Mawaweel web application are as follows [20]:

1) Heterophonic variation of the improvised melody

The vocal improvisation is accompanied with one instrument playing a heterophonic variation of the vocal melody. *i.e.* the instrument plays the same melody but with a possible slight modification to the onset and duration of each note. The instrument used in this accompaniment is the qanoun.

2) Structural notes of the improvised score

The vocal melody is accompanied with one instrument performing only the main, or structural, notes of the improvised melody. This way of accompaniment gives both feelings of continuity and variety. Continuity is achieved because the structural notes (usually long or extreme) are always performed, and variety is made because other less important notes are substituted with silence or prolonged main notes. The instrument used in this accompaniment is the violin.

3) Imitation

Imitation may be described as a full or partial recurrence of a melody or motivic idea. This way of accompaniment is best used to fill up silences among the different vocal figures, or sentences. In the Mawaweel application, the imitation may be a shrunk or stretched variety of the performed vocal figure. It may be a full repetition of it or a truncated version. Moreover, Imitation may start soon after the end of the vocal figure, or a bit before so this gives a feeling of continuity".

4) Harmonic accompaniment

The vocal improvisation is accompanied with piano chords. Three main chords are used with their inversions, and utilized according to a formula introduced from flamenco music. This is because flamenco has Arab roots and share many things in common with Arab music, such as some scales, intervals, rhythms and ornamentation [21].

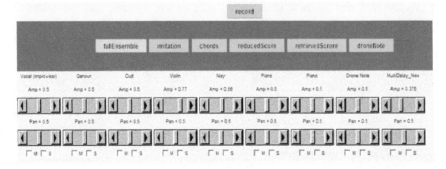

This is an evaluation version of the *Mawaweel Accompaniment System*

- To start, click **"record"**, then improvise on the maqam Hijaz on D, or in harmonic minor on G. Before recording, you may click **"droneNote"** to hear tonic,
- When done, click **"stop"**.
- To listen to your improvisation with a fully automatic instrumental accompaniment, click **"fullEnsemble"**.

not in a mood to improvise, but wanna listen?!,

Click on the following link to listen to examples of automatically accompanied vocal improvisations: Mawaweel uploaded to SoundCloud

Figure 2. Snapshot of the homepage of Mawaweel website [4].

5) Full ensemble

This way of accompaniment combines all the previous ways of accompaniment and forms one comprehensive way performed by several instruments: qanoun, violin, oud, Nay and piano. The full ensemble accompaniment is considered the default way of accompaniment.

4. Methodology and Work Schedule

The main approaches followed in this research project were the statistical and analytical. Yet, the work included tasks within the descriptive and comparative approaches. The project had four stages; the first was inceptive stage in which the Mawaweel website was overviewed. In the second stage, a survey examining the satisfaction of the website visitors was prepared and disseminated to potential users. The survey results were discussed and improvements to the website were proposed in the third stage. In the last stage, the research outcome was documented then published. The approximate durations for the four stages were two weeks, two months, three months and five months, respectively. The stages, tasks, approaches and durations are all depicted in **Table 2**.

5. The Survey

The Mawaweel website was introduced, thoroughly, as an entertainment site to a sample of potential users before disseminating a copy of the survey to each of them. The entire number of respondents was 22 from both sexes and from different ages and backgrounds. The survey included ten points tackling the presentation and the quality of the website. Four points measured the presentation of the contents of the website, and five points measured the quality and usefulness of the website. The last point measured the general opinions on the experience of visiting the Mawaweel website.

Every respondent was requested to fill a three-part form in which she/he rates several aspects of the website. For every aspect, the respondent chooses one out of five available rates: strongly agree, agree, undecided, disagree and strongly disagree. Each of the next three tables shows one or more aspects of the Mawaweel website with the rate of each aspect. In every point of each table, a certain aspect is presented together with the ratio of respondents selecting each rate, and the average rate of that particular aspect. The average rate signifies the general rate of an aspect, and is calculated like this: The rate given by every respondent is translated to a numerical value as follows: strongly agree is translated to 100%, agree to 75%, undecided to 50%, disagree to 25% and strongly disagree to 0%. The numerical values of the rates gathered from all respondents are then combined and divided by the overall number of respondents to get the average rate.

Table 3 presents the respondents' views on the presentation of the contents of the website: domain name, loading time, design & interactivity and finally the instructing steps to get the musical accompaniment. For every aspect, the table displays the ratio of respondents electing each of the five different rates, and the average rate of that aspect. The mean and the standard deviation of average rates are also presented in the table.

Table 4 presents the respondents' views on five elements measuring the quality and usefulness of the website. The elements tackles the following aspects: the quality of the final product (improvisation with musical accompaniment), the diversity of accompaniment options, the possibility to save and retrieve the accompaniment and its settings, the possibility to use the website for educational purposes, and finally, the comprehensiveness of website usability to everybody. Every element is displayed with its average rate and the ratio of respondents electing each of the five different rates.

Table 2. Tasks, approaches and duration for each stage of this project.

N.	Stage		Task	Approach	Duration
1	Inceptive stage	–	Overviewing Mawaweel website: presentation & quality of service.	Descriptive	Two weeks
2	Survey handling	– –	Preparing a survey examining visitors' satisfaction. Disseminating the survey, then collecting results.	Statistical	Two months
3	Analysis & improvement	– –	Analyzing and discussing obtained results. Proposing improvements to the website based on: analysis results & comparison with other websites.	Analytical& comparative	Three months
4	Documentation	–	Documenting and publishing this research experience in conferences, journals and/or press.	Descriptive	Five months

Table 3. Respondents' opinions on the presentation of the contents of the website.

N.	Aspect	Rate					Average
		Strongly agree	Agree	Neutral	Disagree	Strongly disagree	
1	The domain name "mawaweel.com" is easy to remember and memorize	59%	32%	0%	4.5%	4.5%	86.38%
2	The website does not require a long time to load.	36.5%	18.5%	18%	18%	9%	63.88%
3	The website design is clear, attractive and user friendly	13.5%	18%	32%	25%	11.5%	49.25%
4	The presentation of the steps required to get the musical accompaniment is clear and easy	31.5%	50%	9.5%	0%	9%	73.75%
Mean of average rates→							**68.32%**
Standard deviation of average rates→							**15.70%**

Table 4. Respondents' opinions on the quality and usefulness of the website.

N.	Aspect	Rate					Average
		Strongly agree	Agree	Neutral	Disagree	Strongly disagree	
1	From the perspectives of musical composition and sound recording & reproduction, the final product (improvisation with musical accompaniment) is of a high quality	7%	29%	34.5%	13.5%	16%	49.38%
2	The website offers a broad range of different accompaniment ways	9%	22%	27.5%	14%	27.5%	42.75%
3	It is possible to save and retrieve the improvisation, accompaniment or the settings of the mixer.	9%	0%	9%	36.5%	45.5%	22.63%
4	I can use this website to improve my singing skills.	32%	27.5%	27%	9%	4.5%	68.38%
5	Anyone can use this website regardless of musical skills or sound range	19%	53%	9%	19%	0%	68.00 %
Mean of average rates→							**50.23%**
Standard deviation of average rates→							**19.13%**

Table 5 presents the respondents' overall views on their experience of visiting the Mawaweel website. The table displays the average rate and the ratio of respondents electing each of the five different rates. Statistical results presented in these three tables are discussed in the next section.

6. Discussion

The statistics presented in the previous tables reflect a mere satisfaction on some aspects and an obvious dissatisfaction on some other aspects. In **Table 3** showing the respondents' opinions on the presentation of the website contents, the mean of average rates is 68.32%. This might be considered as a mere satisfaction on the general presentation of the website. The standard deviation of those rates is 15.70%. This reveals a sort of inhomogeneity in the value of the different aspects of the presentation. For example, the votes clearly tell that selecting the word "mawaweel" for the domain name is a successful choice, but the votes, on the other hand, express dissatisfaction on the design and user-friendliness of the website.

In **Table 4** which shows the respondents' opinions on the usefulness and quality of the Mawaweel website, the statistics show an expanded inhomogeneity in the quality of the different services delivered by the website. Although the mean of average rates is 50.23%, this ratio is not representative because the standard deviation is high: 19.13%. This means that the different votes are scattered far away from the mean. For example, while the majority of the respondents considered the website as a useful way to improve singing skills with an average rate of 68.38%, only 22.63% of the votes went for the ability of the website to save and retrieve the accompaniment and the settings of the mixer. The latter ratio is not shocking indeed, because this service, save & retrieve, is not actuality supported by this version of the application. So nobody can save or retrieve unless he/she

Table 5. Respondents' general opinions on the experience of visiting the Mawaweel website.

N.	Aspect	Rate					Average
		Strongly agree	Agree	Neutral	Disagree	Strongly disagree	
1	I felt satisfied with my experience of visiting the Mawaweel website for automatic accompaniment of Arab vocal improvisation	27%	55%	9%	9%	0%	75%

performs a workaround such as recording the sound produced by the computer's sound card. Indeed, this is not practical at all.

Table 5 has a special importance as it seeks the respondents' general opinions after visiting the Mawaweel website. It is promising that the average vote is 75%. This expresses a general satisfaction, and assures the importance of such websites. This also tells that the respondents' strict critics on some aspects of the previous tables are targeted at improving the presentation and services of the website rather than criticizing the whole idea.

7. Proposed Improvements to the Website

In order to increase the traffic and thus improving the commercial value of the Mawaweel website, we propose improvements to the aspects that gain a low average rate in the above-discussed survey. Precisely, a rate below 50%. Four aspects fall within this category, as follows:

7.1. Variety of Accompaniment Ways

Line in survey form: *The website offers a broad range of different accompaniment way.*

The website already offers five accompaniment types: full ensemble, imitation, chords, reduced score and retrieved score. Such low average vote for this line (42.75%) tells explicitly that the accompaniment ways are neither sufficient nor satisfying. This may have more than one explanation. In the following lines, we present four explanations for the dissatisfaction together with ideas to achieve satisfaction:

- Lack of guidance or visual illustration in the website; so some of the respondents did not know how to use the web application and get different accompaniment types. Accordingly, it is important to provide the users with written guidance or possibly illustrating videos.
- It is possible that the respondents, or some of them, did not understand the names of the different accompaniment ways. Therefore, it is important to replace the difficult technical terminology with easier names that are are simpler and well-understood by common people regardless of their musical backgrounds.
- The musical quality of some compositional ways is not satisfying. So although there are five ways available, but some of them is not satisfying. In view of this, it is necessary to improve the design of the compositional algorithms in order to ameliorate the accompaniment.
- In the available version of the web application, the user is forced to improvise in one particular maqam, the hijazmaqam. Moreover, the user has no control on the choice of the accompanying musical instruments. Therefore, it is required to expand the choice of the maqam of improvisation, and also to allow the user to choose among the different instruments.

7.2. Quality of the Final Product

Line in survey form: *From the perspectives of musical composition and sound recording & reproduction, the final product (improvisation with musical accompaniment) is of a high quality.*

This line has an average vote of 49.38%, and thus reflects respondents' dissatisfaction. A possible explanation for this discontent may be the structure of the proposed accompaniment tracks. So let us consider the melodic accompaniment as example. The web application offers three different melodic accompaniment choices: the imitation, reduced score and the retrieved score. As mentioned in [22], all the three choices are different representations of the musical score (notation) of the vocal improvisation. *I.e.* there has not been a striking or creative effort from the perspective of music composition. In light of this, we emphasize on a particular point mentioned in the previous subsection, which is the necessity of improving the compositional algorithms of all accompaniment ways whether melodic or harmonic. Indeed, interesting examples on the harmonization and poliphoniza-tion of Arab melodies can be found in [23].

Moreover, we find it important to design an algorithm to handle the instrumentation in a better way. In the current version of the application, the imitation is always performed by the oud, and the retrieved score is always performed by qanoun. Thus, there should be a more sophisticated algorithm that allows for a flexible choice of instruments, just like in real life accompaniment. As for improving the product from the perspective of sound recording and reproduction, we see it advantageous to provide the web application with better audio samples as the current ones are not of a high quality.

7.3. Ability of Saving and Retrieving

Line in survey form: *It is possible to save and retrieve the improvisation, accompaniment or the settings of the mixer.*

This line has an average vote of 22.63%, and this is expected because the services of saving and retrieving the improvisation and accompaniment are not available in the current version of this application. The same applies to the service of saving the settings of the mixer. The user has to perform a workaround in order to record his improvisation or snapshot the mixer's settings. Providing these services can expand the usability of this website and increase the number of users, especially if the users get the ability to share their accompanied improvisa-tions with others on social networks. Such services will require having a user account system in the website. *i.e.* more effort and cost, but it will—for sure—increase the value of the website. Indeed, common talent distribution and sharing websites such as YouTubeand SoundCloudhave user account systems [24] [25].

7.4. Website Design

Line in survey form: *The website design is clear, attractive and user friendly.*

The average vote of this line is 49.25%. This exposes a weakness in the website design. In this subsection, we attempt to clarify the weakness points of the design of the Mawaweel website, and also to suggest ideas toward an improved design.

A snapshot of the homepage of the Mawaweel website is shown in **Figure 2** (see Section 3). Let us discuss four main features of the website design: font, colors, click-buttons and language. As appears in the figure, the website uses a diversity of font sizes, colors and many click-buttons. According to [26], using lots of colors, fonts and click-buttons poisons the website and causes an information overload. So, it is necessary to keep the homepage as simple as possible. This is especially because visitors are not willing to spend more than four seconds to discover the type of service offered by the website [27].

Sometimes, it is necessary to have several options or choices, and thus many click-buttons. For example, there are five different choices for the accompaniment way in the Mawaweel website. In this case, having one drop-down list can be a better alternative than having five click-buttons. To better explain the idea of the drop-down list, let us consider the example shown in **Figure 3**. This example is taken from a music education website [28], and the title of the drop-down list is "topics". Once the user moves the cursor to this button, the drop-down list appears with all possible topics: chords, intervals, key signatures, etc.

Although the Mawaweel website provides a service targeted mainly at the Arab region, the website is only available in English. This is a drawback that can be solved by introducing bilingualism to the website. An

Figure 3. Example of a drop-down list [28].

Figure 4. Example of a language drop-down list [29].

example of allowing bilingualism in Arab-targeted music websites is shown in **Figure 4**. It shows the language drop-down list of awebsite [29]. The menu allows the user to choose between two languages: Arabic and English.

8. Conclusion and Future Work

This contribution was targeted at driving more traffic and thus improving the significance of the Mawaweel website, which was chosen as an example of websites delivering automatic musical accompaniment to Arab vocal performance. We handled a survey to study users' opinions in regard to quality of service and website presentation. Results confirmed the ability of the website to make success, mainly if particular enhancements are applied, such as: improving the compositional algorithms of the Mawaweel application, ameliorating the visual guidance and illustration of the website, proposing an Arabic version of the home page and allowing sharing, saving and retrieving the accompanied performance. Future work can include applying similar studies and approaches to websites providing music composition games as web services.

References

[1]   Nasr, V. (2013) Business, Not as Usual. *Finance & Development*, **50**, 26-29.

[2]   Pingdom (2012) World Internet Population Has Doubled in the Last 5 Years. Tech Blog [Web Log].
       http://royal.pingdom.com/2012/04/19/world-internet-population-has-doubled-in-the-last-5-years/

[3]   Kearney, A.T. (2009) Middle East Media on the Move: An Emerging Growth Industry in a Pivotal Region.
       http://www.atkearney.com/documents/10192/4095877b-119c-492b-a236-219098f229df

[4]   (2013) Mawaweel: Web Applet for Automatic Accompaniment to Arab Vocal Improvisation "Mawwāl".
       http://www.mawaweel.com

[5]   Lee, Y. and Kozar, K. (2006) Investigating the Effect of Website Quality on e-Business Success: An Analytic Hierarchy Process (AHP) Approach. *Decision Support Systems*, **42**, 1383-1401.
       http://dx.doi.org/10.1016/j.dss.2005.11.005

[6]   Hoffman, D., Novak, T. and Chatterjee, P. (1995) Commercial Scenarios for the Web: Opportunities and Challenges. *Journal of Computer-Mediated Communication*, **1**.

[7]   Swatman, P.M.C., Krueger, C. and van der Beek, K. (2006) The Changing Digital Content Landscape: An Evaluation of e-Business Model Development in European Online News and Music. *Internet Research*, **16**, 53-80.
       http://www.emeraldinsight.com/doi/abs/10.1108/10662240610642541
       http://dx.doi.org/10.1108/10662240610642541

[8]   Nantel, J. and Glase, E. (2008) The Impact of Language and Culture on Perceived Website Usability. *Journal of Engineering and Technology Management*, **25**, 112-122. http://dx.doi.org/10.1016/j.jengtecman.2008.01.005

[9]   Savage, J. (2005) Information Communication Technologies as a Tool for Re-Imagining Music Education in the 21st Century. *International Journal of Education & the Arts*, **6**. http://www.ijea.org/v6n2/

[10]   Korkofingas, C. and Macri, J. (2013) Does Time Spent Online Have an Influence on Student Performance? Evidence for a Large Business Studies Class. *Journal of University Teaching & Learning Practice*, **10**.

[11]   Waldron, J. and Veblen, K. (2008) The Medium Is the Message: Cyberspace, Community, and Music Learning in the Irish Traditional Music Virtual Community. *Journal of Music, Technology & Education*, **1**, 99-111.

[12]   Al-Ghawanmeh, F., Haddad, R. and Al-Ghawanmeh, M. (2014) Proposing a Process for Using Music Analysis Software to Improve Teaching Authentic Arab Singing and Ornamenting. *International Journal of Humanities and Social Science*.

[13] Al-Ghawanmeh, F., Al-Ghawanmeh, M. and Haddad, R. (2009) Appliance of Music Information Retrieval System for Arabian Woodwinds in E-Learning and Music Education. *Proceedings of the International Computer Music Conference*, Montréal, 16-21 August 2009, 17-20.

[14] Haddad, R., Al-Ghawanmeh, F. and Al-Ghawanmeh, M. (2010) Educational Tools Based on MIR System for Arabian Woodwinds. *Journal of Music, Technology and Education*, **3**, 31-45.
http://dx.doi.org/10.1386/jmte.3.1.31_1

[15] Al-Taee, M., Al-Rawi, M. and Al-Ghawanmeh, F. (2008) Time-Frequency Analysis of the Arabian Flute (Nay) Tone Applied to Automatic Music Transcription. *Proceedings of the 6th ACS/IEEE International Computer Systems and Applications*, Doha, 31 March-4 April 2008, 891-894.
http://dx.doi.org/10.1109/AICCSA.2008.4493636

[16] Al-Taee, M., Al-Ghawanmeh, M., Al-Ghawanmeh, F. and Omar, B. (2009) Analysis and Pattern Recognition of Arabian Woodwind Musical Tones Applied to Query-by-Playing Information Retrieval. *Proceedings of the International Conference of Computer Science and Engineering, ICCSE-59, World Congress on Engineering*, WCE 2009, London, 1-3 July 2009.

[17] Al-Ghawanmeh, F., Jafar, I., Al-Taee, M., Al-Ghawanmeh, M. and Muhsin, Z. (2011) Development of Improved Automatic Music Transcription System for the Arabian Flute (Nay). *Proceedings of the 8th International Multi-Conference on Systems, Signals and Devices (SSD-11)*, Sousse, 22-25 March 2011, 1-6.
http://dx.doi.org/10.1109/SSD.2011.5993561.

[18] Racy, A.J. (1998) Improvisation, Ecstasy, and Performance Dynamics in Arabic Music. In: Nettle, B. and Russell, M., Eds., *In the Course of Performance*: *Studies in the World of Musical Improvisation*, Chicago University Press, Chicago, 95-112.

[19] Arabic Musical Forms (2007) In Maqam World. www.maqamworld.com

[20] Al-Ghawanmeh, F. (2013) Automatic Accompaniment to Arab Vocal Improvisation "Mawwāl". Unpublished Master's Thesis, New York University, New York.

[21] Chuse, L. (2003) Cantaoras: Music, Gender and Identity in Flamenco Song. Routledge, New York.

[22] Al-Ghawanmeh, F., Al-Ghawanmeh, M. and Obeidat, N. (2014) Toward an Improved Automatic Melodic Accompaniment to Arab Vocal Improvisation, Mawwāl. *Proceedings of the 9th Conference on Interdisciplinary Musicology-CIM*14, Berlin, 4-6 December 2014, 397-400.

[23] Al-Momani, M. and Al-Ghawanmeh, F. (2015) The Impact of an Arab-Influenced Piano Curriculum on Students with an Arab Background. International Education Studies, Canadian Center of Science and Education, Toronto.

[24] Strickland, J. (2007) How YouTube Works. http://money.howstuffworks.com/youtube3.htm

[25] What's the Difference between Each Subscription Level?
http://help.soundcloud.com/customer/portal/articles/247820-what-s-the-difference-between-each-subscription-level-

[26] Winchel, W. (2012) 5 Ways to Get Your Website Design Back into Shape. Kunocreative Blog (Web Log).
http://www.kunocreative.com/blog/bid/73640/5-Ways-to-Get-Your-Website-Design-Back-into-Shape

[27] Scaglione, J. (2012) Usability Testing: Why Great Design Is Only Half the Battle. Designmodo (Web Log).
http://designmodo.com/usability-testing/

[28] Music Teacher (2014) Music Theory Videos. http://www.musictheoryvideos.com/

[29] I3zif.com (2013) The Oud Is the Most Popular Arabic Musical Instrument. http://www.i3zif.com/en/

5

The *IRIS* Development Platform and Proposed Object-Oriented Data Base

Mihai-Octavian Dima

Institute for Physics and Nuclear Engineering, Bucharest, Romania
Email: modima@nipne.ro

Abstract

Various code development platforms, such as the ATHENA Framework [1] of the ATLAS [2] experiment encounter lengthy compilation/linking times. To augment this situation, the *IRIS* Development Platform was built as a software development framework acting as compiler, cross-project linker and data fetcher, which allow hot-swaps in order to compare various versions of software under test. The flexibility fostered by IRIS allowed modular exchange of software libraries among developers, making it a powerful development tool. The *IRIS* platform used input data ROOT-ntuples [3]; however a new data model is sought, in line with the facilities offered by *IRIS*. The schematic of a possible new data structuring—as a user implemented object oriented data base, is presented.

Keywords

Software Development Platform, User-Defined Object Oriented Data-Base

1. Introduction

The *IRIS* platform originated as an improvement to the work under the ATHENA Framework [1] of the ATLAS [2] experiment. ATHENA is an Object-oriented/Multi-threading software developed at CERN for data-fetching and code running of ATLAS triggering, and reconstruction under a vast array of software contributions to all sub-systems. The platform was under development in 2004 and considerable overhead was encountered when accessing data and running over untuned sections of code pertaining to various sub-systems. The principal problem encountered was the slow code compilation and linking, a much faster framework being needed—with flexibility to allow exchange of software libraries among developers.

IRIS acts both as compiler and running environment, giving flexibility in comparing work of developers, routine hot-swapping and shared-object library creation. It was created to augment the development of LVL-2 trigger code and had as input data ROOT-tuple [3] skimmed data. The aim then was to be able to test 5 - 10 ideas/

hour, and promote a productive development environment. Envisaged was that work be flexibly hot-swapped in/out among developers using shared object libraries and that routines be "un/mounted" at will at any point ("bean-stalk" **Figure 1**).

Such a software development platform is desirable both for its reliability [4] and its applicability to a number of numerical developments [5].

The routines are "mounted" on the framework just like files are attached to i-nodes to populate a file-system (see **Figure 2**). This is in the main program, that basically lists the routines to be mounted—example below:

```
extern field* amix(int, char**)            ;
int main(int argc, char** argv)
{ field* ipx                                ;
  ipx = amix(argc, argv)                    ;
  JOB dataqual(ipx, "job DATA QUAL" ,
                "pre.alfa1"      ,
                "pre.alfa2"      ,
                "run.beta1"      ,
                "run.beta2"      ,
                "end.gamma1"     ,
                "end.gamma2"     ,
            NULL)                           ;
  dataqual.run()                            ;
  delete ipx                                ;
}
```

The *iris* executable will expect the presence in the running directory of *alfa*1.*cc*, *alfa*2.*cc*, *beta*1.*cc*, *beta*2.*cc*, *gamma*1.*cc*, and *gamma*2.*cc*. More "leafs" can be of course added to the iris stalk. After downloading and un-

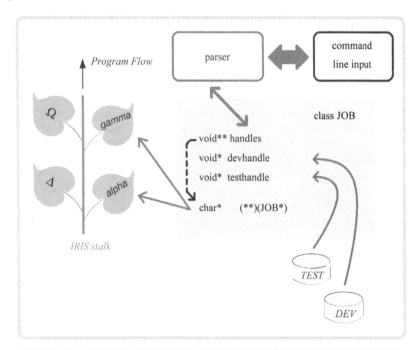

Figure 1. The IRIS platform relies on a mounter singleton defining handles (sockets) to functions found in shared object libraries. These are typed into char* (**)(JOB*) functions that actually are mounted in the exec-loop of the class. Various auxiliary functions are also performed, like compilation of routines that are under development—using the stdlib library. Shared objects are loaded with the dlfcn library.

packing the package, it can be compiled with the standard make. At this point *iris* will take control, compile the above files and make a *dev.so* shared-object library. Issuing the command *iris* will produce the following output:

```
Compiling alfa1  ... DONE ! (1 out of 6)
Compiling alfa2  ... DONE ! (2 out of 6)
Compiling beta1  ... DONE ! (3 out of 6)
Compiling beta2  ... DONE ! (4 out of 6)
Compiling gamma1 ... DONE ! (5 out of 6)
Compiling gamma2 ... DONE ! (6 out of 6)
----------
Building DEV shared lib ... DONE !
```

At this first stage it will not run the job. To run the job, issue: *iris beta*1. In full this means *iris -s dev.run.beta*1, or: shadow and replace the first function from the *RUN*-section with function *beta*1 (found in *dev.so*), and then run the job. The code will open *dev.so* for the default functions set in *t.cc*, and also the **.so* file in which the substitute function *beta*1 is found (also *dev.so*). It will build the necessary function pointers on the "stalk" and:

- run the *PRE*-section in the *JOB*-object constructor;
- in the *JOB.run*() function it will open the ROOT-tuple and run for each event all "leaves" in the *RUN*-section. The ROOT-tuple will close itself at the end of *JOB.run*() and finally
- the *END*-section "leaves" will be run in the destructor section of *JOB*.

2. Usage of *IRIS*

The iris executable is designed to give flexibility in development work: it is fast in data-fetching, fast in function-fetching [6] and versatile in compiling or just fetching functions (owned by the developer, or by other developers in the group). This allows developers to rapidly switch from one hypothesis to another, test single or multiple code pieces, and compare with reference new ideas in the group. Below will be outlined the main use-cases of *iris*. The notation convention of iris is the following: fully qualified name refers to *file.section.function* and denotes that the user wants to place function *function* from file *file* in section section. Omitting the file defaults to *dev*, omitting the section defaults to *run*, and omitting the function defaults to ... a link-fault.

Compiling routines—most development work means having a fixed set of "environment"-routines that run everytime, and 1 - 2 routines that change as the developer improves the algorithm, or makes amendments to it. This requires the fixed set to be mentioned in t.cc as shown in the Introduction, and the amended set to be declared at run-time. First time *iris* is run (command *iris*), it produces the *dev.so* library in which the fixed environment will reside, together with the starting version of the routines to be amended. The developer implements some changes, and issues a command like *iris pre.alfa*1 *beta*1 *-c pre.delta omega*, where *delta* and *omega* are the new versions of *alfa*2 and *beta*2. (Renaming is not necessary, here it is done for code output illustrative purposes only.) This means: compile the new versions *delta* and *omega*, make the *test.so* library with them, shadow *alfa*1 with itself (no change) and likewise with beta1, then shadow *alfa*2 from *dev.so* with the new version from *test.so* and likewise for *beta*2. The output from *iris* will look like this:

```
Compiling delta ... DONE !
Compiling omega ... DONE !
----------
Building TEST shared lib ... DONE !
**************************
PRE jobs
---
ran >> alfa1
ran >> delta
---------------------------
RUN jobs
---
```

```
event nr. 0 ran >> beta1 >> omega ... DONE !
event nr. 1 ran >> beta1 >> omega ... DONE !
event nr. 2 ran >> beta1 >> omega ... DONE !
---------------------------
END jobs
---
ran >> gamma1
ran >> gamma2
*************************
```

Note that the code will print the function's name after it has been executed, which is useful for debugging purposes.

It is easy to see how the "shadowing" convention works: routines preceeded by *-s* (or simply nothing) are considered replacements in their respective sections (if a section is not mentioned, it is defaulted to *run*). Replacements are made until there are none more (as defined in *t.cc*). In the above example only two replacements per section are possible. Addition of routines is possible, as it will be shown below.

If in addition to *-s* the *-c* is also present (as *-sc*, or simply *-c*), then *iris* expects the respective *files.cc* to be present in the running directory: it will compile them, build the *test.so* library and mount them, according to prescription, on the *iris* "stalk".

Swapping routines in/out—it is possible that the developer wants to check a reference library against developed code, or simply check a collegue's *dev.so* library which—for notation purposes—shall be called *ext.so*, the "external" library. This is one of the main strengths of *iris*, the flexibility to accommodate various contributions within the development group.

The same above operations would have been in this case: *iris pre.alfa1 beta1 -s ext.pre.delta ext.run.omega*. The package will skip compilation of any routines and simply load from the file *ext* the required functions to be

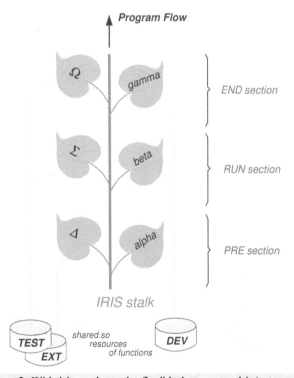

Figure 2. With iris work can be flexibly hot-swapped in/out among developers using shared object libraries—by "un/mount" at any point on a chain resembling a bean-stalk. The iris code compiles *dev.so* and *test.so* libraries and at runtime can open those for desired functions, or override them with functions from other *ext.so* libraries.

attached to the *iris-* "stalk". The output in this case would be:

```
* * * * * * * * * * * * * * * * * * * * * * * *
PRE jobs
---
ran >> alfa1
ran >> delta
-----------------------------
RUN jobs
---
event nr. 0 ran >> beta1 >> omega ... DONE !
event nr. 1 ran >> beta1 >> omega ... DONE !
event nr. 2 ran >> beta1 >> omega ... DONE !
-----------------------------
END jobs
---
ran >> gamma1
ran >> gamma2
* * * * * * * * * * * * * * * * * * * * * * * *
```

It is possible to combine local function compilation with external libraries: *iris pre.alfa*1 *beta*1 *-s ext.pre.delta -c omega*, the output being:

```
Compiling omega ... DONE !
----------
Building TEST shared lib ... DONE !
* * * * * * * * * * * * * * * * * * * * * * * *
PRE jobs
---
ran >> alfa1
ran >> delta
-----------------------------
RUN jobs
---
event nr. 0 ran >> beta1 >> omega ... DONE !
event nr. 1 ran >> beta1 >> omega ... DONE !
event nr. 2 ran >> beta1 >> omega ... DONE !
-----------------------------
END jobs
---
ran >> gamma1
ran >> gamma2
* * * * * * * * * * * * * * * * * * * * * * * *
```

Adding routines—is performed by the *-a* qualifier. For example *iris pre.alfa*1 *beta*1 *-a ext.pre.delta -c omega* would mean hot-swap *alfa*1, immediately after add the list of functions following the *-a* qualifier (up to the next qualifier), compile *omega* and replace *beta*2 with it. The output would look like:

```
Compiling omega ... DONE !
----------
Building TEST shared lib ... DONE !
* * * * * * * * * * * * * * * * * * * * * * * *
PRE jobs
```

```
---
ran >> alfa1
ran >> delta
ran >> alfa2
----------------------------
RUN jobs
---
event nr. 0 ran >> beta1 >> omega ... DONE !
event nr. 1 ran >> beta1 >> omega ... DONE !
event nr. 2 ran >> beta1 >> omega ... DONE !
----------------------------
END jobs
---
ran >> gamma1
ran >> gamma2
**************************
```

3. Persistent Object Data Base

IRIS relied on n-tuples as input data—in the form of ROOT-tuples [3]. This is flat-data and the current section offers a few ideas on how a similar, user designed, but object oriented data base could be written.

Work with C++ (F-90 and any algorithm language) has led mostly to relational data storage. Just like in the case of IRIS above, more was not considered needed. Starting with the early 2000's this began to change, persistent (non-flatened) object storage being more and more of need.

Writing data to permanent storage was formalized starting with the 1960's (relational data bases—RDB) and the 1980's (object oriented data bases—OODB).

The most widely accepted standard for OODB Management System (OODBMS [7]) is the ODMG 3.0 [8]. The ODMG group however is divided over options for a future 4th generation OODBMS standard. ODMG places 2 general sets of demands usually required by an OODBMS:
- DBMS conditions:
  1. persistence
  2. secondary storage management
  3. concurrency
  4. recovery
  5. ad hoc query facility
- OO conditions:
  1. handling complex objects
  2. accommodating object identity
  3. observing encapsulation
  4. handling types or classes
  5. complying with inheritance
  6. overriding combined with late binding
  7. extensibility
  8. having computational completeness

It became apparent in C++ evolution [9] that the objects not only are "constructed" by the user, but also the user should be responsible for their proper disposal (memory management, de-allocation). This can be extended: the user being also responsible for selecting and writing which data needs to go in a data-base (likewise in the destructor section of a class).

Of special attention here is the allocation of memory within objects "construction"—which the machine is not (and should not) be able to interfere with, the management of this resource being entirely up to the user. Such allocation may be virtual by inheritance (*i.e.*—"fish" allocates one size/(type) of memory, while "dog" allocates another, both inheriting "farm animal"). This led to the (correct!) prevalence of destructors and virtual destructors in C++ and the responsibility of the user in managing their memory de/allocation.

Naturally, this also led to a number of problems in large projects involving numerous contributors—that had little Quality Control (memory leaks, segmentation faults, etc.).

Taking a cue from this evolution writing persistent objects to permanent storage should have the same approach: namely making the user responsible for the proper writing of objects to the DB. Basically this proceeds in the same way that the objects are deleted in the destructor.

The model here proposed relies thus on the user, not the DB-software, or the operating system (OS) to realise these demands—just as the application relies on the user to properly write the destructor.

In principle the only memory accounting needed is that of the (new)-allocation of known C++ types. All arrays of user-defined objects need not be known in number, as each object's destructor is called by an iterative loop of the *delete*[] statement, by a (secret) counter held by the OS. Each destructor will know what to do (and what to write).

The same applies for deleting a generic class of objects—say "animal farm", the virtual destructor *delete*[ ]-ing (and writing to DB, relyant on each of its implementations) "cattle", "sheep", "chicken" ... accordingly.

The above become transparent with the use of smart pointers, though these are implementation dependent and perhaps better to be avoided.

Typical flatening of objects would be implemented by writing to 3 DB's (**Figure 3**):

- a *header-DB* (**HDB**): containing the definitions of the classes—indexed by order number
- an *object-DB* (**ODB**): containing flattened objects, indexed by type and order number. Order numbers would be flagged as \visible" and \invisible", depending upon the object being declared self-standing, or within a class—in 2 lists: v1, v2, v3, ... and i1, i2, i3 ... etc. This allows fast DB-querying, both internally and externally
- an *allocation-BD* (**ADB**): containing memory allocations of each object, indexed by order nr. and regarded as bit-streams (their deconvolution interpreted by the object-DB).

Relational keys—between the three are evidently needed; however they are fast, as the above indexing pertains little header volume (little impedance mismatch). A slim-tall example of relation key structure can be found in the JAZELLE-DBMS [10].

JAZELLE keys delete all horizontally related objects, although this is a requirement specific to algorithmic languages (C, C++, F-90, etc.). ADA for instance does not require DB fault-free compliance, as incomplete type declarations are common practice in this language, hence references to missing objects are tolerated.

Take the example "particle" in High Energy Physics, which can reference: "vertex", "track", "cluster", "mc-truth". Any of the objects may be missing, hence "particle" that references all, or themselves referencing among themselves, need not all disappear just because one is absent. Said absence causes a (solved or) unsolved DB-fault and is signalled by a nil-pointer. This feature is useful, as it saves time from loading un-necessary structures into the application, from the DB. This touches also on OO-8 above: "extensibility"—in the sense that

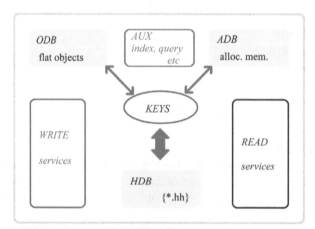

Figure 3. A section showing diagram of the proposed object oriented data base. The user (responsible for the objects' destructors) is also the implementer of the writing of objects. This is performed with the services offered by the DB, however in the structure format here shown.

it can be extended also with missing data types (having no specification), which however, may be added at a later stage, but, which do not prevent the partial-functioning of the DB.

As the user is the implementer of the read-constructor and write-destructor, this job will rely on DB "services" of accessing/storing data in the 3 sub-DB's.

Version-check services would also be provided issuing strong-warnings in case of outdate-mismatches (of the header files).

Transparent persistence of the DB is also fast, updating the ODB/ADB being nearly header free.

Acknowledgements

This work was supported by a grant of the Romanian National Authority for Scientific Research, CNCS-UEFISCDI, grant number ANCS PN09370104. I am also thankful to the Wuppertal Physics Department for the 2004 stay and to the ATLAS Collaboration for access to the ATHENA Framework and Monte Carlo simulation data.

References

[1]   ATLAS Collaboration—Duckeck, G., *et al.* (2005) Atlas Computing: Technical Design Report. CERN-LHCC-2005-022; Lenzi, B. (2009) The Physics Analysis Tools Project for the ATLAS Experiment. ATL-SOFT-PROC-2009-006.

[2]   Aad, G., *et al.* (2008) The ATLAS Experiment at the CERN Large Hadron Collider. *Journal of Instrumentation*, **3**, S08003.

[3]   Antcheva, I., *et al.* (2009) ROOT—A C++ Framework for Petabyte Data Storage, Statistical Analysis and Visualization. *Computer Physics Communications*, **180**, 2499-2512. http://dx.doi.org/10.1016/j.cpc.2009.08.005

[4]   Adam, G. and Adam, S. (2003) Reliable Software in Computational Physics. *Romanian Reports in Physics*, **55**, 488.

[5]   Adam, G., *et al.* (2006) Resolving Thin Boundary Layers in Numerical Quadrature. *Romanian Reports in Physics*, **58**, 155; Balaceanu, V. and Pavelescu, M. (2011) Neutronic Calculation System for CANDU Core Based on Transport Methods. *Romanian Reports in Physics*, **63**, 948; Necula, C. and Panaiotu, C. (2008) Application of Dynamic Programming to the Dating of a Loess-Paleosol Sequence. *Romanian Reports in Physics*, **60**, 157.

[6]   Contrary to Popular Belief, Shared-Object Dynamic Binding Provides Faster Code through Memory "In-Page" Function Fitting and Considerably Faster Hot-Swap Times vs. Static Binding.

[7]   O'Brien, J.A. and Marakas, G.M. (2009) Management Information Systems. McGraw-Hill/Irwin, New York; Atkinson, M., *et al.* (1992) The Object-Oriented Database Manifesto. In: *Building an Object-Oriented Database System*, Morgan Kaufmann Publishers Inc., San Francisco, 1-20.

[8]   Cattell, R.G.G., *et al.*, Eds. (2000) The Object Data Management Standard: ODMG 3.0. Morgan Kaufmann Publishers Inc., San Francisco.

[9]   Bjarne Stroustrup (1989) The Evolution of C++: 1985-1989. *Computing Systems*, **2**, 191; Bjarne Stroustrup (1999) An Overview of the C++ Programming Language, in: The Handbook of Object Technology, Ed. Saba Zamir, CRC Press LLC, Boca Raton; Bjarne Stroustrup (1994) The Design and Evolution of C++, in: Addison-Wesley Publ.; Torsten Sehy (2012) *Evolution of C++*, Seminar on Languages for Scientific Computing. http://hpac.rwth-aachen.de/teaching/sem-lsc-12/EvolutionC++.pdf

[10] Johnson, T. (1990) JAZELLE Users Manual, SLAC-R-362.

6

Enhancing ERS-A Algorithm for Pattern Matching (EERS-A)

Dima Suleiman[1], Mariam Itriq[1], Aseel Al-Anani[2], Rola Al-Khalid[2], Amjad Hudaib[2]

[1]Department of Business Information Technology, King Abdullah II School for Information Technology, The University of Jordan, Amman, Jordan
[2]Department of Computer Information Systems, King Abdullah II School for Information Technology, The University of Jordan, Amman, Jordan
Email: dima.suleiman@ju.edu.jo, m.itriq@ju.edu.jo, a.anani@ju.edu.jo, r.khalid@ju.edu.jo, ahudaib@ju.edu.jo

Abstract

Pattern matching is a very important topic in computer science. It has been used in various applications such as information retrieval, virus scanning, DNA sequence analysis, data mining, machine learning, network security and pattern recognition. This paper has presented a new pattern matching algorithm—Enhanced ERS-A, which is an improvement over ERS-S algorithm. In ERS-A, two sliding windows are used to scan the text from the left and the right simultaneously. The proposed algorithm also scans the text from the left and the right simultaneously as well as making comparisons with the pattern from both sides simultaneously. The comparisons done between the text and the pattern are done from both sides in parallel. The shift technique used in the Enhanced ERS-A is the four consecutive characters in the text immediately following the pattern window. The experimental results show that the Enhanced ERS-A has enhanced the process of pattern matching by reducing the number of comparisons performed.

Keywords

Pattern Matching, Enhanced Two Sliding Windows Algorithm, RS-A Fast Pattern Matching Algorithm, Enhanced RS-A

1. Introduction

Many applications use pattern matching algorithms such as search engines, anti-virus and biological applications such as DNA [1]-[5].

Most of the algorithms have been implemented in order to make the searching process faster and more efficient; this can be achieved either by reducing the number of attempts, comparisons or by both. Some of algorithms made enhancements on preprocessing phase [6]-[9] and searching phase [10]-[12], and others modified the shifting technique [5] [9] [13]-[15] used in a case of a mismatch between the pattern and the text.

Searching process differs from one algorithm to another: some algorithms scan the text from one side only, either from left [15] or from right [5]; other algorithms use two sliding windows to scan the text from the left and the right sides simultaneously [10]-[13].

Some algorithms made modification on the shifting values. The shift value is the amount of shift that the sliding window will move in a case of a mismatch between the text and the window; shift values depend on the number of consecutive characters immediately after the sliding window. Some algorithms use one consecutive character [16] [17]; others use two [10] [12] [15] and few use three [13].

In this paper, we propose a new pattern matching algorithm—Enhanced ERS-A. The algorithm uses two sliding windows such as TSW [12], ETSW [10], ERS-A [11] and EBR [13] algorithms. It also uses four consecutive characters to compute the shift values such as RS-A [5] and ERS-A [11] algorithms. In addition to that, it uses the same comparison technique between the pattern and the text that was used in ETSW [10].

This paper compares between the new algorithms of EERS-A, ETSW [10] and ERS-A [11]. The results showed that the new algorithm is better than others as explained in Section 5. The reminder of this paper is organized as follows: Section 2 consists of related works; Section 3 explains EERS-A algorithm; Section 4 covers the analysis. Finally, the conclusion and the future work are presented in Section 6.

2. Related Works

Pattern matching algorithms were needed in many applications [2] [14] [18]-[20]. Some algorithms made enhancement in a memory used in preprocessing phase, while others try to make the searching process faster and more efficient [8] [9] [21].

The Berry-Ravindran algorithm (BR) [15] made enhancement in Boyer Moore algorithm [16]. In a case of a mismatch between the text and the pattern window Boyer uses one consecutive character in the text immediately to the right of the pattern window to determine amount of shift the window must move, on the other hand Berry-Ravindran uses two consecutive characters.

Many enhancements made in Berry-Ravindran algorithm (BR) [15], some algorithms changed the searching process but on the other hand they used the same bad character shift values, bad character shift depends on using two consecutive characters immediately that follow the text such as TSW [12] and ETSW [10]. Others made enhancement on the shift values such as RS-A [5] and ERS-A [11] these two algorithms changed the shift values by using four consecutive character instead of two, also EBR [13] algorithm made modifications on Berry-Ravindran bad character shift by depending on using three consecutive characters.

Two Sliding Windows algorithm TSW [12] used the same preprocessing technique used in BR [15] but made enhancements on the searching phase. In a case of a mismatch between the pattern and text, it uses two consecutive characters to determine the amount of shift the pattern window must slide which is the same technique used in BR [15], but instead of using one pattern window to scan the text as in BR [15] it uses two sliding windows that scan it in parallel.

Searching process become faster in Enhanced Two Sliding Window algorithm (ETSW) [10]. ETSW [10] made enhancements on TSW [12] by minimizing the number of comparisons needed but it doesn't make any changes on the number of attempts. The reason for this is that two algorithms used the same preprocessing techniques and also used the two sliding window, the only difference between them is related to the idea that TSW [12] compares the text with the pattern from one side of the pattern while ETSW [10] compare the text with the pattern from the both sides of the pattern at the same time, the best time complexity is $O(m/2)$ and the worst case time complexity is $O\big(\big((n/2-m/2+1)\big)(m/2)\big)$. The preprocess time complexity is $O\big(2(m-1)\big)$.

RS-A [5] algorithm used only one window to search for a pattern p in a text t from the right side of the text. In order to make the searching process faster ERS-A [11] algorithms made enhancements on RS-A by using two windows instead of one. The left window aligned with the text from the left and in a case of a mismatch the window will be shifted to the right, and the right window aligned with text from the right and in a case of a mismatch the window will be shifted to the left. The two windows slide in parallel. The search will stop either when the pattern is found or in a case the pattern not found at all.

The EERS-A made enhancement on ERS-A [11], it uses the same preprocessing technique that depends on using four consecutive characters to determine the amount of shift, it also uses two sliding windows to scan the text from the left and right sides at the same time. Enhancements made on a comparison between the text and the pattern, in this case it uses the same method used in ETSW [10], which make comparisons between the text and the pattern from both sides of the pattern at the same time. It is obvious from the results that there are no changes in average number of attempts in both ERS-A [11] and EERS-A, on the other hand there are a clear differences in average number of comparisons. The EERS-A is more efficient and faster.

3. The Enhanced ERS-A Algorithm

EERS-A algorithm improved the searching process by scanning the pattern as well as the text from both sides simultaneously. EERS-A used two sliding windows to scan the text from both sides at the same time; also comparisons between the pattern and the text happened from both sides of the pattern.

EERS-A algorithm used the same searching technique used in ERS-A, they uses two sliding windows to search for a pattern p in a text t. Two sliding windows scan the text from the left and right side at the same time and in a case of a mismatch both algorithms will use RS-A bad character shift function [5]. The searching process will stop either when a pattern is found or in a case a pattern is not found in the text at all.

The main difference between EERS-A and ERS-A [11] algorithms is that in ERS-A [11] comparisons between the pattern and the text happened only from the left side of the pattern while in EERS-A comparisons done from left and right sides of the pattern at the same time.

4. Pre-Processing Phase

Two arrays are generated in this phase *nextl* and *nextr*, each array is one-dimensional array. The values of the *nextr* array are calculated according to RS-A algorithm [5]. Initially the indexes of the four consecutive characters of the text after aligning it with the right window are $(n - m - 4)$, $(n - m - 3)$, $(n - m - 2)$ and $(n - m - 1)$ for a, b, c and d respectively, which are used to calculate the shift values in a case of a mismatch from the right side of the text as in Equation (1).

$$
\text{Right shift value } [a,b,c,d] = \min
\begin{cases}
m+3 & \text{if } p[m-1] = a \\
m+2 & \text{if } p[m-1] = b \\
m+1 & \text{if } p[m-1] = c \\
1 & \text{if } p[0] = d \\
2 & \text{if } p[0][1] = cd \\
3 & \text{if } p[0][1][2] = bcd \\
m-((m-4)-i) & \text{if } p[i][i+1][i+2][i+3] = abcd \\
m+4 & \text{otherwise}
\end{cases}
\tag{1}
$$

On the other hand, the values of the *nextl* array are calculated according ERS-A algorithm [11]. The shift values are calculated by using four consecutive text characters a, b, c and d which are aligned immediately to the right of the left sliding window. Initially, the indexes of the four consecutive characters in the text string needed to search the text from the left side are $(m + 1)$, $(m + 2)$, $(m + 3)$ and $(m + 4)$ for a, b, c and d respectively as in Equation (2).

$$
\text{Left shift value } [a,b,c,d] = \min
\begin{cases}
1 & \text{if } p[m-1] = a \\
2 & \text{if } p[m-2][m-1] = ab \\
3 & \text{if } p[m-3][m-2][m-1] = abc \\
m+1 & \text{if } p[0] = b \\
m+2 & \text{if } p[0] = c \\
m+3 & \text{if } p[0] = d \\
m-i & \text{if } p[i][i+1][i+2][i+3] = abcd \\
m+4 & \text{otherwise}
\end{cases}
\tag{2}
$$

The pre-processing phase is the same in both ERS-A and EERS-A algorithms but the searching phase is enhanced in EERS-A.

5. Searching Phase

In EERS-A algorithm the searching process started by aligning two windows with the text, the left window aligned with the beginning of the text and the right window aligned with the end of the text. In case of a mismatch the proposed window will be shifted according to next array values calculated in a preprocessing phase; the left window will be shifted to the right and the right window will be shifted to left.

Four pointers will be used in a comparison process between the text and the pattern, two for each window. The left window uses the L and temp_newlindex pointers while the right window uses the R and temp_newrindex pointers.

Comparisons between the text and the pattern from both sides is the same, in each window the first character of the pattern is compared with the corresponding text character and at the same time the last character of the pattern is compared with the corresponding character in the text. Each window uses different pointers as explained below:

6. Left_Window Search Process

After aligning the left window with the text from the left, comparisons between the pattern and the text will be done using two pointers, L and temp_newlindex, L pointer points at the last character of the pattern and the temp_newlindex points at the first character of the pattern, comparisons are made between the pointers and the corresponding characters of the text.

If a mismatch occurs in any pointer a shift will occurs according to the ERS-A bad character algorithm.

In case of a match the two pointers will move.

The L pointer will move to the left and the temp_newlindex will move to the right. A movement of pointers in a case of a match will stop either when two pointers reach the middle of the pattern or when the L pointer is less than or equal the temp_newlindex, in either case the pattern is found.

7. Right_Window Search Process

After aligning the right window with the text from the right, comparisons between the pattern and the text will be done using two pointers, R and temp_newrindex, R pointer points at the first character of the pattern and the temp_newrindex points at the last character of the pattern, comparisons are made between the pointers and the corresponding characters of the text.

If a mismatch occurs in any pointer a shift will occurs according to the ERS-A bad character algorithm. In case of a match the two pointers will move. The R pointer will move to the right and the temp_newrindex will move to the left. A movement of pointers in a case of a match will stop either when two pointers reach the middle of the pattern or when the R pointer is less than or equal the temp_newrindex, in either case the pattern is found.

The proposed EERS-A algorithm is explained in **Figure 1**.

8. Working Example

In this section, we will give an example to explain the new algorithm.

Given:

Pattern (P) = "ACCBCBAC", $m = 8$,

Text (T) = "ABCDABADBACEDABACCBCBACABADBCEDABADDDBACCBABCBCBAB", $n = 50$.

9. Pre-Processing Phase

Initially, *shiftl* = *shiftr* = $m + 4 = 12$.

The shift values are stored in two arrays *nextl* and *nextr* as shown in **Figure 2(a)** and **Figure 2(b)** respectively.

To build the two next arrays (*nextl* and *nextr*), we take each four consecutive characters of the pattern and

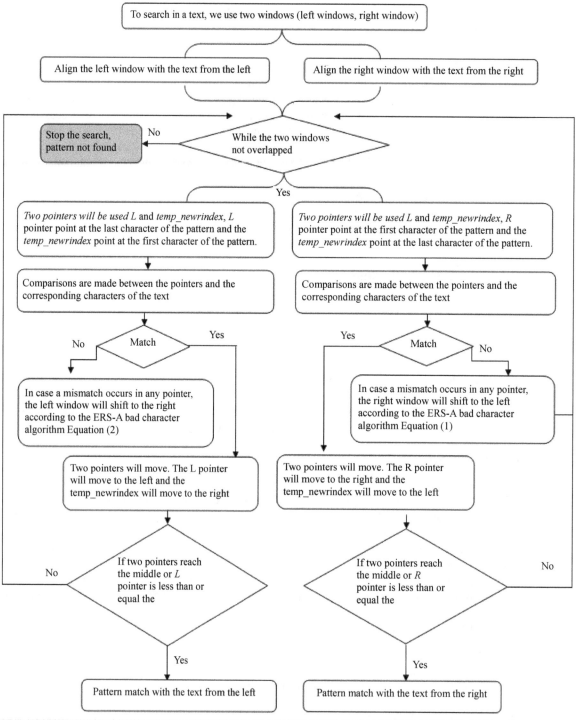

Figure 1. EERS-A flowchart.

Figure 2. The *nextl* and *nextr* arrays.

give it an index starting from 0. For example for the pattern structure ACCBCBAC, the consecutive characters ACCB, CCBC, CBCB, BCBA and CBAC are given the indexes 0, 1, 2, 3 and 4 respectively.

The shift values for the *nextr* array are calculated according to Equation (1) while the shift values for the *nextl* array are calculated according to Equation (2).

10. Searching Phase

The searching process for the pattern P is explained through the working example as shown in **Figure 3**.

10.1. First Attempt

In the first attempt (see **Figure 3(a)**), we align the left sliding window with the text from the left. In this case, a comparison is made between the text character located at index 0 (character A) with the leftmost character in the pattern (character A) although a match occurs, the total result is a mismatch since at the same time a comparison must be made between the text character at index 7 (character D) with the rightmost character in the pattern (character C); therefore we take the four consecutive characters of the text at index 8, 9, 10 and 11 which are (B, A, C and E) respectively. To determine the amount of shift (*shiftl*) we have to do the following:

Since if $p[m-3][m-2][m-1] = abc$; BAC = BAC then according to a preprocessing algorithm the shift value will be 3.

10.2. Second Attempt

In the second attempt (see **Figure 3(b)**), we align the right sliding window with the text from the right. In this case, a match occurs between text character at index 42 (A) and left most character of the pattern character A but a mismatch occurs between the last text character B with the last pattern character C so as a total result,

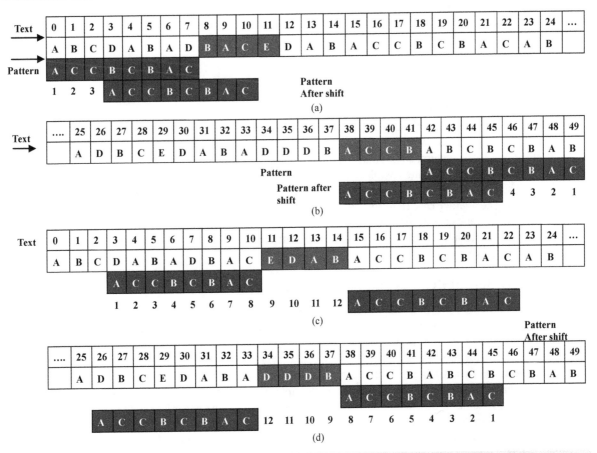

Figure 3. Working example.

there is a mismatch; therefore we take the four consecutive characters from the text at index 38, 39, 40 and 41 which are A, C, C and B respectively. To determine the amount of shift (*shiftr*), we have to do the following:

a) We find the index of ACCB in the pattern which is 0.

b) Since we search the text from the right side we use *nextr* array, and *shiftr* = *nextr*[0] = 4; therefore the window will be shifted to the left 4 steps.

10.3. Third Attempt

In the third attempt (see **Figure 3(c)**), a mismatch occurs from the left between the text character at index 3 (character D) and the leftmost character in the pattern (character A) while there is a match between the text character at index 10 (character C) and the rightmost character in the pattern (character C); therefore we take the four consecutive characters from the text at indexes 11, 12, 13 and 14 which are E, D, A and B respectively, since EDAB is not found in the pattern, so the window will be shifted to the right 12 steps.

10.4. Fourth Attempt

In the fourth attempt (see **Figure 3(d)**), a comparison is made between the text character located at index 38 (character A) with the leftmost character in the pattern (character A) at the same time a comparison must be made between the text character at index 45 (character B) with the rightmost character in the pattern (character C) since there is a mismatch we take the four consecutive characters of the text at index 34, 35, 36 and 37 which are D, D, D and A respectively; since DDDB is not found in the pattern, so the window will be shifted to the left 12 steps.

10.5. Fifth Attempt

We align the left most character of the pattern P[0] with T[15]. A comparison between the pattern and the text characters leads to a complete match at index 15. In this case, the occurrence of the pattern is found using the left window.

11. Analysis

Preposition 1: The space complexity is $O(2(m-3))$ where m is the pattern length.

Preposition 2: The pre-process time complexity is $O(2(m-3))$.

Lemma 1: The worst case time complexity is $O(((n/2 - m/2 + 1))(m/2))$.

Proof: The worst occurs when a match between the text and patterns occurs in all characters except a character at index $m/2$ in the pattern, and if at the same time the shift values in case of a mismatch equal to 1.

Lemma 2: The best case time complexity is $O(m/2)$.

Proof: The best case occurs when the pattern is found in the leftmost or the rightmost sides of the text.

Lemma 3: The average case time complexity is $O(n/(2*(m/2 + 4)))$.

Proof: The average case occurs when the four consecutive characters of the text directly following the sliding window is not found in the pattern. In this case, the shift value will be $(m + 4)$ and hence the time complexity is $O\left(\left[n/(2*(m/2 + 4))\right]\right)$.

12. Experimental Results and Discussion

Several experiments have been done using Book 1 from the Calgary corpus [22] to be the text in most of searching algorithms. Book 1 consists of 141,274 words (752,149 characters). Book 1 consists of 141,274 words (752,149 characters). Patterns of different lengths are also taken from Book 1.

Table 1 shows the results of comparing the algorithms ETSW, ERS-A and EERS-A.

In **Table 1**, the first column related to the pattern length; second column is the number of words in a certain length. It can be clearly seen that the number of attempts in EERS-A and ERS-A are the same since the two algorithms use the same shifting techniques in a case of a mismatch, and according to the results it's clear that the number of comparisons in EERS-A are better than all other algorithms. For example, as shown in **Table 1**, 2896 words of length 6, the average number of comparisons in ETSW is 7633, in ERS-A is 6750 and in the new algorithms is 6212, which is the minimum value among the others values.

ETSW algorithm and EERS-A algorithm use the same comparison technique, they use two sliding windows to scan the text, and in addition to that they use the same technique when comparing the text with the pattern where comparisons happened from both sides of the pattern simultaneously. It is clear that the number of comparisons and attempts in EERS-A algorithm are better than ERS-A algorithm and this refers to using different shifting technique. While ETSW uses Berry-Ravindran (BR) [15] bad character shift values which uses two consecutive characters, EERS-A uses ERS-A [11] bad character shift values that uses four consecutive characters.

Table 2 shows the average number of attempts and comparisons for 100 words taken from the right side of Book1. It is clear that EERS-A is the best among all others according to the number of comparisons and the same results can be seen in **Table 3** and **Table 4**.

Table 5 and **Figure 4** show the average number of comparisons needed to search for patterns with different lengths. The results show that EERS-A finds the patterns with minimum number of comparisons compared with

Table 1. The average number of attempts and comparisons of ETSW, ERS-A and EERS-A algorithms.

Pattern length	Number of words	ETSW		ERS-A		EERS-A	
		Attempts	Comparisons	Attempts	Comparisons	Attempts	Comparisons
5	4535	4456	3549	3533	3880	3533	2813
6	2896	7596	7633	6166	6750	6166	6212
7	1988	9341	9118	7737	8506	7737	7636
8	1167	10056	10115	8451	9319	8451	8525
9	681	9538	9590	8106	8957	8106	8171
10	382	9283	9339	7970	8830	7970	8042
11	191	5451	5482	4701	5146	4701	4742
12	69	6384	6433	5589	6286	5589	5653
13	55	7947	7986	6955	7587	6955	7004
14	139	19437	19535	17115	18776	17115	17242
15	32	19682	19782	17385	19198	17385	17519
16	10	20029	20092	17722	19147	17722	17807
17	3	21897	22147	19521	22669	19521	19855

Table 2. The average number of attempts and comparisons performed to search for (100) patterns selected from the right side of the text.

Pattern length	Number of words	ETSW		ERS-A		EERS-A	
		Attempts	Comparisons	Attempts	Comparisons	Attempts	Comparisons
5	100	185	187	146	163	146	148
6	100	227	230	182	205	182	186
7	100	347	351	286	324	286	291
8	100	504	510	424	476	424	431
9	100	670	677	571	640	571	579
10	100	1160	1170	999	1117	999	1011
11	100	622	628	529	597	529	536
12	100	865	878	756	860	756	774

Table 3. The average number of attempts and comparisons performed to search for (100) patterns selected from the middle of the text.

Pattern length	Number of words	ETSW		ERS-A		EERS-A	
		Attempts	Comparisons	Attempts	Comparisons	Attempts	Comparisons
5	100	13965	11618	11038	11970	11038	10875
6	100	16682	16771	13536	14870	13536	13648
7	100	27267	26242	22607	24971	22607	22179
8	100	27830	28015	23385	25976	23385	23617
9	100	33929	34069	28764	31541	28764	28943
10	100	29676	29845	25471	28193	25471	25689
11	100	23195	23242	19886	21119	19886	19946
12	100	26806	27009	23484	26507	23484	23761

Table 4. The average number of attempts and comparisons performed to search for (100) patterns selected from the left side of the text.

Pattern length	Number of words	ETSW		ERS-A		EERS-A	
		Attempts	Comparisons	Attempts	Comparisons	Attempts	Comparisons
5	100	271	270	216	238	216	218
6	100	364	368	295	326	295	299
7	100	402	405	333	372	333	337
8	100	536	541	451	499	451	457
9	100	776	783	660	730	660	668
10	100	1579	1593	1361	1517	1361	1378
11	100	619	624	531	573	531	537
12	100	1667	1685	1459	1641	1459	1480

Table 5. The average number of attempts and comparisons for patterns with different lengths.

Pattern length	Number of words	TSW	ETSW	RS-A	ERS-A	EERS-A
		Comparisons	Comparisons	Comparisons	Comparisons	Comparisons
5	4535	4896	3549	8191	3880	2813
6	2896	8311	7633	9556	6750	6212
7	1988	10263	9118	10638	8506	7636
8	1167	11087	10115	11922	9319	8525
9	681	10538	9590	12911	8957	8171
10	382	10272	9339	12927	8830	8042
11	191	5967	5482	11672	5146	4742
12	69	7168	6433	9030	6286	5653
13	55	8673	7986	9422	7587	7004
14	139	21319	19535	17845	18776	17242
15	32	21739	19782	18318	19198	17519
16	10	21596	20092	23531	19147	17807
17	3	25404	22147	23119	22669	19855

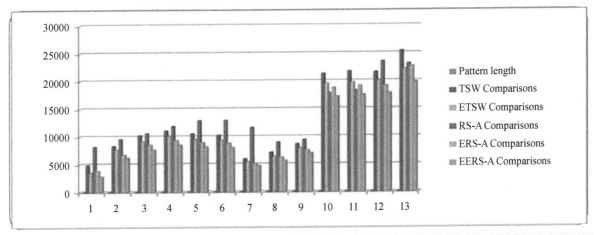

Figure 4. The average number of comparisons of TSW, ETSW, RS-A and ERS-A, EERS-A algorithms.

other algorithms such as TSW, ETSW, RSA and ERS-A. For example, it took EERS-A 8042 comparisons to locate the pattern of length 10 while it took TSW, ETSW, RS-A and ERS-A 10272, 9339, 12927 and 8830 comparisons respectively for the same pattern length. These results show that EERS-A is the best algorithm compared to others.

13. Conclusions and Future Work

In this paper, we presented a new pattern matching algorithm—Enhanced ERS-A algorithm. The Enhanced ERS-A algorithm enhances the ERS-A's process by utilizing the idea of the two sliding windows and by making comparisons with the pattern from both sides simultaneously. The comparisons done between the text and the pattern are done from both sides in parallel. This process gives the proposed algorithm a preference over the ERS-A algorithm.

The Enhanced ERS-A algorithm utilizes the idea of RS shifting algorithm to maximize the shift values. To assess the performance of the proposed algorithm, we considered ETSW and ERS-A algorithms for comparison with the proposed algorithm. The experimental results show that the Enhanced ERS-A shows better results in the number of comparisons performed.

References

[1]   El Emary, I.M.M. and Jaber, M.S.M. (2008) A New Approach for Solving String Matching Problem through Splitting the Unchangeable Text. *World Applied Sciences Journal*, **4**, 626-633.

[2]   Chao, Y. (2012) An Improved BM Pattern Matching Algorithm in Intrusion Detection System. *Applied Mechanics and Materials*, **148-149**, 1145-1148.

[3]   Diwate, R. and Alaspurkar, S. (2013) Study of Different Algorithms for Pattern Matching. *International Journal of Advanced Research in Computer Science and Software Engineering*, **3**, 615-620.

[4]   Bhukya, R. and Somayajulu, D. (2010) An Index Based Forward Backward Multiple Pattern Matching Algorithm. *World Academy of Science, Engineering and Technology*, **4**, 1513-1521.

[5]   Senapati, K.K., Mal, S. and Sahoo, G. (2012) RS-A Fast Pattern Matching Algorithm for Bio-Logical Sequences. *International Journal of Engineering and Innovative Technology (IJEIT)*, **1**, 116-118.

[6]   Bhukya, R. and Somayajulu, D. (2011) Multiple Pattern Matching Algorithm Using Pair-Count. *IJCSI International Journal of Computer Science Issues*, **8**, 1694-0814.

[7]   Faro, S. (2009) Efficient Variants of the Backward-Oracle-Matching Algorithm. *International Journal of Foundations of Computer Science*, **20**, 967-984. http://dx.doi.org/10.1142/S0129054109006991

[8]   Faro, S. and Külekci, M.O. (2012) Fast Packed String Matching for Short Patterns. arXiv:1209.6449v1 [cs.IR]

[9]   Salmela, L., Tarhio, J. and Kalsi, P. (2010) Approximate Boyer-Moore String Matching for Small Alphabets. *Algorithmica*, **58**, 591- 609.

[10] Itriq, M., Hudaib, A., Al-Anani, A., Al-Khalid, R. and Suleiman, D. (2012) Enhanced Two Sliding Windows Algorithm for Pattern Matching (ETSW). *Journal of American Science*, **8**, 607-616.

[11] Suleiman, D., Hudaib, A., Al-Anani, A., Al-Khalid, R. and Itriq, M. (2013) ERS-A Algorithm for Pattern Matching. *Middle East Journal of Scientific Research*, **15**, 1067-1075.

[12] Hudaib, A., Al-Khalid, R., Suleiman, D., Itriq, M. and Al-Anani, A. (2008) A Fast Pattern Matching Algorithm with Two Sliding Windows (TSW). *Journal of Computer Science*, **4**, 393-401. http://dx.doi.org/10.3844/jcssp.2008.393.401

[13] Suleiman, D. (2014) Enhanced Berry Ravindran Pattern Matching Algorithm (EBR). *Life Science Journal*, **11**, 395-402.

[14] Al-Mazroi, A. and Rashid, N. (2011) A Fast Hybrid Algorithm for the Exact String Matching Problem. *American Journal of Engineering and Applied Sciences*, **4**, 102-107.

[15] Berry, T. and Ravindran, S. (2001) A Fast String Matching Algorithm and Experimental Results. In: Holub, J. and Simanek, M., Eds., *Proceedings of the Prague Stringology Club Workshop'99*, Collaborative Report DC-99-05, Czech Technical University, Prague, 16-26.

[16] Boyer, R.S. and Moore, J.S. (1977) A Fast String Searching Algorithm. *Communications of the Association for Computing Machinery*, **20**, 762-772. http://dx.doi.org/10.1145/359842.359859

[17] Pendlimarri, D. and Petlu, P.B.B. (2010) Novel Pattern Matching Algorithm for Single Pattern Matching. *International Journal on Computer Science and Engineering*, **2**, 2698-2704.

[18] Hussain, I., Kausar, S., Hussain, L. and Khan, M. (2013) Improved Approach for Exact Pattern Matching (Bidirectional Exact Pattern Matching). *International Journal of Computer Science Issues*, **10**, 59-65.

[19] Bhandaru, J. and Kumar, A. (2014) A Survey of Fast Hybrid String Matching Algorithms. *International Journal of Emerging Sciences*, **4**, 24-37.

[20] Hussain, I., Kazmi, S., Khan, I. and Mehmood, R. (2013) Improved-Bidirectional Exact Pattern Matching. *International Journal of Scientific & Engineering Research*, **4**, 659-663.

[21] Hlayel Abdallah, A. and Hnaif Adnan, A. (2014) A New Exact Pattern Matching Algorithm (WEMA). *Journal of Applied Sciences*, **14**, 193-196.

[22] Calgary Corpus. ftp://ftp.cpsc.ucalgary.ca/pub/projects/text.compression.corpus/

7

A MATLAB-Based Numerical and GUI Implementation of Cross-Gradients Joint Inversion of Gravity and Magnetic Data

Junjie Zhou[1,2*], Xingdong Zhang[1,2], Chunxiao Xiu[1,2]

[1]Key Laboratory of Geo-Detection (China University of Geosciences, Beijing), Ministry of Education, Beijing, China
[2]School of Geophysics and Information Technology, China University of Geosciences, Beijing, China
Email: [*]zjjs_195@163.com

Abstract

The cross-gradients joint inversion technique has been applied to multiple geophysical data with a significant improvement on compatibility, but its numerical implementation for practical use is rarely discussed in the literature. We present a MATLAB-based three-dimensional cross-gradients joint inversion program with application to gravity and magnetic data. The input and output information was examined with care to create a rational, independent design of a graphical user interface (GUI) and computing kernel. For 3D visualization and data file operations, UBC-GIF tools are invoked using a series of I/O functions. Some key issues regarding the iterative joint inversion algorithm are also discussed: for instance, the forward difference of cross gradients, and matrix pseudo inverse computation. A synthetic example is employed to illustrate the whole process. Joint and separate inversions can be performed flexibly by switching the inversion mode. The resulting density model and susceptibility model demonstrate the correctness of the proposed program.

Keywords

Joint Inversion, Cross Gradients, Gravity and Magnetic Data, Numerical Implementation, Graphic User Interface

1. Introduction

The 3D joint inversion (*i.e.*, imaging) technique of multiple geophysical data often reveals a subsurface structure

---

[*]Corresponding author.

more accurately than an individual inversion of single dataset. The joint inversion process relies on a certain linkage among various models, for which several methodologies have been proposed [1]-[7]. One conventional scheme takes sample property measurements when available, and determines their statistical interrelationships to restrict the inversion process. Unlike this, structural link methods are widely used to perform joint inversion without requiring rock property data. The cross-gradients technique is one such method, and its structural similarity criterion has been shown to give good results [8]. First proposed by Gallardo and Meju [9], the method was based on the assumption that, although petrophysical correlation varies, implicitly common boundaries exist. The method has been successfully applied to both synthetic and real data, but the relevant numerical implementation for practical use has rarely been discussed in previous work.

We now present a simple and general numerical implementation of 3D cross-gradients joint inversion framework for gravity and magnetic data in the MATLAB programming environment, noted for its powerful scientific computing capability (especially for matrix solution) and its graphical utilities. First, the joint inversion theory is briefly reviewed, and the separate design of a graphical user interface (GUI) and computing kernel is analyzed. Second, some key issues concerning numerical emplementation are discussed (e.g., forward difference of cross-gradients, and matrix inverse computation). A synthetic joint inversion experiment was carried out to demonstrate the basic use of the proposed program. A comparative example is presented to indicate the practicality of the program.

2. General Framework of Cross Gradients Joint Inversion

2.1. Inputs and Outputs

Generally, an inversion converts acquired geophysical data into a physical property model, which is then assigned geological information to explain the nature of the subsurface material or its geological structure. Cross-gradients joint inversion uses two or more types of data to reproduce physical models. This is often found to be more accurate than dealing with each data type separately because of the constraints offered by the additional structural information. **Figure 1** shows the basic input and output of a cross-gradients joint inversion of gravity and magnetic data. This data is obviously necessary for the inversion to be carried out, but other information— reference models, boundary constraints and inversion parameters needed to control the procedure—is optional. The standard output comprises 3D density and susceptibility distribution and their corresponding predictions.

The input and output (I/O) dataset is usually stored as observational data, configurations and 3D model files. A commonly adopted approach to organizing such datasets is to use the University of British Columbia Geophysical Inversion Facility (UBC-GIF) format (ASCII encoding) [10]. In this format, observational data is arranged in columns along with observation locations and estimated errors. The models are ordered and sorted into columns with the associated mesh configuration file. To handle the frequent use of the I/O operations of these file formats, several MATLAB functions are written (listed in **Table 1**). These import the revelant datasets that are then processed utilizing a computing kernel module (described below). UBC-GIF tools are again invoked by these functions to export files and 3D graphics of the resultant models and predictions.

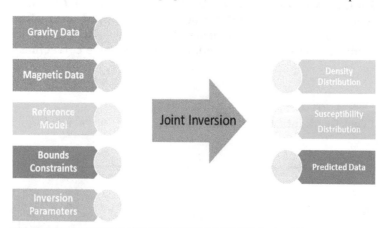

Figure 1. Schematic diagram of the input and output items associated with a joint inversion.

Table 1. I/O functions list for UBC-GIF format file.

Function name	Instruction
ubc_read_grv	read *.grv data file
ubc_save_grv	save *.grv data file
ubc_read_mag	read *.mag data file
ubc_save_mag	save *.mag data file
ubc_read_modl	read *.den or *.sus model file
ubc_save_modl	save *.den or *.sus model file
ubc_read_msh	read *.msh mesh file
ubc_save_msh	save *.msh mesh file
ubc_view_modl	use UBC-GIF tools to visualize 3D model
ubc_view_data	use UBC-GIF tools to visualize 2D data

a. For more information about UBC-GIF tools, please refer to [10].

2.2. Graphical User Interface Design

Cross-gradients joint inversion involves different kinds of observed data, different physical models and various choices of inversion parameters, all of which may cause confusion to users and make the program difficult for them. Some inversion parameters, such as regularization and the structural coupled factor, are usually chosen by trial and error; however, the results may be distorted if incorrect parameters are used, neccessating a data experiment before the inversion is performed. A GUI has been designed to encourage users to perform easy inversions and data experiments without confusion [11].

Figure 2 shows the main interface of this program. The files and their corresponding parameters need to be completed in the editing box controls on the panel. Four graphical box controls display inversion data during processing (blank while initializing). All the available operations are arranged as menu bars above the panel.

The inversion parameters and input file directions are recorded by a customized project file that can be either loaded or saved using the first menu item *Project*. The *View* menu is used to visualize the observational data or the 3D models using UBC-GIF tools, which produce 3D visuals of higher qualitythan the built-in MATLAB functions. The *Inversion* menu contains two modes—joint inversion, and separate inversion without structural constraints. The *Tests* menu helps the user to carry out data experiments and assists in the selection of correct inversion parameters such as depth weighting and regularization. Finally, the *Help* menu is linked to a user's manual and an *About* dialogue box. There is also a status bar displaying the local time and current state of the program.

2.3. Compute-Intensive Module Design

The computation kernel module has been designed to be separate from the GUI for its strict requirement of computing resources, including the CPU loadings and memory allocations. Following Fregoso and Gallardo [8], the inversion equation may be expressed with some slight modification as:

$$\mathbf{p}_{k+1} = \mathbf{p}_k + \mathbf{N}_k^{-1}\mathbf{n}_k + \mathbf{N}_k^{-1}\mathbf{B}_k^T\mathbf{t}_k, \tag{1}$$

where

$$\left(\mathbf{B}_k\mathbf{N}_k^{-1}\mathbf{B}_k^T\right)\mathbf{t}_k = \mathbf{B}_k\mathbf{N}_k^{-1}\mathbf{n}_k - \boldsymbol{\tau}_k$$
$$\mathbf{N}_k = \mathbf{P}_k^T\mathbf{G}^T\mathbf{C}_d^{-1}\mathbf{G}\mathbf{P}_k + \mathbf{L}^T\mathbf{C}_L^{-1}\mathbf{L} + +\mathbf{Z}\mathbf{C}_p^{-1}\mathbf{Z} \tag{2}$$
$$\mathbf{n}_k = \mathbf{P}_k^T\mathbf{G}^T\mathbf{C}_d^{-1}\left[\tilde{g}\left(\mathbf{p}_k\right)-\mathbf{d}\right] + \mathbf{L}^T\mathbf{C}_L^{-1}\mathbf{L}\mathbf{p}_k + \mathbf{C}_p^{-1}\mathbf{Z}\left(\mathbf{p}_k - \mathbf{p}_0\right)$$

Here subscript k denotes the iteration number; 0 is *a priori* information; **d** is a data vector; **p** is a model vector transformed from property model m (in combined manner); matrix $\mathbf{Z}$ is a weighting matrix; **L** is a Laplacian matrix; **C** is a covariance matrix with respect to subscript d, L and p, which indicate data, smoothness and smallness terms; τ is a column vector of assembled cross-gradients components in 3D space; **B** is a Jacobian matrix of cross-gradients; and **P** is a Jacobian matrix of transform function. The final models m_1 and m_2 are extracted from **p** by the inverse transform function when the iteration procedure satisfies the given data and structural misfit thresholds. For more details of Equation (1), please refer to [8]. The parameters (**Table 2**) to be assigned in the GUI partly constitute the arrays described above. The cross-gradients joint inversion procedure for this iterative scheme is illustrated in **Figure 3**.

There are several key considerations when numerically implementing the iterative Equation (1). First, the gradient operator involved in τ, **L** and **B** must be calculated in a 3D difference scheme, preferably by using forward differences to eliminate the chessboard pattern [12]. The discretization of τ_x, τ_y and τ_z are, from [8].

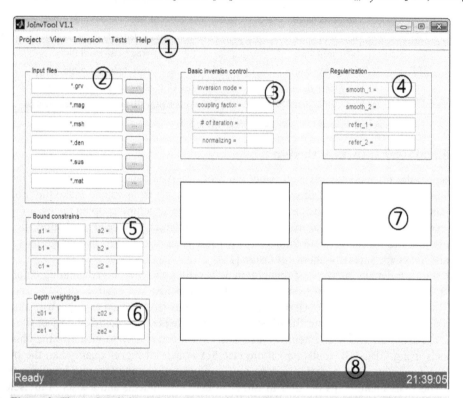

Figure 2. The main window of the cross gradients joint inversion program. 1) Menu bar; 2) Input files textboxes; 3) Basic control parameter textboxes; 4) Regularization textboxes; 5) Bound constraints textboxes; 6) Depth (Distance) weightings parameter textboxes; 7) Data display area; 8) Status bar.

Table 2. Control parameters of the inversion.

Types	Parameter	Instruction
string	gravity data file	(required) *.grv file
string	magnetic data file	(required) *.mag file
string	mesh file	(required) *.msh file
string	density reference model	(optional) *.den file
string	magnetization reference model	(optional) *.sus file
string	sensitivity file	(optional) *.mat file
real	physical property bounds	(optional) lower and upper bounds
real	depth weighting parameters	(required) used to compute Z
string	inversion mode	(required) joint or separate mode
real	structural coupling factor	(optional) a positive number
integer	number of iteration	(required) the maximum # of iteration
real	smoothness factors	(required) regularization parameters
real	smallness factors	(required) regularization parameters

$$\tau_x = \left[\left(m_{1y} - m_{1c}\right)m_{2z} + \left(m_{1z} - m_{1y}\right)m_{2c} + \left(m_{1c} - m_{1z}\right)m_{2y}\right]\Big/\left[dydz\right]$$

$$\tau_y = \left[\left(m_{1z} - m_{1c}\right)m_{2x} + \left(m_{1x} - m_{1z}\right)m_{2c} + \left(m_{1c} - m_{1x}\right)m_{2z}\right]\Big/\left[dxdz\right] ,$$

(3)

$$\tau_z = \left[\left(m_{1x} - m_{1c}\right)m_{2y} + \left(m_{1y} - m_{1x}\right)m_{2c} + \left(m_{1c} - m_{1y}\right)m_{2x}\right]\Big/\left[dxdy\right]$$

where subscripts x, y, z denote the cell adjacent to the center in each direction, and c is the center cell (**Figure 4**). The exact value of B is difficult to compute directly, but by discretizing τ, an approximate value is obtained by a Taylor's expansion of the cross gradients at the zero point and neglecting the higher orders. For most cases, τ takes a value close to zero, so the approximate solution is always sufficiently precise (the reader is referred to [8] [9] for more details). Note that, since the computation for each element is independent, it is suggested that the code be vectorized in order to utilize the full potential of MATLAB's matrix computing capability [13] [14]. A built-in function "sparse" is employed to perform efficient assembling of these matrices [15].

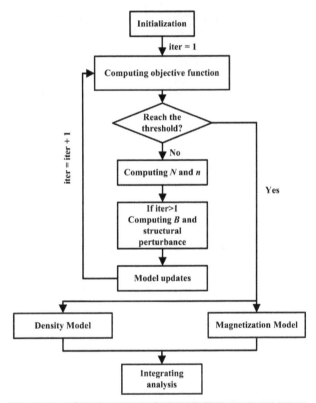

Figure 3. Flowchart of the joint inversion process.

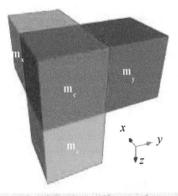

Figure 4. Schematic of forward difference for gradient computations involved in cross-gradients and smoothness operators.

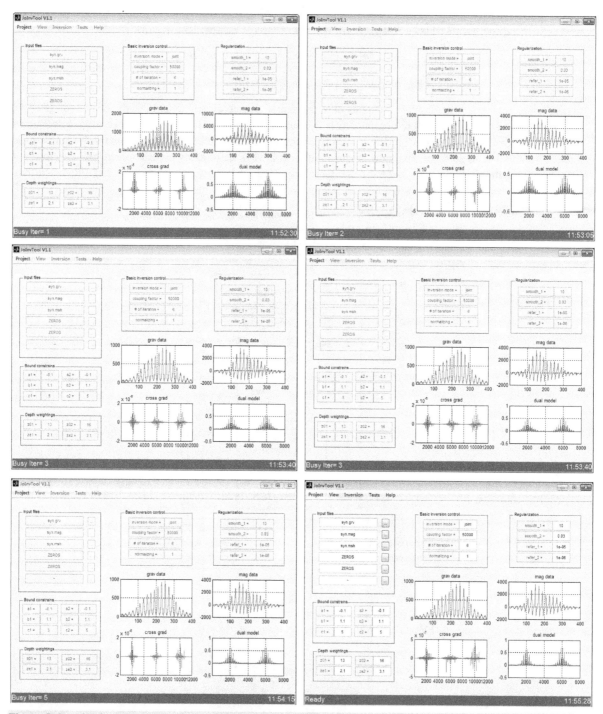

Figure 5. Iterative implementation of cross-gradients joint inversion. Observed data (red lines), current predicted data (blue lines), model updates and cross-gradients array (also blue lines in the following graphs) are displayed at each iteration. The textboxes are locked (grey) during the computation process.

Second, matrix N is inverted by a standard inverse algorithm when its condition number is not too large; fortunately, matrix C_p plays a regulator role to eliminate the ill-conditioned problem [16]. It can generally be solved by the standard inverse solver "inv" with high precision, but the inverse of the composed matrix $[BN^{-1}B^{T}]$ is usually difficult to compute because the production of several of the involved matrices makes it singular. In previous work, truncated singular values decomposition (SVD) has been used to calculate the pseudo inverse [8]; however, here we prefer to resolve the problem using a damped least-squares technique in which a damping factor is introduced:

$$\mathbf{B}_k \mathbf{N}_k^{-1} \mathbf{B}_k^T \approx \mathbf{B}_k \mathbf{N}_k^{-1} \mathbf{B}_k^T + \frac{\max\left(\mathbf{B}_k \mathbf{N}_k^{-1} \mathbf{B}_k^T\right)}{\beta} \mathbf{I}.\tag{4}$$

where $\mathbf{I}$ is the identity matrix, and β is a structural coupling factor. The second term on the right-hand side of Equation (4) in effect makes the total matrix well-posed. Taken together with the composed array $[\boldsymbol{BN}^{-1}\boldsymbol{n}\text{-}\boldsymbol{\tau}]$ on the right-hand side, a linear system emerges which may be solved using the built-in CG solver "bicg" [15].

3. Synthetic Example

A synthetic experiment was carried out to illustrate the basic use of this program. The whole standard iterative process is shown in **Figure 5**. The textboxes are locked until the process is complete. The gravity and magnetic data (**Figure 6**) are generated on a synthetic geological model (**Figure 7**), and with 2.5% Gaussian noise added. The model consisted of two anomalies, A and B, with density contrast 0.5 g/cm³, 1 g/cm³ and susceptibility 1 (SI unit, similarly hereinafter) and 0.5, respectively. The mesh comprised 20 × 20 × 10 regular prisms of 50 m side length. All of the observed and geometry data were collected into the relevant files. The depth weighting parameters were chosen by UBC-GIF tools [10], and the regularization parameters were selected by trial and error aided by L-curve optimization [16].

When the process was complete, the *View* menu invoked UBC-GIF tools to visualize the resulting models and data shown in **Figure 6** and **Figure 7**. It is seen that the inverted density model and susceptibility model reproduced the data very well, indicating the accuracy of the fitting feature of this process. When compared to the true density and susceptibility models, the recovered values reflected the relative amplitude and locations correctly.

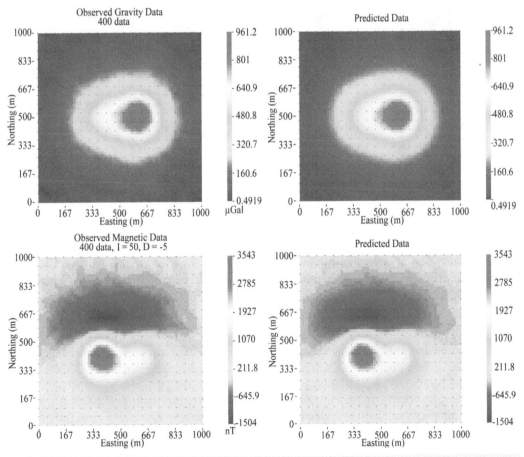

Figure 6. Synthetic gravity (µGal) and magnetic data (nT) and predicted joint inversion using standard mode.

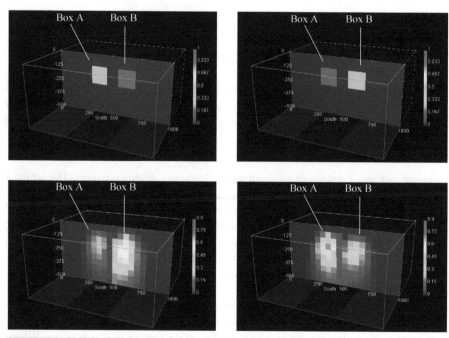

Figure 7. Synthetic density model (left) and susceptibility model (right) in a 3D subsurface and their corresponding joint inversion results using standard mode. The displayed profile is located at $x = 500$ m.

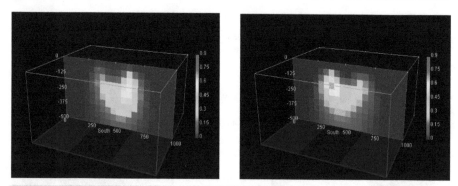

Figure 8. Separate inversion results of density model (left) and susceptibility model (right) in 3D subsurface.

To demonstrate the significant improvement produced by joint inversion, we also conducted a comparative experiment by changing the inversion mode parameter from *joint* to *separate*. The recovered models are shown in **Figure 8**, which show that the anomalies were recovered in the correct location but with low resolution. Note that the boundary between the two anomalies is blurred, making it hard to identify the two independent targets in the separate images.

4. Conclusion

A MATLAB-based numerical implementation of cross-gradients joint inversion of gravity and magnetic data is presented. A user-frendly GUI has also been designed for flexible handling of multiple observations, models and inversion control parameters. The inversion process is carried out using an independent module. Some important issues are discussed, such as cross-gradients computing and matrix inverting. The use of this program has been illustrated by a simple example using synthetic data. The correctness and accessibility of this program have been demonstrated. Although this program is available for both research and practical use, we suggest porting this MATLAB-based program to other professional software platforms (e.g., ArcGIS) for more integrating and convenient applications in the future work.

Acknowledgements

This work was funded by National Natural Science Foundation of China, Beijing Higher Education Young Elite Teacher Project (YETP0650), The National High Technology Research and Development Program ("863" Program) of China (No. 2013AA063901-4 and 2013AA063905-4), R & D of Key Instruments and Technologies for Deep Resources Prospecting (The National R&D Projects for Key Scientific Instruments) (No.ZDYZ2012-1-02-04), Constrained multi-parameter inversion of geophysical technology and software systems (No. 2014AA06 A613), and The Fundamental Research Funds for the Central Universities. We thank the UBC-GIF and Roman Shekhtman, the developer of Meshtools3D and gm-data-viewer, for making the programs available to the scientific community.

References

[1] Zeyen, H. and Pous, J. (1993) 3-D Joint Inversion of Magnetic and Gravimetric Data with *a Priori* Information. *Geophysical Journal International*, **112**, 244-256. http://dx.doi.org/10.1111/j.1365-246X.1993.tb01452.x

[2] Gallardo, L.A., Perez-Flores, M.A. and Gomez-Trevino, E. (2005) Refinement of Three-Dimensional Multilayer Models of Basins and Crustal Environments by Inversion of Gravity and Magnetic Data. *Tectonophysics*, **397**, 37-54. http://dx.doi.org/10.1016/j.tecto.2004.10.010

[3] Bosch, M., Meza, R. and Jimenez, R. (2006) Joint Gravity and Magnetic Inversion in 3D Using Monte Carlo Methods. *Geophysics*, **71**, G163-G156. http://dx.doi.org/10.1190/1.2209952

[4] Pilkington, M. (2006) Joint Inversion of Gravity and Magnetic Data for Two-Layer Models. *Geophysics*, **71**, L35-L42. http://dx.doi.org/10.1190/1.2194514

[5] Shamsipour, P., Marcotte, D. and Chouteau, M. (2012) 3D Stochastic Joint Inversion of Gravity and Magnetic Data. *Journal of Applied Geophysics*, **79**, 27-37. http://dx.doi.org/10.1016/j.jappgeo.2011.12.012

[6] Zhdanov, M.S., Gribenko, A. and Wilson, G. (2012) Generalized Joint Inversion of Multimodal Geophysical Data Using Gramian Constraints. *Geophysical Research Letters*, **39**, L09301. http://dx.doi.org/10.1029/2012GL051233

[7] Williams, N.C. (2008) Geologically-Constrained UBC-GIF Gravity and Magnetic Inversions with Examples from the Agnew-Wiluna Greenstone Belt, Western Australia. Ph. D. Dissertation. The University of British Columbia, Vancouver.

[8] Frogoso, E. and Gallardo, L.A. (2009) Cross-Gradients Joint 3D Inversion with Applications to Gravity and Magnetic Data. *Geophysics*, **74**, L31-L42. http://dx.doi.org/10.1190/1.3119263

[9] Gallardo, L.A. and Meju, M.A. (2004) Joint Two-Dimensional DC Resistivity and Seismic Travel Time Inversion with Cross-Gradients Constraints. *Journal of Geophysical Research: Solid Earth* (1978-2012), **109**, B03311. http://dx.doi.org/10.1029/2003JB002716

[10] Oldenburg, D.W. and Jones, F.H.M. (2007) Inversion for Applied Geophysics: Learning Resources about Geophysical Inversion. The University of British Columbia, Vancouver. http://www.eos.ubc.ca/ubcgif/iag/index.htm

[11] Özgü Arısoy, M. and Dikmen, Ü. (2011) Potensoft: MATLAB-Based Software for Potential Field Data Processing, Modeling and Mapping. *Computers & Geosciences*, **37**, 935-942. http://dx.doi.org/10.1016/j.cageo.2011.02.008

[12] Lelièvre, P.G. and Oldenburg, D.W. (2009) A Comprehensive Study of Including Structural Orientation Information in Geophysical Inversions. *Geophysical Journal International*, **178**, 623-637. http://dx.doi.org/10.1111/j.1365-246X.2009.04188.x

[13] Hahn, B.H. and Valentine, D.T. (2013) Essential Matlab for Engineers and Scientists. 5th Edition, Academic Press, Boston, 129-160. http://dx.doi.org/10.1016/B978-0-12-394398-9.00006-X

[14] Eshagh, M. and Abdollahzadeh, M. (2012) Software for Generating Gravity Gradients Using a Geopotential Model Based on an Irregular Semivectorization Algorithm. *Computers & Geosciences*, **39**, 152-160. http://dx.doi.org/10.1016/j.cageo.2011.06.003

[15] Pidlisecky, A., Haber, E. and Knight R. (2007) RESINVM3D: A 3D Resistivity Inversion Package. *Geophysics*, **72**, H1-H10. http://dx.doi.org/10.1190/1.2402499

[16] Hansen, P.C. (1994) Regularization Tools: A Matlab Package for Analysis and Solution of Discrete Ill-Posed Problems. *Numerical Algorithm*, **6**, 1-35. http://dx.doi.org/10.1007/BF02149761

8

Automatic and Manual Proliferation Rate Estimation from Digital Pathology Images

Lama Rajab[1], Heba Z. Al-Lahham[1], Raja S. Alomari[2], Fatima Obaidat[1], Vipin Chaudhary[2]

[1]The University of Jordan, Amman, Jordan
[2]The University at Buffalo, Buffalo, USA
Email: Lama.rajab@ju.edu.jo, ralomari@buffalo.edu

Abstract

Digital pathology is a major revolution in pathology and is changing the clinical routine for pathologists. We work on providing a computer aided diagnosis system that automatically and robustly provides the pathologist with a second opinion for many diagnosis tasks. However, interobserver variability prevents thorough validation of any proposed technique for any specific problems. In this work, we study the variability and reliability of proliferation rate estimation from digital pathology images for breast cancer proliferation rate estimation. We also study the robustness of our recently proposed method CAD system for PRE estimation. Three statistical significance tests showed that our automated CAD system was as reliable as the expert pathologist in both brown and blue nuclei estimation on a dataset of 100 images.

Keywords

Prolifiration Rate Estimation (PRE), Digital Pathology, Interobserver Variability

1. Introduction

The development and continued growth of cancerous cells involve various changes at both macro and micro levels of the body. Cell proliferation is usually among the major indicators for proliferation of cancerous cells. Specifically, breast cancer proliferation rate estimation (PRE) is a crucial step for determining the cancer level and is used as a prognostic indicator [1]. In conjunction with tumor size and grade, lymph node status and histological grade, PRE is an indicator for the aggressiveness of individual cancers and helps setting the treatment plan [2].

Traditionally, pathologists perform proliferation rate estimation for breast cancer by examining the whole slides via a microscope. Over the past two decades, digital pathology enabled the usage of high resolution digitizers to provide high resolution images that replace the microscope as shown in our previous work [3].

There are many clinically approved techniques to estimate the PRE including: mitotic index, S-phase fraction, nuclear antigen ImmunoHistoChemistry (IHC) including KI-67 and PCNA-staining Cyclins and PET [4] [5]. Each one of these methods has its advantages or disadvantages based on the clinical settings.

In our work, we use Ki-67-stained biopsy images for PRE. In this technique, PRE is estimated by counting the number of brown nuclei and the number of blue nuclei as shown in **Figure 1**. Stromal areas are clinically excluded from counting because stromal area does not become cancerous. In our previous work [6], we performed digital stromal area removal to eliminate this ambiguous area for both junior pathologists and automated PRE systems.

Manual PRE is time-consuming and laborious for pathologists. An average of six minutes per image is required for PRE by an expert pathologist. Our expert pathologist requires over 10 hours estimating the proliferation rate for our dataset containing 100 images. Many authors target automation of PRE including our recent work [7]. However, one major concern was not investigated in all these efforts which was the inter-variability between the expert pathologists [8].

In this paper, we study the statistical inter-pathologist variability for the various manual PRE we have between four expert pathologists. Moreover, we investigate the reliability of our proposed automated PRE compared to the four pathologist opinions for the 100 images in our dataset.

2. Materials and Methods

Manual ground truth estimation is a major area of interest due to the various human factors that influence the experts. Specifically for breast cancer PRE [9] [10], we find that pathologists provide variable ground truth estimations which make it hard to evaluate any automated PRE estimated technique. Many automated PRE techniques have been proposed in the literature and we recently proposed our technique in [7], an exhaustive review of the techniques as well as a detailed description of our techniques are presented in [7]. In this paper, we provide the necessary statistical study for the inter pathologists variability. Furthermore, we study the statistical variability between the four manual ground truth and our automated technique. In [7], we compared the automated results with one expert pathologist and a student trained by a pathologist. In this paper, we run our statistical study to include for expert pathologists and one automated technique.

We study three statistical significance tests to show the inter-observer variability. Moreover, we study the manual vs automated [7] PRE variability. We study three statistical significance measures: correlation coefficient, T-Test, and Ch-Square test. We briefly describe them due to space limitations.

2.1. Correlation Coefficient

The value of the correlation coefficient $\rho_{x,y}$ gives an indication about the strength and the nature of the relationship between two random variables x and y. It ranges between -1 and $+1$. A value of $+1$ means perfect correlation between these two random variables while a -1 values indicates maximal uncorrelated variables [11] the equation for the correlation is shown in Equation (1):

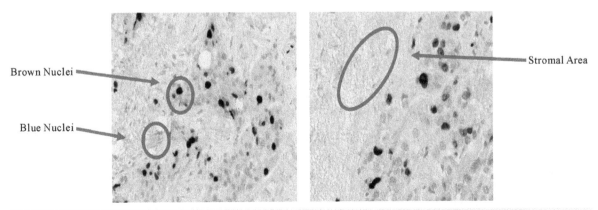

Figure 1. The sample images of Ki-67 stained pathology images showing sample blue nuclei, and stromal areas.

$$\rho_{x,y} = \frac{\sum (x - \bar{x})(y - \bar{y})}{\sqrt{\left(\sum (x - \bar{x})^2 \sum (y - \bar{y})^2 \right)}} \tag{1}$$

where x and y are two random variables, $\bar{x}$ and $\bar{y}$ are the corresponding mean values for each sample.

2.2. Student T-Test

Student T-Test (or t test for short) is one of a number of hypothesis tests. The t-test looks at the t statistic, t distribution and degrees of freedom to determine a t value (probability) that can be used to determine whether the two underlying distributions of the two random variables are different as shown in Equation (2):

$$t = \frac{\bar{X}_T - \bar{X}_C}{\sqrt{\dfrac{\sigma_r^2}{n_T} + \dfrac{\sigma_c^2}{n_C}}} \tag{2}$$

where $\bar{x}_T$ and $\bar{x}_C$ are the two mean values for the corresponding two data samples r and c, σ_r^2 and σ_c^2 are the corresponding variances for the two data samples r and c, n_T and n_C are the number of the corresponding samples. Moreover, the degrees of freedom (df) for the test should be determined. In the t-test, the degree of freedom is the sum of the persons in both groups minus 2. Given the alpha level, the df, and the t value, you can look the t value up in a standard table of significance Typically, when $t > 0.05$, the two random variables (two underlying data samples) are said to be statistically insignificance, $i.e.$, highly correlated [12].

2.3. Chi-Square

Chi square X^2 is a statistical test commonly used to compare observed with unobserved data upon a specific hypothesis as in Equation (3):

$$X^2 = \frac{\sum_{i=1}^{r} \sum_{j=1}^{c} (Oij - Eij)^2}{Eij} \tag{3}$$

where Oij is the observed frequency in the ith row and j^{th} column, Eij is the expected frequency in the ith row and j^{th} column, r is the number of rows and c is the number of columns. The appropriate number of degrees of freedom (df) is calculated as the number of rows-1 multiplied by the number of columns. If X^2 is greater than what is known as the critical value, then the two samples are dependent.

3. Experimental Results and Analysis

Our data set contain 100 Ki-67-stained histopathology digital images for breast cancer. The blue nuclei are negative positive cells while the brown nuclei are the positive ones. Our collaborating pathologists provided us with the ground truth from four different pathologists including herself as the most senior pathologist. We provided each pathologist with anonymized images labeled in sequence along with an sheet to score for the blue and brown nuclei. None of the four pathologists knew about the other and they were scoring independently. Our most senior pathologist (coauthor) spent over 10 hours for scoring the 100 cases which means an average of 6 minutes per case. Moreover, we run our proposed automated PRE system proposed in [7] over the same 100 images and recorded the automated scoring for both the blue and the brown nuclei.

3.1. Correlation Coefficient

The inter-observer reproducibility is first measured by using the correlation coefficient [13] [14]. Overall, there is a higher correlation between pathologists in brown nuclei estimation than blue nuclei estimation. Moreover, our automated CAD system has also a higher correlation coefficient for brown nuclei compared to blue ones. **Table 1** summarizes the inter pathologists correlation coefficient values and manual vs automated correlation coefficient values.

From **Table 1**, we note that the correlation coefficient indicates a very high correlation between the four observers on the brown nuclei counting. However, the correlation is highly variable for blue nuclei counting from an upper value of 0.73 down to 0.768. **Figure 2** and **Figure 3** show the relationship for the manual PRE for

Table 1. Significance values of correlation coefficients.

Expert observers	Correlation coefficient	
	Brown count	Blue count
Observer 1 vs Observer 2	0.987	0.969
Observer 1 vs Observer 3	0.953	0.807
Observer 1 vs Observer 4	0.965	0.806
Observer 2 vs Observer 3	0.959	0.968
Observer 2 vs Observer 4	0.965	0.806
Observer 3 vs Observer 4	0.977	0.973

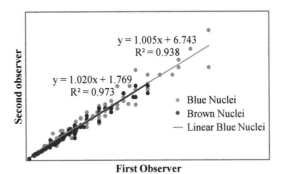

Figure 2. Relationship between first and second observers' nuclei count estimates.

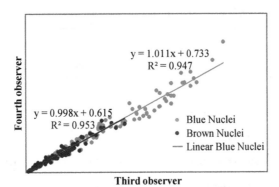

Figure 3. Relationship between third and fourth observers' nuclei count estimates.

observer 1 vs observer 2 and observer 3 vs observer 4, respectively.

On the other hand, we study the correlation coefficients between the manual of each of the four experts and our proposed automated system as shown in **Table 2**. As we examine this table, the brown nuclei counting is highly correlated to the various observers which indicates an almost perfect reliability of our proposed automated system for brown nuclei estimation. Furthermore, the blue nuclei counting are comparable to the correlation between the manual observers. In other words, our automated blue nuclei estimation is as good as the manual estimation which proves its clinical reliability.

3.2. T-Test

We performed a two-tailed paired T-Test on all the pairs between the four observers and the automated system.

Our Null Hypothesis is that there is a difference between the observers in one hand and the automated system on the other hand. All of the reported significance probability values in **Table 3** shows insignificant statistical difference between the manual expert estimations themselves on one hand and between both the 3rd and 4th observers with the automated system on the other hand. In other words according to **Table 4** which shows the interpretation for the p-value. As you see the p value is less than 0.01 which means that we have a strong evidence to reject the hypothesis that says that there is no relationship (there is a difference) between observers on one hand and the automated system in the other hand in both Brown and Blue nuclei counts estimation.

3.3. Chi Square

We computed Chi-square test all pairs, and it compared with the critical chi square value with $df = 1$, confidence level 99% (probability $= 1 - 0.99 = 0.01$). In all pairs (including inter-observer and our automated method), the calculated chi square value is greater than the critical value, which means that each pair of samples are dependent. In other words, it is statistically reliable to consider any of the expert scoring or the automated scoring values. **Figure 4** and **Figure 5** show two samples images where we high agreement between observes, and a low agreement between observers, respectively.

Table 2. Manual vs automated significance values of correlation coefficients.

Expert observers	Correlation coefficient	
	Brown count	Blue count
Observer 1 vs automated	0.974	0.847
Observer 2 vs automated	0.984	0.886
Observer 3 vs automated	0.959	0.661
Observer 4 vs automated	0.963	0.686

Table 3. Significance values resulting from paired T-Test.

Expert observers	p-value	
	p (brown count)	p (blue count)
Observer 1 vs observer 2	8.14×10^{-5}	7.2×10^{-6}
Observer 1 vs observer 3	1.5×10^{-4}	1.5×10^{-15}
Observer 1 vs observer 4	8.7×10^{-5}	2.2×10^{-15}
Observer 2 vs observer 3	8.9×10^{-9}	1.4×10^{-11}
Observer 2 vs observer 4	4.3×10^{-9}	7.1×10^{-12}
Observer 3 vs automated	2.9×10^{-7}	6.9×10^{-11}
Observer 4 vs automated	4.0×10^{-7}	1.5×10^{-11}

Table 4. Interpreting significance probability (p-value).

Significance probability p-value	Interpretation
$p < 0.01$	Strong evidence to reject H_0
$0.01 < p \leq 0.05$	Significant EVIDENCE TO REject H_0
$0.05 < p \leq 0.10$	Weak evidence against H_0
$p > 0.10$	Insignificant evidence to reject H_0

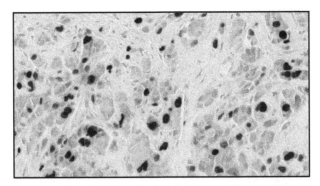

Figure 4. Example of an image has the same value for the brown nuclei in all observers.

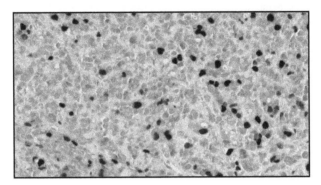

Figure 5. Example of an image where the observers results are completely different.

4. Conclusion

We proposed a detailed statistical study for breast cancer proliferation rate estimation. We studied the inter-observer variability between four expert pathologists on a set of 100 cases. We also studied the reliability of our recently proposed automated PRE system. On the 100 cases, we found that the variability of brown nuclei estimation was statistically insignificant between various pathologists. We also found that our proposed system brown nuclei estimation was statistically reliable. On the other hand, our three statistical significance tests showed fairly high reliability between pathologists for blue nuclei estimation. The same conclusion applies for our proposed automated blue nuclei system.

References

[1] Lord, S.J., Lei, W., Craft, P., *et al.* (2007) A Systematic Review of the Effectiveness of Magnetic Resonance Imaging (MRI) as an Addition to Mammography and Ultrasound in Screening Young Women at High Risk of Breast Cancer. *European Journal of Cancer*, **43**, 1905-1917. http://dx.doi.org/10.1016/j.ejca.2007.06.007

[2] Rakha, E.A., Reis-Filho, J.S., Baehner, F., Dabbs, D.J., Decker, T., Eusebi, V., Fox, S.B., Ichihara, S., Jacquemier, J., Lakhani, S.R., Palacios, J., Richardson, A.L., Schnitt, S.J., Schmitt, F.C., Tan, P.H., Tse, G.M., Badve, S. and Ellis, I.O. (2010) Breast Cancer Prognostic Classification in the Molecular Era: The Role of Histological Grade. *Breast Cancer Research*, **12**, 207.

[3] Alomari, R.S., Allen, R., Sabata, B. and Chaudhary, V. (2009) Localization of Tissues in High-Resolution Digital Anatomic Pathology Images. *Proceedings of SPIE, Medical Imaging: Computer-Aided Diagnosis*, **7260**, Article ID: 726016.

[4] Beresford, M.J., Wilson, G.D. and Makris, A. (2006) Measuring Proliferation in Breast Cancer: Practicalities and Applications. *Breast Cancer Research*, **8**, 216. http://dx.doi.org/10.1186/bcr1618

[5] Urruticoechea, S.A., Lan, E. and Dowsett, M. (2005) Proliferation Marker Ki-67 in Early Breast Cancer. *Journal of Clinical Oncology*, **23**, 7212-7220. http://dx.doi.org/10.1200/JCO.2005.07.501

[6] Alomari, R., Ghosh, S., Chaudhary, V. and Al-Kadi, O. (2012) Local Binary Patterns for Stromal Area Removal in

Histology Images. *Proceedings of the SPIE, Medical Imaging: Computer Aided Diagnosis*, **8315**, Article ID: 831524.

[7]   Al-Lahham, H.Z., Alomari, R.S., Hiary, H. and Chaudhary, V. (2012) Automation Proliferation Rate Estimation from Breast Cancer Ki-67 Histology Images. *Proceedings of the SPIE, Medical Imaging: Computer-Aided Diagnosis*, **8315**, 83152A.

[8]   Gurcan, M.N., Boucheron, L.E., Can, A., Madabhushi, A., Rajpoot, N.M. and Yener, B. (2009) Histopathological Image Analysis: A Review. *IEEE Reviews in Biomedical Engineering*, **2**, 147-171.

[9]   Cheng, H.D., Shan, J., Ju, W., Guo, Y. and Zhang, L. (2010) Automated Breast Cancer Detection and Classification Using Ultrasound Images: A Survey. *Pattern Recognition*, **43**, 299-317. http://dx.doi.org/10.1016/j.patcog.2009.05.012

[10] Phukpattaranont, P., Limsiroratana, S. and Boonyaphiphat, P. (2009) Computer-Aided System for Microscopic Images: Application to Breast Cancer Nuclei Counting. *International Journal of Applied Biomedical Engineering*, **2**, 69-74.

[11] Shao, J. and Wang, H.S. (2002) Sample Correlation Coefficients Based on Survey Data Under Regression Imputation. *Journal of the American Statistical Association*, **79**, 544-552.

[12] Cann, J., Ellin, J., Kawano, Y., Knight, B., Long, R.E., Sam, A., Machotka, V. and Smith, A. (2013) Validation of Digital Pathology Systems in the Regulated Nonclinical Environment. Digital Pathology Association, Madison.

[13] Watkins, M.W. and Pacheco, M. (2001) Interobserver Agreement in Behavioral Research: Importance and Calculation. *Journal of Behavioral Education*, **10**, 205-212. http://dx.doi.org/10.1023/A:1012295615144

[14] Yelton, A.R., Wildman, B.G. and Erickson, M.M.T. (1977) A Probability-Based Formula for Calculating Interobserver Agreement. *Journal of applied behavior Analysis*, **10**, 123-131. http://dx.doi.org/10.1901/jaba.1977.10-127

9

Quantifying Reusability of Object Oriented Design: A Testability Perspective

Mahfuzul Huda[1], Yagya Dutt Sharma Arya[1], Mahmoodul Hasan Khan[2]

[1]Department of Computer Science & Engineering, Invertis University, Bareilly, India
[2]Department of Computer Science and Engineering, IET, Lucknow, India
Email: mahfuzul@iul.ac.in

Abstract

The quality factor of class diagram is critical because it has a significant influence on overall quality of the product, delivered finally. Testability analysis, when done early in the software creation process, is a criterion of critical importance to software quality. Reusability is an important quality factor to testability. Its early measurement in object oriented software especially at design phase, allows a design to be reapplied to a new problem without much extra effort. This research paper proposes a research framework for quantification process and does an extensive review on reusability of object oriented software. A metrics based model "Reusability Quantification of Object Oriented Design" has been proposed by establishing the relationship among design properties and reusability and justifying the correlation with the help of statistical measures. Also, "Reusability Quantification Model" is empirically validated and contextual significance of the study shows the high correlation for model acceptance. This research paper facilitates to software developers and designer, the inclusion of reusability quantification model to access and quantify software reusability for quality product.

Keywords

Reusability, Testability, Object Oriented Design, Design Metrics, Object Oriented Software, Software Quality Model, Software Testing, Effort

1. Introduction

Significant efforts have been made in the field of software measurement for improving the quality of product and most of them pursue the goal of the quality of final product, *i.e.* later phase in system development life cycle [1]. In software engineering it is widely accepted that the quality of finally delivered product is highly dependent on the early decision in the development process [2]. An accurate evaluation of software quality depends on testability estimation, which in turn depends on the factor that can affect testability. Reusability is strongly associated to testability and continuously plays an important role to deliver best quality and high class software within fixed time and given budget [3]. Reusability factor is not new; Mxllroy defines "reusability factor" has been behind many software developments for product's quality. Reusability plays an important role in software quality assessment at design time and also acts as the basis to find testability indices for industry project's ranking. The basic criterion for evaluating testability factor is reusability. If a component is not reusable then the whole concept of component based software development fails. The definitions of reusability from various researchers are summarized in **Table 1**.

Software design is a method in software engineering that produces a model of the system and allows system designers/developers to rotate your computational model into a workable algorithm that resolve the problems by the help of qualitative and quantitative assessment [10]. ISO 9126 quality model defines: "level of quality and performance of design achieves expected functionalities by reusability factor [11]". A reusability criterion constantly supports designer for improved software design at an early stage of software development process. Design phase has direct impact on the product testing cost and effort and plays the backbone role of any product. To design and develop a good quality product, reusability plays a key role for assessment of software testability. Estimating reusability factor early in the development life cycle may greatly reduce the overall product development cost and enhance the customer satisfaction. The object oriented design principle is a suitable language for generalized productivity. The objective of this study is to produce a model that quantifies reusability at design instant of development life cycle. In this regard, research proposes a "Reusability Quantification Framework", which is summarized in **Figure 1**.

This paper is structured in such a approach that it initially describes the reusability: an important factor to testability for quantification process and then lists and describes reusability quantification model with their correlation establishment and also highlights information for statistical significance of the developed model that are significant for further study. The developed model has been empirically validated; furthermore, the research paper concludes with software industry utility of model for project leveling in conclusion section.

2. Reusability: A Testability Perspective

Reusability is recognized as a very important factor to testability evaluation of object oriented software, which consent to the inclusion of changes in a design and gives an early focus to create testable software within development life cycle. The IEEE defines software reusability as the capability of a system or component to perform its required function under its specified condition that means "a component is reusable then the whole component of product design do not required to change [12]". **Table 2** is denoted as the reusability is an important criterion in different quality model.

In general the overall objective of the reusability quantification is to deliver good quality software that is effective in function, easily approachable to user and permit the incorporation of changes in a product design and gives an early focus to deliver testable software within specified condition *i.e.* fixed time and bounded budget because delivering good quality product is no longer an advantage, but a essential factor. Objective of this study

Table 1. Researcher definition.

Name of Researcher	Definition
Freeman [4]	"Reuse is the use of any kind of information which a developer may need in the software creation process".
Basili and Rombach [5]	"Software reuse is the use of everything related with software with a software project, including knowledge".
Tracz [6]	"Reusability is the use of software specification that was designed for reuse".
Braun [7]	"Use of existing software components in a new perspective, either in the same system or in another system".
Cooper [8]	"Reuse is the ability of a previously developed software component to be used again or used repeatedly in part or in it's entirely, with or without modification".
Krueger [9]	"Reuse is the process of developing software systems from existing software rather than building them from scratch".

Figure 1. Research framework for reusability quantification process.

Table 2. Reusability quality criteria in different quality model.

Quality Model	Definition
McCall quality model [13]	This quality model has three quality of software product: according to this model "Reusability quality factor" show the quality of product as a form of product transition that means adaptability to new environment with the help of generality and self documentation quality criteria.
Dromey quality model [14]	Dromey proposed a framework for evaluate requirement design and implementation phase. The high level software product properties for the implementation include 'reusability as the quality criteria of Dromey quality mode.
Boehm quality model [15]	Boehm quality model used reusability as the quality factor to accomplish the completeness criteria to automatics and qualitative evaluate the quality of software.
FURPS model [16]	FURPS model extended by IBM Rational software used "reusability as the quality factor" in FURPS QUALITY MODE to accomplish the consistency and documentation quality criteria.

to evaluate software reusability by using the concept of software quality assessment during the initial stage in development life cycle. Here research is required to develop a structured approach to make sure that software is reusable, effective and high quality.

3. Object Oriented Design Properties

In software development environments, object oriented designing and development is becoming very preferred paradigm in industrial software development environments for large-scale system design. This technology offers support to deliver final software product with higher quality and lower maintenance costs [17]. Classes in object oriented design system provide an excellent structuring principle that allows a structure to be divided into well designed units which may then be implemented separately. One of the major advantage of having object orientation is its support for software reusability, which may be achieved either through the simple reuse of a class in a library or via inheritance among relationship. Object oriented principles direct the designers what to avoid and what to support. Several procedures have been defined in this method so far to estimate object oriented design. There are several essential qualities of object orientation that are recognized to be the basis of internal qualities of object oriented design that support in the context of measurement. These ideas significantly include design properties *i.e.* encapsulation, inheritance, coupling, and cohesion. Encapsulation is a mechanism to realize data abstraction and information hiding. It hides internal specification of an object. Inheritance is the distribution of operations and attributes among classes. Coupling indicates the relationship or interdependency between modules. Cohesion refers to the internal reliability inside the components of the design. A class is cohesive when its components are greatly interrelated and it should be difficult to divide a cohesive class. Cohesion can be used to recognize the defectively designed classes. **Table 3** summarize as the design properties and their advantages.

4. Object Oriented Design Metrics

Several research works in the object oriented metrics arena were done in recent years [3]. Most of the metric is accepted by practitioners on "heavy usages and popularity" and by academic experts on empirical (post development) validation. This led to the definition of four new metrics, Encapsulation Metrics (ENM), Coupling Metrics (DCC) and Cohesion Metrics (COM), Inheritance Metrics (MFA) which could be calculated from design information only. A suite of object-oriented metrics, covering all the design attributes, has been listed and described in **Table 4**.

5. Correlation Establishment

The correlation establishment among Reusability, OOD Properties and Metrics, describes the quantification process of reusability model in order to establish a multivariate linear model for reusability and OOD constructs. The values of these design metrics can be identified by class diagram metrics. Identified metrics will take part in the role of independent variables while reusability will be taken as dependent variable. Evaluation of reusability is very helpful to get testability index of software design for high quality product as early as possible in development life cycle. After rigorously evaluation of existing literature on the topic correlation between reusability and design metrics have been established, shown in **Figure 2** [11] [12] [18] [19]. To establish a correlation between object oriented design properties and reusability, the influence of design metrics are being examined with respect to developed reusability quantification model. It was observed that every Object Oriented Design metrics affect quality factor. Identified independent variables, namely Data Access Metrics (DAM), Measure of functional Abstraction (MFA), Direct Class Coupling (DCC), the values of dependent variable "Y" can be found out by using the "Reusability Quantification Model of Object Oriented Design".

6. Reusability Quantification Model Development

It is clear from in-depth literature survey that reusability is not a new word; rather it has been in conversation among the engineering professionals at various forum, but there is no commonly accepted complete and com-

Table 3. Object oriented design properties and advantages.

Property	Definition	Advantages
Encapsulation	Defined as a kind of data abstraction and information hiding.	Reduces complexity Reusability
Inheritance	A measure of the "is-a" relationship among classes.	Eliminates redundant code Reusability
Coupling	Show the interdependency of an object to other objects in a system design.	Good understandability Reusability
Cohesion	Refers to the internal consistency within the components of design.	Reusability

Table 4. Metrics description.

Metrics	Name	Description
ENM	Encapsulation Metric	This metric count of all the methods defined in a class and hold a single construct behavior so that OOD property prevent access to attribute declaration by protecting the internal structure of the objects.
DCC	Coupling Metric	This metric shows the property of interdependency among objects in a design.
COM	Cohesion Metric	This metric computes the relatedness among methods and attribute in a class.
MFA	Inheritance Metric	This metric count "is-a" relationship between classes. This association is correlated to the level of class in an inheritance structure.

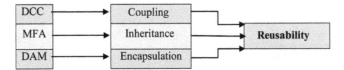

Figure 2. Correlation among reusability, OOD properties and metrics.

prehensive model or framework available to estimating the reusability index of the software product at design phase in development life cycle, that motivate to develop "Reusability Quantification Model of Object Oriented Design", using object oriented principle based on its inner design property in development life cycle. This model used above mentioned design metrics to illustrate a range of measurement for software project. In order to create a model for reusability factor, following multiple regression technique has been selected.

$$\text{Reusability} = \alpha 0 \pm \alpha 1 * \text{Coupling} \pm \alpha 2 * \text{Inheritance} \pm \alpha 3 * \text{Encapsulation} \tag{1}$$

Using "SPSS" math work software values of all design metrics, intercept, and coefficient of the respective metrics are calculated. On the basis of this technique, the multiple regression reusability model has been developed in Equation (2). The developed multiple regression model takes the following form

$$\text{Reusability} = -37.111 + 3.973 * \text{Coupling} + 32.500 * \text{Inheritance} + 20.709 * \text{Encapsulation} \tag{2}$$

Statistical Significance of Reusability Quantification Model

The descriptive statistics of the output table gives the valuable record of statistics that are mean, standard deviation and number of software projects selected for each of the dependent variable and independent variable.

ANOVA examination for dependent variable (reusability) gives the result of F (frequency ratio) with df (degree of freedom). ANOVA output **Table 5** shows frequency ratio of 19.077 with (3, 4) degree of freedom by experimental tryout at the confidence interval level of 95%. The critical values of F is 9.12 [20]. Study obtained F ratio at (3, 4) degree of freedom is 19.077 that is larger than this, so result conclude that F-ratio is likely to occur by chance with a $P < 0.05$ level of significance.

The coefficients part and statistical significance of design metrics and constant for reusability model gives the values, that need in order to write the reusability model and prove that all the three identified design metrics do the statistically significance role at the 95% confidence level. The standardized beta coefficient give a measure of the contribution of each independent variable to the reusability model and significance values give a rough suggestion of the impact of each predictor variable. The data used for developing Reusability model has been collected through large commercial object oriented system (**Table 6**).

The Reusability Quantification Model summary (**Table 7**) of the output is most useful when performing multiple regressions. In this table "R" is the multiple correlation coefficient that used to know how strongly multiple independent variable are related to dependent variable. "R square" gives supportive coefficient of determination.

7. Empirical Validation of Developed Model

Empirical validation of work proves that how significant developed model, where metrics and model are able to quantify the reusability index of object oriented design in design stage. This validation is an essential phase of research to evaluate the developed model for appropriate execution and high level acceptability. It is also the fine approach and practice for claiming the model acceptance. To justify claiming for acceptance of developed model, an experimental validation of the proposed reusability quantification model at design phase has been carried out using tryout data from different versions of two famous windows application frameworks, object windows library (OWL) of four publicly released versions OWL 4.0, OWL 4.5, OWL 5.0, OWL 5.2 and Microsoft foundation class (MFC) of five publicly released versions MFC 1.0, MFC 2.0, MFC 3.0, MFC 4.0, MFC 5.0 [21]. In order to validate developed model, the value of metrics are available by using above data set for following projects in **Table 8**.

8. Statistical Analysis of Reusability Quantification

Charles Spearman's Rank Correlation Coefficient (r_s) was used to test the significance of correlation between

Table 5. Examination of ANOVA for reusability model.

Model (1)	Sum of Squares	Df	Mean Square	F	Sig.
Regression	51197.757	3	17065.919	19.077	0.008[a]
Residual	3578.411	4	894.603		
Total	54776.169	7			

a. Predictors: (Constant), Inheritance, encapsulation, Coupling; b. Dependent Variable: Reusability.

Table 6. Coefficients of independent variables and constant for reusability model.

Model Equation No. 2	Unstandardized Coefficients		Standardized Coefficients	t	Sig.
	B	Std. Error	Beta		
(Constant)	−37.111	77.201		−0.481	0.656
Coupling	3.973	72.513	0.009	0.055	0.959
Inheritance	32.500	7.395	1.017	4.395	0.012
Encapsulation	20.709	84.225	0.056	0.246	0.818

Dependent Variable: Reusability.

Table 7. Model summary for reusability model.

Model	R	R Square	Adjusted R Square	Std. Error of the estimation	Change Statistics				
					R Square Change	F Change	df1	df2	Sig. F Change
1	0.967[a]	0.935	0.886	29.90991	0.935	19.077	3	4	0.008

a. Predictors: (Constant), Encapsulation, Coupling, Inheritance.

Table 8. Known and calculated reusability ranking and project acceptance under charles spearman's rank correlation coefficient.

Projects	Calculated Reusability Index	Calculated Reusability Rating	Known Reusability Index	Known Reusability Rating	d^2	r_s	$r_s > 0.6563$
P1	162.73716	11	195.92	14	9	0.983929	√
P2	218.71919	12	204.37	15	9	0.983929	√
P3	267.08929	14	56.84	9	25	0.955357	√
P4	278.69338	15	81.94	10	25	0.955357	√
P5	265.89075	13	11.29	7	36	0.935714	√
P6	36.3647	7	157.71	12	25	0.955357	√
P7	48.33769	8	168.81	13	25	0.955357	√
P8	127.42131	9	54.62	8	1	0.998214	√
P9	127.78604	10	82.53	11	1	0.998214	√
P10	0.461	1	10.50	5	16	0.971429	√
P11	17.4928	4	10.50	6	4	0.992857	√
P12	14.1456	3	8.00	2	1	0.998214	√
P13	34.9219	5	8.70	3	4	0.992857	√
P14	34.9219	6	7.20	1	25	0.955357	√
P15	12.9665	2	9.00	4	4	0.992857	√

calculated index values of reusability by *Reusability Quantification Model of Object Oriented Design* and its known index values given by expert shown in **Figure 3**. The "r_s" was calculated using the following formula

$$r_s = 1 - \frac{6 \sum d^2}{n(n^2 - 1)} \qquad -1.0 \leq r_s \leq +1.0$$

where

r_s is coefficient of Rank Correlation,

d is the difference between calculated index values and known values of reusability,

n is the number of software projects for experiment, (In this research n = 15 software projects)

$\sum$ is notification symbol, significance "The Sum".

Comparison between calculated reusability rank correlation coefficient and threshold value (0.6563) at 95% confidence level is shown in following line graph **Figure 4**.

Study results have proved that the correlation is acceptable with high degree of confidence that is 95%. Therefore research is concluded without any loss of generality the "*Reusability Quantification Model of Object Oriented Design*" highly significant, because estimation values are more reliable and valid in the context.

9. Key Contributions and Findings

Developed "Reusability Quantification of Object Oriented Design" for object oriented design. The Model has been validated using the same set of try-out data. An empirical validation of the developed model is also performed using try-out data.

Some of the major findings are as given below:

1) Reusability has been identified as a key factor to software testability, addressed in design phase of object oriented software development to produce quality software.

2) The three metrics DAM (Data Access Metrics), MFA (Measure of functional Abstraction), DCC (Direct class Coupling) are identified for each of object oriented design constructs such as encapsulation, inheritance and coupling respectively.

3) Software design constructs are most appropriate and power full for controlling software quality factors in design phase.

4) A guideline produced by developed framework to be followed right from beginning of development so as to design class hierarchy as per the prescriptive reusability index for the project under development.

5) Developed Framework may be used to get reusability metric in design phase for reusability measuring.

6) Reusability indexing (RI) can be done using the proposed model "Reusability Quantification of Object Oriented Design".

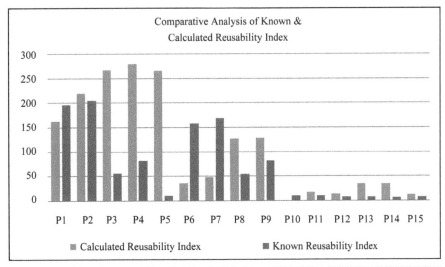

Figure 3. Line graph comparing between known and calculated reusability index for software projects.

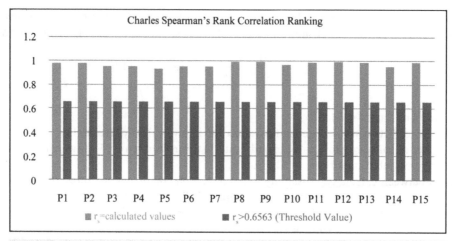

Figure 4. Line graph comparison between calculated correlation values and threshold value.

7) "Reusability Quantification of Object Oriented Design" provides a Reusability indexing (RI) benchmark for other researchers and designers.

8) For Industry project ranking, Reusability indexing (RI) is possible using the "Reusability Quantification of Object Oriented Design". The developed model may be generalized and used by others researchers.

10. Conclusion

This paper has developed an efficient and accurate model for reusability quantification through object oriented design metrics using the technique of multiple regressions. The developed model proposed the possibilities to estimate overall reusability from designed information. Developed model has been demonstrated using functionally equivalent projects and the assessment of reusability index in OOD has been validated using structural and functional information from object oriented software. This paper also validates the quantifying ability of developed model. That validation study on this research work proves that proposed reusability quantification model is highly acceptable, more practical in nature and helps the software industry in project ranking.

Acknowledgements

First and foremost, I would like to express my sincere gratitude to my supervisor Prof. Dr. YDS Arya & Co-supervisor Associate Prof. Dr. M H Khan for the continuous support of my PhD study and research, motivation, enthusiasm. Their guidance helped me in all the time of research. Last but not the least; I would like to thank my parent for their patience, understanding and support that drive me to complete my study.

References

[1] Binder, R.V. (1994) Design for Testability in Object-Oriented Systems. *Communications of the ACM*, **37**, 87-101. http://dx.doi.org/10.1145/182987.184077

[2] Huda, M., Arya, Y.D.S. and Khan, M.H. (2014) Measuring Testability of Object Oriented Design: A Systematic Review. *International Journal of Scientific Engineering and Technology* (*IJSET*), **3**, 1313-1319.

[3] Huda, M., Arya, Y.D.S. and Khan, M.H. (2015) Evaluating Effectiveness Factor of Object Oriented Design: A Testability Perspective. *International Journal of Software Engineering & Applications* (*IJSEA*), **6**, 41-49. http://dx.doi.org/10.5121/ijsea.2015.6104

[4] Freeman, P. (1983) Reusable Software Engineering Concepts and Research Directions. In Tutorial: Software Reusability, 10-23.

[5] Basili, V.R. and Rombach, H.D. (1988) Towards a Comprehensive Framework for Reuse: A Reuse-Enabling Software Evolution Environment. Technical Report CS-TR-2158, University of Maryland, Maryland.

[6] Tracz, W. (1995) Confessions of a Used Program Salesman: Institutionalizing Software Reuse. Addison-Wesley. http://dx.doi.org/10.1145/211782.211785

[7] Braun, C.L. (1994) Reuse. In Marciniak, 1055-1069.

[8]   Cooper, J. (1994) Reuse-the Business Implications. In Marciniak, 1071-1077.

[9]   Krueger, C.W. (1992) Software Reuse. *ACM Computing Surveys*, **24**, 131-183.

[10]   Huda, M., Arya, Y.D.S. and Khan, M.H. (2015) Testability Quantification Framework of Object Oriented Software: A New Perspective. *International Journal of Advanced Research in Computer and Communication Engineering*, **4**, 298-302. http://dx.doi.org/10.17148/IJARCCE.2015.4168

[11]   ISO (2001) ISO/IEC 9126-1: Software Engineering—Product Quality—Part-1: Quality Model. Geneva.

[12]   IEEE Press (1990) IEEE Standard Glossary of Software Engineering Technology. ANSI/IEEE Standard 610.12-1990.

[13]   McCall, J.A., Richards, P.K. and Walters, G.F. (1977) Factors in Software Quality. RADC TR-77-369, Rome Air Development Center, Rome.

[14]   Dromey, R.G. (1996) Concerning the Chimera (Software Quality). *IEEE Software*, **13**, 33-43. http://dx.doi.org/10.1109/52.476284

[15]   Boehm, B.W., Brow, J.R., Lipow, M., McLeod, G. and Merritt, M. (1978) Characteristics of Software Quality. North Holland Publishing, Amsterdam.

[16]   Grady, R.B. (1992) Practical Software Metrics for Project Management and Process Improvement. Prentice Hall, Englewood Cliff.

[17]   Khan, R.A. and Mustafa, K. (2004) A Model for Object Oriented Design Quality Assessment. *Proceedings of the Integrated Design and Process Technology Symposium*, Izmir, 28 June-2 July 2004.

[18]   Fu, J.P., Liu, B. and Lu, M.Y. (2010) Present and Future of Software Testability Analysis. *Proceedings of the International Conference on Computer Application and System Modeling* (*ICCASM*), Taiyuan, 22-24 October 2010, V15-279-V15-284.

[19]   Gao, J. and Ming-Chih, S. (2005) A Component Testability Model for Verification and Measurement. *Proceedings of the* 29*th Annual International Computer Software and Applications Conference*, Edinburgh, 26-28 July 2005, 211-218. http://dx.doi.org/10.1109/COMPSAC.2005.17

[20]   http://homepages.wmich.edu/~hillenbr/619/AnovaTable.pdf

[21]   Bansiya, J. (2002) A Hierarchical Model for Object Oriented Design Quality Assessment. *IEEE Transaction of Software Engineering*, **28**, 4-17.

10

Four Sliding Windows Pattern Matching Algorithm (FSW)

Amjad Hudaib[1], Rola Al-Khalid[1], Aseel Al-Anani[1], Mariam Itriq[2], Dima Suleiman[2]

[1]Department of Computer Information Systems, King Abdullah II School for Information Technology, The University of Jordan, Amman, Jordan

[2]Department of Business Information Technology, King Abdullah II School for Information Technology, The University of Jordan, Amman, Jordan

Email: dima.suleiman@ju.edu.jo, m.itriq@ju.edu.jo, a.anani@ju.edu.jo, r.khalid@ju.edu.jo, ahudaib@ju.edu.jo

Abstract

This paper presents an efficient pattern matching algorithm (FSW). FSW improves the searching process for a pattern in a text. It scans the text with the help of four sliding windows. The windows are equal to the length of the pattern, allowing multiple alignments in the searching process. The text is divided into two parts; each part is scanned from both sides simultaneously using two sliding windows. The four windows slide in parallel in both parts of the text. The comparisons done between the text and the pattern are done from both of the pattern sides in parallel. The conducted experiments show that FSW achieves the best overall results in the number of attempts and the number of character comparisons compared to the pattern matching algorithms: Two Sliding Windows (TSW), Enhanced Two Sliding Windows algorithm (ETSW) and Berry-Ravindran algorithm (BR). The best time case is calculated and found to be $O\left(\dfrac{m}{4}\right)$ while the average case time complexity is $O\left(\dfrac{n}{4m}\right)$.

Keywords

Pattern Matching, FWS, Enhanced Two Sliding Windows Algorithm, RS-A Fast Pattern Matching Algorithm

1. Introduction

String matching is a challenging subject in computer science. Many researchers proposed and designed different techniques and algorithms to find all possible occurrences of a pattern P of size m from the text string T of size n [1]-[3]. The researchers focus on reducing the number of character comparisons and processing time. String matching algorithms are used in various applications such as matching DNA sequences [4] [5], voice recognition, image processing, text processing [6]-[8], network security, real-time problem, web applications and information retrieval from databases [9] [10].

In this paper, we combine the searching strategy of the ETSW algorithm and the shifting process of the BR algorithm [11] [12]. This paper ends up with a new algorithm (FSW) that uses four sliding windows which are equal to the length of the pattern. FSW divides the text into two parts; each part is scanned from both sides simultaneously using two sliding windows. The four windows slide in parallel in both halves of the text. The comparisons done between the text and the pattern are done from both of the pattern sides in parallel. The FSW algorithm finds the first occurrence of the pattern from either the left windows or the right windows from both parts of the text. In all the cases we tested and the comparisons we performed with other matching algorithms such as BR, TSW and ETSW, the proposed algorithm FSW proved to be the best in reducing the number of comparisons and attempts needed to find the pattern [13] [14]. This paper is organized as follows: Section 2 provides an overview of the related works; Section 3 explains the FSW algorithm; Section 4 includes the performance analysis and Section 5 concludes the paper.

2. Related Works

Recently, several new pattern matching algorithms have been proposed to minimize the number of comparisons done to locate a pattern in a text [15]-[17]. Enhancements are made on both the searching process by using several sliding windows that scan the text in parallel and on the preprocessing phase by determining the shift value that the pattern should move in the process of searching the text for the pattern [18].

The Berry-Ravindran algorithm (BR) uses the bad character shift function to calculate the shift value for the two consecutive characters in the text immediately to the right of the pattern window. In BR the searching time complexity is calculated to be $O(nm)$ and the pre-processing time complexity is $O(\sigma 2)$ [14]. The Two-Sliding Window algorithm (TSW) determines the shift value by using the idea of Berry-Ravindran bad character shift function. The pre-processing time complexity is found to be $2(m-1)$.

In the searching phase, TSW uses two sliding windows to scan the text from both sides in parallel. The search process continues until the first occurrence of the pattern is found or until both windows reach the middle of the text. The size of each sliding window is equal to the length of the pattern. In TSW, the best time complexity is $O(m)$ and the worst case time complexity is $O\left(\left(\frac{n}{2}-m+1\right)(m)\right)$ [12].

The Enhanced Two Sliding Windows algorithm (ETSW) utilizes the idea of Berry-Ravindran bad character shift function to get better shift values during the searching phase. In the searching phase, ETSW scans both of the text and the pattern from both sides in parallel. Both the text and the pattern are divided into left and right parts. So, the text is searched from both parts simultaneously and the comparisons with the pattern are done from both its parts at the same time. ETSW algorithm stops when the pattern is not found. In ETSW, the best time case is $O\left(\frac{m}{2}\right)$ while the average case time complexity is $O\left(\frac{n}{2m}\right)$ [11]. The Enhanced RS-A algorithm (ERS-A) [19] utilizes the idea of RS-A algorithm to get better shift values. ERS-A algorithm uses four consecutive characters in the text immediately to the right of the pattern window.

The ERS-A algorithm uses two sliding windows to search for a pattern in a text. The two windows slide from both sides of the text simultaneously. The searching process continues until a match is found. It stops immediately if the pattern is not found in the text. In ERS-A, the best case complexity is $O(m)$ while the average case time complexity is $O\left(\frac{n}{2*(m+4)}\right)$ [19].

In this paper enhancements are made on the ETSW algorithm, the preprocessing phase is the same while the searching process is made better using four sliding windows to scan the text simultaneously. The comparisons with the pattern are also done from both of the pattern sides in parallel.

3. The FSW Algorithm

The FSW algorithm scans the text as well as the pattern from both sides simultaneously in order to improve the search process. The proposed algorithm (FSW) scans the text using four sliding windows, allowing multiple alignments in the searching process. Each window size is equal to the length of the pattern. In the searching phase, the text is divided in into two parts; each part is scanned from both sides simultaneously using two sliding windows. The four windows slide in parallel in both halves of the text. The comparisons done between the text and the pattern are done from both sides of the pattern in parallel.

Two of the siding windows are aligned with the left and the right sides of the first part of the text and at the same time the other two sliding windows are aligned with the left and the right sides of the second part of the text resulting in four sliding windows that scam the text simultaneously. FSW algorithm stops when a sliding window finds the pattern or the pattern is not found within the text string at all.

FSW algorithm enhances the searching process in the ETSW algorithm. Both the FSW and ETSW algorithms utilize the idea of BR bad character shift function to get better shift values during the searching phase.

The main difference between the FSW and the ETSW algorithms lies in the searching process. During the search the comparisons between the pattern and the text in the FSW are made using four sliding windows while in the Enhanced TSW algorithm two sliding windows are used. Using two additional windows during the search process decreases the number of comparisons and attempts done.

3.1. Pre-Processing Phase

The pre-processing phase of the FSW algorithm is the same as in ETSW algorithm. Two arrays *nextl* and *nextr* are generated. Each array is a one-dimensional array. The shift values are calculated according to Berry-Ravindran bad character algorithm (BR). The shift values needed to search the text from the left side are stored in the *nextl* array. On the other hand *nextr* array contains the shift values needed to search the text from the right side.

To build the two arrays (*nextl* and *nextr*), we take each two consecutive characters of the pattern and give it an index starting from 0. For example for the pattern structure abcd, the consecutive characters ab, bc and cd are given the indexes 0, 1 and 2 respectively.

The shift values for the *nextl* array are calculated according to Equation (1) while the shift values for the *nextr* array are calculated according to Equation (2). In Equation (1), we compare between the last character in the pattern $m - 1$ with a if there is a match the window is shifted 1 character to the right. If there is a mismatch the shift is the minimum of $m - i$ in case of $p[i]\,p[i+1] = $ ab, $m + 1$ in case of $p[0] = $ b and $m + 2$ otherwise. In Equation (2), if the first character of the pattern matches b then the window is shifted 1 character to the left otherwise we take the minimum of $m - ((m-2)-i)$ in case of $p[i]\,p[i+1] = $ ab, $m + 1$ in case of $p[m-1] = $ a, $m + 2$ otherwise.

$$\text{Bad Char } shiftl\,[\text{a},\text{b}] = \min \begin{cases} 1 & \text{if } p[m-1]=\text{a} \\ m-i & \text{if } p[i]\,p[i+1]=\text{ab} \\ m+1 & \text{if } p[0]=\text{b} \\ m+2 & \text{otherwise} \end{cases} \tag{1}$$

$$\text{Bad Char } shiftr\,[\text{a},\text{b}] = \min \begin{cases} m+1 & \text{if } p[m-1]=\text{a} \\ m-((m-2)-i) & \text{if } p[i]\,p[i+1]=\text{ab} \\ 1 & \text{if } p[0]=\text{b} \\ m+2 & \text{otherwise} \end{cases} \tag{2}$$

3.2. Searching Phase

In the four sliding windows algorithm, the text is divided into two parts. The left part is named part 1 while the right part is named part 2. Four windows are created for the whole test. Two windows are created for each part of the text, to search for the pattern in parallel. The left and right windows of part 1 are named p_{1L} and p_{1R} respectively. The left and right windows of part 2 are named p_{2L} and p_{2R} respectively. At the beginning of the search, p_{1L} and p_{2R} windows are aligned with the left most and rightmost sides of the text. p_{2L} window is aligned with the text at index $n/2 + m - 1$ while p_{1R} window is aligned with the text at index $n/2 - 1$ where n is the text length and m is the pattern length. The alignments of p_{2L} and p_{1R} are calculated taking into consideration the case where some characters of the pattern may appear in part1 of the text and the rest may appear in the second part of the text.

Figure 1 explains the algorithm of the FSW algorithm.

```
L1 = m − 1; //text index used from left in part 1
R1 = n/2 − 1; //text index used from right in part 1
L2 = n/2 + m − 1; //text index used from left in part 2
R2 = n − m; //text index used from right in part 2
T index = 0; //text index used to control the scanning process
While (T index <=  ⌈ n/4 ⌉ )
    begin
        found Part 1 Left = false.
        found Part 1 Right = false.
        found Part 2 Left = false.
        found Part 2 Right = false.
        l1 = m − 1; // pattern index used at left side of part 1
        r1 = 0; // pattern index used at right side of part 1
        l2 = m − 1; // pattern index used at left side of part 2
        r2 = 0; // pattern index used at right side of part 2
        //keep record of the text index where the pattern match the text during comparison
        temp-l index 1 = temp-r index 1 = 0, temp-l index 2 = temp-r index 2 = 0;
        templ = 0; tempr = m − 1;
        if (P[m − 1] = T[L1] and P[0] = T[L1 − m + 1]) //search from left of part 1
        begin
                    temp-l index 1 = L1
                    L1 = L1 − 1
                    templ++
                    while ((l1 >= 0 and P[l1] = T[L1]) and (P[templ] = T[L1 − l1 + templ]))
                    {L1 = L1 − 1, l1 = l1 − 1; templ++;
                if ((L1 − l1 + templ) >= L1)
                    {foundPart1Left = true; exit from while loop;}
                    }
        end
        if (P[0] = T[R1] and P[tempr] = T[R1 + m − 1]) //search from right of part 1

        begin
                    temp-r index 1 = R1
                    R1 = R1 + 1
                    tempr--;
                    while ((r1 < m and P[r1] = T[R1]) and P[tempr] = T[R1 + tempr − r1])
                    {R1 = R1 + 1, r1 = r1 + 1; tempr--;
        if (R1 + tempr − r1 <= R1)
                    {foundPart1Right = true; exit from while loop;}
                    }
        end
        templ = 0; tempr = m − 1;
        if (P[m − 1] = T[L2] and p[0] = T[L2 − m + 1]) //search from left of part 2

        begin
                    temp-l index 2 = L2
                    L2 = L2 − 1
                    templ++
                    while ((l2 >= 0 and P[l2] = T[L2]) and (P[templ] = T[L2 − l2 + templ]))
                    {L2 = L2 − 1, l2 = l2 − 1; templ++;
                if ((L2 − l2 + templ) >= L2)
                    {found Part 2 Left = true; exit from while loop;}
                    }
        end
        if (P[0] = T[R2] and P[tempr] = T[R2 + m − 1]) //search from right of part 2

        begin
                    temp-r index 2 = R2
                    R2 = R2 + 1
                    tempr--;
                    while((r2 < m and P[r2] = T[R2]) and P[tempr] = T[R2 + tempr − r2])
                    {R2 = R2 + 1, r2 = r2 + 1; tempr--;
        if (R2 + tempr − r2 <= R2)
                    {found Part 2 Right = true; exit from while loop;}
                    }
        end

        if (found Part 1 Left) {display "match at left of part 1:" +L1 + 1); exit from outer loop;}
        if (found Part 1 Right) {display "match at right of part 1:" +R1 − m); exit from outer loop;}
        if found Part 2 Left) {display "match at left of part 2:" +L2 + 1); exit from outer loop;}
        if found Part 2 Right) {display "match at right of part 2:" +R2 − m); exit from outer loop;}
        //To avoid skipping characters after partial matching
        L1 = temp-l index 1; R1 = temp-r index 1;
        L2 = temp-l index 2; R2 = temp-r index 2;
        if (L1 > R1){ display ("not found"); exit from outer loop;}
        //from pre-processing step
        L1 = L1 + get (shiftl); R1 = R1 − get (shiftr);
        L2 = L2 + get (shiftl); R2 = R2 − get (shiftr);
        T index = Tindex + 1;
    End
```

Figure 1. FSW pattern matching algorithm.

3.3. Working Example

In this section we will present an example to clarify the FSW algorithm.

Given:

Pattern (P) = "abcd", $m = 4$,

Text (T) = "abaccbacdacdbadcbbcacbbcaaddcaabcbaaacbddababcdddabdaabaabccdabccdbacbdcbcdacc dbcbddaadddbcabdb", $n = 100$.

3.3.1. Pre-Processing Phase

Initially, $shiftl1 = shiftr1 = shiftl2 = shiftr2 = m + 2 = 6$.

The shift values are calculated using equations 1 and 2. The values are then stored in two arrays *nextl* and *nextr* as shown in **Figure 2(a)** and **Figure 2(b)** respectively.

3.3.2. Searching Phase

The searching process for the pattern P is illustrated through the working example as shown in **Figure 3**.

First attempt: (see **Figure 3(b)**)

We align p_{1L} with the text from the left of part 1. In this case, comparisons are made between the text character located at index 0 (character a) with the leftmost character in the pattern (character a). At the same time, comparisons are made between the text character at index 3 (character c) with the rightmost character in the pattern (character d). As a result, a mismatch occurs between text character c and pattern character d; therefore we take the two consecutive characters from the text at index 4 and 5 which are c and b respectively. To determine the amount of shift (*shiftl*) we have to do the following two steps:

a) We look for the index of cb in the pattern.

b) Since cb is not found in the pattern, so the window is shifted to the right 6 steps (see Equation (1)).

As explained in the example the number of comparisons needed to determine if there is a match or not is one; this is because two character comparisons between the text and the pattern are performed at the same time.

Second attempt: (see **Figure 3(c)**)

We align p_{1R} with the text from the right of part 1. In this case, a match occurs between the text character at index 52 (d) and the rightmost character in the pattern d while there is a mismatch between the text character at index 49 (b) and the leftmost character in the pattern a; therefore we take the two consecutive characters from the text at index 47 and 48 which are b and a respectively. To determine the amount of shift (*shiftr*), we have to do the following two steps:

a) We look for the index of ba in the pattern.

b) Since ba is not found in the pattern, but the $p[0]$ which is a matches the text character at index 48 then according to the pre-processing phase the sliding window will be shifted 1 step to the left.

Third attempt: (see **Figure 3(d)**)

We align p_{2L} with the text from the left of part 2. In this case, a mismatch occurs between the text character at index 50 (c) and the leftmost character in the pattern a while there is a match between the text character at index 53 (d) and the rightmost character in the pattern d; therefore we take the two consecutive characters from the text at index 54 and 55 which are a and b respectively. To determine the amount of shift (*shiftl*) we have to do the following two steps:

a) We look for the index of ab in the pattern, which is found 0.

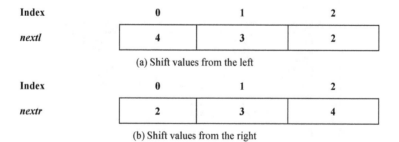

Index	0	1	2
nextl	4	3	2

(a) Shift values from the left

Index	0	1	2
nextr	2	3	4

(b) Shift values from the right

Figure 2. The *nextl* and *nextr* arrays.

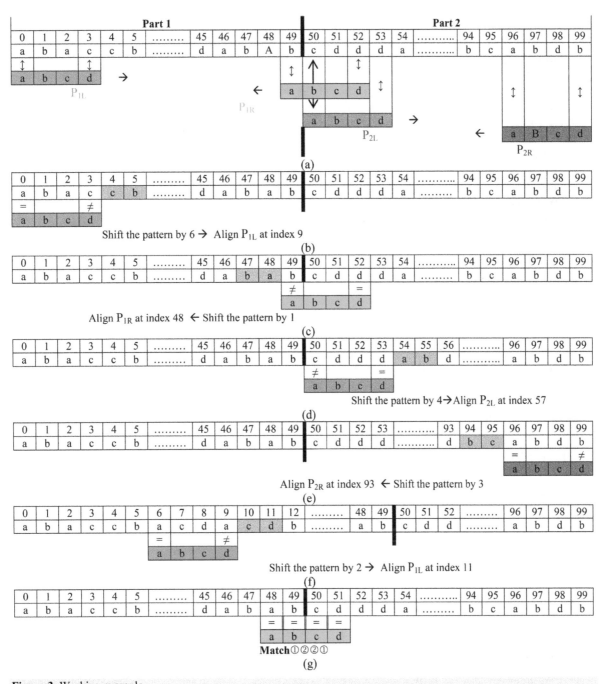

Figure 3. Working example.

b) Since we search from the left side we use *nextl* array, and *shiftl* = *nextl* [0] = 4.

Therefore the window will be shifted to the right 4 steps.

***Fourth attempt*:**

In the fourth attempt (see **Figure 3(e)**), we align the fourth sliding window with the text from the right of part 2. In this case, a mismatch occurs between the text character at index 99 (b) and the rightmost character in the pattern (character d) while there is a match between the text character at index 96 (character a) and the leftmost character in the pattern (character a); therefore we take the two consecutive characters from the text at index 94 and 95 which are b and c respectively. To determine the amount of shift (*shiftr*), we have to do the following two steps:

a) We look for the index of bc in the pattern.

b) Since we search from the right side, we use *nextr* array, and *shiftr* = *nextr* [1] = 3.
Therefore the window is shifted to the left 3 steps.

Fifth attempt:

In the fifth attempt (see **Figure 3(f)**), we align the first sliding window with the text from the left of part 1. In this case, a match occurs between the text character at index 6 (a) and the leftmost character in the pattern (character a) while there is a mismatch between the text character at index 9 (character a) and the rightmost character in the pattern (character d); therefore we take the two consecutive characters from the text at index 10 and 11 which are c and d respectively,

a) We look for the index of cd in the pattern.

b) Since we search from the left side we use *nextl* array, and *shiftl* = *nextl* [2] = 2.
Therefore the window is shifted to the right 2 steps.

Sixth attempt:

In the sixth attempt (see **Figure 3(g)**), we align the second sliding window with the text from the right of part 1. A comparison between the pattern and the text characters leads to a complete match at index 48. In this case, the occurrence of the pattern is found using the right window of part 1.

4. Analysis

Preposition 1: The space complexity is $O(2(m-1))$ where m is the pattern length.

Preposition 2: The pre-process time complexity is $O(2(m-1))$.

Lemma 1: The worst case time complexity is $O\left(\left(\dfrac{n}{2}-\dfrac{m}{4}+1\right)\left(\dfrac{m}{4}\right)\right)$.

Proof: The worst case occurs when at each attempt, all the compared characters of both pattern sides at 4 windows that slide simultaneously are matched the corresponding text characters except the pattern character indexed (m), and at the same time the shift value is equal to 1.

Lemma 2: The best case time complexity is $O\left(\dfrac{m}{4}\right)$.

Proof: The best case occurs when the pattern is found at the first index $\dfrac{n}{2}-1$, $\dfrac{n}{2}+m-1$, or at the last index

($n-m$), in this case the number of comparisons made to compare m pattern characters are $\dfrac{m}{4}$.

Lemma 3: The average case time complexity is $\left(\dfrac{n}{4m}\right)$.

Proof: The average case occurs when the two consecutive characters of the text directly following the sliding window is not found in the pattern. In this case, the shift value will be ($m + 2$) for each window from 4 available windows.

5. Results

In order to ensure that the FSW algorithm gives extraordinary results in the searching process, several experiments were performed. The FSW algorithm searches the text using four sliding windows. All the windows slide in parallel. Comparisons done with the pattern is also done from both sides simultaneously. **Tables 1-5** as well as **Figures 4-7** show the results of comparing FSW with ETSW, TSW and BR algorithms.

Table 1, **Figure 4** and **Figure 5** show the average number of attempts and comparisons for patterns with different lengths. It is noticeable that the number of comparisons and attempts in FSW is much better than the others. This is because in FSW four windows are used while in both ETSW and TSW algorithms two sliding windows are used. On the other hand, BR algorithm uses only one sliding window. For example, if the text has 1167 words, each of length 8, then the average number of comparisons and attempts made by FSW is 3577 and 3502 respectively. The number of comparisons and attempts made by ETSW is 10115 and 10056 respectively. Looking at **Table 1**, the number of comparisons and attempts of TSW and BR are also greater than FSW. This makes FSW algorithm better than the other algorithms in terms of the average number of comparisons and attempts.

Table 1. The average number of attempts and comparisons for patterns with different lengths.

Pattern length	Number of words	FSW		ETSW		TSW		BR	
		Attempts	Comparisons	Attempts	Comparisons	Attempts	Comparisons	Attempts	Comparisons
4	8103	2525	2488	3904	3875	3904	4213	6409	7039
5	4535	3133	2856	4456	3549	4456	4896	9577	10645
6	2896	3232	3252	7596	7633	7596	8311	10898	12173
7	1988	3723	3697	9341	9118	9341	10263	11953	13345
8	1167	3502	3577	10056	10115	10056	11087	13256	14807
9	681	3330	3350	9538	9590	9538	10538	14149	15892
10	382	3708	3822	9283	9339	9283	10272	14127	15799
11	191	3341	3363	5451	5482	5451	5967	12808	14243
12	69	3232	3255	6384	6433	6384	7168	9598	10923
13	55	4781	4807	7947	7986	7947	8673	10334	11370

Table 2. The average number of attempts and comparisons performed to search for (100) patterns selected from the middle of the text.

Pattern length	FSW		ETSW		TSW		BR	
	Attempts	Comparisons	Attempts	Comparisons	Attempts	Comparisons	Attempts	Comparisons
4	875	879	2726	2737	2726	2959	3645	4070
5	4706	4730	11582	11618	13965	15140	11558	12793
6	5152	5175	16682	16771	16682	18317	12878	14337
7	1895	1907	26104	26242	26104	30095	19547	22006
8	3511	3530	27830	28015	27830	30915	20831	23336
9	2021	2029	33929	34069	33929	37200	23284	25852
10	4152	4176	29676	29845	29676	32817	20546	22989
11	1333	1341	23195	23242	23195	24646	20264	22005
12	2413	2435	26806	27009	26806	30222	21113	24235

Table 3. The number of attempts and comparisons performed to search for a set of patterns that do not exist in the text.

Pattern length	FSW		ETSW		TSW	
	Attempts	Comparisons	Attempts	Comparisons	Attempts	Comparisons
4	135592	136887	136188	137630	136188	152137
5	116040	1173911	116644	118058	116644	130485
6	101652	102826	102076	103338	102076	113994
7	90480	91359	90854	91798	90854	101469
8	81472	82381	81700	82691	81700	91419
9	74080	74886	74326	75157	74326	83085
10	68012	68698	67984	68722	67984	75863
11	62648	63220	62738	63405	62738	70012
12	58220	58816	58412	59073	58412	65315

Table 4. The average number of attempts and comparisons performed to search for (100) patterns selected from the beginning of the text.

Pattern length	FSW		ETSW		TSW		BR	
	Attempts	Comparisons	Attempts	Comparisons	Attempts	Comparisons	Attempts	Comparisons
4	278	280	143	145	143	157	76	85
5	359	361	185	187	185	206	100	115
6	443	448	227	230	227	255	121	142
7	686	691	347	351	347	388	195	226
8	967	975	504	510	504	568	270	310
9	1340	1349	670	677	670	750	363	417
10	2269	2285	1160	1170	1160	1290	640	727
11	1243	1251	622	628	622	705	331	396
12	1729	1747	865	878	865	972	478	557

Table 5. The average number of attempts and comparisons performed to search for (100) patterns selected from the end of the text.

Pattern length	FSW		ETSW		TSW		BR	
	Attempts	Comparisons	Attempts	Comparisons	Attempts	Comparisons	Attempts	Comparisons
4	251	253	133	135	133	148	6899	7719
5	508	510	268	270	268	297	12930	14404
6	716	720	364	368	364	402	21315	23957
7	792	797	402	405	402	447	22237	24731
8	1056	1063	536	541	536	592	21495	23841
9	1489	1498	776	783	776	859	24919	28257
10	3047	3067	1579	1593	1579	1756	31603	35360
11	1238	1244	619	624	619	669	32797	36438
12	3269	3296	1667	1685	1667	1872	30928	35069

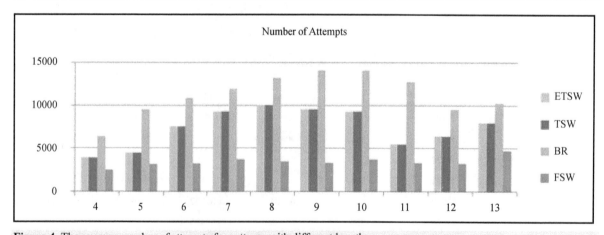

Figure 4. The average number of attempts for patterns with different lengths.

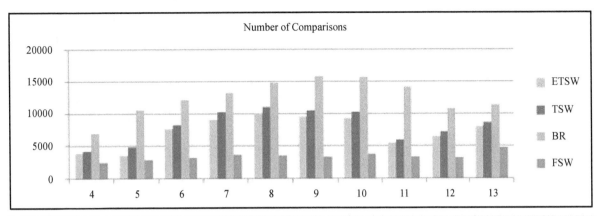

Figure 5. The average number of comparisons for patterns with different lengths.

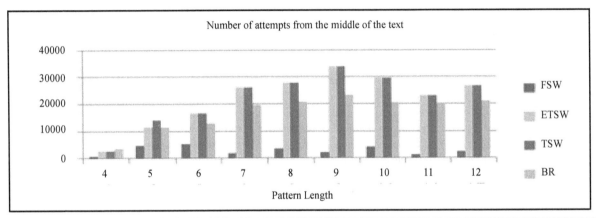

Figure 6. The average number of attempts performed to search for (100) patterns from the middle of the text.

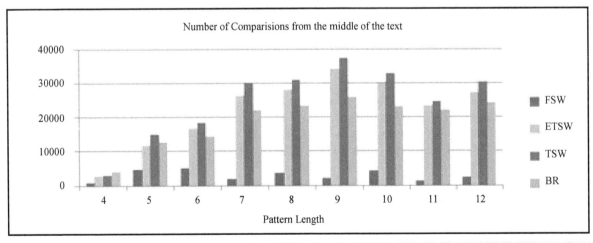

Figure 7. The average number of comparisons performed to search for (100) patterns from the middle of the text.

Table 2, **Figure 6** and **Figure 7** show the average number of attempts and comparisons performed to search for 100 patterns selected from the middle of the text. FSW algorithm shows the best results in both number of comparisons and attempts.

This is expected since FSW search the text using four windows, two of them starts from the middle of the text. On the other hand, ETSW and TSW uses two windows aligned at the rightmost and the leftmost sides of the text.

BR algorithm uses only one sliding window starting from the left of the text.

For example, to search for a pattern of length 4, the average number of comparisons and attempts made by FSW is 879 and 875 respectively. Compared to ETSW, TSW and BR, the results are far better in FSW than in the other algorithms.

FSW algorithm has the minimum number of comparisons and attempts performed to search for patterns of different lengths that are not found in the text as shown in **Table 3**.

Table 4 show the average number of comparisons and attempts performed to search for 100 patterns selected from the beginning of the text. BR algorithm has the minimum number since it searches the text using only one window from the left, *i.e.* from the beginning of the text. On the other hand, ETSW and TSW use two sliding windows that slide from the left side and the right side of the text which increases the number compared to BR algorithm. FSW algorithm's results show that there is an increase in the number of comparisons and attempts performed especially if the pattern is found in the middle of the text. This is expected since four sliding widows are used.

Table 5 show the average number of comparisons and attempts performed to search for 100 patterns selected from the end of the text. The results of FSW are reasonable since the pattern is found at the end of the text. BR on the other hand performed a large number of comparisons and attempts since it searches the text starting from the left side of the text.

6. Conclusions

In this paper, we presented a new pattern—matching algorithm (FSW) which finds all occurrences of a given pattern p in a given text t using four sliding windows. The new algorithm enhances the ETSW algorithm which uses only two sliding windows. Extensive experiments have been conducted. The results show that FSW best performance appears when the pattern is found in the middle of the text. If the pattern is in the beginning or the end of the text, the number of comparisons and attempts in FSW increases compared to other algorithms.

Using four sliding windows that search the text in parallel as well as comparing the pattern from both sides simultaneously makes the FSW performance better and decreases the searching time. In the future we intend to apply the FSW algorithm to additional applications such as computational biology and search engines. Also we intend to use threads to implement the FSW algorithm.

References

[1]   Simone, F. and Thierry, L. (2013) The Exact Online String Matching Problem: A Review of the Most Recent Results. *ACM Computing Surveys*, **45**, 13.

[2]   Yang, Z., Yu, J. and Kitsuregawa, M. (2010) Fast Algorithms for Top-k Approximate String Matching. *Proceedings of the Twenty-Fourth AAAI Conference on Artificial Intelligence*, Atlanta, 11-15 July 2010.

[3]   Pendlimarri, D. and Petlu, P.B.B. (2010) Novel Pattern Matching Algorithm for Single Pattern Matching. *International Journal on Computer Science and Engineering*, **2**, 2698-2704.

[4]   Bhukya, R. and Somayajulu, D. (2011) Article: Exact Multiple Pattern Matching Algorithm Using DNA Sequence and Pattern Pair. *International Journal of Computer Applications*, **17**, 32-38. http://dx.doi.org/10.5120/2239-2862

[5]   Alsmadi, I. and Nuser, M. (2012) String Matching Evaluation Methods for DNA Comparison. *International Journal of Advanced Science and Technology*, **47**, 13-32.

[6]   Bhandaru, J. and Kumar, A. (2014) A Survey of Fast Hybrid String Matching Algorithms. *International Journal of Emerging Sciences*, **4**, 24-37.

[7]   Linhai, C. (2014) An Innovative Approach for Regular Expression Matching Based on NoC Architecture. *International Journal of Smart Home*, **8**, 45-52. http://dx.doi.org/10.14257/ijsh.2014.8.1.06

[8]   Diwate, R. and Alaspurkar, S. (2013) Study of Different Algorithms for Pattern Matching. *International Journal of Advanced Research in Computer science and Software Engineering*, **3**, 615-620.

[9]   Singla, N. and Garg, D. (2012) String Matching Algorithms and Their Applicability in Various Applications. *International Journal of Soft Computing and Engineering (IJSCE)*, **I**, 218-222.

[10]   Guo, L., Du, S., Ren, M., Liu, Y., Li, J., He, J., Tian, N. and Li, K. (2013) Parallel Algorithm for Approximate String Matching with K Differences. *IEEE Eighth International Conference on Networking, Architecture and Storage*, 17-19 July 2013, 257-261. http://dx.doi.org/10.1109/NAS.2013.40

[11]   Itriq, M., Hudaib, A., Al-Anani, A., Al-Khalid, R. and Suleiman, D (2012) Enhanced Two Sliding Windows Algorithm for Pattern Matching (ETSW). *Journal of American Science*, **8**, 607- 616.

[12] Hudaib, A., Al-Khalid, R., Suleiman, D., Itriq, M. and Al-Anani, A, (2008) A Fast Pattern Matching Algorithm with Two Sliding Windows (TSW). *Journal of Computer Science*, **4**, 393-401. http://dx.doi.org/10.3844/jcssp.2008.393.401

[13] Suleiman, D. (2014) Enhanced Berry Ravindran Pattern Matching Algorithm (EBR). *Life Science Journal*, **11**, 395-402.

[14] Berry, T. and Ravindran, S. (2001) A Fast String Matching Algorithm and Experimental Results. In: Holub, J. and Si-manek, M., Eds., *Proceedings of the Prague Stringology Club Workshop*'99, Collaborative Report DC-99-05, Czech Technical University, Prague, 16-26.

[15] Khan, Z. and Pateriya, R.K. (2012) Multiple Pattern String Matching Methodologies: A Comparative Analysis. *International Journal of Scientific and Research Publications*, **2**, 2250-3153.

[16] Claude, F., Navarro, G., Peltola, H., Salmela, L. and Tarhio, J. (2012) String Matching with Alphabet Sampling. *Journal of Discrete Algorithms*, **11**, 37-50. http://dx.doi.org/10.1016/j.jda.2010.09.004

[17] Zhang, P. and Liu, J. (2011) An Improved Pattern Matching Algorithm in the Intrusion Detection System. *Applied Mechanics and Materials*, **48-49**, 203-207. http://dx.doi.org/10.4028/www.scientific.net/AMM.48-49.203

[18] Faro, S. and Lecroq, T. (2012) A Multiple Sliding Windows Approach to Speed Up String Matching Algorithms. SEA, 172-183.

[19] Suleiman, D., Hudaib, A., Al-Anani, A., Al-Khalid, R. and Itriq, M. (2013) ERS-A Algorithm for Pattern Matching. *Middle East Journal of Scientific Research*, **15**, 1067-1075.

11

Semantic Enrichment of XML Schema to Transform Association Relationships in ODL Schema

Doha Malki, Mohamed Bahaj

Department of Mathematics and Computer Science, University Hassan 1st, Settat, Morocco
Email: doha.malki@uhp.ac.ma, mohamedbahaj@gmail.com

Abstract

This paper presents an approach for transforming an XML schema we enriched in ODL (Object Definition Language) schemas. It is possible to realize the concepts of ODL in a model of XML schema, we propose to introduce an enrichment concretizing these concepts in the XML Schema models. We chose oriented object database as a target database because there are many common characteristics between XML and object-oriented model, thus the mapping from XML data into object-oriented databases is more interesting. Also the object-oriented data bases have become very widespread and acceptable and they offer an evolutionary approach, so we agree that it is time to develop a translation between XML and OO databases. The purpose of this article is to automate transformation process of an XML schema to an ODL database. Our work focuses on preserving semantics transformation of association relationships and we describe set of rules to create ODL classes from an enriched XML schema. The experimental study shows that the approach is feasible, and results are the same, the source database is transformed into target one without loss of data.

Keywords

XML Schemas, ODL, Mapping, Association, OODB

1. Introduction

Extensible Markup Language, a met language that allows users to define their own customized markup languages, is characterized by its flexibility and extensibility. Due to all its qualities, it's considered as hot topic for describing and interchanging data through internet between different systems.

The migration of database appears today very interesting and promotes organizations to move towards new technology. Since information is valuable resources for organizations, the mapping process must be submitted before any shift to a new technology [1]. Furthermore, the characteristics of the XML Schema standard [W3C, 2008] are supported by the standard ODMG 3.0 [2], and query languages are more powerful, which encourage to attempt to migrate existing database into new environment.

Database migration is a process wherein all the components of a source database are converted to their equivalents in the environment of the target one.

ODL is designed to support semantic constructs of ODMG object model. It is used to define the pattern of a compatible ODMG database independently of any programming language.

In this article, we present techniques for enriching the XML Schema. Our goal is to introduce the richness of ODL formalism to facilitate the migration of XML Schemas to ODL schema. The introduction of ODL formalism in the XML schema is obtained by extension. To do this, we proceed in several stages:

- Defining the concepts supported by XML Schema;
- Defining XML Schema extensions to take into account all the specificities of ODL objects. These extensions exploit the extension mechanisms supported by XML Schema to remain compliant with the W3C standard.

The content of this document provides a brief introduction to XML Schema and ODL. The rest of the paper is organized as follows. In Section 2, we review some closest related work. Section 3 presents XML Schema conceptual enrichment, we will explain how XML and ODL implement association relationship; several rules to transform an XML schema enriched in ODL schema focusing on transforming association relationship are described in Section 4. In Section 5, we present the processing steps and an example for each type of association relationship is given. Section 6 presents evaluation of our approach by comparing the results of queries; finally Section 7 concludes the paper.

2. Related Work

There are many works that explain the mapping from XML to object-oriented databases, In [3], it discuss the modeling of XML and the need for transformation. A number of generic transformation rules of the conceptual model OO to the XML schema are presented, accentuated on transforming inheritance and aggregation relationships.

Most existing work focuses on a method that was designed to map an object database into an XML database for the interoperability of databases. Schema translation process is supplied with a UML class model [4]. In this paper, set of rules to translate a simple database schema specified in ODL into XML Schema are presented focusing on transforming association relationships (1:M) and (M:M),

In [5], the paper covers XML modeling and the need for transformation. It presents a number of XML schema transformation steps to ORDB, focusing on the transformation of association relations. Different types of these conceptual relationships (one-to-one, one-to-many and many-to-many) and their transformations are mainly discussed.

In [6], it address the mapping of the contents of an existing object-oriented database into XML using object graph; the reverse process is also proposed to store XML data in object-oriented database. In this work, the author use object graph for the transformation, but it does not cover all possible types of relationships.

3. Conceptual Enrichment of XML Schema

Associations allow complete modeling object states. The ODMG support bidirectional binary associations, cardinality (1: 1), (1: N) or (N: M). An association from A to B defines two opposite paths crossing, A- > B and B- > A. Each path must be defined in the ODL object type source by a relationship keyword.

A class in ODL is specified using the class keyword, an attribute is specified using the attribute keyword and relationship is specified using the relationship keyword. Although it is possible to materialize these concepts implicit in a XML schema, we propose to introduce an enrichment embodying these concepts explicitly in the XML Schema.

To do this, we use the extension mechanism advocated by XML Schema, this addition used to include the specific subjects of ODL and to highlight relationships between concepts. In our mapping process, these new concepts help to preserve the semantic of relationships.

3.1. ODL

A Class in ODL is defined as follows:

    class <name>
    (extent <names> key <attribute>...
    {
    <list of elements = attributes, relationships, methods>
    };

A relationship between a class C1 and class C2 is defined by attributes in both classes of types according to the cardinality of the relationship [7]:

- One-to-one: an attribute of type C2 * is included in C1 and another one of type C1 * is included in C2.
- One-to-many: an attribute of type collection < C2 *> (a set or a bag) is contained in C1 and C1 contains an attribute of type C2*.
- Many-to-many: C1 contains an attribute of type collection< C2 *> and *vice-versa*.

A relationship must be specified in both directions. In ODL, the inverse keyword is used to designate the relationship in the opposite direction. For example, if we delete an object of C1, links with all C2 objects will be automatically dereferenced, also all objects C2 links back to the C1 objects will be dereferenced. If we relate an object of C1 to a set of C2 objects, the reverse links will automatically be created. In other words, it will create a link to each of C2 objects to the C1 object.

3.2. XML Schema

XML Schema represents integrity constraints using the XPath expression [8]. It is possible to specify constraints that correspond to unique values, primary keys and relationships in ODBS.

The tags unique is used to define unique, key is to define primary key, and key ref for key reference which defined by refer attribute to specify attribute or element corresponds to the key element or unique specified. The XPath expression selector defines the domain of a constraint, and the field XPath defines the elements or attributes that represent the constraint.

For two complex types CT_1 and CT_2, participating in association relationship (see **Figure 1**), XML schema is defined as follows:

Figure 1. Example of association relationship.

```
<xsd:element name="CT1">
<xsd:complexType>
    <xsd:sequence>
    <xsd:element name="EL1" type="xsd:EL1_type"/>
    ...
    </xsd:sequence>
    <xsd:attribute name="attr1" type="xsd:att1_type" use="required"/>
</xsd:complexType>
</xsd:element>
<xsd:element name=" CT2">
<xsd:complexType>
    <xsd:sequence>
    <xsd:element name="EL2" type="xsd:EL2_type"/>
    ...
    </xsd:sequence>
    <xsd:attribute name="attr2" type="xsd:att2_type" use="required"/>
</xsd:complexType>
</xsd:element>
```

```
<xsd:key name="CT1_K">
<xsd: selector xpath=".//E1"/>
<xsd: field xpath="attr1"/>
</xsd:key>
<xsd:key name="CT2_K">
<xsd: selector xpath="// CT2"/>
<xsd: field xpath="attr2"/>
</xsd:key>
< xsd: keyref name="CT1_CT2_Ref" refer=" CT1_K">
< xsd: selector xpath = "CT2"/>
< xsd: field xpath="@attr1"/>
</keyref>
< xsd: keyref name="CT2_CT1_Ref" refer="CT1_K">
< xsd: selector xpath = "CT1"/>
< xsd: field xpath="@attr1"/>
</keyref>
```

3.3. Enrichment of Semantics in the XML Schema

In this section, we will conceptually enrich XML Schema for the purpose of establishing correspondences between two technologies: XML and ODL. These connections allow us to specify mappings between the two schemas.

The semantic enrichment of an XML schema involves the extraction of its data semantics, to be enriched and converted into a CDM. To do this, we have applied the approach in [9] to enrich semantically XML schema. The process starts by extracting the basic metadata information about an existing XML schema, including relation types and attribute|element properties (*i.e.*, names, types, occurrence, required or not), and keys (K), keyrefs (KR). We assume that data dependencies are represented by keys and keyrefs. As for each keyref tag, there is a reference to a key of a complex type, which can be considered as a value reference.

We extend the semantics of the XML schema above as follows:

We add an element in both of the complex types (CT_1 and CT_2) that we called "elementrole" (ele_rol) whose name expresses the relationship role, its type is the same as the key element of the other complex type, and its cardinality is the same expressed in the relationship, e.g. we add in the element CT_2, an element "ele_rol" with the same cardinality near CT_2 (*) as:

```
<xsd:element name="ele_rol" type="xsd:attr1_type" maxoccurs="unbounded"/>.
```

4. Rules of Mapping from Enriched XML Schema to ODL Schema

Now we present the mapping rules between XML Schema elements and ODL, including concepts describing dependency relationships.

Rule 1: An XML element (<xsd: element>) with complex structure or a global complex type element (<xsd: complex Type>) are transformed into a class in ODL with the same name.

Rule 2: Simple XML elements <xsd: element>, with basic data types <xsd: type> data type (string, short, date, float, etc.), which is enclosed by an <xsd: sequence>, must be converted into attribute in the class ODL resulting from rule 1. XML attributes <xsd: attribute > are also converted into attribute in the corresponding class, with the same name and the same type, except the "elementrole", it will be transformed in a relationship included in the corresponding class. XML attributes < xsd: minOccurs > and < xsd: maxOccurs > carried by the element can carry on associations (see rule 4).

Rule 3: Each field XPath in the element key is transformed into key attribute of the corresponding class.

Rule 4: Referring to the CDM, the relationship will be as follow:

```
Relationship set|bag|<CTname_referred_to> elan inverse CTname_referred_to:: fiels_xpath_of_
Ctname_referred_to.
```

Depending on the cardinality we add set or bag or nothing.

Definition of CDM: The CDM is defined as a set of complex types: CDM: = {CT|CT:= ⟨ctn, AEcdm, Rel⟩}, where each complex type CT has a name ctn. Each CT has a set of elements|attributes AEcdm, and a set of relationships Rel.

Attributes (A|Ecdm): A complex type CT has a set of elements|attributes AEcdm. AEcdm:= {ela|ela: = ⟨elan, t, tag⟩}, where each element | attribute *ela* has a name elan, data type t and a tag, which classifies ela as a non-key "NK", a key "K", or a relationship as R.

Relationships (Rel): A complex type CT has a set of relationships Rel. Each relationship rel ∈ Rel between CT_1 and complex type CT_2 is defined in CT_1 to represent an association. Rel: = {rel|rel: = ⟨CTn_referred_to, Occ, F_xpath_of_CTn_referred_to⟩}, where CTn_referred_to is the name of CT_2, Occ:= minOcurs. maxOccurs is the cardinality constraint of rel from the CT_1 side, and F_xpath_of_CTn_referred_to denotes the *elementrole* name representing the inverse relationship from the CT_2 side.

Since we are focusing on association relationship, we don't discuss the relation type.

5. Application Mapping of Association Relationship from an Enriched XML Schema to ODL

We presented in the previous section a specification of mappings of basic elements of XML schema. In this section, we will apply these mappings to XML Schema enriched. An association expresses a bidirectional semantic connection between two types. Each instance sharing a kind of relationship with others, it could be of any type as: one-to-one, one-to-many or many-to-many. By default, an association is navigable in both directions [10].

Association verbal active: specifies the reading direction of the main association; roles: specifies the function of a type for a given association; cardinality: specifies the number of instances that participate in a relationship.

5.1. One-to-One Association: (Rarely Applied in Practice)

In this section we use an example of (1:1) relationship between professor and class, we assume that each professor teaches at most one class and *vice-versa*. Keep in mind that this kind of relationship is not very common (see **Figure 2**).

Figure 2. One-to-one association.

The steps below explain how to transform the one-to-one association relationship from enriched XML Schema to ODL.

Enriched XML Schema for one-to-one relationship:

```
<xsd :element name = "professor">
< xsd :complexType>
< xsd :attribute name = "professorId" type = "xsd :string" use = "required" />
< xsd :sequence>
....
< xsd :element name="teaches" type= " xsd :string" minOccurs="0" maxOccurs="1">
</ xsd :sequence>
</ xsd :complexType>
</ xsd :element>

< xsd :element name = "class">
< xsd :attribute name = "classId" type =" xsd :string" use = "required"/>
<xsd :sequence>
....
< xsd :element name="teachedby" type= " xsd :string" minOccurs="0" maxOccurs="1">
< /xsd :sequence>
```

```
</xsd :element>
<xsd:key name="professor_K">
<xsd:selector xpath=".//professor"/>
<xsd:field xpath="@professorId"/>
</xsd:key>
<xsd:key name="class_K">
<xsd:selector xpath=".//class"/>
<xsd:field xpath="@classId"/>
</xsd:key>
<xsd:keyref name="professorRefclass" refer="classK">
<xsd:selector xpath=".//professor"/>
<xsd:field xpath="teaches"/>
</xsd:keyref>
<xsd:keyref name="classRefprofessor" refer="professorK">
<xsd:selector xpath=".//class"/>
<xsd:field xpath="teachedby"/>
</xsd:keyref>
```

5.2. One-to-Many Association

Let's consider the example below: a department may have one or many employees. But an employee works in only one department (see **Figure 3**).

Figure 3. One-to-many Association.

Enriched XML Schema for one-to-many relationship:

```
<xsd:element name="Department">
<xsd:complexType>
<xsd:sequence>
<xsd:element name="departmentId" type="xsd:string"/>
....
<xsd:element name="has" type="xsd:string" maxOccurs="unbounded"/>
</xsd:sequence>
</xsd:complexType>
</xsd:element>
<xsd:element name="employee">
<xsd:complexType>
<xsd:sequence>
<xsd:element name="employeeid" type="xsd:string"/>
....
<xsd:element name="worksin" type="xsd:string" maxOccurs="1"/>
</xsd:sequence>
</xsd:complexType>
</xsd:element>
<xsd:key name="department_K">
<xsd:selector xpath=".//department"/>
<xsd:field xpath="departmentId"/>
</xsd:key>
<xsd:key name="employee_K">
 <xsd:selector xpath=".//employee"/>
```

```
<xsd:field xpath="employeeid"/>
</xsd:key>
<xsd:keyref name="departmentRefemployee" refer="employee_K">
<xsd:selector xpath=".//department"/>
<xsd:field xpath="has"/>
</xsd:keyref>
<xsd:keyref name="employeeRefdepartment" refer="department_K">
<xsd:selector xpath=".//employee"/>
<xsd:field xpath="worksin"/>
</xsd:keyref>
```

5.3. Many-to-Many Relationship

In the example below: a student is teached by one or more professors. The same professor teaches lots of students (see **Figure 4**).

Figure 4. Many-to-many Association.

Enriched XML Schema for many-to-many relationship:

```
<xsd:element name="professor">
<xsd:complexType>
<xsd:sequence>
<xsd:element name="professorId" type="xsd:string"/>
....
<xsd:element name="teaches" type="xsd:string" maxOccurs="unbounded"/>
</xsd:sequence>
</xsd:complexType>
</xsd:element>
<xsd:element name="student">
<xsd:complexType>
<xsd:sequence>
<xsd:element name="studentId" type="xsd:string"/>
....
<xsd:element name="teachedby" type="xsd:string" maxOccurs="unbounded"/>
</xsd:sequence>
</xsd:complexType>
</xsd:element>
<xsd:key name="professor_K">
<xsd:selector xpath=".//professor "/>
<xsd:field xpath="professouId"/>
</xsd:key>
<xsd:key name=" student_K">
<xsd:selector xpath=".// student "/>
<xsd:field xpath="studentId"/>
</xsd:key>
<xsd:keyref name=" professorRefstudent " refer="student_K">
<xsd:selector xpath=".// professor "/>
<xsd:field xpath="teaches"/>
</xsd:keyref>
<xsd:keyref name=" studentRefprofessor " refer=" professor_K">
```

```
<xsd:selector xpath=".// student "/>
<xsd:field xpath="teachedby"/>
</xsd:keyref>
```

5.4. Generation Canonical Data Model (CDM) of XML Schema

Let's consider the XML schema shown in the example in Section 5.2 above, the corresponding CDM is as **Table 1**.

Table 1. CDM of XML schema for one-to-many association relationship.

CTn	ela			Rel		
	Elan	T	Tag	CTn_referred_to	Occ	F_xpath_of_CTn_referred_to
Department	departmentId	string	K			
	Name	string	NK			
	has	string	R	employee	0.. unbounded	worksin
Employee	employeeid	string	K			
	empName	string	NK			
	DOB	date	NK			
	worksin	string	R	Department	0..1	has

5.5. Algorithm for Schema Translation

Figure 5 shows the algorithm map XML_ODL for mapping XML schema into ODL schema. The algorithm reads each XML complex type one by one and maps it to ODL. In line 4, the complex type is mapped to a class, the algorithm maps all its elements to attributes of the class and forms the relationship with other classes. Specifically, if the relationship is one-to-one, in line 13 the algorithm adds the relationship in the corresponding class as follow:

```
Relationship < CTn_referred_to > elan inverse CTn_referred_to ::
F_xpath_of_CTn_referred_to;
```

If the relationship is one-to-many, in line 17 the algorithm add the relationship as:

```
Relationship set|bag < CTn_referred_to > elan inverse CTn_referred_to ::
F_xpath_of_CTn_referred_to;
```

Algorithm mapXML_ODL
Input:
cdm : CDM

    1.   **for** (complex type CTn in the CDM cdm CTn∈cdm)
    2.   {
    3.   // map CTn into a class with the same name
    4.   Procedure map_CT_Class(CTn)
    5.   **if** ela.tag <> R then
    6.   {
    7.   // map all elements | attribute to attributes with the same name and data type in class CTn
    8.   Procedure map_elan_t(ela.elan, ela.t)
    9.   **if** ela.tag==K then
    10. // Mention elan as a key
    11. Procedure key(ela.elan)
    12. }
    13. **Else if** Rel.Occ == 0..1
    14. // map elementrole to relationship as one
    15. //add relationships
    16. Procedure add_rel_one (Rel. CTn_referred_to, ela.elan,Rel. F_xpath_of_CTn_referred_to)
    17. **Else** Rel.Occ == unbounded then
    18. // map elementrole to relationship as many
    19. //add relationships as set|bag
    20. Procedure add_rel_may (Rel. CTn_referred_to, ela.elan,Rel. F_xpath_of_CTn_referred_to)
    21. }
    22. }

Figure 5. An algorithm for mapping XML schema into ODL.

The output ODL schema of one-to-many association relationship example is shown as follow (see **Figure 6**).

```
Class department
(extent departments key departmentId )
{ attribute string departmentId;
  attribute string Name;
  relationship set<employee> has inverse employee::worksin;
};
Class employee
(extent employees key employeeid )
{ attribute string employeeid;
attribute string empName;
attribute date DOB;
relationship <department> worksin inverse department::has;
};
```

Figure 6. Sample output ODL schema of one-to-many association relationship example.

6. Experimental Study

To demonstrate the validity of our method, a prototype has been developed, realizing the algorithm above. The algorithm was implemented using Java and EyeDB. To evaluate our approach, we examined the differences between source XML schema and the ODL schema generated by the prototype; we test the query results provided by OQL in EyeDB, and XQuery in stylus studios. Queries returned the same results. The source XML database is transformed into target object database ODL without loss of data.

This section presents two queries applied on the XML schema shown in Section 5.3 and the equivalent ODL generated by the prototype. **Table 2** shows the description and the result of each query.

Table 2. The description and the result of each query.

Description	OQL	XQuery	Result
List the departments and the number of employees in each department	Select D. Name, headCount: count (select E.employeeid from Employee E where E.worksin = D. departmentId) from Departments D, dept. has emp group by Name: D. Name;	for $dept in //Department let $headCount:= count(//Employee[worksin=$dept/ departmentId]) return <Department> {$deptartment/Name} <HeadCount>{$headCount}</HeadCount> </Department>	Accounting 2 Administration 3 Finance 2
Find the names of all employees in Accounting	Select Employee JOIN Department ON Employee. worksin = Department.departmentId WHERE Department.Name =' Accounting'	let $dept: = //Department [Name ='Accounting']/departmentId return//Employee[worksin = $dept]/empName	Smith Scott

7. Conclusion

In this article, we present a method of translation from XML schema into ODL schema, focusing on mapping association relationships; we extend the semantic of XML schema, our proposed method describes a process from the conceptual model to the implementation in the classes. With this method, the results preserve the semantics specified in the conceptual level, either to XML or ODL; our future work will be the development of a better mapping taking into account the concepts that we have not discussed in this paper, such as inheritance relationship.

References

[1]   Alhajj, R. and Polat, F. (2001) Reengineering Relational Databases to Object-Oriented: Constructing the Class Hierarchy and Migrating the Data. *Proceedings of the* 8*th Working Conference on Reverse Engineering* (*WCRE*'01), Stuttgart, 2-5 October 2001, 335-344. http://dx.doi.org/10.1109/WCRE.2001.957840

[2]   Cattell, R.G.G. and Barry, D.K., Eds. (2000) The Object Data Standard: ODMG 3.0. Morgan Kaufmann Publishers Inc., San Francisco.

[3]   Xiao, R.G., Dillon, T.S., Chang, E. and Feng, L. (2001) Modeling and Transformation of Object-Oriented Conceptual Models into XML Schema. *Proceedings of* 12*th International Conference, DEXA* 2001, Munich, 3-5 September 2001, 795-804.

[4]   de Sousa, A.F., Pereira, J.L. and Carvalho, J. (2002) From ODL Schemas to XML-SCHEMA Schemas: A First Set of Transformation Rules. *Proceedings of the Baltic Conference, Baltic DB&IS* 2002, Volume 1, 281-296.

[5]   Widjaya, N.D., Taniar, D., Rahayu, J.W. and Pardede, E. (2003) Association Relationship Transformation of XML Schemas to Object-Relational Databases. *Revised Papers of* 3*rd International Workshop, IICS* 2003, Leipzig, 19-21 June 2003, 251-262.

[6]   Naser, T., Alhajj, R. and Ridley, M.J. (2009) Two-Way Mapping between Object-Oriented Databases and XML. *Informatica*, **33**, 297-308.

[7]   SYSRA (2007) EyeDB Object Definition Language Version 2.8.8. SYSRA, Yerres.

[8]   Berglund, A., Boag, S., Chamberlin, D., Fernndez, M.F., Kay, M., Robie, J. and Simon, J. (2007) XML Path Language (XPath) 2.0 W3C Recommendation 23 January 2007. http://www.w3.org/TR/xpath20/

[9]   Maatuk, A., Akhtar Ali, M. and Rossiter, N. (2010) Converting Relational Databases into Object-relational Databases. *Journal of Object Technology*, **9**, 145-161. http://www.jot.fm/issues/issue_2010_03/article3.pdf

[10]   Hoffer, J.A., Prescott, M.B. and McFadden, F.R. (2005) Modern Database Management. 7th Edition, Prentice Hall, Upper Saddle River.

12

E-Government Strategy and Plans in Jordan

Yousef Kh. Majdalawi, Tamara Almarabeh, Hiba Mohammad, Wala Quteshate

Department of Computer Information Systems, King Abdullah II School for Information Technology, The University of Jordan, Amman, Jordan
Email: ymajdal@ju.edu.jo, t.almaraabeh@ju.edu.jo, h.khadrawi@ju.edu.jo, w.qutechate@ju.edu.jo

Abstract

Life is being developed every day in all of the life aspects. One of the major developing aspects is information technology (IT), and communication technology which makes life easier, faster, and more connected. ICT is evolving fast in Jordan and offering the government to deliver multiple delivery services with different characteristics among E-government services. The Jordanian government has invested heavily in E-government initiatives for the last 10 years to transform from traditional service delivery to more effective and efficient service to deliver high-quality customer-centric and performance-driven services to E-government stakeholders. However the global rank of E-government readiness as well as regional rank of Jordan is still in low rank according to the global countries but it is still quite according to the Arab countries. This research provides a trend analysis to find the trends (positive or negative) in the UN E-government indicators in Jordan and provides an overview to the E-government in Jordan where the researchers analyze the development of E-government in Jordan by introducing a general framework for the E-government through discussing the past, present status and the future plans for E-government in Jordan to get better service to their recipients and to improve overall progress of Jordan achievements compared with regional and global countries.

Keywords

Jordan, Readiness, ICT, EGDI, E-Government

1. Introduction

Governments play a major roles in societies as the administration of government functions and the facilitation of providing services to citizens and civil society institutions through their project in a convenient an efficient way [1]. The improvements in information and communication technologies (ICTs) increase the number of people in both private and public sectors, who benefit from a wide range of services through the Internet and web. The governments try to use ICT as a way to improve their interactions with citizens through providing them with real time access to information and many e-services via the Internet which led to a phenomenon called electronic government or E-government.

Some researchers defined E-government as the use of ICT to transform government institutions and processes into IT-based enablers [2]-[4]. Others define E-government is the implementation of ICT to improve all governmental transactions with all stakeholders' categories (within government, between government agencies, businesses and citizens) [5]-[8]. According to (Bose [9]) E-government is the application of ICT to the innovation in, and improvement of government services.

The United Nations defined E-government as the use of Information and Communication Technology (ICT) and its application by the government for the provision of information and public services to the people [10].

Other researchers added E-government definition with purpose to support good governance in the government organization for example, Jeffry (2008) [11] defined E-government as a continuous innovations in the delivery of services, citizen participation, and governance through the transformation of external and internal relationships by the use of information technology, especially the internet.

E-government added new concepts such as: transparency, accountability, citizen participation in the evaluation of government performance [12]. As one of the developing countries, the Jordanian government has made an initial effort to define E-government as "the ability to submit governmental transactions on-line and make payments electronical where they are required" [13].

Generally, E-government is considered as a new and emerging area of interest in the field of E-business that employs ICTs to enhance the access to and delivery of government information and services to citizens, businesses, government employees, and other agencies [14] [15].

Jordanian government is offering multiple business and technical services to support interaction between government entities and their customers through E-government. Government program in Jordan was launched by his Majesty King Abdullah II to achieve greater efficiency in government performance by raising the level of service delivery to clients and investors from all segments of society easily, quickly, accurately and efficiently and to become a new type of performance of government employees and government transactions [12]. E-government in Jordan is dedicated to delivering services to people across society, irrespective of location, economic status, education or ICT ability.

This paper analyzes the trends (positive or negative) in the UN E-government indicators in Jordan which can help in the development of proposals, plans and strategies to improve the level of E-government in Jordan.

This paper is organized as follows: Section 2 shows literature review of E-government program in Jordan, its vision and mission. Section 3 discusses E-government Readiness in Jordan through United Nations Readiness reports. Section 4 addresses the challenges and opportunities with different factors for achieving the success for E-government projects, especially in Jordan. Section 5 explains the new strategy of E-government in Jordan. Finally the conclusion is drawn in Section 6.

2. Literature Review of E-Government Program in Jordan

His Majesty King Abdullah II, king of Hashemite kingdom of Jordan, announced in 1999, that more efforts should be done to focus on the information technology (IT) industry, as a main generator of economic growth, and integrate it to the daily lives of Jordanians. As a result, and to insure this vision comes true, national E-government initiatives were conducted to cope with the governmental processes, and to make information available to the people on the internet. At that time, the ministry of Post and Communications (MOPC), which changed later to MOICT, was in charge of these initiatives, and it had to establish new departments and staff, just for the purpose of IT issues including organizational restructuring and legal reform. However, the transformation process of the ministry needed highly skilled IT human resources, in addition to high technology resources.

In 2001, (MOPC) transformed into the Ministry of Information and Communications Technology (MOICT) and launched its E-government Program, also a new office was established called Program Management office (PMO) to assist the Ministry, and to coordinate E-government projects, in addition to study the benefits that can be available to the people, and raise their perception to the e-services in the same time.

Two researchers, Michael Blakemore and Roderic Dutton, in their research "E-government, e-Society and Jordan: Strategy, theory, practice, and assessment", analyzed the strategy statements of E-government project implementations in several countries and summarized the expectations' of these nations from implementing an

E-government project such as [16]:

1. Government to citizen (G2C), with the citizen being treated as customer not administrative objects:

- Receiving services that are citizen-, not agency-focused
- Disintermediation of civil service staff—means making services delivered directly to the citizens.
- Intelligent authentication like smartcard
- Providing an access to the governmental information.
- Being provided with access to the physical ICT infrastructure
- Being made "more equal" (reductions in digital and other divides)
- Enhancing trust and make it stronger.

All of these expectations can be included in Jordan in transports Registration, insurance, unemployed compensation, collecting income taxes, leaving work programs (retiring), licensing, and welfare benefits.

2. Government to Government (G2G), involving good governance and a well-governed society, where this kind of relationship between G2G can be found in the United States, like state to local government, integrated justice system, or state to federal government.

- Reducing the fractured nature of individual department and agencies, and moving towards "joined-up" government. Like join all the governmental departments together, and make related data to be transferred between them easily, and safely. This will reduce time consuming, and makes the progress more effective.
- Make the culture of the civil service changed from reactive to proactive.
- Accountable and open government.
- Cost-effective procurement.

3. Government to Business (G2B), this is to achieve a powerful business development.

- De-regulation and legislative reform
- A national economy with flexibility and competitiveness within the global markets.
- Skilled, IT literate, and flexible citizens for the labor market

G2B could be found in Jordan in the clearing house for cheques, clearing between central bank from one side and the other banks in the economy. The submission of tax assessment by any business establishment to the department of Taxation of the government through the Internet (online).

4. An integrated society, where long distances and borders are not a problem anymore in it, in the contrary, saving time and fast services will be the new trend.

Results of achieving the E-government in this way will be noticed as follows:

- Connect rural and far areas with high-speed Internet access, so all the people can get the same services provided online.
- Citizens will be able to do their payments for many governmental charges from home.
- Overcome some barriers that used to be a problem in the normal government such as disability and gender barriers , even though this point depends on the country or culture, for example, disabled people in most of the developed countries can do their duties by themselves, as everything is ready for them. But in the developing countries it is almost impossible for some disabled people to do most of their governmental procedures by themselves, as there are no facilities to help them. That means e-services will be really effective for disabled people and almost ideal.
- Increase the sense of community.

Increase the involvement in the electoral process in a very democratic and reliable way. This is a very advanced level, that still under study in many developed countries to make sure to implement it away from fraud.

To achieve the previous expectations E-government in Jordan has offered E-government Portal. To deliver informational and directory services related to the Government of Jordan in the first stage. Then in the second phase of the E-government Portal will fully integrate the Portal with the E-government Enterprise Federated Architecture and Shared services, finally enabling transactional E-government services (Transactional Portal). Ultimately, the portal will be a "one stop shop" for user interaction with all Government of Jordan entities.

In 2004, thirteen initiatives were implemented, plus thirty individual projects, that included connecting six ministries to e-mail system and government network, implementing some e-services like income tax filling, and giving training courses to more than 4000 government employees about computer literacy and IT.

Despite this ambitious initiative, it was faced by several obstacles, one of the major obstacles was social awareness and readiness, where most of users (especially citizens) were not informed or trained properly on such implementation, which forced the government to stop the implementation process for more reassessment at a later stage.

The E-government strategy report [17], which was done by the MOICT, has addressed many different useful information about the E-government in Jordan, includes the four Pillars of E-government in Jordan (*i.e.* Institutional framework, Legal framework, ICT infrastructure, and Business), the National E-government vision ("E-government in Jordan is dedicated to delivering services to people across society, irrespective of location, economic status, education or ICT ability. With its commitment to a customer-centric approach, E-government will transform government and contribute to the Kingdom's economic and social development), and new strategy of the E-government in Jordan at that time which was covering the years (2007, 2008, and 2009).

3. E-Government Readiness in Jordan

E-Readiness is briefly defined as the degree to which a country is prepared to participate in the networked world (McConnell report, 2000 [18]). The United Nations Department of Economic and Social Affair (UNDESA) issued every two years a report measuring the development of E-government of 193 member states by calculating the E-government development Index value (EGDI). It is a composite index includes a: 1) telecommunication connectivity; 2) scope and quality of online services; and 3) human capacity as in Equation (1). Seven E-government surveys have conducted from 2003 until now. The purpose of UN surveys is to achieve better understanding for the status of E-government across the world to governments, the private sectors, and the researchers.

$$\text{The United Nations E} - \text{government development index}\left(\text{EGDI}\right)$$
$$= 1/3*\left(\text{OSI}_{normalized} + \text{TII}_{normalized} + \text{HCI}_{normalized}\right) \tag{1}$$

In this study, the researchers used government publications, newspapers, and research papers to collect data and hence analyze the current status of Jordanian E-government. The MOICT worked on a long term initiative to implement E-government. To achieve this, E-government in Jordan has set measurable goals and objectives [17]:

✓ Improve service delivery and the quality and speed of government's interaction with citizens and businesses as well as among government entities.

✓ Improve responsiveness to customer needs by using new modes of contact to provide public sector information and services.

✓ Increase transparency of government by increasing the availability of information and accessibility to services.

✓ Save time and money by improving efficiency in government processing, in part through use of common technology standards, policies and a federated architecture, as well as contributing to financial reform within the public sector.

✓ Create positive, spin-off effects on Jordanian society through the promotion of ICT skills development within government, businesses and households that will strengthen Jordan's economic competitiveness.

This strategy covered the years 2007, 2008 and 2009 which is good enough at the that time to support King Abdullah II vision which is a very ambitious vision, and efforts are being done to achieve this target, but in real life, and in the researchers point of view, it will take longer time from what is expected, as infrastructure like ICT tools, and skilled people are still not completely ready, as a result this strategy need update during the next years to keep abreast with the technological development.

As a result of the this strategy, the Jordanian E-government achieved the best improvement in 2008 and 2010 [11] as shown in **Figure 1**, in 2008 Jordan achieved 0.1693 degree in the telecommunication infrastructure index, 0.6054 in the online services index and 0.8677 in the human capital index as you see in **Figure 2**, the reasons of this improvement are the understanding of the importance of E-government websites and service from the society [19].

But in year 2012, the ranking dropped down 47 positions. It is obvious that the drop in ranking is basically return to the slowness in introducing e-services to the public. The lack of financial allocations for E-government services is negatively affecting the progress in this regard. The lack of necessary funds is also affecting the upgrade of infrastructure required for introducing additional E-government services [20].

In year 2014, Jordan ranked 79 globally in United Nations Report of the 2014, ahead 19 positions. This pro-

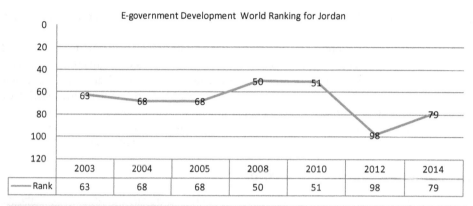

Figure 1. E-government development world ranking for Jordan.

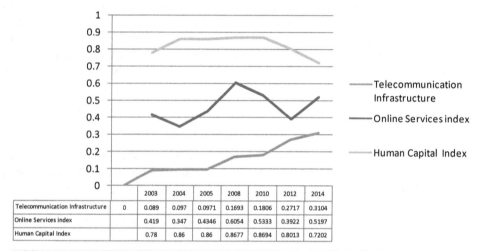

Figure 2. Telecommunication infrastructure, online services, and human capital indices of Jordan.

gress came within the continued efforts of the Ministry of Information and Communication Technology (MOICT) through the E-government program, where the number of electronic services provided through the E-government portal is increased, activate the e-participation and the means of social communication, and start activating the open data on the gate, in addition to the work and cooperation with the most important ministries that represent key sectors such as health, education, environment, finance, labor and social development to improve the quality of services provided to citizens [21]. As you see in **Figure 2**, Jordan achieved 0.5197 points in the overall index for online services which is higher than the global average which stood at 0.3919 degrees, and achieved 0.3104 in the telecommunication infrastructure index which is less than the global average of 0.3650 degree with small drop. This indicator measures the spread of fixed telephone lines, internet users, personal computers, use of mobile, in year 2008 new indicator added to them which is fixed broad band. In year 2012 the availability of personal computers changed to fixed internet subscriptions and in year 2014 changed to wireless broadband subscriptions. The third indicator, which measures the human capital, Jordan has recorded 0.7202 degree outperforming the global average of 0.6566 degree. This indicator reflects the literacy rate and enrollment in primary and secondary education [22].

In this research, the researchers have adopted trend analysis method to find the trends (positive or negative) in the UN E-government indicators in Jordan. Trend analysis is a special case of regression analysis where the dependent variable is the data to be forecasted and the independent variable is the time. To calculate the trends four to seven year data were needed for telecommunication infrastructure index and three year data for the online services index where the data for the other years isn't available.

As shown in **Table 1**, Jordan telecommunication infrastructure index has continuously improved during the period (2003-2014) [10] [11] [22], all indicators with positive trend except the main fixed phone lines with negative trend of −1.151 and this is normal due to the spread of use mobile devices. In 2003, the overall telecom-

Table 1. Telecommunication infrastructure indicators (per 100 persons)—trend analysis.

Year	Index	Estimated Internet Users	Main Fixed Phone lines	Mobile Subscribers	Personal Computers/ Fixed internet subscriptions (2012) /wireless broad band (2014)	Fixed Broadband
2003	0.089	4.516	12.76	16.71	3.28	-
2004	0.097	5.77	12.66	22.89	3.75	-
2005	0.0971	8.100	11.36	24.19	4.500	-
2008	0.1693	13.65	10.52	74.40	6.22	0.83
2010	0.1806	24.46	8.46	86.60	7.20	2.09
2012	0.2717	38.00	7.84	106.99	4.06	3.18
2014	0.3104	41.00	6.20	128.17	10.86	2.76
Trend	0.038	6.795	−1.151	20.178	0.931	0.688

munication infrastructure was low as 0.089 but the value increased to 0.3104 in 2014. The trend analysis showed as that Jordan telecommunication infrastructure index is improving every year with positive trend value of 0.038.

The improvement in global ranking for Jordan in the year 2014 is basically return to the E-services to the public which is one of the main goals of the new strategy of E-government in Jordan as will be discussed in details in another section. The local Government of Amman, the capital of Jordan, has launched an SMS services portal [21] aimed at increasing the channels of communications between citizens and governments. It is now recognized as the most prevalent communication tool with all segments of the Jordanian community, helping in enhancing the quality and efficiency of governmental services. It provides citizens with two types of services: 1) push messages by governmental institutions and departments such as reminders and awareness campaigns; and 2) pull messages that are sent by citizens as an SMS inquiry and are automatically responded to by the relevant governmental department [22].

Jordan online service index has continuously improved during the period (2010-2014), all stages with positive trend as shown in **Table 2**. Best trend in stage 1 "Emerging information services" where Jordanian government websites provide information on public policy, governance, laws, regulations, relevant documentation and types of government services provided. They have links to ministries, departments and other branches of government. Citizens are easily able to obtain information on what is new in the national government and ministries and can follow links to archived information. Good progress on stage 2 "Enhanced information services, until now government websites deliver enhanced one-way e-communication between government and citizen, such as downloadable some forms for government services and applications. Not bad progress in stage 3 "Transaction services", No engagement between government websites in two-way communication with the citizens, including requesting and receiving inputs on government policies, programs, regulations, etc. Good progress in stage 4 is "Connected services" which means that government websites have changed the way governments communicate with their citizens. They are proactive in requesting information and opinions from the citizens using Web 2.0 and other interactive tools. E-services and e-solutions cut across the departments and ministries in a seamless manner. Information, data and knowledge is transferred from government agencies through integrated applications. Governments have moved from a government-centric to a citizen-centric approach, where e-services are targeted to citizens through life cycle events and segmented groups to provide tailor-made services [20]. Actually Now Jordan at the end of stage 2 and MOICT issued a new strategy for E-government which will be discussed in details in another section.

4. Challenges and Opportunities Affecting the Success of E-Government in Jordan

Nowadays governments around the world are racing to implement the E-government concept in their countries, but some of them have suffered failure in adopting E-government concept [23]. According to Heeks (2004),

Table 2. Online services indicators-trend analysis.

Year	Emerging information services (stage 1)	Enhanced information services (stage 2)	Transactional services (stage 3)	Connected services (stage 4)
2010	0.5	0.44	0.57	0.17
2012	0.83	0.48	0.31	0.20
2014	0.91	0.41	0.21	0.50
Trend	0.298	0.123333	0.042333	0.162

most of E-government project in developing countries have failed, 35% of E-government project are total failures, 50% are partial failures and only 15% are success [24].

The most challenges that are expected to be faced during the implementation of an E-government program have been summarized from the E-government handbook of developing countries [25], presented in **Table 3**. A set of recommendations has been provided to assist in overcoming the challenges and obstacles in the road for developing a successful E-government.

Most researches on E-government have focused on developed countries. Of those that are focused on E-government in developing countries, a few have highlighted several issues that need to be faced [26]-[30].

Jordan is one of such developing countries, M. Al-Shboul *et al.* (2014) [31] declared in their research that key factors and challenges affect E-government services adoption in Jordan can roughly categorized under four heading; political factors, social factors, organizational factors, and technological factors [32] [33].

- Political factors: Implementing E-government projects needs huge financial investments. As a result of the lack of available financial resources top leadership gradually lose their enthusiasm to implement E-government.
- Social factors: People who don't have internet access will be unable to advantage from online services which form an important barrier to E-government.
- Organizational factors: Successful implementation of E-government should involve restructuring the existing organizational model, roles, responsibilities, training, and employee's needs [34], thus lack of employee training will be a considerable challenge.
- Technological factors: Required information technology standards to achieve citizens' needs and to pass up any hardware and system barriers that might delay the implementation of E-government. One of the most significant technological challenges is computer security. Stability of E-government services is important for availability and service delivery as well as for Building citizen confidences. Moreover privacy is a core challenge to E-government implementation and acceptance, it concern sharing information among participating government agencies and exposing or mishandling private information.

Moreover, they expose other additional factors affect E-government adoption, implementation, and usage in the Hashemite kingdom of Jordan: legislation and legal framework; human resistance to change, security and privacy issues; culture issues; trust in E-government; usefulness and complexity issues; website design issues; access and IT skill issues; operational cost; organizational issues; technical infrastructure; usability, availability, and accessibility issues. These challenges are relatively similar to challenges cited in [35].

This study suggested some recommendations based on the knowledge gained from the research:

- Transforming into E-government services should not be treated as only a computerization of governmental operation but also as a restructuring process.
- Using the existing academic institutions to enhance peoples' awareness by adopting training courses on E-government knowledge.
- Collaboration with the private sector, which can be helpful in cost-sharing, project and technology management expertise.
- Controlling and getting over the resistance to change by clarifying the transformation aims to employee.

5. New Strategy of E-Government in Jordan Covering the Years (2014, 2015, 2016) [36]

The MOICT presented the new strategy of E-government in Jordan covering the years (2014, 2015, and 2016),

Table 3. Challenges to be faced during the implementation of an E-government and recommendations to overcome these challenges.

Challenges	Recommendations
1. Infrastructure Development **All countries implementing E-government have struggled to develop a basic infrastructure to take advantage of new technologies and communications tools. Many developing countries, even if possessing the will, do not have the infrastructure necessary to immediately deploy E-government services throughout their territory**	• Develop projects that are compatible with the nation's telecom infrastructure. • Use public access kiosks and mobile centers if telecommunication density is low. • Introduce telecom competition and lift regulations on wireless and other digital technologies to accelerate their deployment. • Build on the microenterprise model to bring connectivity to underserved areas and ensure sustainability. • Consider the government's current use of technology and learn from past successes and failures. • Establish an action framework at the beginning of the process to allow for a rational and coordinated investment effort down the road.
2. Law and Public Policy **The application of Information Technology and Communication (ICT) to government may encounter legal or policy barriers. Legislatures must ensure that laws are updated to recognize electronic documents and transactions. Policymakers implementing E-government must consider the impact of law and public policy.**	• Consult with stakeholders to assess how existing laws may impede the desired results. • Give legal status to online publication of government information. • Clarify laws and regulations to allow electronic filings with government agencies. • Reform processes by simplifying regulations and procedures.
3. Digital Divide **The digital divide is the gap between people who have access to the Internet and those who do not. Those without access cannot learn essential computer skills, cannot access information that can provide economic opportunities, and cannot share in the benefits of E-government.**	• Provide communal access through village computer centers or kiosks. • Combine access with training. • Provide incentives to the private sector to donate equipment and training. • Emphasize local language and content tailored to different communities. • Use for-profit entrepreneurs to build and sustain access points in small communities.
4. E-Literacy **E-Literacy refers to marginalized groups who are unable to make use of information and communication technologies because they are not computer literate. With the digital revolution there is a very real danger that the world will be divided into the "information rich" and the "information poor". E-government has the potential of either equalizing access to government and its services or increasing the barriers to participation.**	• Ensure that content is in local languages and that interfaces are easy to use. • Develop applications that use speech or pictures in addition to, or instead of, written text. • Include an educational component in E-government projects. • Provide aides at access points who can train citizens in basic computer skills. • Create programs that include traditional media, like radio programs or newspaper columns, where citizens can learn about E-government. • Special attention should be given to groups difficult to integrate (women, elderly, immigrants).
5. Accessibility **Governments must serve all members of society irrespective of their physical capabilities (disabled people: those who are blind, deaf or otherwise handicapped). Online services will have to be designed with appropriate interfaces.**	• From the outset, design applications that accommodate the disabled, such as an audio option for the blind. • Establish as a legal requirement that the government must adopt technology to assist the disabled. • Set performance criteria and measure progress
6. Trust **To be successful, E-government projects must build trust within agencies, between agencies, across governments, and with businesses, NGOs and citizens**	• Map key internal and external partners and build a strategy to keep open lines of communications. • Start with short-term projects that yield early results. This helps build trust and could help point to areas for larger scale ventures. • Strong leadership can help build confidence in programs.
7. Privacy **Governments must be responsible custodians Of the enormous amounts of personal information they hold. Governments collect vast quantities of data on their citizens through everyday transactions. Protecting the privacy of citizens' personal information stored on these databases while making effective use of the information contained in them is a vitally important issue.**	• Educate and train government officials on the importance of privacy. • Design applications that integrate privacy protections. • Follow "fair information practices". Minimize the collection and retention of personal information. • Limit access to personally identifiable information—do not automatically allow employees to tap into databases of personally identifiable information.

Continued

8. Security

Security is costly, but must be addressed in the design phase, as security breaches can shatter public trust in E-government. Trust is a vitally important component of E-government projects. Without trust, citizens who may already be leery of using technology may avoid and even shun the use of online services that ask for detailed personal information.

- Designate a senior official responsible for computer security.
- Continually assess systems to make sure that security precautions are being implemented.
- Backup information regularly and store backups in a separate location.
- When it comes to personal information, keep information collection to a minimum and do not disclose personal information without express prior consent.
- Provide ongoing training to employees on computer security.
- Evaluate performance of system managers in adhering to sound security practices.

9. Transparency

Citizens too rarely understand how government decisions are made. This lack of transparency prevents the public from actively participating in government and from raising questions or protesting unfair or ill-advised decisions. A lack of transparency can conceal official graft or favoritism.

- Post online rules, regulations and requirements for
- government services (such as requirements for obtaining
- A license) to minimize subjective actions by officials.
- Highly-placed public officials can expedite transparency and accountability efforts by making their offices positive examples of openness.
- When putting services online, give citizens the ability to track the status of their applications.
- Train civil servants and provide incentives to reform.
- Integrate transparency and process reform to simplify regulations and procedures.

10. Interoperability

Putting incompatible record formats online neither simplifies nor reduces the workload imposed on people and government officials. Reliable E-government requires a comprehensive overhaul of legacy systems.

- Map and assess existing record systems.
- Identify and reform regulatory schemes that make interaction with the government onerous.
- Use common standards throughout the government to shorten development time and ensure compatibility.
- Adopt a common IT infrastructure for the government.

11. Records Management

Better information management can help officials identify barriers to more efficient government. An information management framework is necessary to make sense of available data. Without this framework, policy makers could not derive useful analysis quickly enough to react to social and economic developments.

- Encourage data sharing and cooperation between government departments.
- Streamline offline record keeping processes to make the transformation to online publication easier.
- Creation and standardization of meta-data is critical for conducting successful data searches across institutions and networks.

12. Permanent availability and preservation

Historical documentation is of special importance for governments. ICT not only allows for quick and cheap dissemination of data, but also for its compact and convenient storage.

- Design applications according to need.
- Consider relevance, usability, language compatibility and affordability.
- Encourage cooperation between departments and with the private sector in collecting, storing and utilizing data but proceed continuously with personally identifiable information.

13. Education and Marketing

E-government services are only useful if people know about them. Education and outreach programs will be needed.

- Develop publicity and training campaigns that will engage the public about E-government initiatives.
- Conduct research to ensure that online services respond to actual needs and that the implementation suits the target audience.

14. Public/Private competition/collaboration

Answering the question of where government controls end and the private sector takes over in E-government efforts.

- Forge multi-sector partnerships.
- Review and reassess laws and policies that impede public/private cooperation.
- Ensure that agreements with contractors and partners are equitable and can be reviewed and revised over time.
- Seek assistance and involvement from organizations that already have experience in providing services and information using the same or similar technologies

15. Workforce issues

Human resources must be structured and managed with E-government goals in mind. A well-trained and motivated workforce is critical to E-government success.

- Articulate a timeline for implementation in a step by-step manner so the reforms will not seem overwhelming to the bureaucracy.
- Hold regular meetings between E-government policy leaders and the affected workforce so employees are active participants in the process.
- Create incentives by rewarding individuals and agencies that apply the reforms rapidly.

Continued

16. Cost structures **While planning and budgeting in a changing climate is difficult, governments should seek to invest in sustainable programs that can produce savings.**	• Avoid advertising-based or fee-based services. They have generally not been sustainable. • Articulate functionalities clearly and try not to add details that will push budgets into deficit. • Develop projects that are achievable with resources available. • Consider the government's current use of technology and study past successes and failures. • Designate an officer or organizing body that will oversee cost.
17. Benchmarking **Governments must regularly evaluate the progress and effectiveness of their E-government investments to determine whether stated goals and objectives are being met on schedule**	• Create measurable goals during early planning stages. • Designate an office to oversee E-government implementation. • Make sure the office is sufficiently funded and is recognized by all relevant agencies and departments. • Conduct regular audits to ensure progress is being made to achieve stated goals. • Review benchmarks regularly to ensure that accurate measures are appropriate for rapidly changing technology. • Create a data collection system to support program operations and "before and after" surveys of knowledge, skills, and applications among participating organizations to assess program impact. • A common IT infrastructure and architecture standard is key to ensuring that ongoing development takes place in a coherent and integrated way. • Advanced planning of common IT infrastructure standards result in shortened development time and system compatibility. • Quantitative measures can be as beneficial as qualitative ones.

which emphasize on encouraging and motivating government entities to deliver high-quality customer-centric and performance-driven services to E-government beneficiaries while transforming from traditional service delivery to more effective and efficient service providers to their beneficiaries (Citizens, Residents, Visitors, Businesses, Government Entities and Government Employees). In UN report 2012, the participation of all in E-government is imperative to promote economic and social empowerment through ICT for all citizens including vulnerable groups pre-identified by the UN as the Poor, illiterate, blind, old, young, immigrants and women.

The new strategy presents priority of E-government initiatives, tools and projects (as shown in **Figure 3**). The Jordan E-government will launch three main initiatives during the period of this strategy that aim to provide incentives for government entities to pay more efforts toward e-Transformation to better serve their beneficiaries and improve the overall progress of Jordan achievements compared with regional and global countries.

1) E-government Award: The goal of it is to encourage entities, individuals and organizations succeed and develop their creativity in the field of E-government in information and communication technology to promote e-community.

2) Measuring E-government E-Transformation "MADA": The goals of this measurement determining the challenges facing government entities in the process of e-Transformation, enable decision makers and E-government Program to outline corrective policies that correspond to such challenges, and motivating government entities to give more priority to become e-Transformation leaders.

3) Business Development "DALEEL": The goal is promote E-government consulting services toward business development and employ accumulative knowledge and experience in enabling government entities to achieve e-Transformation.

The four stages of e-transformation are evolving around the maturity of service delivery (emerging, enhanced, transactional, and connected). Government of Jordan is aiming to achieve the transactional stage by end of this strategy. Jordan is currently is in the late enhanced stage given that government of Jordan offer more sources of information through the National Government Portal, the National Contact Center (NCC), the National Mobile Portal and National SMS Gateway.

6. Conclusions

Government is a dynamic mixture of goals, structures and functions. After the technological revolution the government is extended to produce E-government. Many researches discussed and worked on E-government in developing and developed countries. Jordan is one of developing countries that has embarked on the E-government initiative and is expected to take several years to complete and E-government in Jordan is not a policy standing

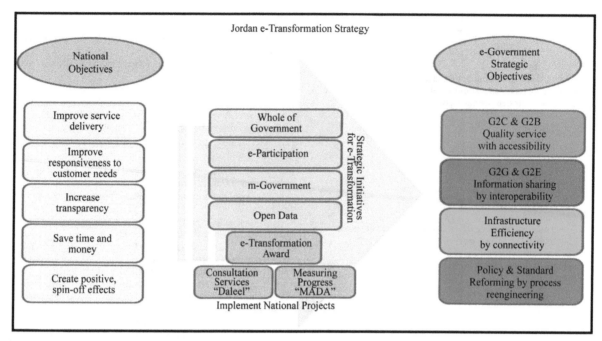

Figure 3. New strategy of E-government in Jordan for the years (2014, 2015, and 2016).

in isolation; it is an integral element of the Kingdom's National Agenda.

This research provided an overview of the past, current, and future status of E-government in Jordan by taking all aspects and sides of E-government program in Jordan which can help in the development of proposals, plans and strategies to improve the level of E-government in Jordan and give trend analysis to get the Jordan trends (positive or negative) in the UN E-government indicators.

References

[1] Pardo, T. (2000) Realizing the Promise of Digital Government: It's More than Building a Web Site. Center of Technology in Government, University of Albany.

[2] Al-Mashari, M. (2007) A Benchmarking Study of Experiences with Electronic Government. *Benchmarking: An International Journal*, **14**, 172-185. http://dx.doi.org/10.1108/14635770710740378

[3] Sprecher, M.H. (2000) Racing to E-government: Using the Internet for Citizen Service Delivery. *Government Finance Review*, **16**, 21-22.

[4] Schware, R. and Deane, A. (2003) Deploying E-Government Programs: The Strategic Importance of "I" before "E". *Info*, **5**, 10-19. http://dx.doi.org/10.1108/14636690310495193

[5] Tambouris, E., Gorilas, S. and Boukis, G. (2001) Investigation of Electronic Government. 8*th Panhellenic Conference on Informatics*, 8-10 November 2001, Nicosia.

[6] Fang, Z.Y. (2002) E-Government in Digital Era: Concept, Practice and Development. *International Journal of the Computer, the Internet and Management*, **10**, 1-22.

[7] Carter, L. and Belanger, F. (2004) Citizen Adoption of Electronic Government Initiatives. *HICSS* 2004—*Proceedings of the 37th Annual Hawaii International Conference on System Sciences*, Hawaii, 5-8 January 2004. http://dx.doi.org/10.1109/HICSS.2004.1265306

[8] Wang, Y.S. and Liao, Y.W. (2008) Assessing eGovernment Systems Success: A Validation of the DeLone and McLean Model of Information Systems Success. *Government Information Quarterly*, **25**, 717-733. http://dx.doi.org/10.1016/j.giq.2007.06.002

[9] Bose, R. (2004) Information Technologies for Education & Training in E-Government. *International Conference on Information Technology: Coding and Computing*, 5-7 April 2004, 203-207.

[10] United Nations (2005) Global E-Government Readiness Report 2005—from E-Government to E-Inclusion. United Nations Division for Public Administration and Development Management. http://unpan1.un.org/intradoc/groups/public/documents/un/unpan021888.pdf

[11] United Nations (2008) Global E-Government Readiness Report 2008—From E-Government to Connected Governance. United Nations Division for Public Administration and Development Management. http://unpan1.un.org/intradoc/groups/public/documents/un/unpan028607.pdf

[12] Abu-Samaha, A. and Samad, Y. (2007) Challenges to the Jordanian Electronic Government Initiative. *Journal of Business Systems, Governance and Ethics*, **2**, 101-109.

[13] AbuShanab, E. and Pearson, J. (2007) Internet Banking in Jordan: The Unified Theory of Acceptance and Use of Technology (UTAUT) Perspective. *Journal of Systems and Information Technology*, **9**, 78-97. http://dx.doi.org/10.1108/13287260710817700

[14] Elsheikh, Y., Cullen, A. and Hobbs, D. (2008) E-Government in Jordan: Challenges and Opportunities. *Transforming Government: People, Process and Policy*, **2**, 83-103.

[15] Mohammad, H., Almarabeh, T. and Abu Ali, A. (2009) E-Government in Jordan. *European Journal of Scientific Research*, **35**, 188-197.

[16] Blakemore, M. and Dutton, R. (2003) E-Government, E-Society and Jordan: Strategy, Theory, Practice, and Assessment. http://dx.doi.org/10.5210/fm.v8i11.1095

[17] The Hashemite Kingdom of Jordan, Ministry of Information and Communications Technology (2006). http://www.moict.gov.jo/HOme.aspx

[18] McConnell International Report (2000) Risk E-Business: Seizing the Opportunity of Global E-Readiness. http://www.mcconnellinternational.com/index.php?option=com_content&view=article&id=10&Itemid=6

[19] Almarabeh, T. and Abu Ali, A. (2010) A General Framework for E-Government: Definition Maturity Challenges, Opportunities, and Success. *European Journal of Scientific Research*, **39**, 29-42.

[20] Almarabeh, T. and Adwan, O. (2013) A Detailed Study of E-Government Readiness in Jordan. *International Journal of Computer Science Issues*, **10**, 88-96.

[21] Greater Amman Municipality, Jordan. http://www.ammancity.gov.jo/en/gam/index.asp

[22] United Nations (2014) Global E-Government Readiness Report 2014—E-Government for the Future We Want. United Nations Division for Public Administration and Development Management. http://unpan3.un.org/egovkb/Reports/UN-E-Government-Survey-2014

[23] Gagne, J.C.D. and Walters, K. (2009) Online Teaching Experience: A Qualitative Meta Synthesis (QMS). *The MERLOT Journal of Online Learning and Teaching*, **5**, 577-589.

[24] Heeks, R. (2004) Causes of E-Government Success and Failure: Factor Model. Institute for Development Policy and Management, University of Manchester, Manchester.

[25] The E-Government Handbook for Developing Countries, Center of Democracy and Technology, 2002.

[26] Wagner, C., Cheung, K., Lee, F. and Ip, R. (2003) Enhancing E-Government in Developing Countries: Managing Knowledge through Virtual Communities. *Electronic Journal on Information Systems in Developing Countries*, **14**, 1-20. www.seu.ac.lk/cedpl/research%20and%20thesis/89-89-1-PB.pdf

[27] Heeks, R. (2002) E-Government in Africa: Promise and Practice. *Information Polity*, **7**, 97-114.

[28] Reffat, R. (2003) Developing a Successful E-Government. *Proceedings of the Symposium on E-Government: Opportunities and Challenge*, Muscat Municipality, 10-12 May 2003, IV1-IV13.

[29] Ndou, V. (2004) E-Government for Developing Countries: Opportunities and Challenges. *Electronic Journal on Information Systems in Developing Countries*, **18**, 1-24.

[30] Bose, R. (2004) Information Technologies for Education & Training in E-Government. *Proceedings of the ITCC 2004 International Conference on Information Technology: Coding and Computing*, Las Vegas, 5-7 April 2004, 203-207.

[31] Al-Shboul, M., Rababah, O., Ghnemat, R. and Al-Saqqa, S. (2014) Challenges and Factors Affecting the Implementation of E-Government in Jordan. *Journal of Software Engineering and Applications*, **7**, 1111-1127. http://dx.doi.org/10.4236/jsea.2014.713098

[32] Weerakkody, V., El-Haddadeh, R. and Al-Shafi, S. (2011) Exploring the Complexities of E-Government Implementation and Diffusion in a Developing Country: Some Lessons from the State of Qatar. *Journal of Enterprise Information Management*, **24**, 172-196. http://dx.doi.org/10.1108/17410391111106293

[33] Bonham, G., Seifert, J. and Thorson, S. (2001) The Transformational Potential of E-Government: The Role of Political Leadership. *Proceedings of the 4th Pan European International Relations Conference*, Canterbury, 6-10 September 2001, 1-9.

[34] Ebrahim, Z. and Irani, Z. (2005) E-Government Adoption: Architecture and Barriers. *Business Process Management Journal*, **11**, 589-611. http://dx.doi.org/10.1108/14637150510619902

[35] Al-Shafi, S. (2009) Factors Affecting E-Government Implementation and Adoption in the State of Qatar. Ph.D. Thesis,

Brunel University, London.

[36] Jordan E-Government (2013) E-Government Strategy 2014-2016.
      http://inform.gov.jo/Portals/0/Report%20PDFs/7.%20Role%20&%20Performance%20of%20Government/i.%20Public
      %20Sector%20Reform%20&%20Development/2014-2016%20MOICT-E-government%20Strategy-Draft.pdf

13

Automatic Synchronization of Common Parameters in Configuration Files

Moupojou Matango Emmanuel[1], Moukouop Nguena Ibrahim[2]

[1]Department of Computer Science, University of Yaounde 1, Yaounde, Cameroon
[2]National Advanced School of Engineering, Department of Computer Science, University of Yaounde 1, Yaounde, Cameroon
Email: moupojouemma@yahoo.fr, imoukouo@gmail.com

Abstract

In an information system, applications often make use of services that they access using the parameters described in their configuration files. Various applications then use different codes to denote the same parameters. When access parameters of a service are modified, it is necessary to update them in every configuration file using them. These changes are necessary, for example because of security policies involving regular changes of passwords, or departure of some system administrators. The database password could be changed for example. When system administrators can not immediately identify all services affected by a change or when they feel they don't have the skills to edit these files, these parameters remain unchanged, creating critical security flaws. This was observed in more than 80% of the organizations we studied. It then becomes necessary to ensure automatic synchronization of all affected files when changing certain settings. Conventional synchronization solutions are difficult to apply when the relevant applications have already been developed by third parties. In this paper, we propose and implement a solution to automatically update all configuration files affected by a change, respecting their structure and codification. It combines a parameters database, a mapping between the configuration files parameters codes and those of the database, and templates for the generation of files. It achieves the objective for all non-encrypted configuration files.

Keywords

System Administration, Configuration File, Parameter, Update, Synchronization

1. Introduction

A configuration file is a file that contains configuration information used by a computer program to adapt or customize its operation. File synchronization (or syncing) in computing is the process of ensuring that computer files in two or more locations are updated via certain rules.

The password change of a critical service (database, email...) that can occur repeatedly (according to security policies), or following the departure of a system administrator is a regular event. Such a change may involve changing parameters of dozens of applications using this service. Although in theory all services affected by a change must be documented, in practice, not only this is not always the case, but in addition to that, many administrators are afraid to make changes in configuration files for applications they do not have control. These manual changes may be associated with errors or false manipulations.

To better understand the problem exposed here, consider the following example which is a usual situation in production environments: Let us consider a set of five services (or applications), each with its particular configuration file that contains, among others, the access parameters to the same database. Those common parameters have different names from one file to the other. If the administrator changes the access parameters to the database, then it will require to also change them in all five configuration files, without forgetting one (if he doesn't use a traceability matrix[1]), without mistake, otherwise some services will then cease running: which turns out being a tedious task. It would then be wise to manage those common settings on a unified way. The two-way file synchronization is then required[2], to ensure that when a parameter in a file undergoes an update, this update is propagated to all other parameters files having a parameter supposed to contain the same value.

The MDAL[3] applications have for example the following configuration files, **Figure 1** and **Figure 2**, used by different services:

These two configuration files used by different services, have several common configuration settings that should have the same value at any time for the system remains in a consistent state of configuration (dbuser, dbpassword, applipassword...). Also note that those common parameters might have different names from one file to the other, which could in turn be in different formats as we will see in the implementation example in-Subsection 3.2.

2. Materials and Methods

2.1. State of the Art on File Synchronization

2.1.1. Whole Files Synchronization

This approach considers that files at different locations are identical, and shall have exactly the same content when an update is made upon one of them. Many whole file synchronization techniques and their applications are described [1]-[3], and many tools performing this kind of synchronization are available [4]. Andrew Tridgell proposed an efficient algorithm called rsync for performing this synchronization [5] [6]. Many rsync enhancements and optimizations where also proposed [7] [8]. But rather than synchronizing the whole configuration file, we shall synchronize only some common parameters inside those files, because of the fact that the files are different.

2.1.2. Synchronizing Particular Elements in Files

This is the purpose of this paper. Some elements in configuration files shall be synchronized with other elements in other files in order to keep the consistency of the system. The parameters are semantically equivalent, but can

```
url=jdbc:mysql://emmanuel-PC:3309/evaluation
dbuser=root
dbpassword=manager10
dbdriver=com.mysql.jdbc.Driver
appliuser=system
applipassword=mongui
```

Figure 1. Configuration file mailerdaemonparams.txt of MDAL applications.

---

[1]Document that correlates any two base-lined documents that require a many-to-many relationship to determine the completeness of the relationship.

[2]Updated files are copied in both directions, usually with the purpose of keeping the two locations identical to each other.

[3]Megasoft Data Access Library: written in Java Framework, facilitating the development, deployment, operation and maintenance of applications accessing databases.

```
url=jdbc:mysql://emmanuel-PC:3309/bdqo
dbuser=root
dbpassword=manager10
dbdriver=com.mysql.jdbc.Driver
appliuser=system
applipassword=mongui
folder=D:\"Program Files"\"deploiementmdal"\srcbackyp
destinationfolder=D:\"Program Files"\"deploiementmdal"\srcbackypmail
sizelimit=6000000
backupid=backup_
compte=1000000074
expediteur=imoukouo@gmail.com
destinataire=imoukouo@gmail.com
repeat_interval=120
```

Figure 2. Configuration file folder mailerparams.txt of MDAL applications.

have completely different codes from one file to another.

Existing approaches to do this are:

1. Centralized configuration settings

The principle here is to have a single file containing all the parameters of all applications/services.

The various applications read their functional parameters in this file; and when an update is made, the new value is immediately visible to all other applications. Hyena[4], for example, allows centralized management of common configuration settings to multiple services by bringing them together in a single file [9].

2. Distributed configuration files with inclusions

This approach is used to preserve the distributed aspect of configuration files; each service having its own configuration file, but containing only its private parameters. Common settings among several configuration files are placed in a common file, and individual files wishing to include them in their settings then have, in their structures, inclusion directives pointing to that or those common files. Thus, when loading the parameters of a file, they are also added, and so recursively, the parameters contained in the files to which it points. Thus, the update of these parameters is only done in the common file and is thus taken into account in the different files including it.

a) The JNLP Protocol[5] uses this technique when loading .Jnlp files for downloading and running Java applications upon the network. Indeed, a .jnlp file may, in its structure, have a link to another .jnlp file; and when loading the original file resources (different .jar files), the JNLP protocol also loads all the resources listed in the referenced file.

b) The "MS CF Manager"[6] application, developed during this project, also uses this technique.

Besides ordinary settings, a configuration file can also have the "mdal.include" parameter that contains the different paths, separated by semicolons, of other configuration files whose parameters should be added to those of the original one.

The two approaches mentioned above are valid only if they were taken into account during the development phase of the application. Care is then taken to define how to access configuration files, taking into account their structures. Now considering the case applications/services are already developed, and that the synchronization of different configuration settings shall be done as described above, the problem becomes very different. Anne Jonassen Hass describes the architecture and processes of a configuration manager [10] without addressing our specific problem, which is how to ensure common parameters synchronization among many configuration files. Bob Aiello and Leslie Sachs where able to bridge the language gap between the myriad of communities involved with successful Configuration Management implementations [10]. They describe practical, real world practices that can be implemented by developers, managers, standard makers, and even Classical CM Folk.

2.2. New Configuration files Synchronization Approach and Model

2.2.1. Identification of the Solution

Configuration Management is a multidisciplinary science (computer science, aeronautics, automobile, wea-

---

[4]Software to simplify and centralize nearly all daily management tasks of Windows network, Active Directory management and adding new capabilities to existing native tools.
[5]Java Network Launching Protocol.
[6]MegaSoft Configuration Files Manager.

pons...) consisting in the management of the technical description of a system and its various components, as well as change management made during the evolution of that system. The diagram showing the general structure and operation of a configurations manager is shown in **Figure 3** [10]:

Used in monitoring different versions of documents in computer science, it allows archive and tracking of all changes that have occurred in these documents. Relying on this science for which a standard exists, it will issue to propose and implement a model of configuration files synchronization for solving the problem. This synchronization should be possible even for existing applications.

Configuration management consists in four main modules:

- **Unique Identification**: It allows determining a configuration item's metadata, to uniquely identify it, and to specify its relations with the outside world and other configuration elements.
- **Storage**: This module ensures that a configuration item will not disappear, or will not be damaged, but it can be found and made available in the desired state.
- **Change Control**: This module is fully in control of all changes requests to the system, and all implemented changes.

In the case of our problem, this automatically implies an automatic traceability, which is not often done when the administrator directly modifies the configuration files, and this often causes difficulties to return after unfortunate changes.

- **Status Reporting**: It allows providing legible and useful information to ensure effective management of the development and maintenance of a product.

In the context of the problem to solve, change control will be suitable. Indeed, it is usually a modification proposal made by the end user, in the case where configuration management has been applied to the development of an application for example. The problem is then found in a more specific area called "Version Control". Changes implemented here therefore simply consist in the various updates of different values of the configura-

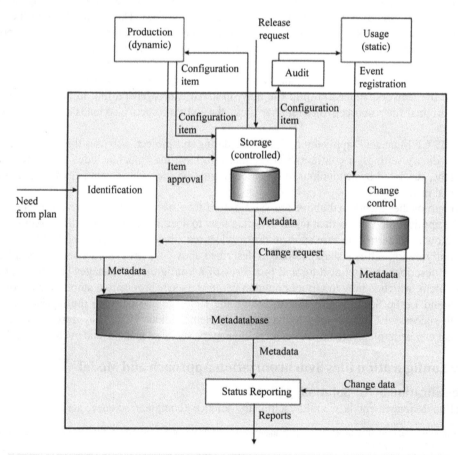

Figure 3. Operation of a configuration manager [10].

tion parameters. The various elements under the control of the configuration manager, which corresponds to the configuration settings in this case, shall in no case be modified, but new versions will be created: this should allow returning to a previous configuration state. It is therefore necessary to make a full scan of the system to establish, in taking into account the specificity of configuration managers architecture, and proceed subsequently to an implementation of this model.

2.2.2. Modeling Solution

Generally, the configuration files synchronization problem may be represented by **Figure 4**.
With:

- Ai: Application i
- AiSj: Service j of the application i
- AiSjFk: Configuration File k of service j of application i
- Pijkl: Parameter l of the configuration file k of service j of application i
- Vijkl: Value of parameter Pijkl
- Fijk: Type (format) of the configuration file k of the service j of application i
- Rel 1: Parameter P_{111n} corresponds to Parameters P_{1121} and P_{1pm}
- Rel 2: Parameter P_{1pr1} corresponds to Parameter P_{n11n}

The problem is the following: at any time the parameters (P_{111n}, P_{1121}, P_{1pm}) a part, and (P_{1pr1}, P_{n11n}) on the other, must have the same value so that settings of applications A1 and An remain consistent. The equalities $V_{111n} = V_{1121} = V_{1pm}$ and $V_{1pr1} = V_{n11n}$ should therefore always be checked. If a parameter is changed, its correspondents must also be changed in cascade.

Let P be the set of parameters under the control of the configuration files synchronization module. We assume that every parameter is inside a group of parameters, and every group has at least one element, the parameter itself. The following functions can be defined:

1. correspondence: $P \times P \rightarrow$ Boolean
correspondence(p,q) $\equiv$ p.group = q.group[7]

2. update: $P \times$ Char $\rightarrow$ Unit
update(p,val) $\equiv$ $\forall q \in P$ if correspondence(p,q) then q.value := val

The realization of this solution is based on the use of templates. A template is a file having the same structure as a configuration file, but wherein parameters values are replaced by their identifiers in the system. Thus, to add

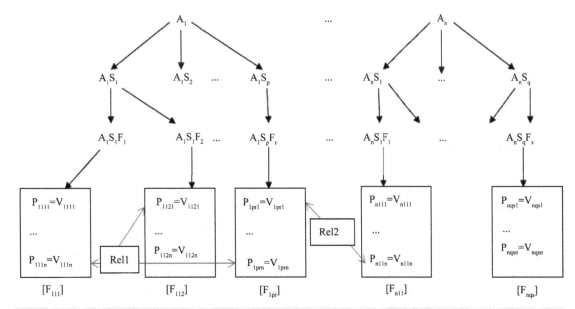

Figure 4. Configuration files synchronization problem.

[7]Two parameters are in correspondence when they contain exactly the same information. So at any time they must have the same value. This is our traceability matrix.

or delete a configuration parameter, this will be from the template. The analysis of the system led to the following relational schema for entities to use to implement the solution:

- application (code, label, description)
- template (code, name, filepath[8], description)
- application_template (application_code,template_code)
- parametersgroup (code, groupname, description)
- parameter (code, identifier[9], parametersgroup_code, parameter_type, begin_date, end_date)
- template parameter (template_code, parameter_code)
- value (code, value, creationhour)
- parametersgroup_value (parametersgroup_code, value_code)

When a parameter p is updated, the following operations are performed:

1. A new value is created for the parameters group containing p, and saved.

The following operations are repeated for all configuration parameters q in the same group with p.

2. A copy of q's template content is made.

3. In that copy, all parameters identifiers are replaced by their last saved values in the system.

4. The result then overwrites the template's target file, which is the original configuration file.

The procedure for updating a configuration parameter is as follows:

Algorithm 1 updateParameter (Parameter: p, String: newValue)
/*p: parameter that needs to be updated; newValue: new value of the parameter */

1: p.getGroup().setLastValue(Value (newValue));
/* creating a new value and adding it in the list of parameter's group values */

/* Updating all parameters in the same groupwith p; p.getGroupedParameters() returning at least {p}*/
2: **for all** par ∈ p.getGroupedParameters()**do**

    3: Template template = par.getTemplate();
    /* reading the template file containing the parameter */

    4: String file = template.filepath;/*reading file effectively containing the parameter */

    5: String templateCopy = readFile (template.name);/* reading template file content */

      6: **for all** param ∈ template.getParameters() **do**

        7: templateCopy = templateCopy.replace(param.identifier, param.getGroup().getLastValue());
        /* setting values of parameters in the template*/

      8: **end for**

    9: wrieteFile (file, templateCopy) ;/*updating the target file of the template */

10: **end for**

---

3. Results and Example

3.1. Results

As result of the model presented in Subsection 2.2.2, a configuration files synchronization tool was proposed called "Configuration Files Synchronizer" ensuring that correspondent parameters in those files may be synchronized in an easy way. Concretely, the result consists in an application allowing the management of those common settings on a unified way; so that when a parameter undergoes an update, this update is propagated to all other configuration files having a parameter supposed to contain the same value.

To do this, it must be set in the application the configuration files that are to be synchronized, and their respective template files. After this, the different common parameters must be regrouped in appropriate groups. When a parameter has to be updated, the update is not directly done in the configuration file. It is done through

---

[8]Path to the original configuration file for which this template was created.
[9]Unique identifier of a parameter in the database, which is mapped (same name) to the parameter's value in the template file.

the application, which also updates all the parameters in the same group than the first one, while updating their respective configuration files. An example of this is given in the Subsection 3.2 below.
Notice that an implementation of this solution was proposed in Java programming language.

3.2. Implementation Example

We consider two applications A1 and A2, with respective configuration files CF11.txt and CF12.properties for A1, and CF2.xml for A2, as shown on the **Figures 5-7**:

The parameters that are corresponding and that must be synchronized are: appli_name of CF11.txt, and application_name of CF12.properties.

1. Building Configuration Files Templates

Remind that a template has the same structure than its configuration file, the difference being that parameters values are replaced by their identifiers in the system. Proceeding like that, we have the following templates, where **Figures 8-10** are respectively the template files of configuration files represented by **Figures 5-7**:

2. Creating corresponding parameters groups

Now, parameters that are to be synchronized must be placed in the same group, so that, when a parameter will be updated, all parameters in the same group will also be updated, as described in Section 2.2.2. To do this, the following parameter group is created using the equivalent parameters and the template files:
A1 application name (A1_CF11_appli_name, A1_CF12_application_name)

3. Tables content

- application (code, label, description)
  (1, Application 1, "")
  (2, Application 2,"")
- template (code, name, filepath , description)
  (1, CF11_template.txt, {path}\CF11.txt, "")
  (2,CF12_template.properties, {path}\CF12.properties, "")
  (3,CF2_template.xml, {path}\CF2.xml, "")
- application_template (application_code, template_code)
  (1, 1)
  (1, 2)
  (2, 3)

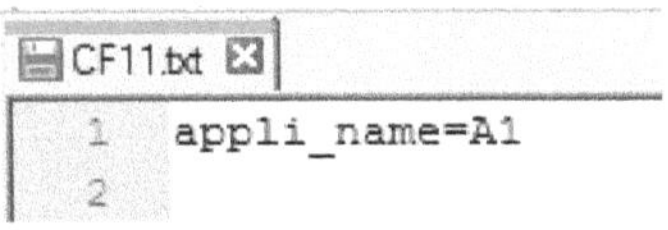

```
CF11.txt
appli_name=A1
```

Figure 5. CF11.txt.

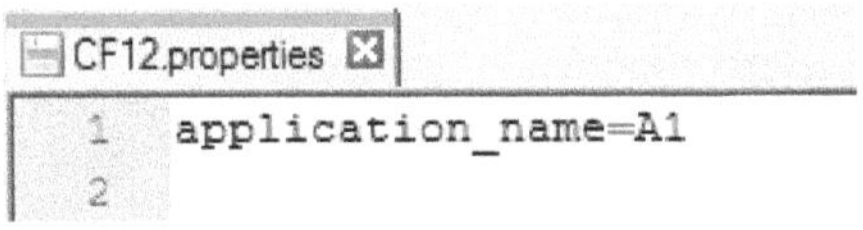

```
CF12.properties
application_name=A1
```

Figure 6. CF12.properties.

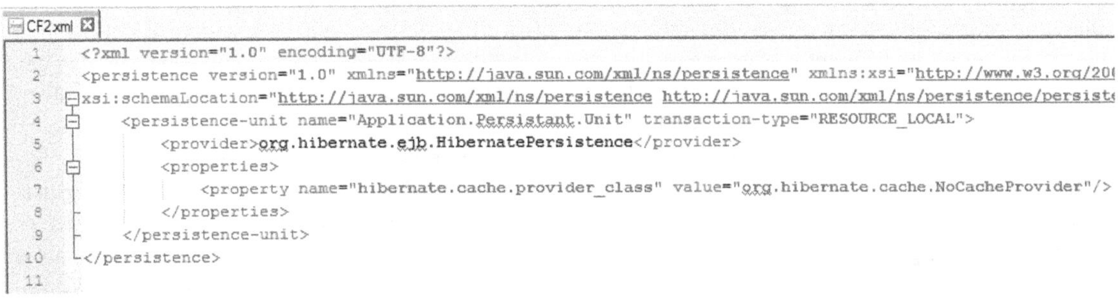

```
CF2.xml
<?xml version="1.0" encoding="UTF-8"?>
<persistence version="1.0" xmlns="http://java.sun.com/xml/ns/persistence" xmlns:xsi="http://www.w3.org/20
xsi:schemaLocation="http://java.sun.com/xml/ns/persistence http://java.sun.com/xml/ns/persistence/persist
    <persistence-unit name="Application.Persistant.Unit" transaction-type="RESOURCE_LOCAL">
        <provider>org.hibernate.ejb.HibernatePersistence</provider>
        <properties>
            <property name="hibernate.cache.provider_class" value="org.hibernate.cache.NoCacheProvider"/>
        </properties>
    </persistence-unit>
</persistence>
```

Figure 7. CF2.xml.

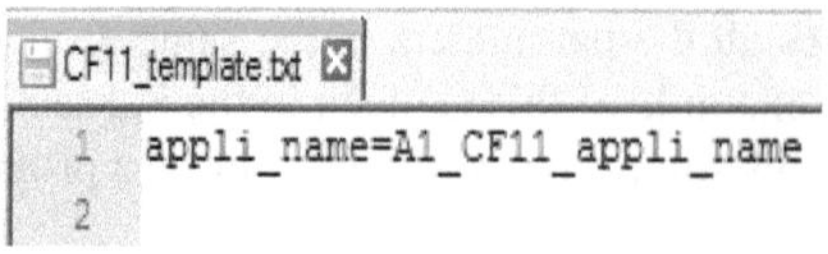

Figure 8. CF11_template.txt.

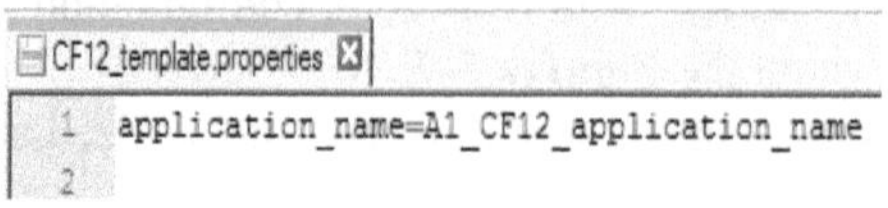

Figure 9. CF12_template.properties.

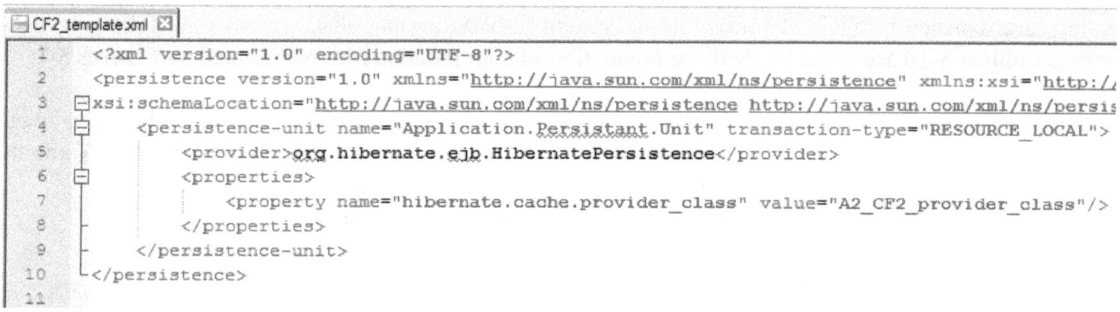

Figure 10. CF2_template.xml.

- parametersgroup (code, groupname, description)
  (1, A1_application_name, "")
  (2, A2_CF2_provider_class, "")
- parameter (code, identifier , parametersgroup_code, parametertype, begin_date, end_date)
  (1, A1_CF11_appli_name, 1, ordinary, 10/02/2015, null)
  (2, A1_CF12_application_name, 1, ordinary, 10/02/2015, null)
  (3, A2_CF2_provider_class, 2, ordinary, 10/02/2015, null)
- template_parameter (template_code, parameter_code)
  (1, 1)
  (2, 2)
  (3, 3)
- value (code, value, creationhour)
  (1, A1, 10/02/2015;07:30)
  (2, org.hibernate.cache.NoCacheProvider, 10/02/2015;07:30)
- parametersgroup_value (parametersgroup_code, value_code)
  (1, 1)
  (2, 2)

4. Conclusion

The multiplicity of configurations files creates a problem of parameters synchronization, when the same parameters are found in different configuration files and with different names. Such parameters are then equivalent and must at all times have the same value, so the update of a parameter must then be propagated to other files in order to maintain the system configuration in a coherent state. Existing approaches to solve this problem, such as centralization or files referencing are limited because they cannot be used for applications already developed. A model for the resolution of this problem (even for existing applications) has been proposed in this paper. Configuration files are represented by their templates, and links are established between equivalent parameters. When a parameter undergoes an update, this update is propagated to all other configuration files having a parameter supposed to contain the same value. This solution results in a very useful tool for system administrators to synchronize configuration files. In perspective, this tool may be improved in order to take into account configuration files security aspects when they are secured by security tools such as mRemote or Secure CRT.

Acknowledgements

We thank the government of Cameroon for premium sought they gave us in funding for our research.

We thank CETIC[10] for funding our research. We thank MEGASOFT SARL Company for allowing us to undertake this work.

References

[1] Tridgell, A. and MacKerras, P. (2002) The Rsync algorithm. Academic Press, Cambridge.

[2] Ramsey, N. and Csirmaz, E. (2001) An Algebraic Approach to File Synchronization. *Proceedings of the 9th ACM International Symposium on Foundations of Software Engineering*, 175-185. http://dx.doi.org/10.1145/503229.503233

[3] Balasubramaniam, S. and Pierce, B. (1998) What Is a File Synchronizer? *Proceedings of the ACM/IEEE MOBICOM 98 Conference*, 1998, 98-108.

[4] Basso, M. and Mann. J. (2013) MarketScope for Enterprise File Synchronization and Sharing. Gartner.

[5] Tridgell, A. (2000) Efficient Algorithms for Sorting and Synchronization. Ph.D. Dissertation, The Australian National University, Canberra.

[6] Torsten, S. and Memon, N. (1996) Algorithms for Delta Compression and Remote File Synchronization. Technical Report TR-CS-96-05.

[7] Rasch, D. and Burns, R. (2003) In-Place Rsync: File Synchronization for Mobile and Wireless Devices. *Proceedings of the USENIX Annual Technical Conference*, 2003.

[8] Suel, T., Noel, P. and Trendaflov, D. (2004) Improved File Synchronization Techniques for Maintaining Large Replicated Collections over Slow Networks. *Proceedings of the 20th International Conference on Data Engineering*, 30 March-2 April 2004, 153-164. http://dx.doi.org/10.1109/ICDE.2004.1319992

[9] (2014) Hyena. Shared Settings. http://www.systemtools.com/HyenaHelp/sharedsettings.htm

[10] Hass, A.M. (2002) Configuration Management Principles and Practice. DELTA.

---

[10]Centre d'Excellence Africain en Technologies de l'Information et de la Communication.

14

Reusable Function Discovery by Call-Graph Analysis

Dan Zhao, Li Miao, Dafang Zhang

College of Information Science and Engineering, Changsha, China
Email: dzhao34@hnu.edu.cn, miaoli@hnu.edu.cn, dfzhang@hnu.edu.cn

Abstract

Nowadays, one of the IT challenges faced by many enterprises is the maintenance of their legacy system and migration of those systems to modern and flexible platform. In this paper, we study the network properties of software call graphs, and utilize the network theories to understand the business logic of legacy system. The call graphs turn out approximately scale-free and small world network properties. This finding provides new insight to understand the business logic of legacy system: the methods in a program can be naturedly partitioned into the business methods group and supportive methods group. Moreover, the result is also very helpful in reusing valuable functionality and identifying what services should be to expose in the migration from legacy to modern SOA context.

Keywords

Call Graph, Network Properties, Legacy System, Service-Oriented Architecture

1. Introduction

In today's Internet-driven economy, one of the IT challenges faced by many enterprises is the maintenance of their legacy system and migration of those systems to modern and flexible platform [1]. Legacy systems generally consist of invaluable assets with embedded critical business logic representing many years of coding, developments, enhancements and modification. However, they are always undocumented, tightly coupled, and relative closed and inflexible. Thus, legacy systems present a dilemma: on the one hand, enterprises cannot simply remove/replace those systems as they are mission critical and their failure can have a significant impact on business. On the other hand, maintaining them incurs unjustifiable expense. A viable solution to this dilemma is to migrate those systems into new technological environments in which the legacy features can be reused. Service-Oriented Architecture (SOA) [2] has gained significant attention from academic and industry as a promising architectural style enabling legacy system to expose and reuse their functionalities. The objective of SOA is extracting and modularizing the valuable functionality in legacy system into shared, reusable service. The service here is some encapsulated component with well-defined interface and interoperability protocol, which composes SOA-style application flexibly and quickly. But both in commercial and academic context, currently most legacy system are extremely large and complex. They easily contain hundreds of thousands or even millions of lines of code, and different parts may be developed by different developers with various styles and documentation never catches up with the code change. Therefore, it is almost impossible to comprehend the whole system for developer when they migrate legacy to SOA, let alone find valuable functionalities and wrapper them into services [3]. Therefore, it would be quite helpful for developers to have some "intelligent and knowledgeable searching" technique to understand the business logic of legacy system and highlight the valuable functionality which has potential to be wrapped into service.

A call-graph is one kind of internal graph structure of software program, and reflects the essential function and behavior of programs. It is a directed graph $G = (N,E)$, which maybe has loops, where N is the set of nodes which represent methods, and E is the set of edges which represents invocation relations between methods. For every node $n \in N$, in-degree is the number of the in-coming edges of this node, which indicates the times that this method is invoked by other methods; Out-degree is the number of the out-going edges of this node, which indicates the times that this method invokes other methods. We made three empirical analyses to investigate the network properties of software call-graph, and utilize the network theories to understand the business logic of legacy system. The reason we make use of the network theories is that the invocation relationship underlying call-graph is very similar to the link relationship in network:

- *They both have same static structure.*

In software programs, the caller method invokes the callee method and the callee method is invoked by caller method; while in network, the source web page links to the target web page and the target web page is linked to the source web page. Both of them are directive connection relationships within different systems.

- *They both perform their functions through dynamic connection*

In software programs, different modules execute step-by-step invocation then they can provide computing capability; while in network, different web pages can be dynamically linked together then they can provide information service. Both of them reflect the essential function by the runtime characteristics. This characteristics has already used in the Google web crawling, which is done by analyzing this link relationship underlying webpages.

The most interesting observation in the empirical analyses is that there are a few key nodes in software call graphs with the in-degree above average or the out-degree above average. Re-checking our testing cases, we found that the nodes with the out-degree above average correspond to those methods which provide high-level business functions; and the nodes with the in-degree above average correspond to those methods which provide low-level supportive functions. For example, the method init() has the out-degree above average, which performs the business function "initialization" to initialize the whole system; the methods initDB(), initCache() and buildConc() invoked by init() have high in-degree, which can provide some supportive functions, such as initializing database, clearing cache and building socket connection. These key methods provide new insight to understand the business logic in legacy systems: the methods in a program can be naturedly partitioned into the business methods group and supportive methods group. Moreover, the result is also very helpful in reusing valuable functionality and identifying what services should be to expose in the migration from legacy to SOA context.

The rest of this paper is structured as follows: Section II explains our approach; Section IV makes three empirical analyses to investigate network properties of software call graphs. Section V presents and the findings as lessons learned. Section VI the paper concludes with some potential work.

2. Approach

We generate and analyze call-graph by static program analysis [4], which is a significant technique to determine the properties of program behavior without execution, has already been adopted in the software comprehension, debugging and testing field in the past twenty years. There have already many algorithms to construct a call graph from the software program, such as Class Hierarchy Analysis (CHA), Rapid Type Analysis (RTA) and Control Flow Analysis (CFA) [5]. We select CHA algorithm [6], which means scanning the class inheritance graph and constructing call-graph based on class hierarchy information. This is a relative simple algorithm and there is no reduplicate edge in the call-graph generated, which means even if a caller method invokes the callee method multiple times, there is only one edge existed between the caller method to the callee method. So for every node in our call-graph, in-degree indicates the number of the methods which invoke this method, and out-degree indicates the number of the methods which are invoked by this method. The reason we select this algorithm is that what we focus on the happiness of invocation relationship, not the time of the invocation relationship.

We use Java programming language as the target language and analyze ten widely used Java programs, whose code are publicly available and can be downloaded from the open-source website. They are listed as following **Table 1**.

We implement our analysis tool "Spotglitter" as a plugin for Eclipse. The tool is based on T.J. Watson Libraries for Analysis (WALA) [17], which is a bytecode analysis framework for Java. The tool first accept Java programs input, no matter source code or bytecode, and then generate call-graph for the program based on class hierarchy information. After that, It analysis the call-graph and visualize the result. We make three empirical analyses to detect characteristic of the degree distribution, node distribution, clustering degree and the separation degree of software programs call-graph. The detail is introduced in the Section 3.

3. Empirical Analysis

3.1. Empirical Analysis 1

For call-graph is a directed graph, where an invocation relationship corresponds to a directed link pointing from the caller method to the callee method, in this empirical analysis, we explored the in-degree distribution and out-degree distribution respectively in order to give an exact analysis for the invocation relationship underlying software programs. The results are illustrated in **Figure 1(a)** and **Figure 1(b)**. Here the X axis represents the percentage of the total methods and the Y axis represents the percentage of the max in-degree (in **Figure 1(a)**) or max out-degree (in **Figure 1(b)**).

From the results, we observed that both the in-degree distribution and out-degree distribution can be approximately characterized by the following algebraic scaling behavior:

$$P(k) \sim k^{-r} \tag{1}$$

where k is the variable that measures the number of links at different nodes and γ is the scaling exponent. We calculate the mathematical expectation and variance for the ten programs, the scaling exponent γ in in-degree distribution (in **Figure 1(a)**) is 1.6 and the scaling exponent γ in out-degree distribution (in **Figure 1(b)**) is 2.1 ± 0.1.

Table 1. Summary of analyzed programs.

Programs	Comments	Number of methods in the program
JBPM [7]	A powerful workflow and BPM engine to createand analyze business processes.	1418
SableCC [8]	An object-oriented framework to generate compilers and interpreters in Java.	2191
JUNG [9]	A software library that provides the common and extensible language of modeling, analysis, and visualization of data.	1973
JGraph [10]	A most powerfulgraph component available for Java.	1278
Azureus [11]	A Java BitTorrent client.	12,942
Apache James [12]	Java SMTP and POP3 Mail server and NNTP News server	2127
Java PetStore [13]	A sample application to demonstrates how to use J2EE 1.3 platform.	1894
Damls_ Matcher [14]	An ontology toolkit providing semantic matchmaking for web service based on DAML-S.	337
JTB [15]	A syntax tree builder to be used with JavaCC parser generator	1126
LGMA [16]	A grid network environment demo.	298

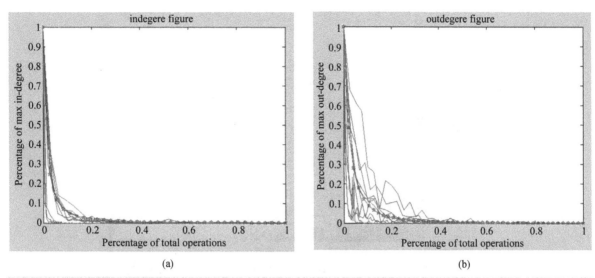

Figure 1. (a) In-degree Distribution ($\gamma = 1.6$); (b) Out-degree Distribution ($\gamma = 2.1$).

3.2. Empirical Analysis 2

The aim of this experiment is to analyze the nodes distribution in call-graph based on the result in empirical analysis 1. The result is shown in **Figure 2**. Here the X axis represents the percentage of the max in-degree and the Y axis represents the percentage of the max out-degree.

We observe in **Figure 2** that most of the nodes are located in the left-lower area, namely that both the in-degree and out-degree of those nodes are below average in-degree and out-degree. But in the right-upper area there isn't any node existed, which indicates that there existed no nodes in the call-graph which have both above average in-degree and out-degree. Another interesting observation is that there are nearly 20% nodes with the out-degree above average out-degree, whose out-going edges cover over 70% of total out-going edges, and there are nearly 13% nodes with the in-degree above average in-degree, whose in-coming edges cover over 50% of total in-coming edges.

3.3. Empirical Analysis 3

In this empirical analysis, we try to analyze the clustering degree and the separation degree of the call-graph by computing the clustering coefficient and the characteristic path length. The characteristic path length L is defined as the average over all the links in the shortest path connecting the two nodes in the call-graph, which is used to measure the typical separation between two nodes in the network (a global property). The characteristic path length L can be computed with the Dijkstra algorithm [18]. The clustering coefficient C is defined as the average fraction of pairs of neighbors of a node that are also neighbors of each other, which can measure the cliquishness of a typical neighborhood (a local property). The clustering coefficient C can be computed by the following equation:

$$C = \langle C_v \rangle_v = \left\langle \frac{2E_v}{k_v (k_v - 1)} \right\rangle \tag{2}$$

Suppose that a nodev has k_v neighbors; then the clustering coefficient C_v of a node n is given by theratio of existing links E_v between its k_v first neighbors to the potential number of such ties $k_v (k_v - 1)/2$. By averaging C_v over all nodes one arrives at the clustering coefficient C of the call-graph. We also compare these values to the random networks with the same number of nodes N. Toa given N and μ, where μ is the average number of links per node, the value of the clustering coefficient C and the characteristic path length L of random network are very small. In particular, for $N \to \infty$ and μ fixed, the characteristic path length in the largest connected component approaches the logarithmic behavior of a Moore graph,

$$L_{\text{rand}} \approx \frac{\ln N}{\ln \mu} \tag{3}$$

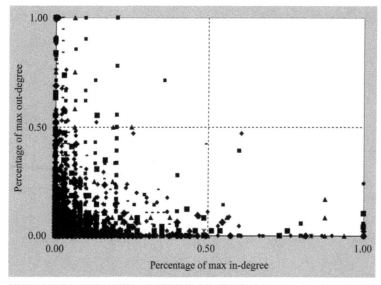

Figure 2. Distribution of in-degree and out-degree.

and the clustering coefficient approaches zero,

$$C_{\text{rand}} \approx \mu/N \tag{4}$$

The result is listed in **Table 2**. From **Table 2**, we see that the call-graph has large clustering, $C \gg C_{\text{rand}}$, and the characteristic path length, $L \approx L_{\text{rand}}$, where C_{rand} and L_{rand} are the respective statistical quantities for a random network with the same parameters N and μ.

4. Finding and Discussion

4.1. Findings

From our preliminary empirical analysis, we can propose that these call-graph generated from software programs show the properties in both scale-free network [19] [20] and small-world network [21] [22], which has already shown in many physical networks, such as cellular network [23], scientific literature [24], WWW [25] and telephone network [26].

- *Scale-free network characteristics*

Scale-free networks, including the Internet, are characterized by an uneven distribution of connectedness. Instead of the nodes of these networks having a random pattern of connections, some nodes act as "very connected" hubs, a fact that dramatically influences the way the network operates. Scale-free networks are characterized by a power-law distribution of a node's degree (*i.e.* the number of its next neighbors). From the empirical analysis 1, we have observed that the in-degree distribution and out-degree distribution of call graphs can be approximated by the power law, where the scaling exponent γ in in-degree distribution is 1.6 and the scaling exponent γ in out-degree distribution is 2.1 ± 0.1. While other scale-free network, such as WWW, Social network, Cellular network, phone call network, the scaling exponent is between 2.0 to 3.0. The power law distribution brings out the result that the structure and dynamics of scale-free network are strongly affected by a few nodes covering a great number of connections. This result is proved in empirical analysis 2. We have seen that nearly 20% nodes with the out-degree above average out-degree, whose out-going edges cover over 70% of total out-going edges, and there are nearly 13% nodes with the in-degree above average in-degree, whose in-coming edges cover over 50% of total in-coming edges. Comparing with the internet, the methods with high out-degree are very similar to hub nodes on the internet, *i.e.*, pages with many links to authorities pages, based on only the links between web pages [27]. The number of hub nodes is very small but they are very highly connected, which means deleting them is far more destructive to the whole internet.

- *Small-world network characteristics*

Roughly speaking, small-world network are those with high clustered subsets of nodes that there are a few steps away from each other. More precisely, the defining properties of small-world network rest on two structural properties: clustering and separation. In term of network topology, clustering, a local property, is used to measure the probability that two neighbors of one node are connected themselves, which is expressed by clustering coefficient. And separation, a global property measured by the characteristic path length, is used to evaluate the separation degree between two nodes in the network. In a small-world network, the characteristic path length compares to that in a random network with the same number of edges, whilst the clustering coefficient of its nodes can be orders of magnitudes larger on average. Watts [7] discusses several models for generating graphs simultaneously satisfying these two properties. From empirical analysis 3 (**Table 2**), we find that obviously the call-graph lies in these two extremes: they have large clustering, $C \gg C_{rand}$, and small characteristic path length, $L \approx L_{rand}$. Therefore, we conclude that the call-graph of software program can be described by small-world network. With the localization attribute in small-world network, we can also give some explanation to the separation of the nodes with the in-degree above average and the out-degree above average in the second empirical analysis. Because of the large clustering coefficient and the small average shortest path, the nodes in the call-graph will be concentrated in several local areas with large numbers of edges. These local areas are composed of those key nodes with in-degree above average or out-degree above average and the nodes which are directly connected to the key nodes.

4.2. Discussion

Based on scale-free network and small-world network theories, we conclude that the key methods in the software programs contain about 20% of the total programs. This result provides extremely valuable and useful information to perform the reusing action to existing applications. In SOA context, most services should be mapped to business functions. So we believe that those methods with the out-degree above average, about 20% of total methods, should be extracted as services first of all. The other methods with large in-degree should also take into consideration because they can be used as atomic services to compose complex services. Based on this conclusion, developers can "search" in existing programs quickly and reuse proper methods based on this degree distribution. Moreover, as we explained in Section 1, the connectivity properties reflect essential function and behavior of programs. So from the analysis of degree distribution, maybe we can give an appropriate measurement to "reusage quality". Similar to the Pareto Principle (also known as 20 - 80 rule), we can assume that the methods with large connections are quite possibly be connected again in future, which means these methods are more useful than the others. Then we can get a conclusion that these methods can have higher reusage quality than the other methods. In addition, most of the test cases are well known and regarded as good-design programs. The out-degree distribution in a few programs cannot be identified with a scale-free regime, which is due to the limited size of the sample and some fine difference among different programming models. So what is the best distribution model for the invocation relationship in software programs? How can we use the degree distribution for call-graph as a criterion to evaluate the design of the software programs? Can this power law distribution or the key methods ratio be used as an indicator to measure the quality of the software? These are also very interesting but critical problems in software engineering area.

Table 2. Clustering coefficient and average shortest path in call-graph and random network.

Program	N	μ	C	C_{rand}	L	L_{rand}
JBPM	1418	1.70	0.107	0.002	4.03	3.66
SableCC	2191	1.64	0.139	0.003	1.85	3.77
JUNG	1973	2.71	0.082	0.001	2.71	3.74
JGraph	1278	1.55	0.075	0.002	9.13	3.63
Azureus	12942	1.58	0.025	0.001	5.78	3.86
Apache James	2127	1.70	0.138	0.001	2.99	3.75
Java Pet Store	1894	2.81	0.104	0.001	2.29	3.73
Damls-Matcher	337	2.02	0.010	0.005	4.40	3.30
JTB	1126	2.11	0.217	0.004	10.91	3.60
LGMA	298	2.36	0.036	0.009	3.29	3.27

5. Conclusions

With the quickly changing requirements and the ever growing high cost for software programs, how to reuse legacy system asset and extend current software lifecycle has already become an urgent problem in IT field. SOA technology emerges as a promising approach. But a basic problem for SOA is how to find the similar functions and evaluate the "reusage quality" of these functions rapidly. For invocation relationship reflects the essential function and behavior of programs, in this paper we try to investigate the properties of this relationship in order to evaluate the reusable functions in existing software programs. Here we use Java programming language as the testing language, and make use of call-graph analysis technique, which is a new application for traditional static program analysis techniques. From the empirical analysis, we have found that the call-graph generated from software programs exhibited the properties both in scale-free network and small-world network: the distributions of in-degree and out-degree follow the low-power; a few nodes cover most of connections; and the call-graph shows large clustering and small characteristic path length. According to scale-free network and small-world network, we can differentiate the business methods and supportive methods in software programs. More precisely, those methods with high out-degree provide high-level business functions; and those with high in-degree provide low-level supportive functions. Based on this conclusion, developer can select appropriate functions to reuse. Especially in SOA context, those methods with high out-degree, about 20% of total methods, should be extracted as services first of all; and those methods with high in-degree, about 13% of total methods, should also be extracted as atomic services to compose complex services. Further, this connectivity may also be used as a measurement to evaluate reusage quality of different methods, which also provide strong supportive information to reuse of existing programs.

We plan to continue to study the reason why the software programs present such properties in scale-free network and small-world network. Also we want to explore how to expose and package these methods with strong connectivity as reusable services, because as programming paradigms move, we need to expose these services into new form factors too. We would also like to understand if we can use these properties to measure the quality of the design and software programs.

References

[1] Heckel, R., Correia, R., Matos, C., EI-Ramly, M., Koutsoukos, G. and Andrade, L. (2008) Software Evolution. Chapter Architectual Transformations: From Legacy to Three-Tier and Service, Springer, Berlin, 139-170.

[2] Papazoglou, M., Traverso, P., Dustdar, S. and Leymann, F. (2007) Service-Oriented Computing: State of the Art and Research Challenges. *Computer*, **40**, 38-45. http://dx.doi.org/10.1109/MC.2007.400

[3] Khadka, R., Saeidi, A., Idu, A., Hage, J. and Jansen, S. (2012) Legacy to SOA Evolution-A Systematic Literature Review. In: Ionita, A.D., Litoiu, M. and Lewis, G., Eds., *Migrating Legacy Applications*: *Challenges in Service Oriented Architecture and Cloud Computing Environments*, IGI Global, 40-71.

[4] Binkley, D. (2007) Source Code Analysis: A Roadmap. 2007 Future of Software Engineering, Minnesota, 23-25 May 2007, 104-119.

[5] Ali, K. and Lhoták, O. (2012) Application-Only Call Graph Construction. *Proceedings of the* 26*th European conference on Object-Oriented Programming*, Beijing, 11-16 June 2012, 688-712. http://dx.doi.org/10.1007/978-3-642-31057-7_30

[6] Dean, J., Grove, D. and Chambers, C. (1995) Optimization of Object-Oriented Programs Using Static Class Hierarchy Analysis. *Proceedings of the 9th European Conference on Object-Oriented Programming* (*ECOOP'95*), arhus Denmark, 7-11 August 1995, 77-101.

[7] JBPM. http://www.jboss.com/products/jbpm

[8] SableCC. http://www.sable.mcgill.ca/software/

[9] JUNG. http://jung.sourceforge.net/index.html

[10] JGraph. http://www.jgraph.com/

[11] Azureus. http://sourceforge.net/projects/azureus/

[12] Apache James. http://james.apache.org/download.cgi

[13] Java Pet Store. http://java.sun.com/developer/releases/petstore/

[14] Damls Matcher. http://kbs.cs.tu-berlin.de/ivs/Projekte/damlsmatcher/download.html

[15] JTB. http://compilers.cs.ucla.edu/jtb/

[16] LGMA. http://121.37.58.35:8080/LGMA.jar

[17] WALA. http://wala.sourceforge.net/wiki/index.php/Main_Page

[18] Rosen, K.H. (2000) Handbook of Discrete and Combinatorial Mathematics. CRC Press, Boca Raton.

[19] Barabási, A.L. and Albert, R. (1999) Emergence of Scaling in Random Networks. *Science*, **286**, 509-512. http://dx.doi.org/10.1126/science.286.5439.509

[20] Baccaletti, S., Latora, V., Moreno, Y., Chavezf, M. and Hwanga, D. (2006) Complex Networks: Structure and Dynamics. *Physics Reports*, **424**, 175-308. http://dx.doi.org/10.1016/j.physrep.2005.10.009

[21] Milgram, S. (1967) The Small World Problem. *Psychology Today*, **1**, 61-67.

[22] Watts, D.J. and Strogatz, S.H. (1998) Collective Dynamics of "Small-World" Networks. *Nature*, **393**, 440-442. http://dx.doi.org/10.1038/30918

[23] Brin, S. and Page, L. (1998) The Anatomy of a Large-Scale Hypertextual Web Search Engine. In: *Seventh International World-Wide Web Conference* (*WWW* 1998), Brisbane, 14-18 April 1998, 107-117.

[24] Karp, P.D., Riley, M., Saier, M., Paulsen, I.T., Paley, S.M. and Pellegrini-Toole, A. (2000) The EcoCyc and MetaCyc Databases. *Nucleic Acids Research*, **28**, 56-59. http://dx.doi.org/10.1093/nar/28.1.56

[25] Wasserman, S. and Faust, K. (1994) Social Network Analysis: Methods and Applications. Cambridge University, Cambridge.

[26] Broder, A., Kumar, R., Maghoul, F., Raghavan, P., Rajagopalan, S., Stata, R., *et al.* (2000) Graph Structure in the Web. *Computer Networks*, **33**, 309-320. http://dx.doi.org/10.1016/S1389-1286(00)00083-9

[27] de Moura, A.P.S., Lai, Y.C. and Motter, A.E. (2003) Signatures of Small-World and Scale-Free Properties in Large Computer Programs. *Physical Review E*, **68**, Article ID: 017102.

15

ADTEM-Architecture Design Testability Evaluation Model to Assess Software Architecture Based on Testability Metrics

Amjad Hudaib, Fawaz Al-Zaghoul, Maha Saadeh, Huda Saadeh

Department of Computer Information Systems, King Abdullah II for Information Technology Department, The University of Jordan, Amman, Jordan
Email: Ahudaib@ju.edu.jo, Fawaz@ju.edu.jo, Saade_m87@ju.edu.jo, Hsaadeh@uop.edu.jo

Abstract

Architectural design is a crucial issue in software engineering. It makes testing more effective as it contribute to carry out the testing in an early stage of the software development. To improve software testability, the software architect should consider different testability metrics while building the software architecture. The main objective of this research is to conduct an early assessment of the software architecture for the purpose of its improvement in order to make the testing process more effective. In this paper, an evaluation model to assess software architecture (Architecture Design Testability Evaluation Model (ADTEM)) is presented. ADTEM is based on two different testability metrics: cohesion and coupling. ADTEM consists of two phases: software architecture evaluation phase, and component evaluation phase. In each phase, a fuzzy inference system is used to perform the evaluation process based on cohesion and coupling testing metrics. The model is validated by using a case study: Elders Monitoring System. The experimental results show that ADTEM is efficient and gave a considerable improvement to the software testability process.

Keywords

Software Testability, Testability Metrics, Software Architecture Evaluation, Software Cohesion, Software Coupling, Fuzzy Inference System

1. Introduction

Researches show that more than forty percent of software development efforts are spent on testing, with the percentage for testing critical systems being even higher [1] [2]. Many studies have been conducted to address software testing to reduce software testing efforts by handling software testability at early stages in the software development life cycle (SDLC) [1] [3]-[6].

Software Testability (ST) is the quality attribute about the easiness degree to which system's defects can be detected at testing phase [3]. The better the testability of particular software, the lower the testing effort required in testing phase. Moreover, the earlier the testability is considered, the lower the cost of testing phase. Thus, ST should be considered at the early phases of software development life cycle (SDLC), specifically in the software architecture (SA) [2] [3].

Software Architecture (SA) provides a high level of abstraction of software represented by software components and the connections between them. Software architect should consider the testability metrics while building the SA in order to improve software testability.

In this paper, we present a model (Design Testability Evaluation Model (ADTEM)) to conduct an early evaluation of the software architecture in order to make the testing process more effective.

ADTEM assesses the SA based on cohesion and coupling testability metrics. Fuzzy inference system is used in the evaluation process to assess the testability of SA according to a proposed set of inference rules. The model is implemented and applied on a case study (Elders Monitoring System) to ensure its applicability and effectiveness. The main activities of this model are:

1. Assess software system testability based on cohesion and coupling testability metrics.
2. Assess software system components testability based on cohesion and coupling testability metrics.
3. Classify software system components based on their level of testing effort.
4. Highlight the set of components in SA that should be improved to increase ST.

The rest of this paper is organized as the following: Section 2 summarizes some related works and discusses how they differ from the proposed model. The proposed model is discussed in details in Sections 3, 4 and 5. In Section 6, the proposed model is applied on a case study. Finally, Section 7 concludes the paper and discusses possible future work.

2. Related Work

Some studies focus on assessing system testability based on object-oriented metrics derived from system design [6]-[8]. In [4] a set of object-oriented metrics are defined to assess the testability of classes in a Java system. The relationships between these metrics and the testing process are evaluated. These metrics are: depth of inheritance tree, fan out, number of children, number of fields, number of methods, response for class, and weighted methods per class. Another class based testability metrics is proposed in [5]; which detects potential testability weaknesses of a UML class diagram and points out parts of the design that need to be improved to reduce the testing effort. In addition, it proposes a methodology for improving design testability. In [6], statistical analysis techniques, mainly correlation and logistic regression, are used in order to evaluate the capability of lack of cohesion metric to predict testability of object oriented classes collected from two java software systems.

Chidamber and Kemerer (CK) proposed a set of object oriented testability metrics [8]. The CK metrics were evaluated in [7] [9] [10], to investigate the relationship between these metrics and unit testing. A CK metrics are also used as a base for a fuzzy inference system to assess the testability efforts [1] [11]-[13].

In [14], object-oriented modeling techniques are used to help the product development team on the generation of the best fitted hardware/software architecture for a given problem under given constraints. It uses object and system testability metrics. The main focus of this work is to select near-optimum clustering of methods and attributes into objects with moderate cohesion and coupling. However, this approach applied to Data Flow Diagrams (DFD) that does not express information about process hierarchy.

In this paper, the evaluation is based on coupling and cohesion testability metrics that are derived from the software architecture. Both software system and software system components are considered in the evaluation process.

3. Proposed Model

In this paper, SA evaluation model is proposed. The evaluation is based on cohesion and coupling testability metrics. The fuzzy inference system is used to perform the evaluation process based on these metrics. The proposed approach consists of two phases (as shown in **Figure 1**). In the first phase, software system architec-

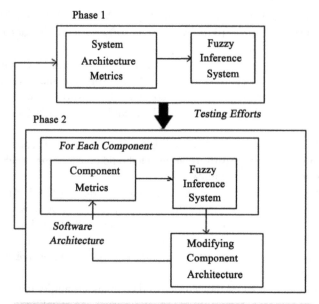

Figure 1. Proposed model.

ture is assessed according to the studied testability metrics (is discussed in Section 4). This assessment gives an indication on the required testing efforts for the entire software system. If software system required significant testing efforts, the second phase is performed to help in improving software system testability and reducing testing efforts. Moreover, in this phase, each component in the SA is assessed using the fuzzy inference system. Components' assessment specifies the testing efforts required for each component. After assessing all components, the architect can tell which component(s) required more effort for testing. Then, this component is modified to increase its testability; consequently, the whole software system testability. This process can be iterated as long as the system and components functionalities are maintained. In the following sections, the proposed model is discussed in details.

4. Software Architecture Testability Metrics

Two testability metrics: cohesion and coupling, are applied on architectural design. In the next subsections, these metrics are computed for each component as well as for the entire system.

4.1. Cohesion

The component cohesion (CCoh) is calculated for the system architecture to compute testing efforts. CCoh is the connectivity between system component, and it represents the component connectivity [3]. It is calculated by Equation (1); where the ratio between the numbers of component edges (E) and the maximum connectivity of the system (MC) is calculated [14]. The maximum connectivity corresponds to a complete graph which the total number of component is calculated by Equation (2).

$$CCoh = \left(\frac{E}{MC} \right) \tag{1}$$

$$MC = \frac{1}{2} \times n(n-1) \tag{2}$$

where, n is the number of component. If $n = 1$, then CCoh = 1.

System cohesion (SCoh) is the average of the summation of components' cohesion, and it is calculated using Equation (3).

$$SCoh = \left(\frac{\sum_{i=1}^{n} CCoh(i)}{n} \right) \tag{3}$$

where, CCoh(i) is the cohesion of the ith component.

4.2. Coupling

Coupling describes the interconnection between system components. Both component coupling (CCop) and system coupling (SCop) are considered. Component coupling can be described as the relation between component i and other components in the system as the number of fan-in and fan-out. It is calculated by Equation (4); as the ratio between the number of edges interconnecting component i and the total number of edges within system architecture [14].

$$CCop = \frac{\sum_{i=1}^{n-1} e(i)}{E} \tag{4}$$

where n is the number of components, $e(i)$ is the number of edges of component i, and E is the total number of edges in the system architecture.

In addition, component coupling describes the component dependence (CDep), which is the number of components that depend on component i. CDep is calculated using Equation (5).

$$CDep = \frac{\text{The ith component dependency tree}}{n} \tag{5}$$

where the ith component of dependency tree is the tree rooted at component i. All other components that depend on component i are its children and its descendants.

Figure 2 shows the dependency tree in which **Figure 2(a)** presents the original architecture, and **Figure 2(b)** presents the corresponding dependency tree for component A.

System coupling can be described as the Cumulative Component Dependency (CCD) [15] which calculates the dependences for all components in the system using Equation (6).

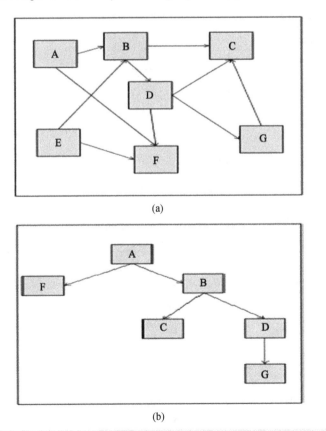

(a)

(b)

Figure 2. An example on dependency tree. (a) The original architecture; (b) The corresponding dependency tree for component A.

$$CCD = \frac{\sum_{i=1}^{n} \text{The ith component dependency tree}}{n^2} \qquad (6)$$

The interconnection between system components (SCop) is calculated by Equation (7).

$$SCop = \frac{\sum_{i=1}^{n-1} CCop}{n} \qquad (7)$$

where n is the number of components in the system.

5. Fuzzy Inference System

The Mamdani fuzzy inference system is used to control the model and combine it with a set of linguistic control rules. The Mamdani uses three inputs and one output inference system. Mamdani inference system consists of three steps represented in **Figure 3**. In input fuzzification step, the value of each input variable is mapped to a fuzzy value according to the corresponding membership function. The second step is rules evaluation and aggregation. In this step, input fuzzy values are evaluated according to the inference rules which are listed in **Table 1**, where values: L is Low; M is Moderate; H is High; VL is Very Low; and VH is Very High. Then, all matched rules are aggregated to generate the fuzzy output value. The third step is the defuzzification step where the output is mapped from fuzzy domain to an output value.

The first input variable is the cohesion (Coh). It could be CCoh or SCoh. It has three values; low, medium, and high, each has a membership function illustrated in **Figure 4(a)**. The second input variable is the coupling (Cop), which could be CCop or SCop. Cop has three values; low, medium, and high. The corresponding membership functions are illustrated in **Figure 4(b)**. Finally, the third input variable is the dependency (Dep), which could be CDep or SDep. Dep is also has low, medium, and high values. The corresponding membership function

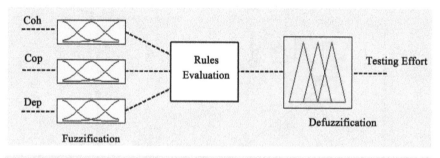

Figure 3. Fuzzy inference system steps.

Table 1. Fuzzy inference rules. Output values: L is Low; M is Moderate; H is High; VL is Very Low; and VH is Very High.

Coh	Cop	Dep		
		Low	Moderate	High
Low	Low	M	M	H
Medium	Low	L	M	M
High	Low	VL	VL	L
Low	Medium	M	H	VH
Medium	Medium	M	H	H
High	Medium	VL	M	H
Low	High	H	VH	VH
Medium	High	M	H	H
High	High	L	H	H

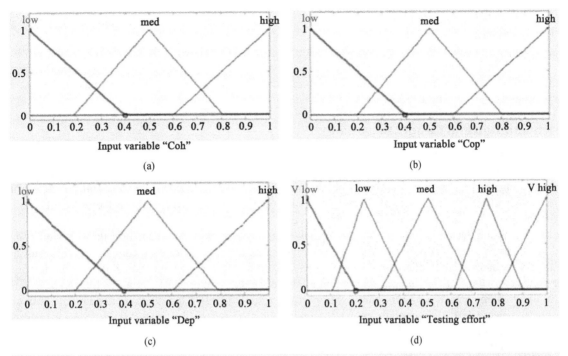

Figure 4. Membership function for (a) Coh; (b) Cop; (c) Dep input variables; and (d) testing effort output variable.

is illustrated in **Figure 4(c)**. The range of membership functions for all input variables is between 0 and 1. The membership functions are uniformly distributed over the range. The output from the fuzzy inference is the testing effort. This variable has five values; very low, low, medium, high, and very high. The membership functions for these values are illustrated in **Figure 4(d)**. The higher the value of this variable, the worse the testing effort required to test the system/component. As for input variables, the membership functions are uniformly distributed over the range 0 to 1.

Proposed Model Phases

The proposed model consists of two phases; system assessment and components assessment. In this section these phases are discussed in details.

- **Phase One: System Assessment**

In this phase, the system architecture is assessed based on SCoh, SCop, and CCD. These metrics are calculated using equations 2, 6, and 5 respectively. The calculated values are entered to the fuzzy inference as Coh, Cop, and Dep respectively. The output from the fuzzy inference is the effort required for system testing. If this value is significant, phase two can be performed to reduce this value as much as possible.

- **Phase Two: Components Assessment**

The purpose of this phase is to classify system components into different classes according to its testing efforts. This will direct the architect to the group of components that require a high testing effort. Then, he/she can modify them to decrease their required testing effort which means increasing the system testability. To assess components testability, component CCoh, CCop, and CDep are calculated according to Equations (1), (3), and (4) respectively. These values are evaluated using the fuzzy inference to know the testing efforts for that component. This process is repeated for each component. At the end of this phase, components are classified according to their testing efforts.

6. Case Study: Elders Monitoring System

The model has been tested using fall detection-response subsystem from Helping Our People Easily (HOPE) [16] [17]. The subsystem works as follows: Once a fall is detected, the network availability (cellular or Wi-Fi) is checked. For displaying user location in map view, the location co-ordinates are scanned and sent to one of map services using a Java Script Object Notation (JSON) query to retrieve and detect the location. If there is no network available, then a recently cached location is used and GPS-based positioning scanning is stopped to prevent battery drainage.

For sending out an alert, the value of network status is checked. If cell network is available, then a call is dialed. In case there is no cell network but Wi-Fi network is available, then a message is sent out with the user location. For the worst case scenario of no networks being available, the alarm signals for help nearby. The architecture design is shown in **Figure 5**.

Implementation and Results Discussion

The model was implemented using Matlab software and applied on the elders monitoring system architecture. As illustrated in **Figure 5**, the architecture consists of seven components; four of them have several modules. When applying the proposed model, firstly, phase one will evaluate the testability of the entire system. Since system testing effort that results from phase one is moderate, phase two will evaluate the testability of each component.

Table 2 lists the evaluation results for elders monitoring system architecture. It lists the cohesion and the coupling values for each phase. In addition, it shows the testing effort (TE) for each component that result from the fuzzy inference system. Notice that, three components out of seven have high testing effort (the highlighted components: *network scanner*, *power source* and *alert transmitter* component). As a result, the architect can modify these components in order to reduce entire system testing efforts. This is can be done by increasing the cohesion and decreasing the coupling of the components that required high testing efforts. As a result, the cohesion of alert trasmitter component is increased by connecting call dialer and message transmitter modules to alert raiser module.

By this modification, the coupling between call dialer and alert switcher, and message transmitter and alert switcher are eliminated. Thus, reducing the total coupling of alert transmitter component. Another modification, to increase the cohesion of power resource component is to separate the charger module into different component since it does not have any connection with battery module or any other external modules. **Figure 6** shows the architecture after the modifications. The architecture is assessed again to evaluate the modification results.

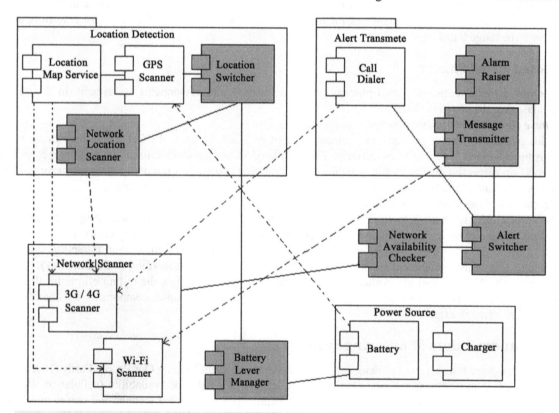

Figure 5. Elders monitoring system architecture.

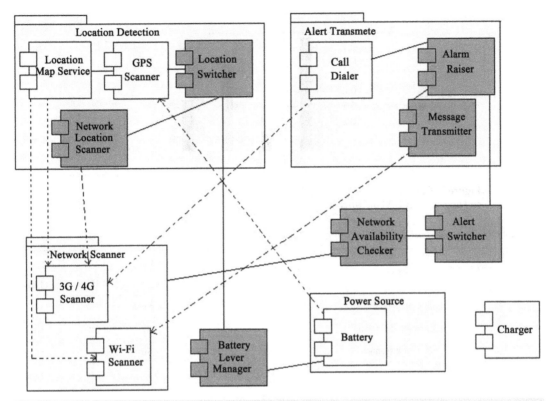

Figure 6. Elders monitoring system architecture after modifications.

Table 2. The evaluation results for elders monitoring system architecture before modification.

Phase 1		SCoh	SCop	CCD	TE	
	System	0.5	0.28	0.75	0.60	Moderate
	Component	CCoh	CCop	CDep	TE*	
	Location detection	0.5	0.30	1.0	0.62	Moderate
	Network scanner	0.0	0.35	0.57	0.68	High
	Power source	0.0	0.15	1.0	0.75	High
Phase 2	Alert transmitter	0.0	0.4	0.57	0.75	High
	Battery level manager	1.0	0.2	1.0	0.26	Low
	Network availability checker	1.0	0.2	0.57	0.09	Very Low
	Alert switcher	1.0	0.40	0.57	0.50	Moderate

The results are listed in **Table 3**. **Table 4** expresses the percentage values of the testing efforts improvement, where "-" means the decreasing of testing efforts.

Table 4 shows that the system testing effort is reduced by 42% since the testing effort for *power source* and *alert transmitter* is reduced by 67% and 35% respectively.

Figure 7 shows the comparison between system cohesion, coupling, dependency, and testing efforts before (called System_B) and after (called System_A) the architecture modifications. As illustrated in **Figure 7**, SCoh increases after architecture modifications. In addition, SCop and CDD is reduced by 14% and 21% respectively. These enhancements results in reducing system testing effort by 42%.

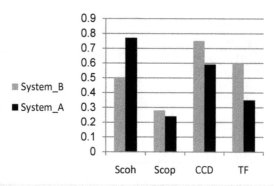

Figure 7. Comparison between system testability metrics before (System_B) and after (System_A) modification.

Table 3. The evaluation results for elders monitoring system architecture after modification.

Phase 1	System	SCoh	SCop	CCD	TE*	
		0.77	0.24	0.59	0.35	Low
	Component	CCoh	CCop	Cdep	TE*	
	Location detection	0.50	0.37	0.87	0.71	High
	Network scanner	0.0	0.43	0.50	0.75	High
	Power source	1.0	0.18	0.87	0.25	Low
Phase 2	Alert transmitter	0.66	0.25	0.50	0.49	Moderate
	Battery level manager	1.0	0.25	0.87	0.42	Moderate
	Network availability checker	1.0	0.25	0.50	0.29	Low
	Alert switcher	1.0	0.25	0.50	0.29	Low
	Charger	1.0	0.0	0.12	0.07	Very Low

Table 4. The percentage values of the testing efforts improvement. *Testing Effort, "-" means decreased.

Phase 1	System	SCoh	SCop	CCD	TE*
		54	−14	−21	−42
		CCoh	CCop	CDep	TE*
	Location detection	0	23	−13	15
	Network scanner	0	23	−12	10
	Power source	100	20	−13	−67
Phase 2	Alert transmitter	66	−38	−12	−35
	Battery level manager	0	25	−13	62
	Network availability checker	0	25	−12	222
	Alert switcher	0	−38	−12	−42
	Charger				

7. Conclusion and Future Work

In this paper, we proposed an evaluation model to assess software architecture (Architecture Design Testability Evaluation Model (ADTEM)) based on testability metrics. The model directs software architects on how to improve software architecture testability. A fuzzy inference system was built to assess both software and component testability according to inference rules. The model was implemented and applied on a case study. The results showed that the model is applicable and efficient and it can improve the testability efforts. As future works, we propose an adjustment fuzzy rules and membership functions based on testable architectures.

References

[1]   Dahiya, S., Bhutani, S., Oberoi, A. and Singh, M. (2012) A Fuzzy Model for Object Oriented Testability and Its Performance. *International Journal of Information and Technology and Knowledge Management*, **5**, 484-489.

[2]   Sommerville, I. (2011) Software Engineering. 9th Edition, Pearson.

[3]   Evaluating Software Architecture (2008) Software Architecture Book, Advanced Topics in Science and Technology in China, 221-273.

[4]   Bruntink, M. (2003) Testability of Object-Oriented Systems: A Metrics-Based Approach. Master Thesis, Universiteit van Amsterdam, Amsterdam.

[5]   Baudry, B., Traon, Y.L. and Sunyé, G. (2002) Testability Analysis of a UML Class Diagram. *Proceedings of the 8th IEEE Symposium on Software Metrics*.

[6]   Badri, L., Badri, M. and Tour, F. (2011) An Empirical Analysis of Lack of Cohesion Metrics for Predicting Testability of Classes. *International Journal of Software Engineering and Its Applications*, **5**, 69-85.

[7]   Badri, M. and Toure, F. (2012) Empirical Analysis of Object-Oriented Design Metrics for Predicting Unit Testing Effort of Classes. *Journal of Software Engineering and Applications*, **5**, 513-526.

[8]   Chidamber, S.R. and Kemerer, C.F. (1994) A Metrics Suite for Object Oriented Design. *IEEE Transactions on Software Engineering*, **20**, 476-493. http://dx.doi.org/10.1109/32.295895

[9]   Magiel, B. and Deursen, A.V. (2004) Predicting Class Testability Using Object-Oriented Metrics. *Proceedings of the 4th IEEE International Workshop on Source Code Analysis and Manipulation*, 136-145.

[10] Singh, Y. and Saha, A. (2008) A Metric-Based Approach to Assess Class Testability. *Agile Processes in Software Engineering and Extreme Programming Lecture Notes in Business Information Processing*, **9**, 224-225. http://dx.doi.org/10.1007/978-3-540-68255-4_30

[11] Gupta, V., Aggarwal, K. and Singh, Y. (2005) A Fuzzy Approach for Integrated Measure of Object-Oriented Software Testability. *Journal of Computer Science, Science Publications*, **1**, 276-282.

[12] Ahuja, H.K. and Kumar, R. (2012) Fuzzy Logic Driven Testability Measurement for an Object Oriented System. http://dspace.thapar.edu:8080/dspace/handle/10266/2064?mode=full&submit_simple=Show+full+item+record

[13] Kaur, N. (2011) A Fuzzy Logic Approach to Measure the Precise Testability Index of Software. *International Journal of Engineering Science and Technology*, **3**, 857-865.

[14] Dias, O.P. (1999) Metrics and Criteria for Quality Assessment of Testable Hw/Sw Systems Architectures. *Journal of Electronic Testing: Theory and Applications*, **14**, 149-158. http://dx.doi.org/10.1023/A:1008374027849

[15] Cumulative Component Dependency (CCD) (2013) http://baruzzo.wordpress.com/2009/08/22/how-testable-is-a-software-architecture/

[16] Helping Our People Easily (HOPE) (2013) http://www.utdallas.edu/~rym071000

[17] Chung, L., Lim, S., Chung, Y., Mehta, R.Y. and Chembra, A.B. (2010) AAC for Elderly People with Hearing, Speech or Memory Loss Due to Aging. Proceedings of the 25th *Annual International Technology & Persons with Disabilities Conference*, San Diego.

The Research of Event Detection and Characterization Technology of Ticket Gate in the Urban Rapid Rail Transit

Yunfeng Hou, Chaoli Wang*, Yunfeng Ji

Department of Control Science and Engineering, University of Shanghai for Science and Technology, Shanghai, China

Email: houyunfeng0930@163.com, *clclwang@126.com, jyf123456789@126.com

Abstract

Making events recognition more reliable under complex environment is one of the most important challenges for the intelligent recognition system to the ticket gate in the urban rapid rail transit. The motion objects passing through the ticket gate could be described as a series of moving sequences got by sensors that located in the walkway side of the ticket gate. This paper presents a robust method to detect some classes of events of ticket gate in the urban rapid rail transit. Diffused reflectance infrared sensors are used to collect signals. In this paper, the motion objects are here referred to passenger(s) or (and) luggage(s), for which are of frequent occurrences in the ticket gate of the urban railway traffic. Specifically, this paper makes two main contributions: 1) The proposed recognition method could be used to identify several events, including the event of one person passing through the ticket gate, the event of two consecutive passengers passing through the ticket gate without a big gap between them, and the event of a passenger walking through the ticket gate pulling a suitcase; 2) The moving time sequence matrix is transformed into a one-dimensional vector as the feature descriptor. Deep learning (DL), back propagation neural network (BP), and support vector machine (SVM) are applied to recognize the events respectively. BP has been proved to have a higher recognition rate compared to other methods. In order to implement the three algorithms, a data set is built which includes 150 samples of all kinds of events from the practical tests. Experiments show the effectiveness of the proposed methods.

Keywords

Intelligent Recognition, Ticket Gate, Motion Objects, Infrared Sensors, Time Sequence

---

*Corresponding author.

1. Introduction

The automatic fare collection (AFC) system has received a great deal of attention from the industrial and scientific communities over the past several decades owing to its wide range of applications in preventing stealing a ride, access control, law enforcement, etc. Obviously, it is a significant value study in the intelligent recognition system. Especially in the urban rapid rail transit, the fare evasion phenomenon is coming to rampant. The main difficulty of recognition of these events is that there are many ways for passengers to pass through the walkway of the ticket gate. For example, people can walk through the walkway without anything or pulling a suitcase; two walking passengers also can pass through the walkway closely to each other for a fare evasion. However, as far as I know, few researches have been reported on this problem. Since 1970s, Samsung [1], Gun Nebo [2], Nippon Signal [3], and Omron [4] have successively set up their AFC systems. However, intelligence recognition system was hardly found in their product, or merely equipped with few simple recognition functions. Quri [5] presented a recognition algorithm based on event driven. In that paper, the method combines event recognition technology, human gait recognition technology and human body contour recognition technology. But this method has somewhat difficulty in dealing with the transit without a big gap between two walking passengers. The relatively low recognition rate (85%) is also far from the requirement of market. In order to improve the recognition rate, a novel method is proposed.

This paper focuses mainly on the issue of a robust recognition to several events of ticket gate in the urban rapid rail transit. According to the actual conditions, as shown in **Figure 1**, three types of events are discussed.

The overall process of recognition system can be viewed as a pipeline as shown in **Figure 2**. A single-chip microcomputer is used to collect signals sent by infrared sensors and communicate with an upper computer. During motion objects passing through the walkway, the measurement data from infrared sensors would be combined into a vector according to time order, as shown in **Figure 5**. The vector as the feature descriptor makes the characteristics of events more manifest. All feature descriptors of different events are used to train the

(a) One person

(b) With handbag and knapsack

(c) Two consecutive people

(d) With a suitcase

Figure 1. Events defined in this paper: (a) One person without anything walking through the ticket gate; (b) One person with handbag and knapsack walking through the ticket gate; (c) Two consecutive passengers passing through the ticket gate without a big gap between them; (d) A passenger walking through the ticket gate pulling a suitcase. Note that situations described in (a) and (b) are defined into event of one person passing through the ticket gate in this paper; situation described in (c) is defined into event of two consecutive passengers passing through the ticket gate without a big gap between them; situation described in (d) is defined into event of a passenger walking through the ticket gate pulling a suitcase.

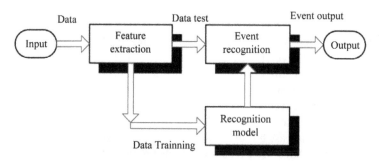

Figure 2. The overall process of recognition system.

recognition model. Finally, these recognition models are evaluated on the task of events recognition of ticket gate. Various methods [6]-[8] are used to train the recognition model.

Tripod turnstile gate, slide-stile gate and flap-stile gate are the three main types of ticket gates in the market. For slide-stile gate is often used as the preferred ticket gate, in this paper, it will be selected as the main research object. The rest of the paper is organized as follows. Section 2 introduces a topological graph of the sensors-array scheme. Section 3 presents a data preprocessing process. Section 4 is the design of recognition. Section 5 shows experimental results, and Section 6 is a conclusion.

2. Topological Graph of Sensors-Array

Eight diffuse reflectance infrared sensors are used to detect the movement sequence of the motion objects in the recognition system. All of the sensors are arranged in an array which we call sensors-array. For every diffuse reflectance infrared sensor, its emitter is integrated with its receiver. When no motion objects detected by a sensor, its output value is 1 (high level signal), otherwise, its output value is 0 (low level signal).

All of the diffuse reflectance infrared sensors are situated in the walkway side of the ticket gate in this paper. As shown in **Figure 3**, the walkway of the ticket gate is divided into three zones, which are defined as import area, gait detection area, export area.

Import area and Export area are used for charging and installing the roller brake respectively, witches are not within the scope of this article.

Gait detection area, No. 1 to No. 8 sensors are 15 cm off the ground, which are used to detect shanks of human body. **Figures 4(a)-(c)** describe the movement sequences of one passenger passing through the walk gate, two consecutive passengers passing through the ticket gate without a big gap between them, and one passenger walking through the walkway pulling a suitcase got by No. 1 to No. 8 sensors respectively, which show a big difference both in data representation and data length. As a whole, the data of above event types show a good sense of distinction.

3. Data Preprocessing

In order to improve the recognition rate, it is very important to maintain the integrity of the data. During one passenger passing through the walkway, according to **Figure 4**, the working stage of No. 1 to No. 8 infrared sensors would be represented by a matrix which consists of n rows and 8 columns (every row describes eight sensors' working stage at a point in certain time; every column describes a sensor's working stage at different points in time). Then we translate the matrix into a vector which contains $8 \times n$ elements as the input vector for the event representation, as shown in **Figure 5**. At last, we will unify the input vector to the same length as training vector.

4. Event Feature

In this section, machine learning is used to identify events. For a good recognition, the machine learning model must be robust and efficient. Robustness refers to insensitivity to slight difference within the same event. Efficiency refers to a high identification to different events. Although many machine learning models can be used for event identification, the challenge of identifying events is finding a robust and efficient method. In this paper, an extensive set of publicly available machine learning models, deep learning (DL), back propagation neural

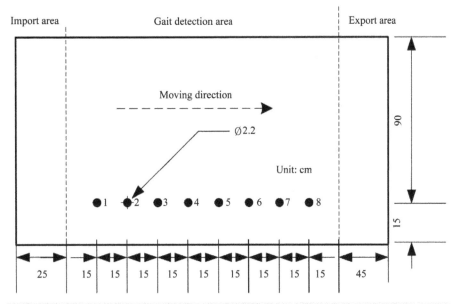

Figure 3. Location of diffuse reflectance infrared sensors.

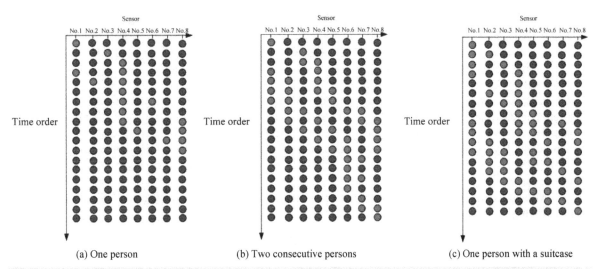

(a) One person   (b) Two consecutive persons   (c) One person with a suitcase

Figure 4. Movement sequences of different events defined in this paper got by No. 1 to No. 8 sensors. Red color means sensor detects a motion object, blue color means sensor detects nothing. (a) Movement sequences of one passenger passing through the walk gate got by No. 1 to No. 8 sensors; (b) Movement sequences of two consecutive walking passengers passing through the walk gate without a big gap between them got by No. 1 to No. 8 sensors; (c) Movement sequences of a passenger walking through the walkway pulling a suitcase got by No. 1 to No. 8 sensors.

network (BP), support vector machine (SVM), are used to evaluate the effectiveness of solving recognition problem respectively. Feature descriptor described in the previous section is put into the learning models as the input value.

4.1. Deep Learning (DL)

Recently, deep learning (DL) has been the leading technique to learn good information representation that exhibits similar characteristics to that of the mammal brain. It has gained significant interest for building hierarchical representations from unlabeled data. A deep architecture consists of feature detector units arranged in multiple layers: lower layers detect simple features and feed into higher layers, which in turn detect more complex features. In particular, deep belief network (DBN), the most popular approach of deep learning, is a multilayer generative model in which each layer encodes statistical dependencies among the units in the layer below, and it

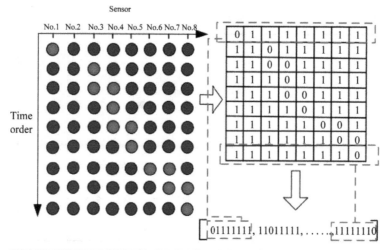

Figure 5. Process of data preprocessing.

can be trained to maximize (approximately) the likelihood of its training data. A great deal of deep belief network (DBN) models have been proposed so far [6] [9]-[11]. Particularly, the model proposed by Hinton *et al.* is a breakthrough for training deep networks. It can be viewed as a composition of simple learning modules, each of which is a Restricted Boltzmann Machine (RBM) that contains a layer of visible units representing observable data and a layer of hidden units learned to represent features that capture higher-order correlations in the data. Today, including machine transliteration [12], hand-written character recognition [9] [13], object recognition [14], various visual data analysis tasks [15]-[17] etc., DL have been successfully applied to above applications.

Restricted Boltzmann Machine (RBM) [13] [18]-[20] is a bipartite, two-layer, undirected graphical model consisting of a set of (binary or real-valued) visible units (random variables) $\mathbf{v}$ of dimension D representing observable data, and a set of binary hidden units (random variables) $\mathbf{h}$ of dimension K learned to represent features that capture higher-order correlations in the observable data. Hidden units $h_j \in \mathbf{h}$ are independent of each other when conditioning on $\mathbf{v}$ since there are no direct connections between hidden units. Similarly, the visible units $v_i \in \mathbf{v}$ are also independent of each other when conditioning on $\mathbf{h}$. **Figure 6** illustrates the undirected graphical model of an RBM.

RBM is an energy-based model. We define the energy of joint distribution over the visible and hidden units by $E(\mathbf{v}, \mathbf{h})$.

$$E(\mathbf{v}, \mathbf{h}) = -\sum_{i=1}^{D}\sum_{j=1}^{K} v_i w_{ij} h_j - \sum_{j=1}^{K} b_j h_j - \sum_{i=1}^{D} c_i v_i \tag{1}$$

where w_{ij} is the weight between the visible units v_i and hidden units h_j, c_i and b_j are respectively visible and hidden units bias.

$$p(\mathbf{v}, \mathbf{h}) = \frac{1}{Z} e^{-E(\mathbf{v}, \mathbf{h})} \tag{2}$$

$$Z = \sum_{v,h} e^{-E(\mathbf{v}, \mathbf{h})} \tag{3}$$

where Z is normalized factor, also known as the partition function.

The probability that the network assigns to a visible vector $\mathbf{v}$ (training vector), is given by summing over all possible hidden vectors:

$$p(\mathbf{v}) = \frac{1}{Z} \sum_{h} e^{-E(\mathbf{v}, \mathbf{h})}. \tag{4}$$

We can raise the probability that the network assigns to a training vector by adjusting the weights and bias to lower the energy of the training vector. The derivative of the log probability of a training vector with respect to a weight is surprisingly simple.

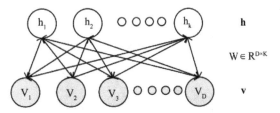

Figure 6. Undirected graphical model of an RBM.

$$\frac{\partial \log p(\mathbf{v})}{\partial w_{ij}} = \langle v_i h_j \rangle_{\text{data}} - \langle v_i h_j \rangle_{\text{model}} \tag{5}$$

where the angle brackets represent expectations under the distribution specified by the subscript that follows. $\langle \rangle_{\text{data}}$ is the distribution of the training data, and $\langle \rangle_{\text{model}}$ is the equilibrium distribution defined by RBM. We can get a very simple learning rule for performing stochastic steepest ascent in the log probability of the training data:

$$\Delta w_{ij} = \xi \left(\langle v_i h_j \rangle_{\text{data}} - \langle v_i h_j \rangle_{\text{model}} \right) \tag{6}$$

where ξ denotes a learning rate.

DBN is a probabilistic generative model that composed by several layers of hidden variables, in which each layer captures high-order-correlations between the activities of hidden features in the layer below. DBN is mainly made up by Restricted Boltzmann Machine (RBM) and two adjacent layers of DBN including a RBM, as shown in **Figure 7**; the DBN is composed by three hidden layers $\mathbf{h}^1$, $\mathbf{h}^2$ and $\mathbf{h}^3$, $\mathbf{v}$ is the input layer.

A marked feature of DBN is that to learn a deep hierarchical model we should repeat a greedy layer by layer unsupervised training for several times. In 2006, a fast, unsupervised learning algorithm for these deep networks is proposed by Hinton *et al.* [9].

4.2. Back Propagation Neural Network (BP)

BP network is basically a gradient decent algorithm designed to minimize the error function in the weights space. During training of the neural network, weights are adjusted to decrease the total error. In principle, it has been proved that any continuous function can be uniformly approximated by BP network model with one or more hidden layer. However, it is not easy to choose the appropriate number of hidden layers because currently there is no definite rule to determine it. Using too many hidden layers maybe lead to local optimum and increase training time. But using too few hidden layers impairs the neural network and prevents the correctly mapping of inputs and outputs. In the next section, we will test the performance of BP with different numbers of hidden layers.

4.3. Support Vector Machine (SVM)

Support vector machine (SVM) is a technique developed by Vapnik (1999) [7], which is used to train the classifiers according to structural risk minimizations concept. SVM has been used in various classification problems and pattern recognition field since 90s.

Data can be classified into two classes (positive and negative) with SVM. Assuming a group of points that belong to these two classes, SVM description can be referred as follows: a SVM establishes the hyper plane which allocates the majority of points of the same class in the same side, which maximizes the distance between the two classes to the hyper plane. Define the optimal separating hyper plane as the distance between one class and a hyper plane which is the small distance between the hyper plane and the other points of the same class. The hyper plane created by SVM contains a subset of points of these two classes, which we call support vectors.

Assuming training set $\{\mathbf{x}_i, y_i\}$ $i = 1, \cdots, k$, where $\mathbf{x} \in \Re^N$ is an N-dimensional input data and $y \in \{-1, +1\}$ is the required classification.

The goal is to estimate a function with the training set that classifies the pairs $\{\mathbf{x}_i, y_i\}$ which haven't been correctly used yet. The optimal hyperplane is defined by:

$$\mathbf{w}x + b = 0 \tag{7}$$

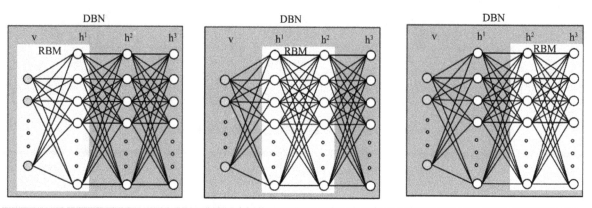

Figure 7. Deep belief network with three hidden layers h^1, h^2 and h^3.

where $\mathbf{w} \in R^n$ is the weight vector and b is the bias. A vector $\mathbf{x}_i$ that labeled as the same class y_i must satisfy the follow equation:

$$y_i\left(\mathbf{w}\mathbf{x}_i + b\right) - 1 \geq 0 \tag{8}$$

where $\mathbf{w}$ is normal to the hyperplane. The Euclidian distance between these points over the separating margin and the hyperplane is determined by Equation (9).

$$\frac{y_i\left(\mathbf{w}\mathbf{x}_i + b\right)}{\|\mathbf{w}\|} = \frac{1}{\|\mathbf{w}\|} \tag{9}$$

Thus, for maximizing the separating hyperplane, we should minimize $\|\mathbf{w}\|$. The following equation can be established with Lagrange multipliers theory.

$$J\left(\mathbf{w}, b, \alpha\right) = \frac{1}{2}\|\mathbf{w}\|^2 - \sum_{i=1}^{N} \alpha_i \left[y_i\left(\mathbf{w}\mathbf{x}_i + b\right) - 1 \right] \tag{10}$$

where α_i is the Lagrange multiplier. The optimization problem solution is obtained through minimization of $J\left(\mathbf{w}, b, \alpha\right)$.

For nonlinear decision surfaces, the input data generated by machines in a higher dimension space tends to decrease computational efforts of the support machines. By introducing variables that enlarge the margin by relaxing the linear SVM, to allow a few misclassification errors in the margin, and penalize these errors through penalty parameter C in Equation (12), the not linearly separated problem can be solved. These changes allow that the Equation (8) can be violated, or:

$$y_i\left(\mathbf{w}\mathbf{x}_i + b\right) + \zeta_i \geq 1 \tag{11}$$

where ζ_i is non-negative variables associated to each training vector. The cost function can be given by Equation (12).

$$\phi\left(\mathbf{w}, \zeta\right) = \frac{1}{2}\|\mathbf{w}\| + C\sum_{j=1}^{N} \zeta_j \tag{12}$$

where C is the training parameter that decides the balance between the training error and model complexity, which is known by regulating constant.

A detailed discussion of the computational aspects of SVM can be found in [21] and [22], with many examples also can be found in [23]-[26].

5. Experiment

We will illustrate the effectiveness of the method by presenting experiments on three events data got by sensors 1 - 8. The database used in our experiment was constructed by 150 samples (with 50 samples per class). 90 samples (with 30 samples per class) are used to train DL, BP, SVM and 60 samples (with 20 samples per class) are used to test recognition rates.

5.1. Experimental Settings

In this paper, deep learning (DL), neural networks based on error back-propagation algorithms (BP), support vector machine (SVM), are used for learning the data respectively. Events of one person with a bag or without anything walking through the ticket gate, two consecutive passengers passing through the ticket gate without a big gap between them, a passenger walking through the ticket gate pulling a suitcase are defined as event 1, event 2, and event 3. The definition of all events refers to the assembly of event 1, event 2 and event 3. The running environment of experiments is Matlab 2013a.

5.2. Results for Events Classification

To aid comparison with previous work, **Table 1** summarizes the average recognition rates of the recognition system and Quri's recognition system at a false acceptance rate of 0.1%. Note that the method gives perfect recognition results for database build in this paper: DL gives 89.2%, BP gives 92.5%, and SVM gives 90.0%. While, limited by the fixed sensors' position, method proposed in Quri's paper gets a relatively low recognition rate with 85.0%.

Figure 8 illustrates the recognition performance of recognition manners (DL, BP, SVM) referred in this paper. BP gives better performance than DL, SVM overall. All recognition manners got a 100% recognition rate to event of one person walking through the ticket gate. While all recognition manners got a relatively low recognition rate to event of two consecutive passengers passing through the ticket gate without any gap between them. While, BP shows a higher recognition rates both in events 3 (100%) and all events referred in this paper (92%), with recognition rates of DL and SVM 90%, 89% and 90%, 90%.

Table 1. Average recognition rates obtained with using different recognition methods on database built in this paper. 90 samples (30 samples per class) are used for training and 60 samples (20 samples per class) are used for test. Note that recognition of Quri's methods is got with his recognition scheme and database defined in his paper.

Method	Average recognition rates			
	Test samples/train samples	Min	Max	Average
Quri [1]	-	-	-	0.850
DL	60/90	0.833	0.900	0.892
BP	60/90	0.916	0.933	0.925
SVM	60/90	0.900	0.900	0.900

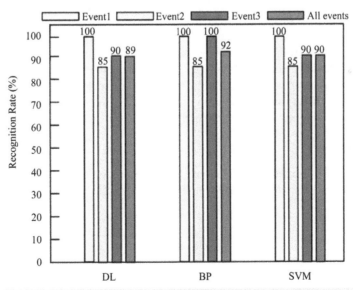

Figure 8. Recognition performance of methods proposed.

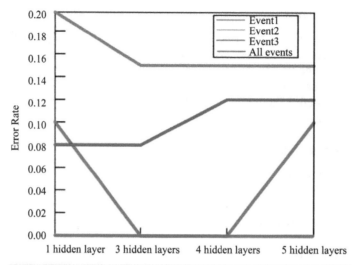

Figure 9. Recognition error rates of BP.

In order to have an estimate of the performance of BP with different numbers of hidden layers, we test the recognition rate of BP with 1, 3, 4, 5 hidden layers. The results shown in **Figure 9** are average recognition error rate of BP with 1, 3, 4, 5 hidden layers respectively. The results show that the proposed BP models with 3 hidden layers reach a relatively satisfactory recognition rates. In this paper, the BP model contains three hidden layers by default. In theory, the more hidden layer neurons are often with more high recognition accuracy. But too much of the hidden layer neurons can greatly increase the training time, at the same time, the increase of the hidden layer neurons will cause the loss of the tolerance of the network. So the numbers of neurons in 3 hidden layers are empirically selected as 500, 400, and 100 respectively in this paper.

6. Conclusions

This paper refers to the event recognition technology on the ticket gate in the urban railway traffic. We put forward a recognition manner according to the different moving sequence of various events. The main contributions are as follows: 1) We integrate the moving sequence matrix to a one-dimensional vector as the feature descriptor. Several recognition algorithms (DL, BP, and SVM) are applied to recognize the events. It has been found that BP has a higher recognition rate compared to other methods with 3 hidden layers. 2) Several events that often happened in the scene of the ticket gate could be identified effectively in this paper. Experiments proved method proposed in this paper have a higher recognition rate.

Eight sensors are used in the senor-array; the hardware of the intelligent recognition system is very simple and inexpensive. Experiments show that the method gets a satisfactory result.

Moreover, we just provide a new insight into the role of machine learning played in dealing with events recognition of ticket gate in the urban railway station. More events should be defined in the follow-up study. Also, more high recognition accuracy is required in the reality need of engineering. Feature selection or recognition system remains an interesting and important research topic in events recognition.

Acknowledgements

This paper was partially supported by the National Natural Science Foundation (61374040), the Hujiang Foundation of China (C14002), Scientific Innovation Program (13ZZ115), and Graduate Innovation Program of Shanghai (54-13-302-102).

References

[1]   http://www.samsungsds.com.cn

[2]   http://www.gunneboentrance.com

[3]   http://www.signal.co.jp

[4]   http://www.omron.com

[5]   Qu, R., Bao, Y.-R. and Ren, C.-M. (2007) The Study of Event Recognition Technology of Ticket Gate in Urban Railway Traffic. *Sensors and Actuators A: Physical*, **134**, 641-649. http://dx.doi.org/10.1016/j.sna.2006.06.053

[6]   Hinton, G.E. and Salakhutdinov, R.R. (2006) Reducing the Dimensionality of Data with Neural Networks. *Science*, **313**, 504-507. http://dx.doi.org/10.1126/science.1127647

[7]   Vapnik, V. (1999) Support Vector Method for Function Estimation. US Patent 5,950,146. Google Patents.

[8]   Hornik, K., Stinchcombe, M. and White, H. (1989) Multilayer Feed forward Networks Are Universal Approximators. *Neural Networks*, **2**, 359-366. http://dx.doi.org/10.1016/0893-6080(89)90020-8

[9]   Hinton, G.E., Osindero, S. and Teh, Y. (2006) A Fast Learning Algorithm for Deep Belief Nets. *Neural Computation*, **18**, 1527-1554. http://dx.doi.org/10.1162/neco.2006.18.7.1527

[10] Hinton, G. (2012) A Practical Guide to Training Restricted Boltzmann Machines. *Momentum*, **9**, 599-619.

[11] Bengio, Y. (2009) Learning Deep Architectures for AI. Foundations and Trends® in Machine Learning.

[12] Deselaers, T., Hasan, S., Bender, O. and Ney, H. (2009) A Deep Learning Approach to Machine Transliteration. *Proceedings of the European Chapter of the Association for Computational Linguistics Workshop on Statistical Machine Translation*, Athens, 30-31 March 2009, 233-241.

[13] Hinton, G.E. (2002) Training Products of Experts by Minimizing Contrastive Divergence. *Neural Computation*, **14**, 1771-1800. http://dx.doi.org/10.1162/089976602760128018

[14] Hinton, G. (2007) To Recognize Shapes, First Learn to Generate Images. In: *Computational Neuroscience: Theoretical Insights into Brain Function*, 535-547.

[15] Horster, E. and Lienhart, R. (2008) Deep Networks for Image Retrieval on Large-Scale Databases. *Proceedings of the 16th ACM International Conference on Multimedia*, ACM, Vancouver British Columbia, 643-646.

[16] Chen, E., Yang, X., Zha, H., Zhang, R. and Zhang, W. (2008) Learning Object Classes from Image Thumbnails through Deep Neural Networks. *Proceedings of the International Conference on Acoustics, Speech and Signal Processing*, Las Vegas, 31 March-4 April 2008, 829-832.

[17] Liu, Y., Zhou, S. and Chen, Q.C. (2011) Discriminative Deep Belief Networks for Visual Data Classification. *Pattern Recognition*, **44**, 2287-2296. http://dx.doi.org/10.1016/j.patcog.2010.12.012

[18] Fischer, A. and Igel, C. (2012) An Introduction to Restricted Boltzmann Machines. *Progress in Pattern Recognition, Image Analysis, Computer Vision, and Applications, Lecture Notes in Computer Science*, **7441**, 14-36. http://dx.doi.org/10.1007/978-3-642-33275-3_2

[19] Smolensky, P. (1986) Information Processing in Dynamical Systems: Foundations of Harmony Theory. In: Rumelhart, D.E. and McClelland, J.L., Eds., *Parallel Distributed Processing*, Vol. 1, MIT Press, Cambridge, 194-281.

[20] Freund, Y. and Haussler, D. (1992) Unsupervised Learning of Distributions on Binary Vectors Using Two Layer Networks. *Proceedings of Advances in Neural Information Processing Systems*, 912-919.

[21] Vapnik, V.N. (1995) The Nature of Statistical Learning Theory. Springer-Verlag, New York. http://dx.doi.org/10.1007/978-1-4757-2440-0

[22] Cristianini, N. and Shawe-Taylor, J. (2000) An Introduction to Support Vector Machines and Other Kernel-Based Learning Methods. Cambridge University Press, Cambridge. http://dx.doi.org/10.1017/CBO9780511801389

[23] Pal, M. and Mather, P.M. (2004) Assessment of the Effectiveness of Support Vector Machines for Hyperspectral Data. *Future Generation Computer Systems*, **20**, 1215-1225. http://dx.doi.org/10.1016/j.future.2003.11.011

[24] Melgani, F. and Bruzzone, L. (2004) Classification of Hyperspectral Remote Sensing Images with Support Vector Machines. *IEEE Transactions on Geoscience and Remote Sensing*, **42**, 1778-1790. http://dx.doi.org/10.1109/TGRS.2004.831865

[25] Foody, G.M. and Mathur, A. (2004) A Relative Evaluation of Multiclass Image Classification by Support Vector Machines. *IEEE Transactions on Geoscience and Remote Sensing*, **42**, 1335-1343. http://dx.doi.org/10.1109/TGRS.2004.827257

[26] Camps-Valls, G. and Bruzzone, L. (2009) Kernel Methods for Remote Sensing Data Analysis. Wiley, Chichester. http://dx.doi.org/10.1002/9780470748992

Towards Designing an Intelligent Educational Assessment Tool

Thair Hamtini, Shahd Albasha, Marwa Varoca

Department of Computer Information Systems, University of Jordan, Amman, Jordan
Email: thamtini@ju.edu.jo

Abstract

Assessment is an important part of learning process. It can be defined as the process of gathering information for the purpose of making judgments about a current state of affairs presumably for the purpose of enhancing future outcomes [1]. It determines whether or not the goals of education are being met. Typically, most assessment tools give a numerical score as the result of the assessment. This may not be enough to improve the student's progress. In this paper we defined main problems in current assessment tools and proposed a new assessment model that uses notions in knowledge space theory to overcome the shortage of the current assessment models. The experiment result showed that this new prototype made the assessment process easier and more effective. However, assessment affects decisions about grades, instructional needs and curriculum. This is an important phase of the learning process being showed in this paper in knowledge states framework. Future research will focus on making the tool behave intelligently to improve students' learning momentum.

Keywords

Artificial Intelligent, Evaluation, Knowledge Space Theory, Precedence Relation, Competences

1. Introduction

Educational assessment helps decision makers in any educational institution to make decisions about grades, advancement, instructional needs and curriculum, it also inspires us to ask the hard question: "Are we teaching what we think we are teaching?".

In most current assessment tools, the system gives the learner an indicator of the level of his/her knowledge in a specific field. However, they don't give any guidance to the learner or instructor about the next learning step, this is one of the main problems in current assessment models. Many assessment methods, performed by many specialists in schools and universities, are systematically based on the numerical evaluation. Such form of evaluation may not be very accurate and may not give the needed feedback to both student and instructor. Assessment is more like a movie rather than a snapshot. What we really want to know is how students are progressing over time, not where they stand on a particular point of time [1]. According to Camacho, Ortigosahas, Pulido, and RMoreno [2], the application of AI (artificial intelligence) techniques in pedagogical and educational environments originated new possibilities to develop learning processes.

A considerable amount of research has been conducted about assessing the learners [1] [3] [4]. However, it is a challenging problem to capture and represent the amount of knowledge the learner has in a specific field. Furthermore, it is essential to give a valuable feedback or guidance to both instructor and learner about the next learning that must be followed.

According to the BEAR (Berkeley Evaluation & Assessment Research Center), there are four principles that any assessment and adaptation system or approach must address to be useful in e-learning settings [5]. These principles are:

1) Assessments should be based on a developmental perspective of student learning;

2) Assessments in e-learning should be clearly aligned with the goals of instruction;

3) Assessments must produce valid and reliable evidence of what students know and can do;

4) Assessment data should provide information that is useful to teachers and students to improve learning outcomes [6].

Most current assessment tools cover the first three assessment principles. However, the fourth principle seems to present a challenge and is not well covered.

In this research, we aim to design and implement an assessment model to propose a solution for issues and problems in current assessment tools, the model employs the notion of knowledge space theory [7]-[10]. In this theory, a field of knowledge is represented by a finite set of knowledge skills (knowledge states). Moreover, knowledge space theory assumes dependencies between these states in that knowledge of a given skill or a subset of skills may be a prerequisite for knowledge of another more difficult or complex skill.

The proposed model in this paper should provide guidance to both learner and instructor smoothly to move from one state of knowledge to a more advanced state using concepts of knowledge space theory. It will contribute to design a new concept of assessment that would hopefully add value to learning process and make it more efficient and effective. We shall investigate the usefulness of such concepts in assessing student competence rather than just using the traditional tests that provide numerical scores only.

2. Related Work

A considerable amount of research has been conducted about assessing the learners [1] [3] [5]. However, it is a challenging problem to capture and represent the amount of knowledge the learner has in a specific field.

There are many assessment concepts and tools based on different techniques. One of them was designed in 2004 by using the (concept mapping) techniques. The research was working on the idea of making a diagnosis of learners' knowledge based on different categories of errors. For example, the result of the assessment for learner will be one of the following: unknown concepts, incomplete understanding, and false beliefs [4]. In [11], another assessment concept is designed to help instructor generate tests and correct them. It focuses on enhancing the cognitive aspects of assessment: while editing a question, the teacher tells which cognitive domain (from the six outlined by Bloom) he wants to assess, then the tool guides the instructor in designing the examination. Thus, writing an evaluation must be planned in order to enrich its educational value.

On the other hand, Clements and Sarama [6] have found that teachers' use of measurement learning trajectories facilitate all children's learning, especially those children who may have missed opportunities to develop higher levels of thinking strategies. When evaluating and comparing students' achievement gains across classrooms, Clements and Sarama [6] found the large gains for students in classrooms where teachers used number and measurement learning trajectories to assess student understanding and guide instructional decisions compared to the achievement scores of students in a control group. All of the models we mentioned above help learners and instructors somehow to assess their progress [11] [12], but they still have a problem in accurately capturing the learner knowledge state. Furthermore, it is essential to give a valuable feedback or guidance to both instructor and learner about the next learning that must be followed.

3. Knowledge Space Theory

According to Doignon and Falmagne [3] [9], knowledge space theory (KST) is the most recent psychological development applied in the field of e-learning. It is a set-theoretical framework, which proposes mathematical formalisms to operationalize knowledge structures in a particular domain. In this theory, a field of knowledge is represented by a finite set of knowledge skills (knowledge states) [13]. Moreover, knowledge space theory assumes dependencies between these states in that knowledge of a given item or a subset of items may be a prerequisite for knowledge of another more difficult or complex item [14].

The idea is that a knowledge skill and competences are interrelated and embedded. For instance, skill C requires both skill A and Skill B as prerequisite. A student who shows a high degree of mastery of skill C can be judged to have mastered both skill A and skill B. The key question is, given a particular subject, to partition it into appropriately related skill and to find the most appropriate prerequisite/embedment relationship between these skills as shown in **Figure 1**.

In the notion knowledge space theory, a precedence diagram is used to show precedence relations and dependencies between skills and competences [15]. For example, in the precedence diagram (**Figure 1**), the precedence relation between problems is symbolized by the downward arrows. For example, problem (e) is preceded by problems (d) and (a). In other words, the mastery of problem (e) implies that of (d) and (a).

Note that this precedence relation is part of a much bigger one, representing a comprehensive coverage of a greater knowledge space; knowledge space is a combinatorial structure, describing the possible states of knowledge of a human learner in a specific field.

4. Framework of the Proposed System

In this paper, we are going to propose a sophisticated framework to enhance student learning. The framework simulates the knowledge state of the learner; it doesn't give the learner a numerical value in the end of assessment process but gives instead the current knowledge state of the student in addition to guiding the learner to the next knowledge state he is ready to learn in the current time.

The learning objectives will be declared at the beginning of the process, and then a matching process takes a place between the learning objectives and questions saved in the data base that were provided by the teacher in the first place. The prerequisite relation is an important part of the framework because it also takes a place in the matching process while creating quizzes. In other words, it helps construct questions by taking the knowledge states order respectively.

The framework has two main parts: one for teacher and one for student as shown in **Figure 2**. The teacher after signing up, he can define his classes and then define the objectives of each class with the dependences between them, as shown in the precedence diagram in **Figure 1**. For every objective the teacher will specify the prerequisite objective(s) of it in an easy way as shown in **Figure 2**.

The framework would also provide an efficient way for creating quizzes to assess the students, the teacher can create quizzes using this framework with questions in four different forms: Fill in the blank, Multiple choice, Multiple choice with more than one correct answer, True or False. The teacher can also add picture to the question and the student can provide answers with pictures, too.

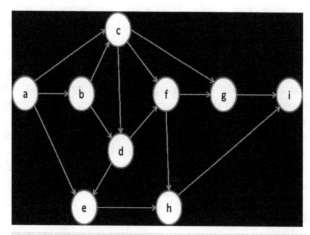

Figure 1. Precedence diagram.

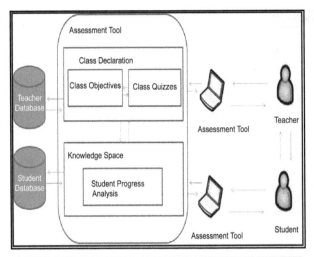

Figure 2. The proposed framework.

After the teacher finished creating the quiz, he can export the quiz for students who are registered in his class, and when the student finish answering the quiz, the teacher will import the answered quizzes from his students. On the other hand, students must sign up to have an account on the system and register in their classes.

4.1. Output of the Framework

After analyzing the imported answered quizzes from students, the framework relying on the notions of the knowledge space theory and the dependencies between objectives the teacher has provided; it will output the following as shown in **Figure 3(a)** and **Figure 3(b)**.

1) The current knowledge state for the student;

2) Mastered skills list: A list contains the skills that the student mastered so far;

3) Uncompleted skills: A list contains the skills that the student doesn't master yet;

4) Student's readiness list: A list that offers the student a selection of only the skills he is ready to learn at the current time.

4.2. Unites of the Framework

In this sub-section, a more detailed view of the framework architecture is represented, the framework mainly consists of four main units as shown in **Figure 4**. A detailed description of each unit job is expressed below in addition to the interaction between units.

The class definer: In this unit the teacher will be able to define a class with a description of it, in addition to viewing students who are enrolled in the class. This unit is also responsible for declaring the objective or main outcomes of the class plus the dependency relation between them (dependency notions of knowledge space theory). The dependency relation can be inserted easily to the system.

The quiz creator: In this unit it is responsible for creating and building quizzes. It helps instructor in many ways in creating tests. It provides 4 types of questions (Multiple choice, Fill in the blank, True/False, Multiple choices with more than one correct answer) as shown in **Figure 5** below. Teachers can also add diagrams and pictures to their questions for more clarifications, in addition to providing the correct answer for each question for the purpose of evaluation. One important thing has to be mentioned here is that every question can also be matched with one or more of the class objectives that have been defined by the teacher.

Knowledge state recognizer: In this unit, the system will match the students' answers with the correct answers provided by teachers, this comparison with result to recognition of the students' mastered skills and students' weakness points by matching his answers with the objectives of the class in the first place.

Knowledge state visualizer: In this unit the knowledge state of the student specified on the dependency diagram of the class will be viewed for teacher for the purpose of easier analysis of the student results. For example, as shown in **Figure 6**, the student is in knowledge state "b" and he is ready to move to the knowledge state "c".

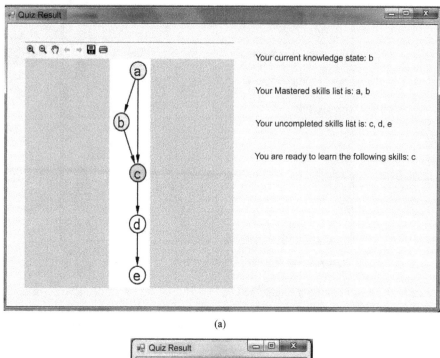

(a)

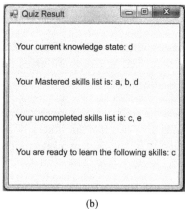

(b)

Figure 3. a) Output of the framework; b) List in the output of the framework.

5. Experiment and Results

We implemented a prototype for the proposed framework and tested it with the help of graduate students in an e-learning course in University of Jordan in spring 2014. The students were divided into groups; each group has developed an e-learning course for a specific topic. However, students after building the e-course they tested the prototype for assessment purposes.

A questionnaire was given to the student to evaluate the tool and to give future suggestions for improving. The dimensions included in the questionnaire were mainly about:

1) Ease of use;

2) The indicator of the student progress during the assessment process;

3) Creating quizzes easily and efficiently;

4) Enabling the instructor to define the precedence relation in a clear form;

5) The ability of the framework to judge whether the student masters a specific objective of the material or not.

Students filled the questionnaire based on their testing with one of the following options (agree, neural, disagree) and the result of the questionnaire is showed in **Figure 7** below.

After doing this experiment and analyzing the results, it was clear that 75% of people who have tested the framework have agreed on three dimensions of the testing criteria which are:

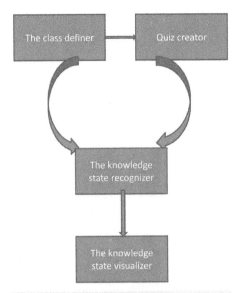

Figure 4. Framewok main units.

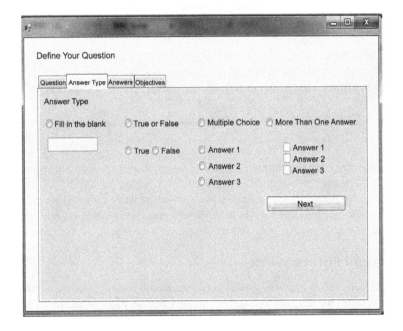

Figure 5. Quize creator unit.

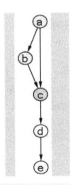

Figure 6. Knowledge state visulaizer.

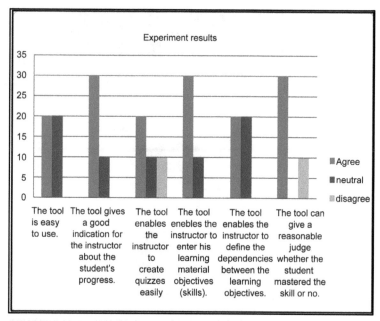

Figure 7. Experiment result.

1) The indicator of the student progress during the assessment process;

2) Enabling the instructor to define the learning objective in a clear form;

3) The ability of the framework to judge whether the student masters a specific objective of the material or not.

On the other hand, 50% of people who have tested the framework disagreed on the testing dimensions which are:

1) Ease of use;

2) Creating quizzes easily and efficiently;

3) The tool enables the instructor to define the precedence diagram easily.

The result of the questionnaire helped us put a plan for future work by focusing on the dimensions that were disagreed by most of the research samples. In addition, it helped us in planning how to enhance this framework to be more effective.

6. Conclusions and Future Work

In this paper, an educational assessment model was proposed by using notions of knowledge space theory to overcome the shortage of the current assessment models and to provide guidance for instructor and learner through the educational process. The framework was tested in University of Jordan e-learning class and the experiment results are shown in this paper. The results showed that this framework contributes to make the assessment process easier and more effective and clarifies the way for future enhancement on this model.

The proposed model may be used in any educational institution through enabling the instructor to define the learning objects of the material and the dependencies between them, it also enables the student to answer the created quiz depending on those dependencies in order to give guidance to instructor and learner on the knowledge state of the learner.

In the future, we will continue the research in this area by working on the notions of skills and competencies in an intelligent way. Which means not only relying on the class objectives inserted by the instructor, but dealing with underlying skills and competencies of the class, which may need working on the notions of domain ontology in order to extract skills and competencies in an intelligent and scientific way. This approach will ultimately improve the tool and make it behave intelligently.

References

[1]   Glaser, R., Chudowsky, N. and Pellegrino, J.W., Eds. (2001) Knowing What Students Know. The Science and Design

of Educational Assessment. National Academies Press, Washington DC.

[2]   Camacho, D., Ortigosa, A., Pulido, E. and RMoreno, M. (2008) AI Techniques for Monitoring Student Learning Process. In: Garcia-Peñalbo, F.J., Ed., *Advances in E-Learning: Experiences and Methodologies*, Information Science Reference-IGI Global, Hershey, 149-172.

[3]   Falmagne, J.-C. and Doignon, J.-P. (2011) Learning Spaces. Springer-Verlag, Berlin. http://dx.doi.org/10.1007/978-3-642-01039-2

[4]   Gouli, E., Gogoulou, A., Papanikolaou, K. and Grigoriadou, M. (2004) Compass: An Adaptive Web-Based Concept Map Assessment Tool. *Proceedings of the 1st International Conference on Concept Mapping*, Pamplona, 14-17 September 2004, 295-302.

[5]   Scalise, K., Bernbaum, D.J., Timms, M., Harrell, S.V., Burmester, K., Kennedy, C.A. and Wilson, M. (2007) Adaptive Technology for E-Learning: Principles and Case Studies of an Emerging Field. *Journal of the American Society for Information Science and Technology*, **58**, 2295-2309. http://dx.doi.org/10.1002/asi.20701

[6]   Clements, D.H. and Sarama, J. (2004) Learning Trajectories in Mathematics Education. *Mathematical Thinking and Learning*, **6**, 81-89. http://dx.doi.org/10.1207/s15327833mtl0602_1

[7]   Albert, D. and Lukas, J., Eds. (1999) Knowledge Spaces: Theories, Empirical Research, and Applications. Psychology Press, London.

[8]   Tatsuoka, K.K. (1991) Boolean Algebra Applied to Determination of Universal Set of Knowledge States. ETS Research Report Series, **1991**, i-36. http://dx.doi.org/10.1002/j.2333-8504.1991.tb01411.x

[9]   Gediga, G. and Düntsch, I. (2002) Skill Set Analysis in Knowledge Structures. *British Journal of Mathematical and Statistical Psychology*, **55**, 361-384. http://dx.doi.org/10.1348/000711002760554516

[10]   Heller, J., Steiner, C., Hockemeyer, C. and Albert, D. (2006) Competence-Based Knowledge Structures for Personalised Learning. *International Journal on E-Learning*, **5**, 75-88.

[11]   Falmagne, J.C., Cosyn, E., Doignon, J.P. and Thiéry, N. (2006) The Assessment of Knowledge, in Theory and in Practice. In: Missaoui, R. and Schmidt, J., Eds., *Formal Concept Analysis*, Springer, Heidelberg, 61-79. http://dx.doi.org/10.1007/11671404_4

[12]   Anghel, C., Godja, C., Dinsoreanu, M. and Salomie, I. (2003) JADE Based Solutions for Knowledge Assessment in E-Learning Environments. University of Limerick, Limerick.

[13]   Stahl, C. (2011) Knowledge Space Theory. http://cran.r-project.org/web/packages/kst/vignettes/kst.pdf

[14]   Albert, D. and Hockemeyer, C. (1997) Adaptive and Dynamic Hypertext Tutoring Systems Based on Knowledge Space Theory. In: du Boulay, B. and Mizoguchi, R., Eds., *Artificial Intelligence in Education: Knowledge and Media in Learning Systems*, IOS Press, Amsterdam, 553-555.

[15]   Nwaogu, E. (2012) The Effect of Aleks on Students' Mathematics Achievement in an Online Learning Environment and the Cognitive Complexity of the Initial and Final Assessments. Ph.D. Thesis, Georgia State University, Atlanta.

18

Content-Based Image Retrieval Using SOM and DWT

Ammar Huneiti, Maisa Daoud

Department of Computer Information Systems, the University of Jordan, Amman, Jordan
Email: a.huneiti@ju.edu.jo, maysa_taheir@yahoo.com

Abstract

Content-Based Image Retrieval (CBIR) from a large database is becoming a necessity for many applications such as medical imaging, Geographic Information Systems (GIS), space search and many others. However, the process of retrieving relevant images is usually preceded by extracting some discriminating features that can best describe the database images. Therefore, the retrieval process is mainly dependent on comparing the captured features which depict the most important characteristics of images instead of comparing the whole images. In this paper, we propose a CBIR method by extracting both color and texture feature vectors using the Discrete Wavelet Transform (DWT) and the Self Organizing Map (SOM) artificial neural networks. At query time texture vectors are compared using a similarity measure which is the Euclidean distance and the most similar image is retrieved. In addition, other relevant images are also retrieved using the neighborhood of the most similar image from the clustered data set via SOM. The proposed method demonstrated promising retrieval results on the Wang Database compared to the existing methods in literature.

Keywords

Image Retrieval, SOM, DWT, Feature Vector, Texture Vector

1. Introduction

Content-Based Image Retrieval (CBIR) is a technique to search and index images in a large collection database based on their visual contents like colors, textures, shapes or spatial layouts instead of using tags or other descripting metadata keywords that might associate with the images in the database [1].

Typically, most CBIR systems work by extracting one or more multi-dimensional vectors from each image in the database, this process is done in a posterior step to start retrieving. At query time, the same vectors are usually extracted from the query image and a similarity based function is used then to quantify the amount of difference between the query image vector and other images vectors in the database. Images that have similar vectors to the query one are finally retrieved as a result.

Content Based Image Retrieval finds its applications in many domains such as medical diagnostics, GIS and military applications, pattern recognition, computer vision and many others [2]. However, in most applications CBIR systems are basically depending on extracting some features, *i.e.* characteristics that can capture certain visual properties of an image either globally for the entire image or locally for its regions [3] [4] and deciding the features that can effectively discriminate images and help in matching the most similar ones is the most challenging issue in CBIR systems.

Color features are widely used in CBIR systems as they are independent of image size and orientation [5]. They are usually extracted from different color spaces, e.g. RGB, HSV, YCbCr, by computing the color histogram, color moments or dominant colors. Zhang *et al.* [6] calculated the color histogram in the HSV color space then he quantized the Hue and Saturation into eight bins while the Value channel was quantized into four bins. Color histograms don't capture the spatial relationships of color regions, so they don't robustly match similar image regions.

Stricker and Orengo [7] suggested using the first three color moments (mean, variance and skewness) for each color channel of the HSV color system in order to store each image as a color vector with (9) features. This technique proved its efficiency in matching similar images better than calculating the color histogram.

Liu *et al.* [8] extracted the dominant colors by segmenting images into regions, obtaining the histogram for every region and taking the bin with the maximum size as a dominant color for this region.

In this paper, we decomposed the HSV images using the Discrete Wavelet Transform (DWT) and then quantized the resulted approximation sub band to extract a set of dominant coefficients to form the color vector.

Extracting the color vectors are easy to compute and don't take long processing time. However, depending on them as a sole factor for deciding the images similarity will usually result it retrieving images with similar color distributions regardless their contents similarity. So extracting texture vectors, which represent the spatial arrangement of pixels in the grey level [9] beside the color ones, becomes an essential step to retrieve more accurate results.

The wavelet-based methods, e.g. standard wavelet t and Gabor wavelet, are the most commonly used techniques to extract the texture vectors as they provide better spatial information [10] [11]. Thirunavuk *et al.* [12] proposed using the 2D Dual Tree Discrete wavelet transform to each color channel of the YCbCr color space. Then the mean, energy, standard deviation and entropy values were calculated for each of the sub bands. Lahmiri and Boukadoum [13] used the Discrete Wavelet Transform (DWT) to obtain the (HH) frequency sub band and then applied the Gabor filter bank at different scales and orientations. Entropy and uniformity were then calculated and stored; this method gives better and more accurate classification results than using any of the DWT or the Gabor filter alone for extracting the features. In this paper we extracted the texture vectors by converting the images into grey scale ones, after that we applied the DWT and calculated the mean value for each block of pixels for the resulted four frequency sub bands.

The main motivation of this work was to retrieve images that best match the query image in colors and textures. So we suggested clustering the images based on their color vectors to group images with similar color characteristics in the same cluster. The decision on images similarity was made by calculating the Euclidean distance between the query image's texture vector and the database images' texture vectors. So the most texturally similar image (I), which is the one that has the minimum Euclidean distance from the query image, was first retrieved and used to identify the index of the cluster within which the search for further similar images was bounded. Results showed that the proposed method allowed retrieving images with better precession average values than others reported in literature [12] [14].

The rest of this paper is organized as follows: Section 2 explains the proposed method, Experimental results and discussions are given in Section 3. And Section 4 concludes the work.

2. Content-Based Image Retrieval Using Self Organizing Map and Discrete Wavelet Transform

Two kinds of vectors were extracted from each image in the database. The first vector held the color information while the other one was used for the texture information. Images were then clustered according to their color vectors and this process yielded in grouping images with similar color trends in the same and neighboring clusters as we applied the Self Organizing Map (SOM) clustering technique to make use of its topology preserving property [15]. For the query image, we only extracted a texture vector, and then we calculated the texture similarity between it and every single texture vector in the database. The most similar image (I) to the query mage (Q) was first retrieved from the database while other texturally similar images were retrieved from the same cluster of (I). **Figure 1** shows the block diagram for the proposed method and the algorithm below concludes the method:

1) Pre-processing: for each image in the database

a) Extract the Color Vector by:

i) Converting the image into the HSV colors space;

ii) Decomposing the image using the DWT for (2) levels;

iii) Quantizing the coefficients the of first color channel of the Approximation (LL2) sub band using SOM;

iv) Taking the most dominant (16) coefficient as color vector;

b) Extract the Texture Vector by:

i) Converting the image into grey scale image;

ii) Decomposing the image using the DWT for (2) levels;

iii) Computing the mean value for each block of pixels for all resulted sub bands.

2) At query time

a) Extract the texture vector in the same way used for the database images;

b) Compare the texture similarity between the query image and the database images;

c) Retrieve the most similar image (I);

d) Define the cluster within which (I) is located;

e) Retrieve other most texturally similar images from the same cluster of (I).

2.1. Extracting Color Vectors

Discrete Wavelet Transformation (DWT) decomposes (analyzes) the image (signal) into a set of approximations and details by passing it through two complementary filters (high pass (H) and low pass (L) filters) [9] (**Figure 2**). This process results in a sequence of spatially oriented frequency channels called sub bands as follows:

1) The Approximation sub band (LL): describes the low frequency components in the horizontal and vertical directions of the image. It presents the general trend of pixel values (wavelet approximation of the original image);

2) The Horizontal detail sub band (LH): describes the low frequency components in the horizontal direction and the high frequency components in the vertical direction, represents the Horizontal edges;

3) The Vertical detail sub band (HL): describes the high frequency components in the horizontal direction and the low frequency components in the vertical direction, it detects the Vertical edges;

4) The Diagonal detail sub band (HH): describes the high frequency components in both directions, detects the corners.

All of these sub bands can be reassembled back to reproduce the original image without loss of information in a process called reconstruction or synthesis.

DWT is able to decompose the image (R × C) into 4 sub bands with lower spatial resolution (R/2 × C/2) by down sampling it by a factor of (2). However, for each level of decomposition (N) a hierarchal structure of different frequency sub bands (3N + 1) will result, *i.e.* three levels of decomposition results in (10) different frequency sub bands as shown in **Figure 3**.

We used the HSV color space to extract the color vectors from each image in the database as it was widely used in the previous works [6] [7] and it corresponds closely to the human visual system [16]. A color in the HSV color space is represented by Hue: which is used to distinguish colors and it also represents the nature of the color; Saturation: measures the degree to which a pure color is mixed by white light; and the Value: represents the perceived light intensity [17]. Zhao *et al.* [18] indicated that the chromaticity component in HSV color pace is separated from the brightness; such that the Value component represents the brightness while Hue and Saturation components represent the chromaticity. To reduce the dimensionality of data and the computation time, we mainly concentrated on the Hue channel as human eye is more sensitive to its variations compared to the variations in Saturation [19].

We have generated a general approximation for every HSV image by decomposing it for two levels. Decomposing images for more levels will result in more generalization (more down samplings) and more loss of details

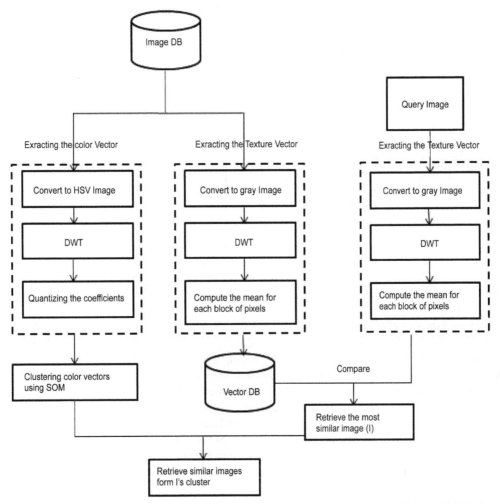

Figure 1. Block diagram for CBIR using SOM and DWT.

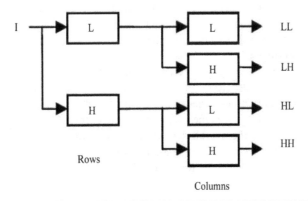

Figure 2. Discrete wavelet sub-band decomposition.

which will affect the retrieving results. Decomposition process can be concluded by the following two steps:

1) Decompose the image for the first level, this step produces the first (4) sub bands (LL1, LH1, HL1, HH1) and each of which was down sampled by a factor of (2).

2) Decompose the resulted Approximation sub band (LL1) for another level to produce (LL2, LH2, HL2, HH2) and each of which was also down sampled by a factor of (2).

We then quantized the coefficients of the first color channel (Hue) of the (LL2) sub band (as it represents a

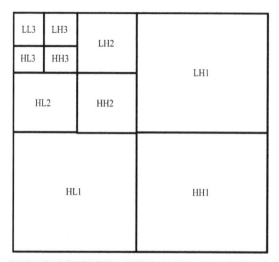

Figure 3. Illustrating the 3 levels of decomposition.

general approximation of the image (image icon)) to obtain the most dominant (16) coefficients as discriminating features for the color vector.

We applied the proposed technique on the Wang database after resizing the images to (256 × 256), so the resulted (LL2) sub band had a (64 × 64) size and we found that extracting more than (16) coefficients increased the computation time without adding any significant improvement on the retrieved results.

After extracting the color vectors from the database images, they were clustered in order to group images with similar color characteristics in the same cluster. Quantization and image clustering were both done using the Self Organizing Map (SOM) technique as neural networks algorithms proved many advantageous in vector quantitation [20] and SOM is a well-known unsupervised neural network algorithm which has been used for many applications [21]. Moreover, Pei and Lo [22] indicate that SOM is a good tool for color quantization because of its topology-preserving property, such that it preserves the neighboring pixel relationship [15] and reflects it on the resulted neighboring clusters [23].

Self Organizing Map (SOM)

SOM is a competitive unsupervised learning clustering technique that is used to classify unlabeled data into a set of clusters displayed usually in a regular Two-Dimensional array [21]. Each cluster in the SOM neural network is referred to as a neuron and associated with parametric reference vector (weight) which has the same dimension as the data to be classified. Self Organizing Map network consists of two layers called the input and the output layers as shown in **Figure 4**.

Each neuron in the input layer is fully connected to every neuron in the output layer using weighted connections (synapses). The output layer structure can have a raw form (One-Dimensional), lattice form (Two-Dimensional) or they can be arranged in Three-Dimensional mesh of neurons.

At the beginning a random value is assigned for each of the output neuron (W) vector elements ($W = w1, w2, \cdots, wn$), these values correspond to the overall density function of the input space and are used to absorb similar input vectors which also have the same dimensionality as the output neurons. Similar input vectors are found according to a predefined similarity measure function, usually the Euclidean distance [23], according to the following Equation:

$$D(w,d) = \left(\sum_{v=1}^{n} (w_v - d_v)^2 \right)^{1/2} \tag{1}$$

$D(w, d)$: Distance function.

w_v: the output neuron vector which consists of (n) number of features.

d_v: the training input vector which consists of (n) number of features.

In training phase, each training input vector d_v (all coefficients of the 1st color channel of the LL2 in the case of color quantization, while the set of all color vectors in the case of image clustering) seeks to find its best similar output neuron Best Matching Unit BMU, which is the one that has the minimum Euclidean distance from

Output Layer

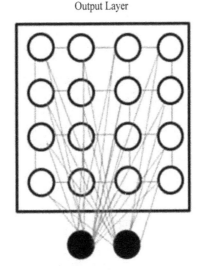

Input Layer

Figure 4. SOM structure.

the currently training input vector, then the weight of the (BMU) and its topological neighbors vectors are stretched toward this training vector according to the following updating rule [21]:

$$W_n(e+1) = W_n(e) + (e) \cdot h_n + \cdots \alpha(e)[d(e) - W_n(e)] \tag{2}$$

e: epoch number as the training phase runs for a specified number of epochs.

$w_n(e+1)$: The weight of neuron (n) in the next epoch.

$w_n(e)$: The weight of neuron (n) in the current epoch.

$\alpha(e)$: Learning rate at current epoch.

$h_n(e)$: The neighbor kernel around the BMU, it defines the region of influence that a training vector has on the SOM.

$d(e)$: The weight of the selected input vector in the current epoch.

By the end of the training phase, the output neurons will have weights that are actually formed by the input space.

In this paper, we used SOM for two purposes: 1) To extract the most dominant coefficients (quantize the coefficients); 2) To group similar images into clusters. In both cases we used the two-dimensional (Grid) output layer structure. However, one input neuron and 16 output neurons were used to extract the most dominant (16) coefficients from the first color channel of the Approximation sub band (LL2). And (16) input neurons (as each color vector has 16 elements) and (9) output neurons were used to cluster images colors vectors for (9) clusters. The number of the extracted coefficients and the number of clusters were experimentally chosen taking into account the computation time.

2.2. Extracting Texture Vectors

To extract the texture vector, all images were converted to grey scale images as [24] defined textures as, "Texture is an attribute representing the spatial arrangement of the grey levels of the pixels in a region or image", and many researchers extracted texture features from grey scale images as well [25] [26]. Images then were decomposed using the DWT method for two levels and the resulted (4) sub bands (LL2, LH2, HL2, HH2) were used to extract the texture vectors by calculating the mean value for each (8 × 8) block of pixels, the block size was experimentally decided as the size of each of the resulted sub bands was (64 × 64). Extracting the mean value from each (8 × 8) block of pixels will result in a texture vector with 64 elements which will be used then to compare images similarity instead of comparing all (256 × 256) image pixels. The same technique of extracting the texture vector was also applied for the query image (Q).

3. Results

The proposed method has been tested using the Wang database, which has (1000) images in the JPEG format and categorized into (10) categories (African People, Beach, Building, Buses, Dinosaurs, Elephants, Flowers, Horses, Mountains and Food).

First of all, images were resized to (265 × 265) and converted from the RGB color space into the HSV color space. They were down sampled then by decomposing them for two levels using the DWT. As a result, the size of each of the resulted sub bands became (64 × 64).

The first color channel of the LL2 sub band is then quantized using SOM and the most dominant (16) coefficients were selected to form the color vector. After extracting the color vectors, images were clustered into a set of (9) clusters using also the SOM technique, to group images with similar colors characteristics in the same and neighboring clusters.

To extract the texture vectors, all images were converted to grey scale images and also decomposed for two levels using the DWT. The mean value for each (8 × 8) block of the all level (2) sub bands coefficients were computed and stored as texture vectors so each image is stored as vector with (64) elements.

For every query image, the texture vector is extracted by the same way used for extracting the database images texture vectors and the most similar image to the query one is then retrieved by calculating the Euclidean Distance between the query (Q) image texture vector and every texture vector (M) in the database according to the following Equation:

$$D = \left(\sum_{f=1}^{64} \left(Q_f - M_f \right)^2 \right)^{1/2} \tag{3}$$

where:

D: Distance between the Query image texture vector (Q) and image texture vector (M) in the database.

f: the features index in the texture vector.

The most similar image (the one that has the smallest distance) to the query image is first retrieved while other texturally similar images are retrieved from the same cluster of that image. Each of the images in the database was taken as a query image and compared to the other (999) images while the top (5) similar images were just retrieved. The performance of the retrieval system was measured by calculating the precision value according to the following Equation as it was found in [12]:

$$P = \frac{R}{T} \tag{4}$$

where:

R: The number of retrieved relevant images.

T: The total number of retrieved images.

Experiments were done by retrieving the most similar images to the query image from the same cluster of the most similar image. Other experiments were also done by retrieving images from neighboring clusters in order to experimentally determine the best retrieval results (**Figure 5**).

Figure 5 shows how the way in which (9) clusters could be arranged in the grid SOM output layer and it also gives an idea about the retrieving process. In (5.A) images were only retrieved from the same cluster (i) of the most similar image, while in (5.B) similar images were retrieved from (5) clusters (cluster (i) and its 4 neighboring clusters). In (5.C) the top (5) similar images were retrieved from (i) and its (8) neighboring clusters.

Figure 6 shows the effect of selecting the top (5) similar images from the same cluster of the most similar image (I) and from its (1, 2, 3, 4, 8) neighboring clusters on the average precision value.

The results showed that retrieving images from the same cluster of the most similar image (I) gives the highest average precision values *i.e.* the best retrieving results as the retrieving process was focusing on selecting the most texturally similar images from a cluster that bounds images with so much similar colors, unlike retrieving from more than one cluster where the focus was on retrieving the nearest texturally similar images from clusters that have images with different degree of colors similarity.

Selecting from two clusters (the cluster that has the most similar image and one of its four neighbors) gives the lowest precision values as we took the average value for four retrieving experiments *i.e.* retrieving from one of the 4 neighbors at a time, the same was done for retrieving from 3 and 4 clusters, and this indicates that the location of the neighboring cluster from which the images were selected affect the retrieving results as the num-

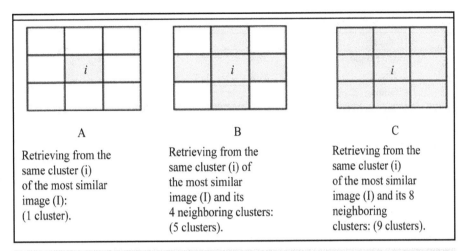

A	B	C
Retrieving from the same cluster (i) of the most similar image (I): (1 cluster).	Retrieving from the same cluster (i) of the most similar image (I) and its 4 neighboring clusters: (5 clusters).	Retrieving from the same cluster (i) of the most similar image (I) and its 8 neighboring clusters: (9 clusters).

Figure 5. Image retrieving process.

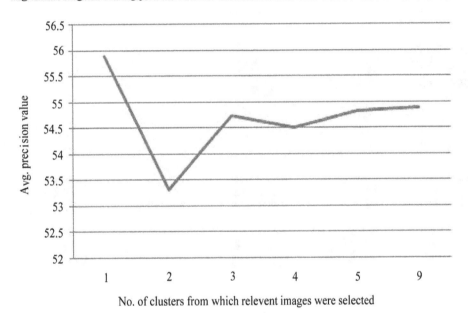

No. of clusters from which relevent images were selected

Figure 6. The effect of retrieving from different number of clusters on average precision value.

ber of similar images that might be grouped in each of the neighboring clusters differs from one cluster to another.

Our results were also compared with others reported in [12] [14] and proved their efficiency over them as depicted in **Table 1** and **Table 2** shows a sample of visual results.

4. Conclusions

In this article, we proposed a method to retrieve relevant content based images using both color and texture vectors. Images were first clustered based on their most dominant (16) color coefficients, while images texture vectors were extracted by converting them to grey images, decomposing them for two levels using the DWT and calculating the mean value for each block of pixels from the (4) sub bands of level (2).

Results showed that the proposed method is able to retrieve images with higher average precision values than other methods proposed in literature by just comparing the texture similarity and without any need to compare color similarities as images are already grouped according to their colors and the top 5 similar images are retrieved from the same cluster of the image that has most similar texture features to the query image.

Table 1. Average precession values.

No.	Category	Precision	Precision [12]	Precision [14]
1	African People	27.8	27	13.3
2	Beach	54.2	33.4	26.15
3	Building	34.4	35	11.05
4	Buses	52.6	32.2	17.25
5	Dinosaurs	52.6	32.2	17.25
6	Elephant	55.6	38.4	34.9
7	Flowers	82.8	29.6	49.5
8	Horses	74.8	34.6	20.8
9	Mountains	50	38	25.9
10	Food	30.4	40	15.6
	Average	55.88	33.86	31.09

Table 2. Visual comparison.

Query Image	Top 5 Retrieved images

Other techniques may be applied in the future by using stochastic artificial neural network like Restricted Boltzman Machine (RBM) to extract features that might help in matching more accurate results.

References

[1] Jain, R. and Krishna, K. (2012) An Approach for Color Based Image Retrieval. *International Journal of Advanced Electronics and Communication Systems*, **2**, Paper ID: 10891.
http://techniche-edu.in/journals/index.php/ijaecs/article/view/36/29

[2] Roy, K. and Mukherjee, J. (2013) Image Similarity Measure Using Color Histogram, Color Coherence Vector, and Sobel Method. *International Journal of Science and Research (IJSR)*, **2**, 538-543.
http://ijsr.net/archive/v2i1/IJSRON2013311.pdf

[3] Selvarajah, S. and Kodituwakku, S.R. (2011) Analysis and Comparison of Texture Features for Content Based Image Retrieval. *International Journal of Latest Trends in Computing*, **2**, 108-113.

[4] Kodituwakku, S.R. and Selvarajah, S. (2010) Comparison of Color Features for Image Retrieval. *Indian Journal of Computer Science and Engineering*, **1**, 207-211.

[5] Mangijao Singha, M. and Hemachandran, K. (2012) Content-Based Image Retrieval Using Color Moment and Gabor Texture Feature. *International Journal of Computer Science Issues (IJCSI)*, **9**, 299-309.

[6] Zhang, L.N., Wang, L.P. and Lin, W.S. (2012) Generalized Biased Discriminant Analysis for Content-Based Image Retrieval. *IEEE Transactions on Systems, Man, and Cybernetics Part B*, **42**, 282-290.
http://dx.doi.org/10.1109/TSMCB.2011.2165335

[7] Stricker, M. and Orengo, M. (1995) Similarity of Color Images Survival Data: An Alternative to Change-Point Models. *Proceedings of SPIE Conference on Storage and Retrieval for Image and Video Databases III*, Vol. 2420, 381-392.

[8] Liu, Y., Zhang, D.S. and Lu, G.J. (2008) Region-Based Image Retrieval with High-Level Semantics Using Decision Tree Learning. *Pattern Recognition*, **41**, 2554-2570. http://dx.doi.org/10.1016/j.patcog.2007.12.003

[9] Singha, M. and Hemachandran, K. (2012) Content Based Image Retrieval Using Color and Texture. *Signal and Image Processing: An International Journal (SIPIJ)*, **3**, 39-57.

[10] Kato, T. (1992) Database Architecture for Content-Based Image Retrieval. *Proceedings of the SPIE—The International Society for Optical Engineering*, **16**, 112-113.

[11] Flickner, M., Sawhney, H., Niblack, W., Ashley, J., Huang, Q., Dom, B., Gorkani, M., Hafne, J., Lee, D., Petkovic, D., Steele, D. and Yanker, P. (1995) Query by Image and Video Content: The QBIC System. *IEEE Computer*, **28**, 23-32.

[12] Thirunavuk, S.K., Ahila, R.P., Arivazhagan, S. and Mahalakshmi, C. (2013) Content Based Image Retrieval Based on Dual Tree Discrete Wavelet Transform. *International Journal of Research in Computer and Communication Technology*, **2**, 473-477.

[13] Lahmiri, S. and Boukadoum, M. (2013) Hybrid Discrete Wavelet Transform and Gabor Filter Banks Processing for Features Extraction from Biomedical Images. *Journal of Medical Engineering*, **2013**, 1-13.
http://dx.doi.org/10.1155/2013/104684

[14] Bhuravarjula, H.H. and Kumar, V.N.S. (2012) A Novel Content Based Image Retrieval Using Variance Color Moment. *International Journal of Computational Engineering Research*, **1**, 93-99.

[15] Chang, C.H., Xu, P., Xiao, R. and Srikanthan, T. (2005) New Adaptive Color Quantization Method Based on Self-Organizing Maps. *IEEE Transactions on Neural Networks*, **16**, 237-249.
http://dx.doi.org/10.1109/TNN.2004.836543

[16] Herodotou, N., Palataniotis, K.N. and Venetsanopoulus, A.N. (1999) A Color Segmentation Scheme for Object-Based Video Coding. *Proceeding of the IEEE Symposium on Advances in Digital Filtering and Signal Processing*, Victoria, 5-6 June 1998, 25-29.

[17] Rasti, J., Monadjemi, A. and Vafaei, A. (2011) Color Reduction Using a Multi-Stage Kohonen Self-Organizing Map with Redundant Features. *Expert Systems with Applications*, **38**, 13188-13197.
http://dx.doi.org/10.1016/j.eswa.2011.04.132

[18] Zhao, M., Bu, J. and Chen, C. (2002) Robust Background Subtraction in HSV Color Space. *Proceedings of SPIE: Multimedia Systems and Applications*, Boston, 29-30 July 2002, 325-332.

[19] Sural, S., Qian, G. and Pramanik, S. (2002) Segmentation and Histogram Generation Using the HSV Color Space for Image Retrieval. *Proceedings of IEEE International Conference on Image Processing*, **2**, 589-592.
http://dx.doi.org/10.1109/ICIP.2002.1040019

[20] Scheunders, P. (1997) A Comparison of Clustering Algorithms Applied to Color Image Quantization. *Pattern Recognition Letters*, **18**, 1379-1384. http://dx.doi.org/10.1016/S0167-8655(97)00116-5

[21] Kohonen, T. (1990) The Self-Organizing Map. *Proceedings of the IEEE*, **78**, 1464-1480.
      http://dx.doi.org/10.1109/5.58325

[22] Pei, S.-C. and Lo, Y.-S. (1998) Color Image Compression and Limited Display Using Self-Organization Kohonen Map. *IEEE Transactions on Circuits and Systems for Video Technology*, **18**, 191-205.

[23] Kangas, J.A., Kohonen, T. and Laaksonen, J.T. (1990) Variants of Self Organizing Maps. *IEEE Trans on Neural Networks*, **1**,93-99.

[24] IEEE (1990) IEEE Standard Glossary of Image Processing and Pattern Recognition Terminology. IEEE Standard, 610.4-1990.

[25] Kavitha, H., Rao, B.P. and Govardhan, A. (2011) Image Retrieval Based on Color and Texture Features of the Image Sub-Blocks. *International Journal of Computer Applications*, **15**, 33-37.

[26] Moghaddam, H.A., Khajoie, T.T., Rouhi, A.H. and Tarzjan, M.S. (2005) Wavelet Correlogram: A New Approach for Image Indexing and Retrieval. *Pattern Recognition*, **38**, 2506-2518.

19

Comparative Analysis of Operating System of Different Smart Phones

Naseer Ahmad, Muhammad Waqas Boota, Abdul Hye Masoom

Department of Computer Science, Virtual University of Pakistan, Lahore, Pakistan
Email: ms120400137@vu.edu.pk, ms120400080@vu.edu.pk, ms140400072@vu.edu.pk

Abstract

Nowadays rapidly increasing technology is mobile phone technology in telecommunication sector. This mobile device technology has great effect on everyone's life. This technology has reduced the burden of people in their daily life. To manage the rising demand for such mobile devices, numerous operating systems came in the market as a platform upon which modern application can be produced. As a result, numbers of platforms and essential depository describe these platforms; customers may or may not be aware of these platforms that are appropriate for their needs. In order to solve this issue, we examine the most famous mobile phone operating systems to decide which operating system is most suitable for developers, business applications as well as casual use. In this paper we make assessment on the popular operating systems of mobile devices available in the business market, and on behalf of such assessment we distinguish that operating system OS is much useful of its particular characteristics compared with other systems.

Keywords

Operating System, Mobile Phone, Communication, Architecture, OS

1. Introduction

Mobile phone device is one of the most widely used technologies in the field of telecommunication. Mobile phone device in the group of mobile technologies contains numbers of portable things like call phones, Personal Digital Assistants (PDAs), palmtops, laptops, global positioning systems, etc. This mobile technology is increasing rapidly around the whole world by the passage of time. We can easily see near around us in our daily life that even a poor person can avail a mobile phone or he/she has access to mobile phone. Mobile phones are widely used in the business environment as well as in our daily life. In the past years people used to go to banks, offices or any other concerned departments for their desired tasks, but in this present period one can easily perform his task with the help of mobile phone. We can see that, few years later the wireless technology is highly developed. We can easily access information by using mobile phones along with the exponential enhancement in performance as well as the capacity of wireless communication system.

One form of telecommunication is mobile phone devices or call phone devices which are used on wireless connection through networks that are broadcasting towers which spread within a specific area on local, national or multinational level. Nowadays maximum growth of mobile devices leads the concerned people to be much more than just voice communication means. But on the other hand, they have begun to be used like mini mobile computers for the purpose of sending or receiving e-mail, internet surfing voice/text chatting, appointments, etc. The most advanced mobile devices of them have the capability to take photos and these photos which are taken from the advanced mobile devices can be compared with the cameras of high resolution. Mobile devices become significant for marketing and advertisement; service provider has great competition among mobile devices and also communication charges of these mobile devices now become affordable for a broad range of people. Hence, in general the number of mobile phone or smart phone of consumers especially in Arabian world is progressively increasing which leads the mobile phone devices to replace the traditional planed line phones or wire phones in households [1].

We go back to 1947 for the history of mobile phone when a company named Lost Technology started its experiments in New Jersey plane. However, the 1st person that achieved mobile device was Martin Cooper. He was a researcher from Motorola in Chicago and he made his first wireless call from cell phone on 3rd April 1973. The mobile device is a sending or receiving circuit using the frequencies among the land-based platforms, but these devices completely perform via satellite. We can say that its principle is similar to the radio communication, but it has the variation in its frequencies that are more powerful as compared to radio communication and can reach to 20 MHZ of receiving or sanding per second. Communication between two persons can take place by using an Integrated Circuit (IC), mobile set, SIM card and the main switch at the service provider company. SIM card consists of a small circuit with a small memory unit and a processing unit which store the user's data for communicating from one end to the other end. Mobile phone device contains a Central Processing Unit (CPU), a sending/receiving circuit, Random Access Memory (RAM) and a flash memory. The main objective of this proposed system is to keep velocity with the development in the area of programming and embedded programs. The purpose of such developed system is to get the privilege knowledge for such kind of operating systems and management systems more important for developing special applications [2].

Mobile networks are consuming a large amount of data in order to enhance their communications and compress the data coverage. Continuously, enhancement in mobile device technology day by day has great impacts on human being. Mobile phone users are availing benefits from the rapid increasing in enhancement of mobile phone devices. We can see this rapid change in mobile device technology in our daily life. In the past period, if someone wanted to mail important document, he/she had to deliver from door to door, but nowadays with current advancement of mobile phone technology, people can easily send the documents in soft copy format via a mobile phone. Enhancement in mobile phone technology also has great impacts on other various fields of life. For example in business sector one can grow his business via a mobile phone; there are many other examples in our daily life and mobile phones play a vital role in the life of human being.

The movement of mobile phone operating system has rapidly increased to contain challengers such as Google Android, Symbian, Apple, BlackBerry, Microsoft, Palm, etc. Such operating system's platforms have come in a very long way because no company provides an operating system that is perfect for the mobile phone users. These companies argue that their platforms of operating system for mobile phones execute best in all ventures and also these companies surely do not announce any weak point of their systems. This situation creates difficulty for the mobile phone users that they do not know which company's platform is the most suitable for their requirements. In order to solve this issue, we perform a broad investigation of popular operating systems of mobile phones in order to point out their strength. After analysis of such operating systems for mobile devices we can get a real idea which mobile phone is the best suitable for end users, business application, gaming and also for multimedia.

For the comparison of different mobile phones in the sense of numerous usage scenarios, we came up with a set of main classifications to compare the operating systems of mobile phones. These classifications are: software features, hardware features, multimedia features, power management and development environment. From these classifications we chose some of them and then concluded on behalf of specific classification which operating system is the most suitable for the users.

The category of software features highlights the operating system features that are supported which express how to improve the operating system to manage system calls, memory management and multitasking. The hardware support category tells us which hardware features are supported by the operating system. The multimedia category specifies audio, video and media applications that are supported by the operating system for mobile phones. The power management features tell us about the features that are available for the operating system to save the energy. The development environment category illustrates how reliable it is for third party developers to make applications for the desired platform.

On behalf of these illustrated classifications, we will select a subset from this comparison domain particularly suitable for every usage model. Software features and development environment are tremendously important for third party developers. Software features, multimedia features and development environment are important categories in gaming zone. Software features and hardware support are the basic categories for business application [3]. In the end, most important categories for casual users are power management, multimedia features and hardware support.

The production of mobile phones is growing rapidly at a tremendous rate and different operating systems for such mobile devices are available in the business market. Different models of mobile phones with different features and options are introduced every month. Some of the main questions which arise in the customer's mind before purchasing a mobile phone are:

- What is the most suitable mobile phone for me?
- What features do I look in mobile phones that are more suitable for my needs?
- What reliabilities in mobile phones are essential that attract me?
- What about the mobile phones, attraction as well as extra features making the particular mobile phone unique?

These surveys have been done by various people for almost the whole range of users markets but the focus has been on single domain or on general domain. Evaluations of mobile phone operating system have typically hit the development market with a few key points so as to illustrate the operating system invaluable for the users. However, vendors of various mobile devices implement cross-platform operating systems, such as Linux kernel including/containing Google's Android. The mobile operating system plays a vital role in the decision-making process of the users. At one stage some companies like IBM, SGI and Sun culminated with their computing stages, but on the other hand we could see the computing environment of Microsoft, Linux and Google. Mobile technologies go forward in order to get closer with the standard of intelligent personal computer. The data in this paper expand the analysis of mobile phone operating system to resolve the users' experience and requirements concerning the mobile computing environment. While the working body is limited to a few number of hardware devices, our focus is on components of the operating system which defiantly describe how well the hardware performs.

We made some assumptions on behalf of performing benchmarks and operating system's rating. Firstly in operating system's rating for a particular user group, we are liable to give intelligent rating for operating systems which give more control to the end users and have more features. First consideration creates an idea in which all operating systems being same like the skills of developers, additional features, and management offer excessive potential for use. Because various features were not easily compared quantitatively, we used the phenomena for rating mobile phones. Secondly, we make assumption while performing the benchmarks in which mobile phones that we are using act like a hardware platform representative and available to each operating system. This was not a problem for Android and iPhone operating system, because at this time one mobile phone is related with each operating system. But on the other hand, in Symbian and Windows mobiles, a large number of mobile phones exist for every operating system where the hardware features differ assumingly. In this paper we try to minimize the effects of hardware variances by ranging the benchmarks with CPU concentrated operations in proportion to the operating system for each mobile phone [1]. We will discuss related work in Section 2, Android in Section 3, iPhone OS in Section 4, BlackBerry in Section 5, Windows Mobile in Section 6 and Symbian in Section 7, and finally we conclude our research work in Section 8.

2. Related Work

Mobile phones now have become popular among users for their numerous features specially the mobile phone that can access the internet and email. But on the other hand the unknown third party developers act behind the screen and protecting all the components is the operating system. The operating system describes the performance, security level, features and active application programming interfaces. Hence the intelligent users of mobile phones depend on the operating systems when they decide to purchase instead of depending on the features of the mobile phone only because they know that good operating system can operate well even the reserved mobile phones can not achieved customers attraction with other operating systems besides performing the casual tasks of Short Message Service (SMS) and multimedia presentation which are not the key features to measure the quality of mobile phones [2].

This is common to make comparison among operating systems for mobile phones. Such type of article paper can easily accessible on the internet since number of users conscious about there mobile phones that how their phones are comparative to other phones in the business environment. This paper generally represents the idea about operating systems that which operating system is most suitable to the end users. Furthermore, this paper does not focus on a specific operating system and user group. The best operating system for mobile phone should be described with different phenomena to satisfy the needs of various mobile phone users. We are going to illustrate in this paper to give a comprehensive analysis relatively simple features checklist. At the end we will conclude that which operating systems is the right choice for the end users based on our analysis. We started by taking a deep look at operating systems for mobile phones. The most common mobile phone's operating systems in the market of mobile phones are Linux, Android, and Symbian, iPhone OS, RIM BlackBerry and Windows Mobile.

3. Android

Android is Linux based operating system designed for mobile devices such as mobile phone and e-reader tablet PCs. Its first public version was released on 12th Nov, 2007 and first mobile phone with this operating system came in business market on 23rd Sep, 2008. It is an open source operating system which is based on Linux kernel which enables the developers to write and modify applications initially in Java. It is also support C/C++. It provides easy access for users to public sites like YouTube, Face book and smooth integration with Gmail and Google calendar etc. It becomes more popular among hardware manufacturers and also in general public in recent years. One best thing which play a very important role in its popularity that it is absolutely free operating system for mobile devices and it has been selected by many hardware manufactures to run it on several devices like mobile phones, net books tablet PCs and others.

3.1. Android OS Architecture

Android OS can be divided into four layers (see **Figure 1**), the Linux Kernel, libraries, application framework, and applications. The libraries in Android OS provide data storage, graphics and media applications. Android

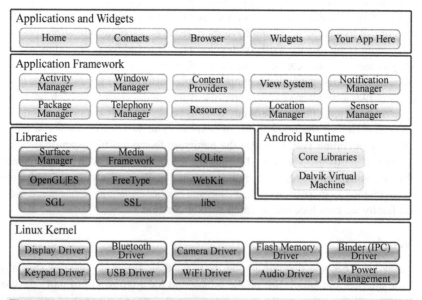

Figure 1. Android OS software architecture [4].

rune time is embedded within the libraries which contains Dalvik Virtual Machine (DVM), which gives power to the applications. The applications from work in which all applications use to access the lowest level's architecture.

In Android OS Linux kernel provides virtual memory, drivers, power management and networking. On observing the kernel dispatched with the Android's source code, there are not any important changes to the main functions of the kernel. The local libraries layer provides Android OS with the potentials for its main features. Packaging of Android OS with SQLite provides most data storage. SGL embedded in local libraries acts as the primary 2D graphics provider and open GL/ES provides 3D graphics support. The WebKit web tendering engine modified to make web pages for smaller screen sizes. The Dalvik VM is a byte code predictor, highly optimized for executing on mobile phone.

The application framework provides most important APIs, in which the applications use sharing data, receiving the notifications and also accessing the telephony system. The software of Android is completely written in Java is interpreted by Dalvik Virtual Machine. Phones and contacts applications reside in applications layer which are most important key features. We may expect in this given modal that Android becomes much stronger and the users will easily identify that what applications should handle specific events.

3.2. Concurrency Model

As we discuss above, Android OS is Linux based. Android offers almost the same features regarding concurrency model. The third party developers are able to run background services but it is not guaranteed that the services will run. The operating system will try to kill the processes when memory will be low it is not harmful for user's experience. It means that foreground running will be alive together with services which are used by the application's Background process can be killed at any moment and these has no effect on the user's experience.

3.3. Virtual Memory

As we know that Android OS is Linux based and it proves that it can run with minimum hardware resources. Application on Android run inside the Dalvik Virtual Machine but not executed as local applications. The Dalvik Virtual Machine allows multiple virtual machine instances to run at once and Dalvik Virtual Machine is registered based virtual machine which optimizes for low memory requirements. The Dalvik Virtual Machine (DVM) is made to run Java applications, but DVM is not a JVM. DVM runs Java applications that are converted into Dalvik executable file format. The lack of a just in time compiler is huge difference between DVM and other JVMs. As it optimized for low memory needs to run the application inside the VM is without any hesitation memory compared to an architecture which uses local application and lack of just in time compiler could minimize the performance.

3.4. Networking

By using standard networking packages like Java.net.org, apache.htt networking functionality can be used. Android OS is marketed in business environment as a mobile phone with "always on" internet. Android mobile phones nearly always connected to the internet using Wi-Fi or cellular network. Programmatic control in Android is outstanding over the Wi-Fi connection. One can scan for Wi-Fi networks using the Android API applications, connect to wireless network and keep the wireless radio active when the mobile device returns to slow. When wireless or Wi-Fi functionality is switched off or when airplane mode is allowed making a Wi-Fi connection is not yet possible it shows that preferences cannot be dominated.

3.5. Security

The Dalvik Virtual Machine (DVM) is main part of Android OS and plays a significant role in the security of the operating system. The main design point of Android security architecture is that by default no application has guaranteed to perform any task that would harmfully effect other applications, operating system and user. This approach is forced by using the DVM and fundamental Linux platform using file permissions and UNIX user identifiers. Unlikely, a large number of Linux desktop operating systems, where applications from the same user execute with the same user ID, and each application executes its own virtual machine in a different process with its own user ID. This clearly indicates that Android applications cannot access the data or code from other programs and all data sharing is done explicitly. By default, Android applications does not allow giving permissions to do anything that may affect the data on mobile phone and the user experience.

4. iPhone OS

Apple released first generation iPhone on June 29, 2007 in USA and the most recent version of iPhone, iPhone 5 released on September 21, 2012 [5]. The mobile device which uses the iPhone OS is similar to Mac OS X. The fundamental organization of iPhone OS is given in **Figure 2**.

The Core OS layer resides in the bottom of iPhone OS architecture. Core services layer contains an additional abstraction layer, media and cocoa touch layer. The Core OS layer also contain the scheduler, Mach kernel, file system, hardware drivers and is in charge of control the memory system, network and inter process communication and security framework to secure the system and program data. As said that the core services layer contain an abstraction setup. It contains access to the network availability, basic framework for objective-C programming, state of mobile device, access to location information and address book.

Media layer includes various frameworks to deal with audio, video, 2D and 3D graphics. The Cocoa Touch layer resides at the top level of iPhone OS architecture and provides basic building blocks to develop graphical event driven applications the iPhone OS. In order to access the higher level APIs objective-C programming is required but as objective-C is a strict superset of C language and possible to contain C code in any objective-C class freely.

4.1. Concurrency Model

Apple has restricted the multitasking capabilities of the iPhone OS in order to maximize the amount of memory available to the foreground application. Apple give permission to only one third party application to run at a same time, when the mobile phone user goes back to the home screen the application is terminated, state information is archived and when the active user goes back then application is reinstated. This is very sensitive obstacle for pervasive computing application since people often want to do work in the background without any user intervention. The restrictions that are imposed by Apple are not natural, near about ten applications or services mostly running concurrently on the iPhone OS, but it is only recommended by Apple's own application. Only one third party service or application can run at the same time and it should be in foreground state, applications and services that run concurrently are core services such as email checking, calling, playback music, mobile synchronization and Bluetooth. Safari is allowed to run continuously when extra free memory is available and it is Apples own application.

4.2. Memory Use

The 1st generation iPhone offer 128 MB memory while 3rd generation iPhone offers 256 MB that is twice as compared to the 1st generation iPhone, allowing to improve the performance as well as multitasking (D. Albazaz). Near about 11 MB of 128 MB is used for virtual RAM and operating system itself uses a large chunk of memory and remaining approximately 76 MB memory is for user. iPhone OS does not contain swap file for virtual memory, this indicates that when RAM is full then there is not any available memory any more. Current 3GS iPhone has quite advantage of much speed when user running the standard Apple applications that supports the multitasking. In previous iPhone models when another application is launched then safari browser is almost always closed, but in new 3GS it can continue running in the background.

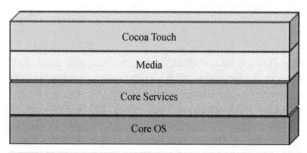

Figure 2. iPhone OS architecture.

4.3. Networking

Inside the iPhone OS the core of network functionality is based on Berkeley Software Distribution (BSD) sockets. Various high level layers of abstraction are also available. The CFNetwork and other software layers on Mac OS X are shown in **Figure 3**.

The CFNetwork layer allows the developers to develop streams and sockets, and by allowing these low level applications can connect to anything to network internally. However, applications can be developed to connect any service that is executing in a particular network, application do not manage over what network to connect do. Without user interaction applications are not allowed to connect a Wi-Fi connection. This show that the applications are restricted to only an inter connection by using the cellular network. iPhone OS make possible for applications to create peer-to-peer network connectivity by using the Bluetooth. The Software Development Kit (SDK) contains the functionality to dynamically discover other mobile phone devices which run iPhone OS and these will have the ability to connect seamlessly to iPhone OS running devices without any pairing. This is Bonjour service discover protocol technology that allows to setup a connection without any configuration. The devices which do not support this standard are not able to connect iPhone OS device.

4.4. Security

iPhone OS offers various APIs to implement security features for developers. Like as desktop counterpart, iPhone OS uses BSD and Common Data Security Architecture (CDSA) to implement the security features. File access permissions a low level features are implemented by the BSD kernel is a form of UNIX operating system. Higher level functionality is given by CDSA for example encryption, security data storage and authentication. With its own API CDSA is an open source standard but it does not follow the standard Macintosh programming convention and due to this reason this not directly accessible.

Like as the dialer and browser with base access the iPhone OS runs applications. This indicates that when security vulnerability is exploited in one service or application the entire operating system may be compromised. This is not same as the Android and BlackBerry OS in which the applications are shielded from the operating system and other service by running in the virtual machine. Because by introducing the iPhone OS various security features have been founded and with firmware updates fixed by Apple that give permission to a hacker to get full control over the mobile device. However, applications that are running with basic rights by default a big threat.

5. BlackBerry

The operating system of BlackBerry is a modest operating system which has been developed by research in motion to be use completely in combination with the family of BlackBerry mobile phone. In the beginning Black-Berry mobile phone were developed with business experts in mind, and provide wireless synchronization with Microsoft exchange in terms of functionality. In this present period BlackBerry still widely used in current market but in past few years number of new mobile devices with different operation systems have been introduce in business market which have great effect on BlackBerry devices.

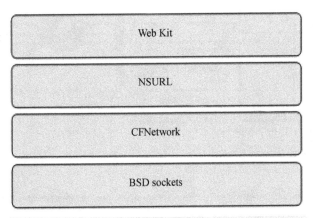

Figure 3. CFNetwork and other software layers on Mac OS X.

As illustrated above that BlackBerry OS is a modest operating system and it does not have much information about there internal functionality of the operating system which have been reveal by RIM. The software development kit (SDK) has course documentation which is available for the application development for operating system but it does not provide technical information about particular operating system. Developers can develop application for BlackBerry mobile device in two ways. In the first way developers can create Java applications by using propriety JVM in order to run on BlackBerry device. Various Java APIs are also available for tasks such as networking, data storage and application integration. In the second way developers can create Mobile Data Service (MDS). This application is optimized to receive data from one end of application and display this data to screen. The BlackBerry MDS Runtime Environment is given in **Figure 4**.

In order to use MDS applications there are different options are visible. These can run in the JVM, web browser, or in MDS runtime. BlackBerry Enterprise Server is essentially required for these applications. It is not possible to make indigenous application such as C/C++ as a third party developer.

5.1. Concurrency Control

Number of applications and processes can run at the same time on BlackBerry OS because of multithreaded nature of BlackBerry OS. In order to handle computationally rigorous tasks these applications can create background threads and also handle network communication without locking the main thread. When an application turned inactive then background threads are allowed to remain active. The truth is that this functionality is available is not a shock, because keeping in mind BlackBerry OS has been developed with running background network processes. For example normal applications use this approach for emails synchronization and calendar events, also third party applications can use these approaches.

5.2. Memory Use

For many third party application JVM handles memory management on the BlackBerry mobile device, if not then specialized MDS runtime is used. The JVM also handles data swapping between flash memory and SRAM, garbage collection and memory allocation. The JVM in BlackBerry must share existing memory between Black-

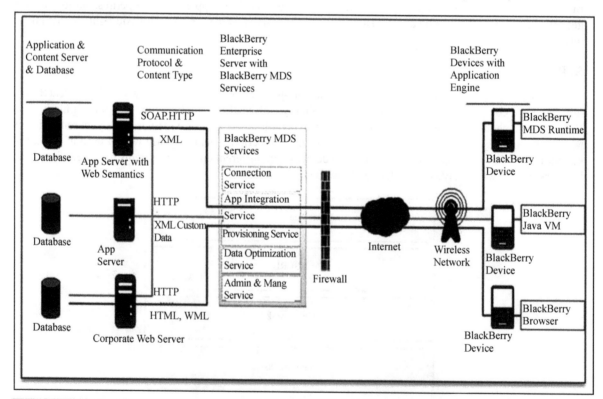

Figure 4. BlackBerry MDS runtime environment [6].

Berry Java Application and BlackBerry device application [7]. A particular low memory manager is running in order to deal with the limited memory capacity of mobile phones. When a large amount of free flash memory decreased under a certain threshold or various available objects drops down under a specific limit then the low memory manager frees the accessible memory. Third party applications and standard application must work with this interface in order to delete the low priority data when the low memory manager receives an event of low memory.

5.3. Networking

In mind BlackBerry OS is developed with background network processes. Making a TCP socket or HTTP socket to create a connection over wireless network is not difficult. In the backend the design of BlackBerry OS is though focused on providing a connection to the internet every time, but not on connecting with mobile phone in the native area of the user like the case in number of persistent computing applications. The API does not have the ability to dynamically discover and connect to the wireless network (Wi-Fi): as we know that a Wi-Fi connection can only be used in one situation if it has been setup by the mobile phone user in the past. However, in order to discover or connect Bluetooth Device is available.

5.4. Security

Historically, the security has been a central point of BlackBerry OS, but on the other hand the present security characteristics are adapted towards the use in endeavor surroundings. When someone uses the BlackBerry Enterprise server then all communication among the mobile phone and external world is encrypted, and the network administrator can add or remove the applications at all as well as change policies that manage, what the user and application can do. Encrypt the all user data on the device is a possible policy. The applications that are used by the JVM are accessible by the BlackBerry OS, access to determine data or virtual memory from other applications is not possible if not access has been specially granted. With these capabilities application potentially may be risky and have to be digitally signed by RIM. This situation is also true for many other APIs that have been labeled as perceptive so that a review experiment is offered when mistreatment of these APIs is noticed.

6. Windows Mobile

The operating system of Windows Mobile has been developed by Microsoft to run this OS on variety of mobile phones. Window Mobile OS is based in Win32 API, and designed to offer a similar services like desktop PCs. A general structure of Windows Mobile kernel is shown in **Figure 5**. In this operating system the kernel is based on Windows Compact Edition (CE), an operating system that is designed for embedded systems and handheld. Windows CE is modular operating system in which the developers choose their required functionality. The size of the operating system including kernel is only few hundred KB, but developers can add components such as web browser or to support for. NET Framework. The main difference among Windows mobile and Windows CE is that the group of components that are fixed and used by Microsoft so that the APIs are reliable between all Windows Mobile Phone devices. However, these APIs are not same. All mobile devices have to manage minimum set of functionalities, but the mobile phone manufactures include the additional APIs in the operating system image freely.

6.1. Concurrency Control

Windows CE came into existence by Microsoft for embedded devices and provides Windows Mobile an interesting attribute that other mobile phone operating system does not provide, in this operating system the kernel offers real time performance. This indicates that users have guaranteed upper bound on the running time of higher priority threads. In order to use this technique Win32 API has to be used because the. NET compact Framework contains a garbage collector that halts all the threads during the garbage collection. As Win32 API is based on such technologies from a period more than 25 years ago dealing with it if possible it should be avoided. In the NET Compact framework the multithreaded functionality offered by Windows Mobile is fully featured, also offers complete functionalities for a developer wish. It is not a problem to run multiple process and multiple threads in background.

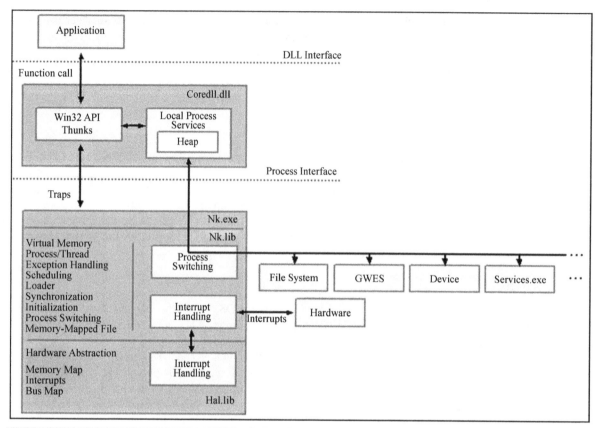

Figure 5. Schematic overview of windows mobile kernel.

6.2. Memory Use

Windows Mobile OS is of 32-bit with maximum of 32 MB of virtual memory that is available for a single application. Windows Mobile 6 is based on Windows CE 5.0 in these days this is common to see the mobile phones with 128 MB or more internal memory but this 128 MB memory is not used by a single application. A large chunk of memory is used by the operating system in order to keep the applications running when the users close the applications, this feature called elegant minimize by the Microsoft. When memory is going low then these applications can be closed by the operating system. Important is that the Windows Mobile offers low level access for programmers to the operating system. The developers can access the Win32 directly by Windows Mobile. This facility maximizes the development options but on the other there are risks the developing of applications with memory leaks. The operating system objects created by this API should be cleaned up manually by the application developers. The controlled wrappers present in the NET Framework are made to make sure that the fundamental Win32 objects are correctly cleaned up. As discussed earlier Symbian OS and iPhone OS also support C/C++, but the APIs to access the operating systems features are cleaner defined and much protected from third party developers. Symbian has the ability to cleanup stack in order to secure memory leaks while Objective C objects can be kept in an auto release team that is cleaned up after a happening loop is finished. Mobile phone operating systems that limit the developers to high level programming languages running internally the virtual machine have surely no memory leak difficulties because the garbage collector takes care of this issue.

6.3. Networking

Windows Mobile offers number of APIs in order to create a network connection for mobile phone users. As discussed above that Windows Mobile allows the developers to access very low level APIs in sense everything that you can imagine is possible. To create standard sockets is not difficult and complete management over the Bluetooth and Wi-Fi connection is accessible by default in the managed. NET Compact framework this facility is not supported, but developers can add this by using freely available wrappers simply.

6.4. Security

As mentioned above that the Windows Mobile is similar to the desktop counterpart in different ways. The developers have access to different low level APIs that give full freedom to the application developers. The reverse of invent is that the implementation in security measures of the operating system are not unlimited. The applications are not sandboxed and secured from one another. The applications cannot access the process space of another process directly but with DLL injection mechanism it is possible to run code within the address space of another process. The process space protection is designed to secure the applications from programming errors in other applications but it is not enough to protect applications from malevolent applications. If a trusted process is initiated there is necessary no restrictions on what it is allowed to do something. However, it is possible that the applications which access the trusted APIs required to be signed before access is allowed but this technique depends on the implemented security plan.

7. Symbian

In the first half of 2009 most popular operating system for mobile devices was Symbian with a market share of 51 percent. However, by far Symbian is huge player on the market of mobile devices, but in last few years its market share decease rapidly more than 20 percent due to the major developments such as the release of iPhone OS and Android OS. Symbian OS has various variants also, because operating system does not contain a user interface itself. Availability of Symbian is found as Series 60 User Interface (S60), User Interface Quartz (UIQ) and Mobile oriented Application Platform of Symbian (MOAP(S)). Nokia mobile company discover the Symbian foundation in the end of first half of 2008 with the aim to unite Symbian OS, S60, UIQ and MOAP(S) in order to create one open mobile software platform, but now in this current period the platform still remain distributed [8]. It also offers a high-level of combination with communication and Personal Information Management (PIM) functionality; it can also provide many services and applications such as play back music, associated libraries, games, routing and many other applications and services in order give more features to users [9].

The UI Framework layer is used by applications implementation and Graphical User Interface (GUI) implementation of the operating system itself (S60, UIQ, and MOAP(S)). In the above given operating system architecture second layer is application service layer to manage the application services. Generic services such as data synchronization and HTTP transport are provided by the Application Services layer. Below this the OS services layer extends the base services layer. The OS Services layer also includes features such as telephony services, task scheduler, multimedia services and network services. The lowest level of user mode services resides in the Base Services layer. The file services also resides in this layer as well as the user library in which applications need to use the interface the kernel. Kernel and hardware drivers form the lowest level layer [10].

7.1. Concurrency Control

Symbian operating system is multithreaded like other operating system for mobile devices. This ability is also allowed to the third party developers of applications to make possible to run the processes in the background. Unlike all types of applications have access to such APIs; it is not a problem for C++ developers. Symbian OS kernel has the facility of hard real time operating system tasks but on the other hand it does not support real time scheduling for the user processes.

7.2. Memory Use

Symbian OS was designed for mobile device with limited resources. Since the out of memory errors may happen any time at the time of memory allocation, to remove these errors and make the program able to go back to a stable and acceptable stat when error occur. In order to make this acceptable Symbian OS is implemented with cleanup stack and leaves. Symbian OS has not the ability to handle exceptions like standard C++, but on the other hand it supplies its own idioms. When an exception or leave occurs, objects that are allocated in the heap would not cleanup dynamically. In order to solve these issue sources of memory leak pointers to all objects that are created should be stored on the cleanup stack. This technique allows the system to cleanup unused objects dynamically (shown in **Figure 6**) [10].

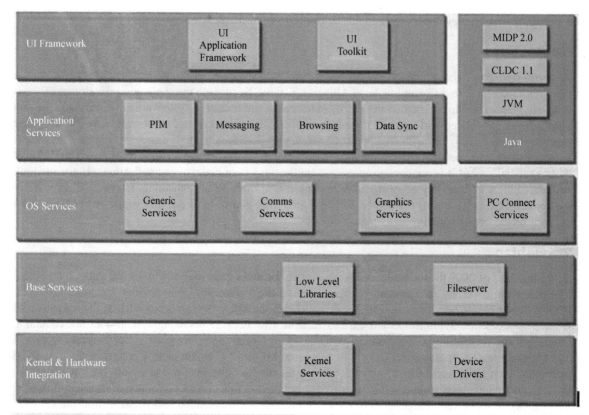

Figure 6. Symbian OS architecture [10].

7.3. Networking

Symbian OS offers limited set of services in order to connect the wireless network. It can detect for Wi-Fi networks retrieve information or data about the cellular network that is being connected. Symbian OS has also offers limited functionality of Bluetooth. It is possible in only one condition the devices that securely connected to each other for Bluetooth I/O. It means that the user input is required before communication among the paired devices. However, this is not a specific problem of Symbian OS. When a connection occurs, the developer has full control over thew transmitted data. Symbian OS sockets are similar to the BSD sockets and it is possible to specify the interface that must be used. New devices are based on Symbian OS platform in order to support open C and C++ and low level socket API is a port of this standard.

7.4. Security

Symbian OS has various features like other mobile device operating systems for the purpose of protection and privacy. The harmful threat is managed by the Symbian OS security architecture is the distribution of malicious applications. This threat is managed by requiring the program to be signed before there installation. Once they installed then access to the resources is restricted. Since application are reviewed before the risk of installing malware is minimized signed by them, but it is not good because there are number of ways for user to obtain the running unsigned applications. In this regard the Symbian OS is similar to the iPhone OS where applications that are divided using the application store are reviewed first by Apple and after Jailbreak this limitation can be circumvented. Symbian offers developers with numerous APIs in order to implement the security features. By default in Symbian OS Cryptographic, hashing and random number generating algorithm are available. In order to setup a secure connection by using SSL is also not difficult.

8. Conclusion

The discussed operating systems for mobile devices have strong and weak points. It is surely not possible to say which one of this operating system is the best. However, it is possible to identify the slightest appropriate

Table 1. Quality comparison of operating systems based on emergent features.

Operating System	Concurrency	Memory Use	Network	Security
Android	***	**	***	***
iPhone OS	*	***	**	**
BlackBerry	***	**	**	***
Windows Mobile	***	***	***	**
Symbian	***	***	**	**

operating system in the list. Summary of strong and weak points of discussed operating system is given in **Table 1**. Unnatural restrictions are imposed by Apple with observations in order to run the background process that makes the latest version of iPhone OS and such version is not suitable for most old applications. The remaining four operating systems have no difficulty in running various applications at the same time or running the background processes, so they all score three points. At the moment Android is the only free open source operating system in this list, so it scores three points but the competition scores only two. These operating systems have different technologies to deal with the restricted memory capacity of mobile devices, but BlackBerry and Android OS score two instead of three since the development of local applications is not possible and all third party applications can run in the virtual machine. Networking is the most important attribute for applications, but approximately all operating systems have restrictions in regard of automatically connecting to Wi-Fi or Bluetooth network. Windows Mobile does not have this type of restrictions and gets three points. Android also gets three points because it has a very strong feature set in place since Android 2.0. Security is an important aspect that gets a reasonable amount of consideration in mobile operating systems. BlackBerry and Android OS both run applications in sandboxed virtual machine and hence get three points. Symbian OS has a complicated system for signing applications and Windows Mobile also has the same situation, while the system is less complicated [8]. Android and iPhone OS are nowadays leading the business market.

Acknowledgements

We are thankful to Dr. Farhan Zaidi who gives us opportunity to do research work. We are also thankful to our friends, colleagues and participants in the interviews to give their feedback.

References

[1]   Wei, M., Chandran, A., Chang, H.-P., Chang, J.-H. and Nichols, C. (2009) Comprehensive Analysis of Smartphone OS Capbilities and Performance.

[2]   Albazaz, D. (2012) Designing a Mini-Operating System for Mobile Phone. *The International Arab Journal of Information Technology*, **9**, 1-2.

[3]   Sharma, T.N., Beniwal, M.Kr. and Sharma, A. (2013) Comparative Study of Different Mobile Operating Systems. *International Journal of Advancements in Research & Technology*, **2**, 1-2.

[4]   Overview of the Android Architecture. http://elinux.org/Android_Architecture

[5]   http://en.wikipedia.org/wiki/IPhone

[6]   The Blackberry MDS Runtime Environment. http://www.rim.com/symposium/press/pdf/BlackBerry_Mobile_Data_System_4.pdf

[7]   BlackBerry Java Development Environment, Fundamental Guide. http://docs.blackberry.com/zh-cn/developers/deliverables/4526/BlackBerry_Java_Development_Environment-4.7.0-US.pdf

[8]   Van der Hoorn, H. (2010) A Survey of Mobile Platforms for Pervasive Computing. Master's Thesis, University of Groningen, Groningen, 16-36.

[9]   Symbian Research Report. http://mad-ip.eu/files/reports/Symbian.pdf

[10]   Symbian OS Architecture. http://benz-second.blogspot.com/2012/06/symbian-os-architecture.html

Timed-Automata Based Model-Checking of a Multi-Agent System: A Case Study

Nadeem Akhtar, Muhammad Nauman

Department of Computer Science and IT, The Islamia University of Bahawalpur, Baghdad-ul-Jadeed Campus, Bahawalpur, Pakistan
Email: nadeem.akhtar@iub.edu.pk

Abstract

A multi-agent based transport system is modeled by timed automata model extended with clock variables. The correctness properties of safety and liveness of this model are verified by timed automata based UPPAAL. Agents have a degree of control on their own actions, have their own threads of control, and under some circumstances they are also able to take decisions. Therefore they are autonomous. The multi-agent system is modeled as a network of timed automata based agents supported by clock variables. The representation of agent requirements based on mathematics is helpful in precise and unambiguous specifications, thereby ensuring correctness. This formal representation of requirements provides a way for logical reasoning about the artifacts produced. We can be systematic and precise in assessing correctness by rigorously specifying the functional requirements.

Keywords

Software Correctness, Formal Verification, Model Checking, Timed-Automata, Multi-Agent System, Timed Computation Tree Logic (TCTL)

1. Introduction

The use of formal methods to define the requirements, design and architecture of a multi-agent system results in precise and unambiguous specifications. These formal specifications provide the basis for systematic, mathematically-proven, well-defined, and unambiguous software development phases of analysis, design, and implementation. Multi-agent systems are distributed, decentralized, consisting of autonomous computing entities known as agents. Correctness is a mathematical property that establishes the equivalence between software and its specifications. Software systems analyzed, designed, and implemented by using agents to offer significant challenges in ensuring their correctness. One of the methods of ensuring the correctness of safety and liveness properties of these agent-based systems is to use formal model checking methods based on timed automata.

2. State of the Art

2.1. Formal Methods

The primary objective of a formal approach is precise and unambiguous specification. A representation of the requirements based on mathematics aids in precise specification of the software, thereby ensuring that the correctness, completeness, and unambiguous properties of the system are preserved [1]. The formal representation of software requirements provides a method for logical reasoning about the artifacts produced. This achieves more precision in the description and allows for a stronger design that satisfies the required properties. Formal methods offer the ability to rigorously prove system correctness, *i.e.* that specifications are consistent with the stated objective; that code is consistent with specification; and that code produces a desired result and none other. To overcome the complexity problems in multi-agent systems and get significant results with formal specifications, we must cope with complexity at each phase: requirements, architecture to design and implementation. We can prove the correctness of a multi-agent system by formalizing critical components in the multi-agent development life-cycle.

The most important reasons to use formal methods in software engineering are: rigorous analysis of system properties; property-preserving transformations; error-free implementation; high quality of each phase of the development process; firm foundation for the adaptation and evolution process; continuous correctness as multi-agent systems are concurrent and often have dynamic environments; formal specification and modeling of a multi-agent system architecture which can change at run-time (*i.e.* dynamic architecture); specification according to the functional and non-functional properties; property-preserving step-by-step transformations from abstract to concrete concepts and then stepwise refinement to implementation code; improved documentation and understanding of specifications.

2.2. Agents and Multi-Agent Systems

An agent is a computer system that is capable of autonomous actions on behalf of its user or owner [2]. Agents are coarse-grained computational systems, each making use of significant computational resources [3]. An agent is a software entity that is able to conduct information-related tasks without human supervision [4]. Intelligent agents (*i.e.* referred to as rational agents) are systems that accomplish their goals by acting rationally. Rational agents can use reasoning to make decisions about their goals. A rational agent is an autonomous computing entity that can accomplish tasks autonomously on the behalf of its user. It can also interact and collaborate with other agents to accomplish its goals. It can also refuse an order or an action that is called from another agent. Intelligent agents must show some degree of autonomy, social ability, and combine proactive and reactive behavior.

- Autonomous: agents have a degree of control on their own actions, they own their thread of control and under some circumstances, they are also able to take decisions;
- Proactive: agents do not only react in response to external events (*i.e.* a remote method call), but they also exhibit a goal-directed behavior and where appropriate are able to take initiative;
- Social: agents are able to and need to interact with other agents in order to accomplish their task and achieve the complete goal of the system [5].

The environment is a first-class abstraction that provides the surrounding conditions for agents to exist and that mediates both the interaction among agents and the access to resources [6]. A generic environment program has been defined by [7]. This simple program gives the agents precepts and receives back their actions; it then updates the state of the environment based on the actions of the agents and other dynamic processes in the environment that are not considered to be agents. Demazeau [8] considers four essential building blocks for agent systems: agents (*i.e.*, the processing entities), interactions (*i.e.*, the elements for structuring internal interactions between entities), organizations (*i.e.*, elements for structuring sets of entities within the multi-agent system), and finally the environment that is defined as the domain-dependent elements for structuring external interactions between entities. The environment is an independent component of the multi-agent system that has its own responsibilities. These responsibilities are not dependent on agents. It provides the medium for agents to exchange messages, and all agent interactions are done through it.

A multi-agent system is composed with autonomous entities (*i.e.* agents) that interact with one another. Multiple agents are necessary to solve a problem, especially when the problem involves distributed data, knowledge, or control [9]. A multi-agent system is a collection of several interacting agents in which each agent has incomplete information or capabilities for solving the problem [10]. In a multi-agent system, agents are autonomous. There is no global system control, data is decentralized, and communication is asynchronous.

2.3. Correctness: Safety and Liveness Properties

A program is functionally correct if it behaves according to its stated functional requirements. Correctness is a mathematical property that establishes the equivalence between software and its specifications [11]. We can be systematic and precise in assessing correctness by rigorously specifying the functional requirements. Software systems provide critical services to users, *i.e.* process control systems in nuclear power plants or in chemical industry, radiation machines in hospitals, transport systems such as cars, trains and airplanes. In these types of systems, correctness is of vital importance.

Safety and liveness properties are correctness properties. The safety property is an invariant which asserts that something bad never happens, that an acceptable state of affairs is maintained. Magee and Kramer [12] have defined safety property S = {a1, a2 ... an} as a deterministic process that asserts that any trace including actions in the alphabet of S is accepted by S. ERROR conditions are like exceptions which state what is not required, as in complex systems we specify safety properties by directly stating what is required. The liveness property asserts that something good happens, which describes the states of a system that an agent must bring about given certain conditions. These properties play a vital role in system verification. Both safety and liveness properties are complementary to each other, safety alone or liveness alone is not sufficient to ensure system correctness. Progress is a type of liveness property. Progress P = {a1, a2 ... an} defines a property P which asserts that in an infinite execution of a target system, at least one of the actions (a1, a2 ... an) will be executed infinitely [13]. We have the safety and liveness properties mathematically based on timed automata and are unambiguous.

2.4. Formal Verification

Formal verification is the mathematical demonstration of the correctness of a system. The basic idea is to construct a mathematical model of the system under investigation, a model which represents the possible behavior of the system. The correctness requirements are specified along with the other functional requirements that represent the desirable behavior of the system. Based on these specifications, we check formal proof whether the possible behavior agrees with the desired behavior. Verification process can be made precise by using formal methods. Formal verification leads to proving or disproving the correctness with respect to this formal correctness notion. Formal verification can achieve complete exhaustive coverage of the system thus ensuring that undetected failures in the behavior are excluded.

In summary, formal verification requires a model of the system consisting of:
1) A set of states incorporating information about values of variables program counters;
2) A transition relation that describes how the system can change from one state to another;
3) A specification method for expressing requirements in a formal way;
4) A set of proof rules to determine whether the model satisfies the stated requirements.

To obtain a more concrete feeling of what is meant, we consider the way in which sequential programs can be formally verified.

2.5. Model Checking

Model checking [14]-[19] is a method for automatic and algorithmic verification of finite state concurrent systems. It takes as input a finite state model of a system and a logical property, it then systematically checks whether this property holds for a given initial state in that model. Model checking is performed as an exhaustive state space search that is guaranteed to terminate since the model is finite. It uses temporal logic to specify correct system behavior. An efficient, flexible search procedure is used to find correct temporal patterns in the finite state graph of the concurrent system. The orientation of the method is to provide a practical verification method. The technical formulation of the Model checking is: Given structure M, state s, and TL formula f, does M, s | = f?. Clarke and Emerson [14] formulated the CTL (Computation Tree Logic) and proposed a CTL Model checking algorithm. They proposed that concurrent programs can be abstracted to finite state synchronization skeletons, suppressing behavior irrelevant to concurrency.

Model checking addresses finite systems but can be scaled up to a more complex system as a multi-agent system. Here, by complex we mean a system with a large number of independent interacting components, with non-linear aggregate activity, with concurrency between components and constant evolution. Model checking basic idea is to use algorithms executed by software tools to verify the correctness of the system. The user inputs a description of a model of the system, the possible behavior, and a description of the requirements specification, *i.e.* the desirable behavior, and leaves the verification up to the machine. If an error is recognized, the tool provides a counter-example showing under which circumstances the error can be generated. The counter-example consists of a scenario in which the model behaves in an undesired way. Thus the counter-example provides evidence that the model is faulty and needs to be revised. This allows the user to locate the error and to repair the model specification before continuing. If no errors are found, the user can refine its model description e.g. by taking more design decisions into account so that the model becomes more concrete and can restart the verification process.

2.6. Timed Automata

A timed automaton is a finite state automaton equipped with a finite set of real value clock variables called clocks, which are used to measure the elapse of time. Timed automata are used to model finite state real-time systems. A state of a timed automaton consists of the current location of the automaton plus the current values of all clock variables. Clocks can be initialized when the system makes a transition. Once initialized, they start incrementing their value implicitly. All clocks proceed at the same rate. The value of a clock thus denotes the amount of time that has been elapsed since it has been initialized. Conditions on the values of clocks are used as enabling conditions of transitions: only if the clock constraint is fulfilled, the transition is enabled, and can be taken; otherwise, the transition is blocked. Invariants on clocks are used to limit the amount of time that maybe spent in a location. Enabling conditions and invariants are constraints over clocks.

A timed automaton A is a tuple (*L, l_0, E, Label, C, clocks, guard, inv*) [21] with
- *L*, a non-empty, finite set of locations with initial location $l_0 \in L$
- *E ⊆ L x L*, a set of edges
- *Label*: *L → 2^{AP}*, a function that assigns to each location *l ∈ L* a set Label(*l*) of atomic propositions
- *C*, a finite set of clocks
- *clocks*: *E → 2^C*, a function that assigns to each edge *e ∈ E* a set of clocks clocks(e)
  clocks: *E → ψ (C)*, a function that assigns to each edge *e ∈ E* a set of clocks clocks(e)
- *guard*: *E → ψ (C)*, a function that labels each edge *e ∈ E* with a clock constraint guard(e) over C, and
- *inv*: *L → ψ (C)*, a function that assigns to each location an *invariant*.

3. UPPAAL

UPPAAL [20] is a toolkit for symbolic model checking of real-time systems developed at the University of Uppsala (Sweden) and Aalborg (Denmark). It provides model checking for verification of behavioral properties as well as simulation of timed automata. It also has some features to detect deadlocks. The model checking algorithms that are implemented in UPPAAL are based on sets of clock constraints, rather than on explicit sets of regions. By dealing with (disjoint) sets of clock constraints, a coarser partitioning of the infinite state space is obtained. A multi-agent system in UPPAAL is modeled as a network of timed automata, called processes. A clock variable evaluates to a real number and clocks progress synchronously. The fulfilled constraints for the clock values only enable state transitions but do not force them to be taken. A process is an instance of a parameterized template. A template can have local declared variables, functions, and labeled locations. State of the system is defined by locations of the automata, clocks, and variables values.

UPPAAL uses a query language (*i.e.* subset of TCTL) for defining requirements. The query language consists of state formulae and path formulae. State formulae describe individual states with regular expressions such as x ≥ 0. State formulae can also be used to test whether a process is in a given location. Path formulae quantify over paths of the model and can be classified into reachability, safety, and liveness properties:
- Reachability properties are used to check whether a given state formula f can be satisfied by some reachable

state. The syntax for writing this property is E $\diamond$ f.

- Safety properties are used to verify that something bad will never happen. There are two path formulae for checking safety properties. A[] f expresses that a given state formula f should be true in all reachable states, and E[] f means that there should exist a path that is either infinite, or the last state has no outgoing transitions, called maximal path, such that f is always true.
- Liveness properties are used to verify that something eventually will hold, which is expressed as A $\diamond$ f.

Processes communicate with each other through channels. Binary channels are declared as **chan x**. The sender **x!** can synchronize with the receiver **x?** through an edge. If there are multiple receivers **x?**, then a single receiver will be chosen non-deterministically. The sender **x!** will be blocked if there is no receiver. Broadcast channels are declared as broadcast **chan x**. The syntax for sender **x!** and receiver **x?** are the same as for binary channels. However, a broadcast channel sends a signal to all the receivers, and if there is no receiver, the sender will not be blocked. UPPAAL also supports arrays of channels. The syntax to declare them is **chan x [N]** or broadcast **chan x [N]**, and sending and receiving signals are specified as **x[id]!** and **x[id]?**. Processes cannot pass data through signals. If a process wants to send data to another process then the sender has to put the data in a shared variable before sending a signal and the receiver will get the data from shared variable after receiving the signal.

4. Case Study: A Multi-Agent Transport System

In this section we present a case study of multi-agent system. It is a system composed of transporting agents. The objective is to specify our system using timed automata and then verify the correctness properties of safety and liveness. The mission is to transport stock from one storehouse to another. They move in their environment which in this case is static, *i.e.* topology of the system does not evolve at run time. We have specified each and every part of the system, *i.e.* agents along with the environment in the form of LTS.

There are three types of agents:

1) Carrier agent: It transports stock from one storehouse to another, it can be loaded or unloaded and can move both forward and backward direction. Each road section is marked by a sign number and the carrier agent can read this number.

2) Loader/Un-loader agent: It receives/delivers stock from the storehouse, it can detect if a carrier is waiting (for loading or unloading) by reading the presence sensor, it ensures that the carrier waiting to be loaded is loaded and the carrier waiting to be unloaded is unloaded.

3) Store-manager agent: It manages the stock count in the storehouse and it also transports the stock between storehouse and loader/un-loader.

4.1. UPPAAL Model

The template of the Carrier agent has eight locations: *Safe, Appr Loaded Carrier, Parking Store House A, Start Loaded Carrier, Crossing, unload Carrier, Parking Store House B* and *Start Empty Carrier*. The templates for Carrier agent and path have been modeled as shown in **Figure 1**.

The Carrier Agent Template: The initial location is *Safe*, which corresponds to a carrier agent has not appeared on crossing loaded yet. The location has no invariant, which means that a carrier agent may stay in this location for an unlimited amount of time. When a carrier agent is approaching, it synchronizes with the controller. This is done by the channel synchronization appr! on the transition to *Appr Loaded Carrier*. The controller has a corresponding appr?. The clock x is reset and the parameterized variable *e* is set to the identity of this carrier agent. This variable is used by the queue and the controller to know which carrier agent is allowed to continue or which carrier agent must be stopped and later restarted.

The location *Appr Loaded Carrier* has the invariant x ≤ 20, which means that the carrier agent must leave the location within 20 time units. The two outgoing transitions are guarded by the constraints x ≤ 10 and x ≥ 10, which corresponds to the two sections before the crossing: can be stopped and cannot be stopped. At exactly 10, both transitions are enabled, which allows us to take into account any race conditions if there is one. If the carrier agent can be stopped (x ≤ 10) then the transition to the location *Parking Store House A* is taken, otherwise the carrier agent goes to location *Crossing*. The transition to *Parking Store House A* is also guarded by the condition e == id and is synchronized with stop?

When the controller decides to stop a carrier agent, it decides which one (sets *e*) and synchronizes with stop!

The location *Parking Store House A* has no invariant: a carrier agent may be stopped for an unlimited amount of time. It waits for the *synchronization go?*. The guard e == id ensures that the right carrier agent is restarted.

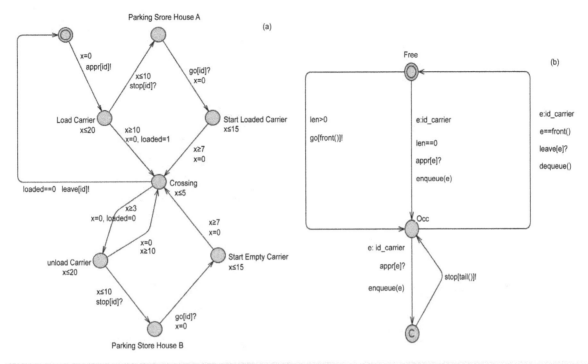

Figure 1. The template for the (a) Carrier agent; and (b) Carrier path.

We can assume that a carrier agent may receive a go? synchronization even when it is not stopped completely, which will give a non-deterministic restarting time. The location *Start Loaded Carrier* has the invariant x ≤ 15 and its outgoing transition has the constraint x ≥ 7.

This means that a carrier agent is restarted and reaches the crossing section between 7 and 15 time units non-deterministically. The location Crossing is similar to *Start Loaded Carrier* in the sense that it is left between 3 and 5 time units after entering it.

The Template of the Path: The path controller synchronizes with the Carrier agent. Some of its locations do not have names. Typically, they are committed locations (marked with a c). The controller starts in the *Free* location (*i.e.*, the path is free), where it tests the queue to see if it is empty or not. If the queue is empty then the controller waits for approaching carrier agent with the appr? synchronization. When a carrier agent is approaching, it is added to the queue with the add! synchronization. If the queue is not empty, then the first carrier agent on the queue is restarted with the go! synchronization.

In the *Occ* location, the controller essentially waits for the running carrier agent to leave the path (leave?). If other carrier agent is approaching (appr?), they are stopped (stop!) and added to the queue (add!). When a carrier agent leaves the path, the controller removes it from the queue.

Table 1 shows the UPPAAL code snippets for system declarations, global declarations, and carrier agent declarations. There is also the UPPAAL verification code which highlights the safety properties.

5. Conclusions and Future Work

A well-defined, precise, timed automaton based model of a multi-agent transport system is proposed. The correctness properties of safety and liveness of this proposed model are verified. The multi-agent system is modeled as a network of timed automata. A clock variable evaluates to a real number and clocks progress synchronously.

Our future work is the proposition, design and implementation of transformation rules for the translation of the current timed automata based formal model into a working system. This working system would have a formal foundation as it would be based on timed automata model.

Acknowledgements

We are grateful to The Worthy Vice Chancellor, The Islamia University of Bahawalpur for motivation and en-

Table 1. UPPAALspecifications (liveness and safety properties).

Declarations		UPPAAL Specifications
System declarations	1 2	//Template instantiations system Carrier_Agent,Path;

Global declarations	1
	2
	3
	4
	5
		//Global declarations
		const int N = 2; //number of carrier agents
		typedef int [0,N-1] id_carrier;
		chanappr[N], stop[N], leave[N];
		urgent chan go[N];

Carrier agent declarations	1
	2
	3
	4
	5
	6
	7
	8
	9
	10
	11
	12
	13
	14
	15
	16
	17
	18
	19
	20
	21
		id_carrier list[N+1];
		int[0,N] len;
		// Postcondition: Put an element at the end of the queue
		void enqueue(id_carrier element)
		{list[len++] = element;}
		// Postcondition: Removes the front element of the queue
		void dequeue()
		{
		int i = 0;
		len -= 1;
		while (i < len)
		{list[i] = list[i + 1];
		i++;}
		list[i] = 0;
		}
		// Postcondition: Returns the front element of the queue
		id_carrier front()
		{return list[0];}
		// Postcondition: Returns the last element of the queue
		id_carrier tail()
		{return list[len - 1];}

Formal verification using UPPAAL verifier	1
	2
	3
	4
	5
	6
	7
		//Collion Detection on Crossing Area
		E<> Carrier_Agent(1).Crossing imply not Carrier_Agent(0).Crossing
		//Reachability
		E<> Carrier_Agent(1).Crossing
		//Check Deadlock For System
		A[] not deadlock

couragement. This work has been possible due to the support of The Department of Computer Science & IT, The Islamia University of Bahawalpur, Pakistan.

References

[1]   George, V. and Vaughn, R. (2003) Application of Lightweight Formal Methods in Requirement Engineering. *Crosstalk: The Journal of Defense Software Engineering*, **16**, 30.

[2]   Wooldridge, M. (2002) An Introduction to MultiAgent Systems. John Wiley and Sons, Chichester.

[3]   Wooldridge, M., Jennings, N.R. and Kinny, D. (2000) The Gaia Methodology for Agent-Oriented Analysis and Design. *Autonomous Agents and Multi-Agent Systems*, **3**, 285-312. http://dx.doi.org/10.1023/A:1010071910869

[4]   Dogac, A. and Cingil, I. (2004) Agent Technology. In: *B2B E-Commerce Technology: Frameworks, Standards and Emerging Issues*, Addison-Wesley, Boston, 103-150.

[5]   Wooldridge, M. and Jennings, N.R. (1995) Intelligent Agents: Theory and Practice. *The Knowledge Engineering Review*, **10**, 115-152. http://dx.doi.org/10.1017/S0269888900008122

[6]   Weyns, D., Omicini, A. and Odell, J. (2007) Environment as a First-Class Abstraction in Multi-Agent Systems. International Journal of *Autonomous Agents and Multi-Agent Systems*, **14**, 5-30.

[7]   Russell, S. and Norvig, P. (2002) Artificial Intelligence: A Modern Approach. 2nd Edition, Prentice Hall, Upper Saddle River.

[8]   Demazeau, Y. (2003) Multi-Agent Systems Methodology. Franco-Mexican School on Cooperative and Distributed Systems (LAFMI).

[9]   Ferber, J. (1999) An Introduction to Distributed Artificial Intelligence. Addison-Wesley, Boston.

[10] Jennings, N.R., Sycara, K. and Wooldridge, M. (1998) A Roadmap of Agent Research and Development. *International Autonomous Agents and Multi-Agent Systems*, **1**, 7-38. http://dx.doi.org/10.1023/A:1010090405266

[11] Ghezzi, C., Jazayeri, M. and Mandrioli, D. (2003) Fundamentals of Software Engineering. 2nd Edition, Prentice Hall, Upper Saddle River.

[12] Magee, J. and Kramer, J. (2006) Concurrency: State Models and Java Programs. 2nd Edition, John Wiley and Sons, Hoboken.

[13] Giannakopoulou, D., Magee, J. and Kramer, J. (1999) Fairness and Priority in Progress Property Analysis. Technical report, Department of Computing, Imperial College of Science, Technology and Medicine, London.

[14] Clarke, E.M. and Emerson, E.A. (1981) Design and Synthesis of Synchronization Skeletons Using Branching Time Temporal Logic. In: Kozen, D., Ed., Logics of Programs, Volume 131, Springer-Verlag, New York, 52-71.

[15] Quielle, J.P. and Sifakis, J. (1982) Specification and Verification of Concurrent Systems in CESAR. *Proceedings of the 5th International Symposium on Programming*, Turin, 6-8 April 1982, 337-351. http://dx.doi.org/10.1007/3-540-11494-7_22

[16] Clarke, E., Grumberg, O. and Peled, D. (1999) Model Checking. MIT Press, Cambridge.

[17] Clarke, E.M., Emerson, E.A. and Sistla, A.P. (1986) Automatic Verification of Finite State Concurrent Systems Using Temporal Logic Specifications. *ACM Transactions on Programming Languages and Systems*, **8**, 244-263.

[18] Clarke, E.M., Grumberg, O. and Long, D.E. (1994) Model Checking and Abstraction. *ACM Transactions on Programming Languages and Systems*, **16**, 1512-1542. http://dx.doi.org/10.1145/186025.186051

[19] Clarke, E.M., Grumberg, O., Jha, S., Lu, Y. and Veith, H. (2003) Counter Example-Guided Abstraction Refinement for Symbolic Model Checking. *Journal of the ACM*, **50**, 752-794. http://dx.doi.org/10.1145/876638.876643

[20] Larsen, K.G., Pettersson, P. and Yi, W. (1997) UPPAAL in a Nutshell. *International Journal on Software Tools for Technology Transfer*, **1**, 134-152.

[21] Katoen, J.P. (1999) Concepts, Algorithms, and Tools for Model Checking. A Lecture Notes of the Course Mechanized Validation of Parallel Systems. For 1998/99 at Friedrich-Alexander Universitat, Erlangen-Nurnberg, 195.

Analyzing the Impact of Different Factors on Software Cost Estimation in Today's Scenario

Deepa Gangwani[1], Saurabh Mukherjee[2]

[1]Research Scholar, Banasthali University, Rajasthan, India
[2]Department of Computer Science, Banasthali University, Rajasthan, India
Email: gangwanideepa@yahoo.com, mukherjee.saurabh@rediffmail.com

Abstract

Software cost estimation is a main concern of the software industry. However, the fact is also that in today's scenario, software industries are more interested in other issues like new technologies in the market, shorter development time, skill shortage etc. They are actually deviating from critical issues to routine issues. Today, people expect high quality products at very low costs and same is the goal of software engineering. An accuracy in software cost estimation has a direct impact on company's reputation and also affects the software investment decisions. Accurate cost estimation can minimize the unnecessary costs and increase the productivity and efficiency of the company. The objective of this paper is to identify the existing methods of software cost estimation prevailing in the market and analyzing some of the important factors impacting the software cost estimation process. In order to achieve the objective, a survey was conducted to find out:

- Nature of projects that companies prefer.
- Impact of training on employees in software cost estimation.
- How many people review the estimated cost?
- How much risk buffer the company keeps for future prospects?

Keywords

Software Cost Estimation, Training, Research method, Nature of Project, Software Review

1. Introduction

Estimating size and cost of a software system is one of the biggest challenges in software project management [1].

In last 50 years many software cost estimation techniques have been evolved in the market to address the different challenges faced by the software industry in software cost estimation. After so much of evolvement, there is still a scope of improvement in effort estimation accuracy. A review of estimation surveys [2] shows that most surveys of effort estimation performance in software development projects report average overruns of 30% - 40%.

The different estimation techniques are divided into two categories *i.e.* algorithmic and non-algorithmic models [3] [4]. Algorithmic models use mathematical formulas whose parameters are based on industrial experience or on historical information that relates some software metric (*i.e.* usually size) to the project cost being used. Algorithmic model is also known as parametric model. These types of models include COCOMO I, COCOMO II, Putnam resource allocation model etc.

In non-algorithmic, no mathematical formulas are used for cost estimation. This model consists of expert estimation, estimation by analogy, top-down estimation, bottom up estimation, Parkinson's Law and price to win.

2. Research Method

The two methods used for this paper are:
- Collecting data with the help of a survey questionnaire (both online and offline), and,
- Interviewing project leaders and project managers of software companies

A survey questionnaire was used to gather information from different IT companies using online and offline method. A random survey was conducted in order to get an overview of current software cost estimation practices. The questionnaire was sent to 35 companies across the country with target participants being project managers, project developers, senior software engineers and infrastructural analysts who contribute to the cost estimation process in software development. A response rate of 80% was attained.

Basic Observations Made on the Survey Data Are

- More than 60% participating organizations are multinational while less than 40% are of Indian origin. This data will enable us present a global view of cost estimation trends existing in the software industry
- More than 60% of the participating organizations had an employee size of greater than 1000 enabling us to evaluate trends in medium to large sized organizations
- 95% participating organizations reflect "Application Development" as their primary work domain. The other key work areas include "Web Development" and "Systems Development". This parameter indicates that we have the right mix of organizations helping us arrive at a conclusion.
- More than 70% of the respondents are "Post Graduates" and are currently working as part of the middle management tier in their respective organizations. This reflects the maturity level of the respondent group.
  I have divided the results of research in to three groups wherein…
- Group 1 represents large companies
- Group 2 represents medium sized companies
- Group 3 contains companies that are smaller in size.
  The results obtained are categorized into five parameters at a group level. The parameters are:
- **Software cost estimation Technique:** As discussed earlier, software cost estimation techniques are categorized into algorithmic and non-algorithmic approach [5].
- **Nature of the Project:** The companies usually engage in two types of projects *i.e.* Fixed bid and Time & Material. Fixed bid projects are contractual agreements to provide specific software services for a specified price while Time & Materials project is a contractual agreement where a client pays the amount based on the number of hours put into the project plus any other added material expenses [6].
- **Training individuals in cost estimation:** Software Cost estimation involves predicting the effort and duration of various projects. Software organizations utilize cost estimators to carefully examine determining factors such as work force, material and equipment. Entry-level cost estimators may receive on-the-job training offered by companies as a part of their on-boarding process [7]. Through these training sessions, new joiners gain sound understanding of software estimation & the importance of estimation in projects.
- **Review process for the estimated software cost:** It is very important to verify the methods used in the estimation process and the results obtained, in order to confirm the integrity of an estimate. It may be tempting to skip this review due to a lack of time, personnel or budget, however, the cost involved in performing a

proper validation/review is likely to be significantly lower than the cost overruns that are likely to develop during a poorly managed software project. When reviewing an estimate one must assess the assumptions made during the estimation process [8].

- **Risk buffer:** As mentioned earlier, most software companies experience cost overruns and unexpected expenses during software development. The main reason is that they begin with uncertain estimates and encounter schedule setbacks. They experience requirement growth and technology change. They are encountered with some essential tasks that weren't planned during estimation. In order to manage such uncertainties, few software companies keep a schedule or budget reserve to deal with such eventualities. To handle these projects' changing realities effectively, it's wise to save a little time and money for the rainy day [9].

3. Result Analysis

3.1. Group 1: Large Sized Companies (Employee Size Is More than 1000)

In this group, companies with more than 1000 employees have been considered

- **Software cost estimation Technique:** These companies use hybrid approach for software cost estimation. Initially they start with algorithmic method for estimation then move to non-algorithmic model. In algorithmic, many companies use function point method in order to calculate the size and complexity of the project based on number of inputs, outputs, files, modules, reports etc. Once the size and complexity is estimated, project managers and project leaders use their experience to estimate the cost by allocating resources and creating a resource pyramid. During the interview, it has also been told by the interviewee that they use their own customized tools based on function point and COCOMO for estimation.
- **Nature of projects:** These companies are majorly into fixed projects and rarely go for time and material type of projects. A possible reason is that companies have an abundant resource pool available to manage crisis. This also helps companies to opt for long term engagements than short term.
- **Training:** In this, companies provide project management training to their employees. These trainings also cover cost estimation. Employees get in-depth knowledge of cost estimation and are also made aware of the tools used by the company to estimate costs of software they would develop. The respondents mentioned that they are quite satisfied with the current software cost estimation technique and the training module has proven beneficial for them.
- **Review:** Any estimation made is reviewed by the team comprising of experienced project managers, system analyst and project leaders. The estimate, along with details of all parameters considered during estimation, is then submitted to the committee for final approval.
- **Risk buffer:** Every company keeps a risk buffer for uncertain situations. This group keeps a buffer of 10% to 30% in order to deal with uncertainties.

3.2. Group 2: Medium Sized Companies

This group includes companies with 200 to less than 1000 employees.

- **Software cost estimation Technique:** This group majorly uses intuition, experience, analogy, price-to-win and capacity related techniques to estimate cost. Some companies also use certain tools for estimation. The elements they consider for estimation are software, hardware, number of delivered units, testing and documentation.
- **Nature of projects:** These companies majorly work on time and material based engagements with fixed cost engagements forming a very small portion of their overall portfolio.
- **Training:** In this, some companies arrange small meetings for providing insights of cost estimation techniques but do not provide targeted training programs for project management modules. The companies believe in intuition and experience for software cost estimation.
- **Review:** The review process involves 2 - 5 individuals that have significant experience in estimating costs.
- **Risk buffer:** This group keeps a buffer of 20% to 40% in order to deal with uncertainties.

3.3. Group 3: Small Sized Companies

This group comprises of companies wherein the size of the employees is less than 200.

- **Software cost estimation Technique:** These companies majorly use price to win, capacity related and software cost models for software cost estimation. Since these companies are at emerging stages, they do not have sufficient historical data to deal with. So they prefer to estimate costs based on individual experiences. The employees, however, are not satisfied with this method as there are situations where companies, despite keeping a risk buffer, are not able to even earn marginal profits.

- **Nature of projects:** These companies deal with time and material type of project as they don't have sufficient resources and dedicated staff for fixed type of projects.
- **Training:** This group does not provide any type of training in software cost estimation. Conducting special training for software cost estimation will require additional cost and effort which these companies can't afford with limited resources.
- **Review:** In this group, the estimate is reviewed by more than 5 individuals before being passed on to the client.
- **Risk buffer:** This group keeps a buffer within a range of 20% to 40% in order to deal with uncertainties. Interviews with stakeholders revealed that there are situations where companies are not able to recover employee costs despite the high risk buffer.

4. Analyzing the Results

In order to analyze the results, three hypotheses have been made *i.e.*

The **"Null hypotheses"** might be:

H01: Training in cost estimation is independent to company size.

H02: Estimated Risk buffer is independent to company size

H03: Number of People reviewing the estimated cost remain same irrespective of company size.

And an **"Alternative hypotheses"** might be:

H11: Training in cost estimation is dependent to company size.

H12: Estimated Risk buffer is dependent to company size.

H13: Number of people review the estimated cost vary according to size of the company

Chi-square test is applied in order to check the association between the two variables by using SPSS 20.0

Research question 1: Is there an association between company size and the training program in software cost estimation.

Interpret results: From **Tables 1-3**, we can interpret, since the P-value (0.002) is less than the significance level (0.05), we cannot accept the null hypothesis (H01). Thus, we conclude that there is a relationship between company size and the training program hence, alternate hypotheses (H11) is accepted.

Research question 2: Is there an association between company size and the risk buffer they keep foe contingencies situation.

In this we will try to find out the relationship between the percentage of risk buffer company keep for handling uncertain situation and the size of the company. The result we got after analyzing the data are:

Interpret results. From **Tables 4-6**, we can interpret, since the P-value (0.034) is less than the significance level (0.05), we cannot accept the null hypothesis (H02). Thus, we conclude that there is a relationship between company size and the risk buffer hence, alternate hypotheses (H12) is accepted

Research question 3: What is the relation between the number of people engaged for the estimated cost review and the size of the company?

Interpret results. From **Tables 7-9**, we can interpret, since the P-value (0.014) is less than the significance level (0.05), we cannot accept the null hypothesis (H02). Thus, we conclude that there is a relationship between company size and number of people review the estimated cost hence, alternate hypotheses (H12) is accepted.

Research question 4: What is the relation between the nature of project and the size of the company?

From **Table 10** simple crosstab formation we can conclude that Mid-Sized & Small Companies still prefer the Time and Material based projects whereas large companies are in favor of Fixed Price Based Project. This is primarily driven by the fact that small companies are still dependent on Body Shopping type of work whereas large organization has moved up on IT Value chain.

Research Question 5: What is the major purpose of estimation of different sized companies?

Here, we have used simple column chart in order to showcase the purpose of estimation of companies depending on their size.

The result which we got is as follows (shown in **Figure 1**)

From **Figure 1**, we can conclude that in large company's purpose of estimation is to determine the manpower requirement which proves the point of managing resource by creating common pool and not assigning resources permanently to project.

Table 1. Company size vs Training program Cross tabulation.

Type of Companies	Training		Total
	Yes	No	
Large Companies	15	2	17
Mid Sized Companies	3	5	8
Small Comapnies	0	3	3
Total	18	10	28

Table 2. Result of Chi Square test.

	Value	df	Asymp. Sig. (2-sided)
Pearson Chi-Square	12.147[a]	2	0.002
Likelihood Ratio	13.598	2	0.001
Linear-by-Linear Associaation	11.631	1	0.001
N of Valid Cases	28		

Table 3. Symmetric measure.

	Value	Asymp. Std. Error[a]	Approx. T[b]	Approx. Sig.
Interval by Interval Pearson's R	0.656	0.119	4.436	0.000[c]
Ordinal by OrdinalSpearman Correlation	0.654	0.138	4.410	0.000[c]
N of Valid Cases	28			

Table 4. Company size vs risk buffer cross tabulation.

Type of Companies	Risk_Buffer			More than 40%	Total
	10%	20%	30%		
Large Companies	10	6	1	0	17
Mid Sized Companies	1	3	3	1	8
Small Comapnies	0	2	0	1	3
Total	11	11	4	2	28

Table 5. Result of Chi Square test.

	Value	df	Asymp. Sig. (2-sided)
Pearson Chi-Square	13.643[a]	6	0.034
Likelihood Ratio	14.550	6	0.024
Linear-by-Linear Associaation	8.265	1	0.004
N of Valid Cases	28		

Table 6. Symmetric measure.

	Value	Asymp. Std. Error[a]	Approx. T[b]	Approx. Sig.
Interval by Interval Pearson's R	0.553	0.127	3.387	0.002[c]
Ordinal by Ordinal Spearman Correlation	0.572	0.123	3.557	0.001[c]
N of Valid Cases	28			

Table 7. Company size vs review of estimated cost.

Type of Companies	Review (in Persons)			Total
	1 - 2	3 - 5	More than 5	
Large Companies	10	5	2	17
Mid Sized Companies	2	6	0	8
Small Comapnies	0	1	2	3
Total	12	12	4	28

Table 8. Result of Chi Square test.

	Value	df	Asymp. Sig. (2-sided)
Pearson Chi-Square	12.582[a]	4	0.014
Likelihood Ratio	12.011	4	0.017
Linear-by-Linear Associaation	5.452	1	0.020
N of Valid Cases	28		

Table 9. Symmetric measure.

	Value	Asymp. Std. Error[a]	Approx. T[b]	Approx. Sig.
Interval by Interval Pearson's R	0.449	0.178	2.565	0.016[c]
Ordinal by Ordinal Spearman Correlation	0.416	0.174	2.330	0.028[c]
N of Valid Cases	28			

Table 10. Nature of projects vs company size.

Type of Companies	Nature_of_Project			Total
	Fixed Projects	Time & Material Projects	Both	
Large Companies	7	6	4	17
Mid Sized Companies	2	6	0	8
Small Comapnies	0	2	1	3
Total	9	14	5	28

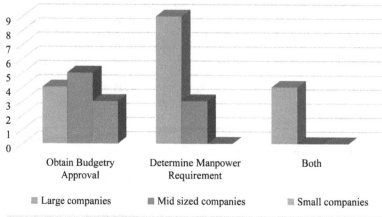

Figure 1. Purpose of estimation vs company size.

5. Limitation

For the purpose of this paper, some of the factors that were considered in order to find the impact on software cost estimation are nature of project, risk buffer, training, review etc. There are other important factors which could be considered for further studies like quality factors (maintainability, portability, flexibility etc.). These quality factors also have an impact on the cost of the software. Now-a-days, software engineers face difficulty when customers demand for the software to be compatible with hand held devices. Changes like these are time consuming and demand extra effort. This paper does not cover impact of such technology driven changes on software cost estimation.

6. Summary

A small survey was conducted to gather information related to software cost estimation techniques existing in the market. As a result we got to know the impact of training provided by the companies on software cost estimation techniques. The survey also helped us gather information on the risk buffer that companies keep to manage contingency situations and how many people review the estimated cost before disclosing it to respective clients. We also got information on company specific purpose of estimation and nature of project the company usually takes based on their time and resource capacity.

References

[1]   Popović, J. and Bojić, D. (2012) A Comparative Evaluation of Effort Estimation Methods in the Software Life Cycle. *ComSIS*, **9**, 455-484.

[2]   Moløkken, K. and Jorgensen, M. (2003) A Review of Software Surveys on Software Effort Estimation. *International Symposium on Empirical Software Engineering*, Rome, 30 September-1 October 2003, 223-230. http://dx.doi.org/10.1109/ISESE.2003.1237981

[3]   Boehm, B. (1981) Software Engineering Economics. Prentice-Hall, Upper Saddle River.

[4]   Yogesh, K. (2014) A Review on Effort Estimation Techniques used in Software Projects. *IJCSMS International Journal of Computer Science & Management Studies*, **14**, 25-31.

[5]   Khatibi, V. and Jawawi, D.N.A. (2010) Software Cost Estimation Methods: A Review. *Journal of Emerging Trends in Computing and Information Sciences*, **2**, 21-29.

[6]   Luschen, T. (2012) Fixed Bid vs. Time and Materials—Pros and Cons. http://www.sundoginteractive.com/sunblog/posts/fixed-bid-vs.-time-and-materials-pros-and-cons

[7]   Education Portal, Study.com, Cost Estimating Courses with Training& Degree Program Info. http://education-portal.com/articles/Cost_Estimating_Courses_Overview_with_Training_and_Degree_Program_Information.html

[8]   Galorath, D. (2008) Step: Estimate Validation and Review. http://www.galorath.com/wp/step-seven-estimate-validation-and-review.php

[9]   Wiegers, K. (2002) Saving for a Rainy Day. http://www.ibm.com/developerworks/rational/library/content/RationalEdge/apr02/RainyDayApr02.pdf

22

A Blind DWT-SCHUR Based Digital Video Watermarking Technique

Lama Rajab[1], Tahani Al-Khatib[1], Ali Al-Haj[2]

[1]Computer Information Systems, The University of Jordan, Amman, Jordan
[2]Princess Sumaya University for Technology, Amman, Jordan
Email: Lama.rajab@ju.edu.jo, tahani.khatib@ju.edu.jo, ali@psut.edu.jo

Abstract

Digital watermarking is one of the most powerful tools used in ownership and copyrights protection in digital media. This paper presents a blind digital video watermarking technique based on a combination scheme between the Discrete Wavelet transform in (DWT) and the real Schur Decomposition. The scheme starts with applying two-level DWT to the video scene followed by Schur decomposition in which the binary watermark bits are embedded in the resultant block upper triangular matrix. The proposed technique shows high efficiency due to the use of Schur decomposition which requires fewer computations compared to other transforms. The imperceptibility of the scheme is also very high due to the use of DWT transform; therefore, no visual distortion is noticed in the watermarked video after embedding. Furthermore, the technique proves to be robust against set of standard attacks like: Gaussian, salt and pepper and rotation and some video attacks such as: frame dropping, cropping and averaging. Both capacity and blindness features are also considered and achieved in this technique.

Keywords

Video Watermarking, Schur Decomposition, Discrete Wavelet Transform (DWT)

1. Introduction

As Digital videos and images are remarkably expanding over the internet due to the development of blogs, video sharing websites and social network applications, it becomes necessary to protect copyrights of the digital contents to guarantee the ownership identification. Digital watermarking in multimedia has become the most efficient technology used in securing digital data. In practice, the watermarking technique embeds a small copyright message, called a watermark, inside the digital media content to identify the ownership.

Effective techniques in watermarking should consider both imperceptivity and robustness of the algorithm. Imperceptibility refers to the watermark perceptual transparency [1], while robustness indicates the ability of extracting the embedded watermark from the digital media under intentional or unintentional attacks such as degradation, cropping, filtering or additive noise [1] [2]. Capacity and blindness of the watermarking techniques are two additional issues to be considered as well. Capacity, also referred as data Payload, includes methods that make it possible to embed the majority of information. Blindness of the algorithms implies that the watermarking extraction does not need the existence of the original image [3].

In literature, many watermarking algorithms have been proposed for video, video frames and images. In general, Digital watermarking techniques are classified into two categories: spatial domain watermarking, as in [4]-[6], and transform domain watermarking, such as in [7]-[10]. In spatial domain methods, watermarking is performed by modifying the pixels values in the host image. However, in frequency domain methods, the watermark is embedded into transformed coefficients of the image. Frequency domain methods are found to be more robust and complex than spatial domain ones; also they are visually more convenient to human and have higher imperceptibility and capacity [11].

All kinds of digital media may be protected in order to guarantee ownership and copyrights identification, and hence watermarking can be applied on digital videos, audios, images or documents. In the case of digital videos, watermarking may be applied on both compressed and uncompressed videos. However, applying watermarking on uncompressed videos is much safer than compressed ones because video frames are considered as consecutive and equally spaced still; and hence, watermark will be embedded without any data loss risk. In contrast, watermarked compressed video such as MPEG-compressed bit stream can be converted to another compression standard which may result in modifying or losing the embedded watermark data [12].

There are many researches on transforming domain watermarking for audio, images, compressed and uncompressed videos. Various proposed algorithms made use of popular transformations such as SVD, DWT, or DCT. Yet, many algorithms combined some of these transformations to form hybrid approaches in order to obtain better embedding and extraction results. In some new researches, SCHUR transform was studied and used in watermarking techniques. Using Schur transform in watermarking embedding and extraction had proved to be a promising area that may compete with other transform domains and make good results for robustness and precision in watermarking.

In [13], authors presented a non blind hybrid watermarking scheme using SCHUR and SVD transforms. They used Schur in embedding and extraction steps after decomposing the image into 8×8 blocks followed by applying SVD on the largest Eigen values. However, in [14], authors proposed a non blind hybrid technique using SCHUR and Cellular Automata Transform (CAT), and made use of the flexibility of CAT domain and the efficiency of the Schur transform. While in [15], a blind image watermarking method based on Schur transform was proposed. The image is transformed into Schur transform and then analyzed to find a non-sensitive zone where embedding procedure take place. On the other hand, the proposed algorithm in [16] embeds the watermark in two decomposition of SCHUR transform, which are the D matrix and the U matrix, the technique improves the robustness of the algorithm since the same watermark information is stored twice in two places.

In this paper, a robust, blind digital video watermarking technique is proposed. The proposed technique combined the Schur decomposition with the DWT transform to produce an efficient technique with high robustness and imperceptibility. The rest of this paper is organized as follows: The Discrete Wavelet transform and the Schur decomposition is described in Section 2. In Section 3 the proposed watermarking technique is discussed in details. In Section 4 the experimental results are discussed and Section 6 concludes the proposed technique.

2. Materials and Methods

2.1. Discrete Wavelet Transform (DWT)

Discrete Wavelet Transform is the multi resolution description of an image, where the decoding can be processed sequentially from a low resolution to the higher resolution [17]. The discrete wavelet transform is based on small waves, called wavelets, of varying frequency and limited duration. Such wavelet transform provides both frequency and spatial description of an image [18]. The Discrete Wavelet Transform DWT splits the signal into high and low frequency parts. The high frequency part contains information about the edge components, while the low frequency part is split again into high and low frequency parts. The high frequency components are usually used for watermarking since the human eye is less sensitive to changes in edges [19]. The discrete wavelet transform decomposes the input image hierarchically to four frequency districts one low (LL) and the other three districts are high: LH, HL, HH as shown in **Figure 1**.

A two dimensional image can be decomposed by DWT by more than one level. In the proposed technique we applied 2 level DWT, and then we used the High level (HL) band in the second level. Each sub-band is a matrix of DWT coefficients at a specific resolution. **Figure 2** shows the sub-bands produced by the 2-level DWT decomposition.

2.2. Schur Decomposition

The Schur decomposition or Schur triangulation is an important mathematical tool in linear algebra used in metrics analysis, which was named after Issai Schur. In fact, SCHUR decomposition represents a major intermediate step in SVD decomposition [20]; and it to be an efficient mathematical tool since it requires about n^3 flops for an n * n matrix; while SVD decomposition requires $11n^3$ flops. Which means that the number of computations performed in SCHUR is less than one third of those performed in SVD decomposition [21].

There are two versions of Schur decomposition transform: complex Schur and real Schur, [22]. The Real Schur decomposition version of a real square matrix A results in two matrices: U and S as shown in Equation (1):

$$\text{Schur}(A) = \left(U \times S \times U^T\right) \tag{1}$$

where S is the block upper triangular matrix called the real Schur form and U is a unitary orthogonal matrix. U^T indicates the conjugate transpose of U. The following example illustrates the Schur decomposition applied on a 3×3 matrix A.

$$A = \begin{bmatrix} 160 & 160 & 159 \\ 160 & 159 & 159 \\ 161 & 160 & 158 \end{bmatrix}$$

Applying real Schur decomposition on matrix A will produce both U and S matrices as follows:

$$U = \begin{bmatrix} 0.5778 & 0.4077 & -0.7071 \\ 0.5765 & -0.8171 & -0.0000 \\ 0.5778 & 0.4077 & 0.7071 \end{bmatrix}$$

$$S = \begin{bmatrix} 478.6664 & -0.7071 & -2.0418 \\ 0 & -0.6664 & -0.5753 \\ 0 & 0 & -1.0000 \end{bmatrix}$$

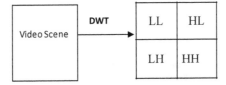

Figure 1. Frame's 2-level DWT sub-bands.

LL$_1$	LL$_2$	HL$_2$
	LH$_2$	HH$_2$
LH$_1$	HH$_1$	

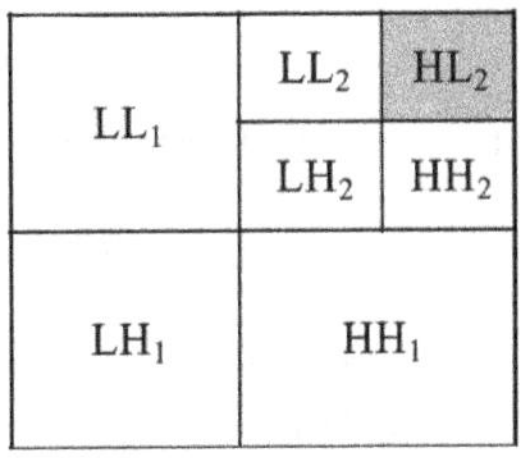

Figure 2. Frame's 2-level DWT sub-bands.

Apparently, Matrix S is a triangular matrix; and it is also similar to A by definition of matrices similarities [20]. Accordingly, matrix S has the same multi set of Eigen values in A. Eigen values set is contained in the main diagonal of the S matrix because S is triangular. Hence, the diagonal in S matrix was selected in our technique for watermarking embedding, because of the fact that Eigen values in Schur decomposition are highly stable [22].

3. The Proposed Technique

3.1. Video Frames and Video Watermarking

The host in any digital watermarking technique is defined as the place where the watermark is embedded. The host can be image, video or audio. A video sequence consists of many frames where each frame can be considered as an image. So image watermarking can be extended to video watermarking. The watermark in the proposed technique is embedded in the frames of a video clip.

3.2. The Proposed DWT-Schur Technique

In this paper a blind robust digital video watermarking technique is proposed. The proposed technique applies both DWT and Schur transforms on the digital video where a binary watermark in embedded and distributed in the video frames. The proposed DWT-Schur watermarking algorithm consists of two procedures, the first embeds the watermark into the original video clip, while the other extracts it form the watermarked version of the clip. The two procedures are described in details in the following sections.

Watermark Embedding Procedure

The proposed DWT-SCHUR Based Watermarking Algorithm begins with embedding the selected binary watermark into the video frames; the embedding procedure is described in details in **Table 1**.

Table 1. Embedding procedure steps.

Input Video

1. Input the video clip V.
2. Divide the video clip into video scenes V_{s_i}
3. Process the frames of each video scene using DWT and Schur as described in steps 4 - 11.
4. Convert every video frame F from RGB to YUV color matrix format.

Apply 2-level DWT

5. Compute the 2-level DWT for the Y (luminance) matrix in each frame F. This operation generates seven DWT sub-bands [LL_1, LL_2, HL_2, LH_2, HH2, LH_1, HH_1].

Apply SCHUR

6. Apply the Schur operator on the HL_2 sub-band (highlighted in **Figure 1**). The Schur operator decomposes the sub-band's coefficient matrix into two independent matrices:

$$HL_2 = \left(U_{HL_2} S_{HL_2} \right) \tag{2}$$

Embedding

7. Rescale the watermark image so that the size of the watermark will match the size of the HL_2 sub-band which will be used for embedding.
8. Embed the binary bits of watermark W_{Vsi} into the diagonal matrix of S_{HL2} by substituting the watermark bit W_i with the eighth LSB (Least significant Bit) bit of $S_{HL_2}(i, i)$:

$$LSB\left(S_{HL_2}(i,i) \right) = W_{Vsi} \tag{3}$$

Video Reconstruction

9. Apply the inverse Schur operator on the modified S'_{HL_2} matrix to get a modified coefficient matrix HL'_2. The inverse Schur operation is as follows:

$$\left(U_{HL_2} \times S_{HL_2} \times U^T_{HL_2} \right) \tag{4}$$

10. Apply the inverse DWT on the modified coefficient matrix HL'_2. This operation produces the final watermarked Video frame F'.
11. Convert the video frames f' from YUV to RGB color matrix.
12. Reconstruct frames into the final watermarked Video scene F'.
13. Reconstruct watermarked scenes to get the final watermarked VXM.

The embedding procedure described previously is depicted in the block diagram shown in **Figure 3**.

3.3. Watermark Extraction Procedure

The Watermark extraction procedure does not need the original video given that the proposed DWT-Schur algorithm is totally blind. Consequently, we can extract the watermark image from the watermarked video frames from the LSBs directly. The watermarking extraction procedure is described in details in **Table 2**.

The watermarking extraction procedure proposed above is illustrated in the block diagram shown in **Figure 4**.

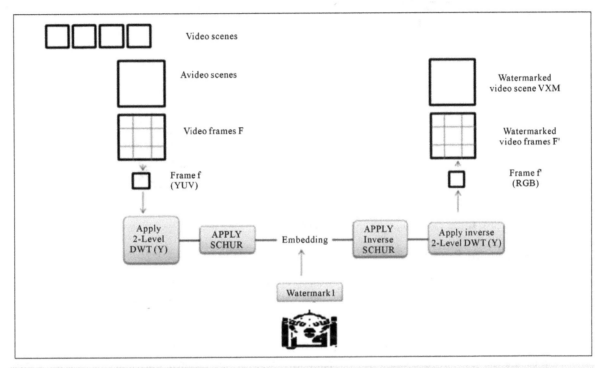

Figure 3. The watrermark embedding procedure.

Table 2. Extraction procedure steps.

Input Video

1. Input the watermarked Video clip V'.
2. Divide the watermarked Video clip V' into watermarked scenes Vsi'.
3. Process the watermarked frames of each watermarked video scene using DWT and Schur as described in steps 4 - 7.
4. Convert the video frame F' from RGB color matrix to YUV.

Apply 2-level DWT

5. Compute the 2-level DWT for the frame F'. Let the seven sub-bands produced after this process be: [wLL$_1$, wLL$_2$, wHL$_2$, wLH$_2$, wHH$_2$, wLH$_1$, wHH$_1$].

Apply SCHUR

6. Apply the Schur operator on the wHL$_2$ sub-band. The Schur operator decomposes the sub-band's coefficient matrix into two independent matrices:

$$W_{HL_2} = U_{wHL_2} S_{wHL_2} \tag{5}$$

Extraction

7. Extract the embedded watermark from the diagonal matrix S_{wHL2} as follows:

$$W_{Vsi}(i) = LSB\left(S_{HL_2}(i,i)\right) \tag{6}$$

Video Reconstruction

8. Construct the image watermark WVsi by cascading all watermark bits extracted from all frames.
9. Repeat the same procedure for all video scenes.
10. The watermarking extraction procedure proposed above is illustrated in the block diagram shown in **Figure 3**.

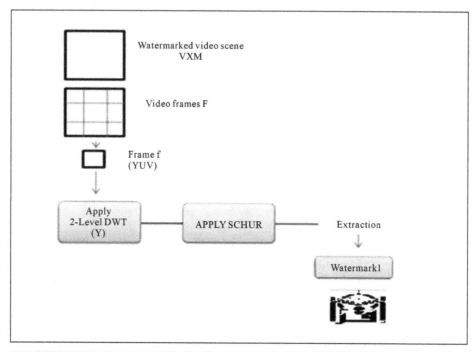

Figure 4. The watermark extraction procedure.

4. Experimental Results

In this section we investigate the robustness of the proposed DWT-Schur technique against different attacks. The cover video clip used for testing has four scenes with 438, 599, 744 and 821 frames respectively. The size for each frame is 352×352 pixels. A snapshot from each scene is shown in **Figure 5**. The watermark is a binary text image with size 363×256 as shown in **Figure 6**. The use of text messages makes it easy to test the robustness. Where we simply read the extracted message and compare it with the original watermark.

To measure the level of robustness and the similarity between the original watermark W and the extracted watermarks W' the correlation shown in the Equation (7) is used. The correlation may take values between 0 and 1. Where 0 indicates that there is no similarity and 1 indicates that both watermarks are same.

$$\text{Corr}\left(W, W'\right) = \frac{x^* x^t}{\sqrt{XX^T}} \tag{7}$$

In the Normal Test the proposed technique shows a high imperceptibility where. No visual degradation was noticed in the video clip after embedding the watermark and the similarity between the embedded and extracted watermark are completely similar as shown in **Figure 7**. The average PSNR for the all watermarked frames was 57.3118. At this PSNR value no quality degradation in the watermarked video was perceived the PSNR is shown in Equation (8).

$$\text{PSNR} = 10 \text{Log} 10\left(255 / \sqrt{\text{MSE}}\right) \tag{8}$$

The robustness for the proposed technique is measured against two types of attacks: standard and frame attacks. Standard attacks include compression, rotation, Gaussian noise, salt & pepper noise, among many others [2]. The video attacks are frames swapping, averaging and dropping. For both types of attacks we measured the similarity between the original and extracted watermarks using the correlation.

Salt & Pepper and Gaussian Noise Addition Attacks The robustness of the proposed technique against salt & pepper and Gaussian noise is acceptable since the watermark is still distinguished and the correlation results are somehow high but the lowest compared with the other attacks which is reasonable since the noise addition attacks affects each pixel in the watermarked frame (the results are shown in **Table 3**).

Table 3. The results after applying the noise addition attacks.

Attacks	Scene 1	Scene 2	Scene 3	Scene 4
Salt & pepper				
Correlation	0.7030	0.6994	0.6956	0.6969
Gaussian				
Correlation	0.9702	0.9628	0.9783	0.9772

Figure 5. Snapshots from the video scenes.

Figure 6. The original watermark.

Rotation Attacks for the rotation attacks we rotated the watermarked image by three different angels 30, 90 and 180 degrees. The proposed techniques shows high robustness against this attack as you see in **Table 4** the watermarks are almost the same as the original with high values of correlation. Hence, the diagonal in S matrix was selected in our technique for watermarking embedding as we discussed before and this is because of the fact that Eigen values in Schur decomposition are highly stable and increase the robustness.

Table 4. The results after applying the rotation attacks.

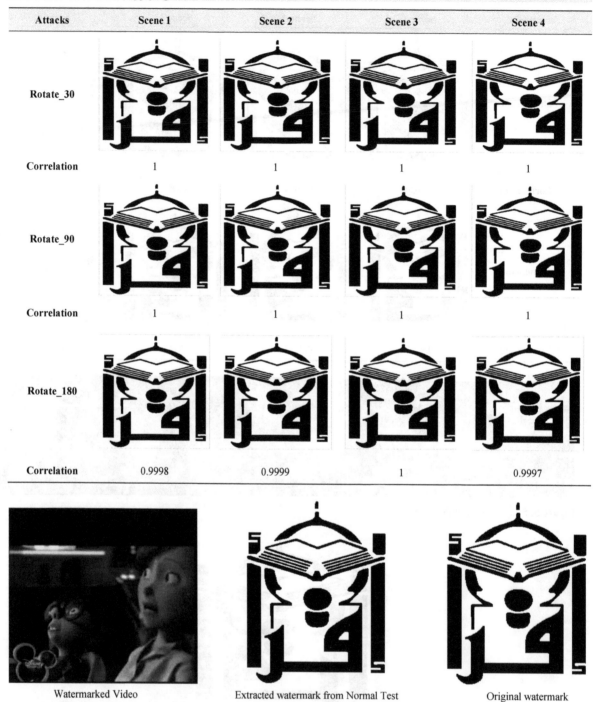

Attacks	Scene 1	Scene 2	Scene 3	Scene 4
Rotate_30				
Correlation	1	1	1	1
Rotate_90				
Correlation	1	1	1	1
Rotate_180				
Correlation	0.9998	0.9999	1	0.9997

Watermarked Video   Extracted watermark from Normal Test   Original watermark

Figure 7. The watermarked and the extracted watermark in the normal test.

Video Attacks for video attacks we test the robustness for the watermarked scenes by applying frames swapping attacks where the fourth and the tenth frames in each watermarked scene are swapped. Then frame averaging video attacks and finally the frame dropping video attacks where we dropped 90% from the watermarked scene and as you see in **Table 5** the results are reflected in the extracted watermark where approximately we see 10% of the watermark and the remaining is dropped with the video. This is because the watermark is distributed in all the frames in each video scene.

Table 5. The results after applying the video attacks.

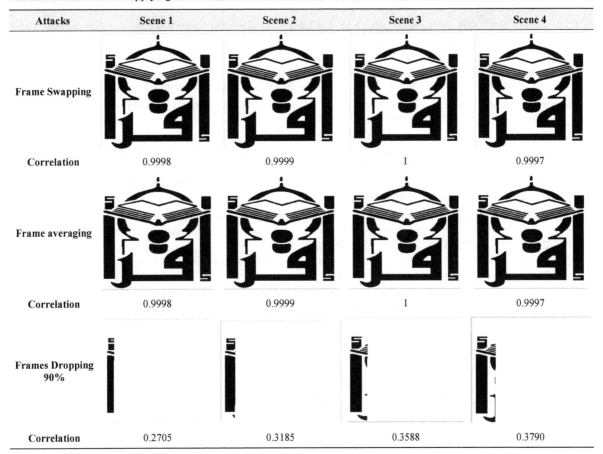

Attacks	Scene 1	Scene 2	Scene 3	Scene 4
Frame Swapping				
Correlation	0.9998	0.9999	1	0.9997
Frame averaging				
Correlation	0.9998	0.9999	1	0.9997
Frames Dropping 90%				
Correlation	0.2705	0.3185	0.3588	0.3790

5. Conclusion

This paper presented a new technique for blind digital video watermarking. The proposed technique made use of two powerful mathematical transforms: Discrete wavelet transforms (DWT) and Schur decomposition. Experimental results demonstrated the imperceptibility, blindness and robustness of the proposed technique. The watermark was successfully extracted without the existence of the original video and no visual distortion appears in the watermarked video. The technique proved its robustness against a set of standard and video attacks, and succeeded in extracting the watermark with minimum distortion. Using Schur decomposition improved the efficiency of the technique due to the small number of computations compared to other similar mathematical decompositions.

References

[1] Khatib, T., Haj, A., Rajab, L. and Mohammed, H. (2008) A Robust Video Watermarking Algorithm. *Journal of Computer Science*, **4**, 910-915. http://dx.doi.org/10.3844/jcssp.2008.910.915

[2] Voloshynovskiy, S., Pereira, S. and Pun, T. (2001) Attacks on Digital Watermarks: Classification, Estimation-Based Attacks, and Benchmarks. *Communications Magazine*, **39**, 118-126. http://dx.doi.org/10.1109/35.940053

[3] Gunjal, B.L. and Manthalkar, R.R. (2010) An Overview of Transform Domain Robust Digital Image Watermarking Algorithms. *Journal of Emerging Trends in Computing and Information Sciences*, **2**, 37-42.

[4] Lancini, R., Mapelli, F. and Tubaro, S. (2002) A Robust Video Watermarking Technique in the Spatial Domain. *Video/Image Processing and Multimedia Communications 4th EURASIP-IEEE Region 8 International Symposium on VIPromCom*, 2002, 251-256. http://dx.doi.org/10.1109/VIPROM.2002.1026664

[5] Hussein, J.A. (2010) Spatial Domain Watermarking Scheme for Colored Images Based on Log-Average Luminance. CoRR, abs/1001.3496.

[6]   Mondal, M. and Barik, D. (2012) Spatial Domain Robust Watermarking Scheme for Color Image. *International Journal of Advanced Computer Science*, **2**, 24-27.

[7]   Mostafa, S.A., Tolba, A.S., Abdelkader, F.M. and Elhindy, H.M. (2009) Video Watermarking Scheme Based on Principal Component Analysis and Wavelet Transform. *International Journal of Computer Science and Network Security*, **9**, 45-52.

[8]   Al-Taweel, S.A., Sumari, P., Alomari, S.A. and Husain, A.J. (2009) Digital Video Watermarking in the Discrete Cosine Transform Domain. *Journal of Computer Science*, **5**, 536-543. http://dx.doi.org/10.3844/jcssp.2009.536.543

[9]   Sathik, M. and Sujatha, S. (2012) A Novel DWT Based Invisible Watermarking Technique for Digital Images. *International Arab Journal of e-Technology*, **2**, 167-172.

[10]   Hernández, M.C., Miyatake, M.N. and Meana, H.P. (2005) Analysis of a DFT-Based Watermarking Algorithm. *2nd International Conference on Electrical and Electronics Engineering*, 7-9 September 2005, 44-47. http://dx.doi.org/10.1109/ICEEE.2005.1529569

[11]   Rajab, L., Al-Khatib, T. and Al-Haj, A. (2009) Video Watermarking Algorithms Using the SVD Transform. *European Journal of Scientific Research*, **30**, 389-401.

[12]   Rajab, L., Al-Khatib, T. and Al-Haj, A. (2008) Hybrid DWT-SVD Video Watermarking. *Proceedings of the International Conference on Innovations in Information Technology*, Al Ain, 16-18 December 2008, 588-592. http://dx.doi.org/10.1109/INNOVATIONS.2008.4781696

[13]   Meenakshi, K., Rao, C.S. and Prasad, K.S. (2014) A Fast and Robust Hybrid Watermarking Scheme Based on Schur and Svd Transform. *International Journal of Research in Engineering and Technology*, **3**, 7-11.

[14]   Panahi, N., Amirani, M., Behnia, S. and Ayubi, P. (2013) A New Colour Image Watermarking Scheme Using Cellular Automata Transform and Schur Decomposition. *Proceedings of the 21st Iranian Conference on Electrical Engineering (ICEE)*, Mashhad, 14-16 May 2013, 1-5. http://dx.doi.org/10.1109/IranianCEE.2013.6599623

[15]   Seddik, H., Sayadi, M. and Fnaiech, F. (2009) A New Blind Image Watermarking Method Based on Shur Transformation. *Proceedings of the 35th Annual Conference of IEEE Industrial Electronics*, Porto, 3-5 November 2009, 1967-1972.

[16]   Mohan, B.C. and Swamy, K.V. (2010) On the Use of Schur Decomposition for Copyright Protection of Digital Images. *International Journal of Computer and Electrical Engineering*, **2**, 781-787. http://dx.doi.org/10.7763/IJCEE.2010.V2.228

[17]   Xia, X.G., Boncelet, C.G. and Arce, G.R. (1997) A Multiresolution Watermark for Digital Images. *Proceedings of the International Conference on Image Processing*, Santa Barbara, 26-29 October 1997, 548-551. http://dx.doi.org/10.1109/ICIP.1997.647971

[18]   Hong, W. and Hang, M. (2006) Robust Digital Watermarking Scheme for Copy Right Protection. *IEEE Transactions on Signal Processing*, **12**, 1-8.

[19]   Kundur, D. and Hatzinakos, D. (1998) Digital Watermarking Using Multiresolution Wavelet Decomposition. *Proceedings of the 1998 IEEE International Conference on Acoustics, Speech and Signal Processing*, Seattle, 12-15 May 1998, 2969-2972. http://dx.doi.org/10.1109/ICASSP.1998.678149

[20]   Golub, G.H. and Van Loan, C.F. (1989) Matrix Computations. Johns Hopkins University Press, Baltimore.

[21]   Mohammad, A.A. (2012) A New Digital Image Watermarking Scheme Based on Schur Decomposition. *Multimedia Tools and Applications*, **59**, 851-883. http://dx.doi.org/10.1007/s11042-011-0772-7

[22]   Mohan, B.C., Swamy, K.V. and Kumar, S.S. (2011) A Comparative Performance Evaluation of SVD and Schur Decompositions for Image Watermarking. *IJCA Proceedings on International Conference on VLSI, Communications and Instrumentation (ICVCI)*, **14**, 25-29.

23

Optimizing Software Effort Estimation Models Using Firefly Algorithm

Nazeeh Ghatasheh[1], Hossam Faris[2], Ibrahim Aljarah[2], Rizik M. H. Al-Sayyed[2]

[1]Department of Business Information Technology, The University of Jordan, Aqaba, Jordan
[2]Department of Business Information Technology, The University of Jordan, Amman, Jordan
Email: n.ghatasheh@ju.edu.jo, hossam.faris@ju.edu.jo, i.aljarah@ju.edu.jo, r.alsayyed@ju.edu.jo

Abstract

Software development effort estimation is considered a fundamental task for software development life cycle as well as for managing project cost, time and quality. Therefore, accurate estimation is a substantial factor in projects success and reducing the risks. In recent years, software effort estimation has received a considerable amount of attention from researchers and became a challenge for software industry. In the last two decades, many researchers and practitioners proposed statistical and machine learning-based models for software effort estimation. In this work, Firefly Algorithm is proposed as a metaheuristic optimization method for optimizing the parameters of three COCOMO-based models. These models include the basic COCOMO model and other two models proposed in the literature as extensions of the basic COCOMO model. The developed estimation models are evaluated using different evaluation metrics. Experimental results show high accuracy and significant error minimization of Firefly Algorithm over other metaheuristic optimization algorithms including Genetic Algorithms and Particle Swarm Optimization.

Keywords

Software Quality, Effort Estimation, Metaheuristic Optimization, Firefly Algorithm

1. Introduction

Effort estimation of software development has been a crucial task for software engineering community. Reliable effort estimation makes it more dependable to schedule project activities, allocate resources, estimate costs, and reduce the probability of project failures or delays. According to the survey in [1], most of the projects face overruns of effort or schedules. The survey also claimed that the lack of accurate estimation models is a main reason for project overruns.

Usually projects seem to be vague at the beginning and become less vague as they progress. At the same time, each project has its special nature that makes it much harder to estimate the required effort for completion. Due to the uncertain nature of projects, authors in [2] [3] suggested developing models that can adapt to a wide range of projects. But for the fact that software project data sets are typically small and the underlying relations are inaccurate or missing, the task of prediction becomes more challenging.

Several effort estimation models have been developed and improved over time for better prediction accuracy and thus better development quality [1] [4]-[8]. Such models range from complex calculations and statistical analysis of project parameters, to advanced machine learning approaches.

Heuristic optimization [9] is a method that relies on several attempts to find an optimal solution. Heuristic optimizers have been used in software effort estimation [10] as the use of genetic programming in [11] for model optimization. Another example is the part that Particle Swarm Optimization took in [12] as a heuristic optimizer. Moreover, the hybrid approaches encompass a combination of heuristic algorithms like the use of Genetic Algorithm and Ant Colony [13].

Despite a large number of experiments on finding the best prediction model, there is no clear evidence of a highly accurate or efficient approach. At the same time it is important to develop a prediction method that is less complex and much more useful. For instance, in some prediction models, a large number of variables that are used to construct the model do not reflect or improve the accuracy of the prediction model. Thus, collecting extra or unrelated variables is time-consuming with no significance. It would be more efficient to build a model with a minimum number of variables, hopefully finding the most important and common variables for generic project development efforts.

This work presents a study of how Firefly Algorithm improves the overall estimation of the software effort estimation. Where the main contributions are:

- Proving the suitability of Firefly Algorithm as predictor towards a generic prediction model for software effort estimation.
- The significant improvement in performance over previously reported methods.
- The suitability of machine learning approaches for effort prediction using a small number of input variables and data set instances.

2. Related Work

Many of Machine Learning (ML) approaches in the literature have been applied to improve the software effort estimation [2]. ML optimization algorithms that are inspired from nature have received much attention to find more accurate estimation for software effort. Nature-inspired ML algorithms include Cuckoo Search [14], Particle Swarm Optimization (PSO) [15], Bat Algorithm [16], Firefly Algorithm [17], and many others.

In [18], the authors compared the performance of different soft computing techniques such as PSO-Tuned COCOMO, Fuzzy Logic with traditional effort estimation structures. Their results showed that the proposed model outperformed traditional effort estimation structures for NASAs software effort data set. In [7], decision trees based algorithm was used to perform the software effort estimation. In addition, the authors presented an empirical proof of performance variations for several approaches that include Linear Regression, Artificial Neural Networks (ANN), and Support Vector Machines (SVM). Also the authors pointed to the suitability of the experimented ML approaches in the area of effort estimation. From their performance comparison results with other traditional algorithms, their results in terms of the error rate were better than other techniques.

A hybrid approach was adopted in [19] for parameter selection and model optimization. The authors used Genetic Algorithms (GA) for optimizing a Support Vector Regression model. The authors clarified the impact of using GA in feature selection and parameter optimization of the effort estimation model. The results of their approach showed that GA is applicable to improve the performance of the SVR model compared to other approaches. A generic framework is proposed in [20] for software effort estimation. The framework tries to simulate the human way of thinking to resolve the effort estimation by adopting fuzzy rules modeling. Therefore the generated models take advantage of experts knowledge, interoperable, and could be applied to various problems as risk analysis or software quality prediction. ANNs gained noticeable attention by researchers for effort estimation as illustrated by the review in [21], but it is insufficient to generalize the applicability of ANN in effort estimation. The authors stated that it is required to have further thorough investigation. The authors in [22] relied on seven evaluation measures to assess the stability of 90 software effort predictors over 20 data sets. According to the empirical results it was found that analogy-based methods or regression trees outperformed in terms of stability. Such conclusions open the door for extensive research towards a superior and generic prediction approach regarding the software effort estimation issue.

3. Firefly Algorithm

Firefly Algorithm (FA) is a multimodal optimization algorithm, which belongs to the nature-inspired field, is inspired from the behavior of fireflies or lightning bugs [17]. FA was first introduced by Xin-She at Cambridge University in 2007 [17]. FA is empirically proven to tackle problems more naturally and has the potential to over-perform other metaheuristic algorithms.

FA relies on three basic rules, the first implies that all fireflies are attracted to each other with disregard to gender. The second rule states that attractiveness is correlated with brightness or light emission such that bright flies attract less bright ones, and for absence of brighter flies the movement becomes random. The last main rule implies that the landscape of the objective function determines or affects the light emission of the fly, such that brightness is proportional to the objective function.

Algorithm 1. Pseudo-code of firefly algorithm.

Objective function $f(x)$

$x = (x1, \cdots, xd) T$

Generate initial population of fireflies $x_i (i = 1, 2, \cdots, n)$

Light intensity I_i at x_i is determined by $f(x_i)$

Define light absorption coefficient γ

while $(t < \text{MaxGeneration})$ **do**

  for $i = 1 : n$ all n fireflies **do**

    for $j = 1 : i$ all n fireflies **do**

      if $(I_j > I_i)$ **then**

        Move firefly i towards j in d-dimension;

      end if

      Attractiveness varies with distance r via $\exp[\gamma r]$

      Evaluate new solutions and update light intensity

    end for

  end for

  Rank the fireflies and find the current best

end while

Post-process results and visualization

The attractiveness among the flies in FA has two main issues that are; the modeling of attractiveness and the various light intensities. For a specific firefly at location X brightness I is formulated as $I(X) \ \alpha f(X)$. While attractiveness β is proportional to the flies and is related to the distance $R_{i,j}$ between fireflies i and j. Equation (1) shows the inverse square of light intensity $I(r)$ in which I_0 represents the light intensity at the source.

$$I(r) = I_0 e^{-\gamma r^2} \tag{1}$$

Assuming an absorption coefficient of the environment γ, intensity is represented in Equation (2) in which I_0 is the original intensity.

$$I(r) = \frac{I_0}{1 + \gamma r^2} \tag{2}$$

Generally the Euclidean distance is illustrated in Equation (3), which represents the distance between a firefly at location X_i and another at location X_j. In which $X_{i,k}$ is the kth component of the spatial coordinate X_i.

$$R_{ij} = \left\| x_i - x_j \right\| = \sqrt{\sum_{k=1}^{d} (x_{i,k} - x_{j,k})^2} \tag{3}$$

A firefly i attracted to a brighter one j as illustrated in Equation (4) where attraction is represented by $\beta_{e^{\gamma r_{ij}^2}}(x_j - x_i)$, and $\alpha\left(rand - \frac{1}{2}\right)$ represents the randomness according to the randomization parameter α.

$$x_i = x_i + \beta_{e^{\gamma r_{ij}^2}}(x_j - x_i) + \alpha\left(rand - \frac{1}{2}\right) \tag{4}$$

Furthermore, variations of attractiveness are determined by γ which on its turn affects the behavior and convergence speed of FA.

4. Effort Estimation Models

One of the Famous and widely used effort estimation models is the Constructive Cost Models COCOMO and its extension COCOMOII. COCOMO is used as cost, effort, and schedule estimation model in the process of planning new software development activity, also known as COCOMO 81. COCOMO was defined between the late 1970s and early 1980s [23]. Where COCOMOII is a later extension of the previously defined model. This research work tries to optimize the parameters of three variations of the COCOMO model. The first is the basic COCOMO model which is represented in Equation (5).

$$E = a_i(\text{KLOC})^{b_i} \tag{5}$$

E is the effort in person-months, KLOC represents the thousand (K) lines of code included in a software project. Typically, the coefficient a_i and the exponent b_i are chosen based on COCOMO pre-set parameters that depend on the software project details.

The other two models are extensions of the basic COCOMO model which are proposed by A. Sheta in [24]. Both models consider the effect of methodologies (ME) as supposed to be linearly related to the software effort. These models are represented in Equations (6) and (7) and named Model I and Model II respectively.

$$E = a_i(\text{KLOC})^{b_i} + c_i(\text{ME}) \tag{6}$$

$$E = a_i(\text{KLOC})^{b_i} + c_i(\text{ME}) + d_i \tag{7}$$

This work tries empirically to optimize the constants a_i, b_i, c_i and d_i using FA, GA and PSO.

5. Data Set and Evaluation Measures

This research considers a famous and public data set in order to produce comparable results; namely NASA projects' effort data set. The data set is challenging due to the small number of instances and limited number of analyzed variables. However, regarding the objectives of this research the data set is considered to be adequate. The data set is split into two parts; training set of about 60% and testing set of about 30% instances.

NASA data set [6] consists of 18 software projects for which this research considers three main variables that are the project size in thousand Lines of Code (KLOC), Methodology (ME), and Actual Effort (AE). Training data set has 13 instances and the records from 14 till 18 are for testing the model. **Table 1** shows the actual values of the training and testing data sets.

In order to check the performance of the developed models, the computed measures are the Correlation Coefficient (R^2),

$$R^2 = \frac{\sum_{i=1}^{n}(y_i - \overline{Y}_i)^2 - \sum_{i=1}^{n}(y_i - \hat{y}_i)^2}{\sum_{i=1}^{n}(y_i - \overline{y}_i)^2} \tag{8}$$

the Mean Squares Error (MSE),

$$\text{MSE} = \frac{1}{n}\sum_{i=1}^{n}(y - \hat{y})^2 \tag{9}$$

Table 1. NASA data set.

Project No.	KDLOC	ME	Measured Effort
1	90.2	30	115.8
2	46.2	20	96
3	46.5	19	79
4	54.5	20	90.8
5	31.1	35	39.6
6	67.5	29	98.4
7	12.8	26	18.9
8	10.5	34	10.3
9	21.5	31	28.5
10	3.1	26	7
11	4.2	19	9
12	7.8	31	7.3
13	2.1	28	5
14	5	29	8.4
15	78.6	35	98.7
16	9.7	27	15.6
17	12.5	27	23.9
18	100.8	34	138.3

the Mean Absolute Error (MAE),

$$\text{MAE} = \frac{1}{n}\sum_{i=1}^{n}\left|y_i - \hat{y}_i\right| \tag{10}$$

the Mean Magnitude of Relative Error (MMRE),

$$\text{MMRE} = \frac{1}{n}\sum_{i=1}^{n}\frac{\left|y_i - \hat{y}_i\right|}{y_i} \tag{11}$$

and the Variance-Accounted-For (VAF).

$$\text{VAF} = \left[1 - \frac{\text{var}\left(y(t) - \hat{y}(t)\right)}{\text{var}\left(y(t)\right)}\right] \times 100\% \tag{12}$$

These performance criteria are used to measure how close the predicted effort to the actual values, where y is the actual value, $\hat{y}$ is the estimated target value, and n is the number of instances.

6. Experiments and Results

The experiments apply FA, GA and PSO for optimizing the coefficients of the basic COCOMO model, COCOMO Model I and COCOMO Model II based on the training part of NASA data set. For FA, the Matlab implementation developed by X.-S. Yang [9] is applied. Number of flies, particles and population size is unified and set to 100 in all the algorithms. The number of iterations is set to 500. The rest of the parameters of FA, GA and PSO are set as listed in **Tables 2-4**. MAE criteria are used as an objective function which is shown in Equation (10). In order to carry out meaningful evaluation results, each algorithm is applied 25 times then the average of the evaluation results is reported. In each run, the optimized models are evaluated based on the testing data using VAF, MSE, MAE, MMRE, RMSE and R^2 evaluation metrics.

Carrying out the experiments, the average convergence curves for FA, GA and PSO are shown in **Figures 1-3** respectively for the three variations of COCOMO model.

Table 2. Firefly algorithm parameter settings.

Parameter	Value
Maximum iterations	500
Number of fireflies	100
Alpha	0.4
Betamin	1
Gamma	0.4

Table 3. GA parameter settings.

Parameter	Value
Maximum iterations	500
Population size	100
Selection method	Tournament selection
Crossover probability	80%
Mutation probability	5%

Table 4. PSO parameter settings.

Parameter	Value
Maximum iterations	500
Particles	100
Acceleration constant	[2.1, 2.1]
Inertia weight	[0.9, 0.6]
Maximum velocity	100

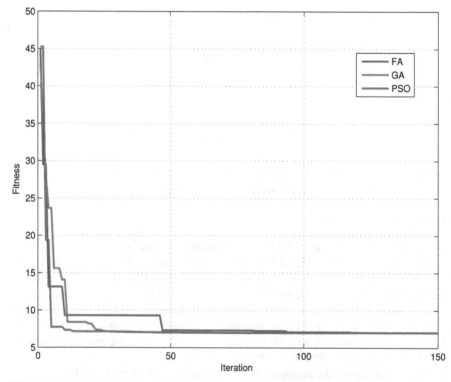

Figure 1. Convergence of FA, GA and PSO in optimizing the basic COCOMO model.

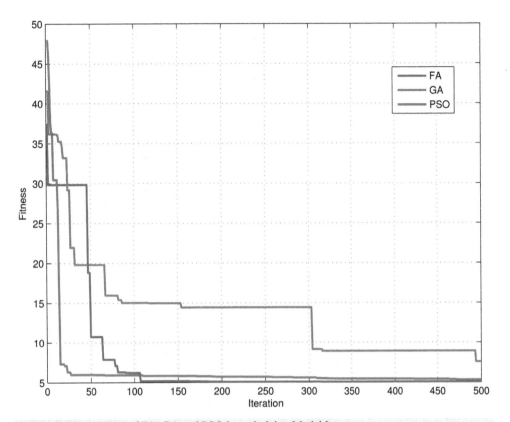

Figure 2. Convergence of FA, GA and PSO in optimizing Model I.

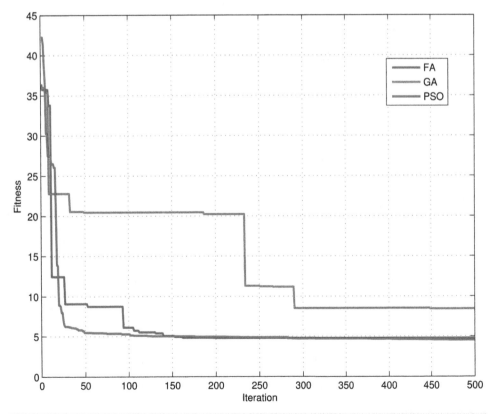

Figure 3. Convergence of FA, GA and PSO in optimizing Model II.

The evaluation results for training and testing cases are shown in **Tables 5-7**. Based on **Table 5** and **Table 6** it can be noticed that Firefly outperforms GA and PSO in optimizing the basic COCOMO model and the Model I by means of all evaluation metrics. For the Model II, Firefly and PSO are very competitive and have very close results. On the other hand GA has the lowest results and it has the slowest convergence.

In summary, FA as a metaheuristic optimization algorithm over-performs GA and PSO in terms of higher estimation accuracy for the software effort COCOMO based models.

Table 5. Basic COCOMO model.

	Training			Testing		
	Firefly	GA	PSO	Firefly	GA	PSO
VAF	93.82%	93.72%	93.73%	98.16%	97.97%	97.98%
MSE	104.88	107.28	107.15	59.14	63.96	63.68
MAE	7.04	7.03	7.03	5.65	6.06	6.04
MMRE	0.24	0.24	0.24	0.11	0.13	0.12
RMSE	10.24	10.36	10.35	7.67	8.00	7.98
R^2	0.9367	0.9352	0.9353	0.9781	0.9763	0.9765

Table 6. COCOMO Model I.

	Training			Testing		
	Firefly	GA	PSO	Firefly	GA	PSO
VAF	96.78%	92.94%	96.96%	98.62%	97.97%	98.52%
MSE	56.05	127.70	54.16	47.74	98.17	60.07
MAE	5.42	8.94	5.16	5.56	7.70	5.63
MMRE	0.41	0.53	0.39	0.24	0.29	0.23
RMSE	7.48	10.95	7.36	6.82	9.39	7.72
R^2	0.9662	0.9229	0.9673	0.9823	0.9637	0.9778

Table 7. COCOMO Model II.

	Training			Testing		
	Firefly	GA	PSO	Firefly	GA	PSO
VAF	96.95%	92.42%	97.48%	98.63%	97.60%	98.70%
MSE	53.74	129.37	45.28	45.02	114.79	52.85
MAE	5.36	8.20	4.43	5.57	7.83	5.29
MMRE	0.38	0.40	0.30	0.24	0.27	0.21
RMSE	7.26	11.05	6.72	6.62	9.86	7.19
R^2	0.9676	0.9219	0.9727	0.9833	0.9575	0.9805

7. Conclusion and Future Work

This work investigated the efficiency of applying the Firefly Algorithm as a metaheuristic optimization technique to optimize the parameters of different effort estimation models. These models are three variations of the Constructive Cost Model COCOMO which are the basic COCOMO model, and other two extensions of the basic model that were proposed previously in the literature. The optimized models are assessed according to different evaluation criteria and compared with models optimized using other metaheuristic algorithms which are Genetic Algorithm and Particle Swarm Optimization. Evaluation results show that developed models using the Firefly Algorithm have higher accuracy in estimating software effort. Further future work is intended to overcome the instability issues, a more generic prediction model that is not highly affected by the size and the type of data set, and preferably an enhancement to the Firefly Algorithm itself. Moreover, it would be important to work towards a hybrid approach that encompasses the best characteristics of different prediction schemes.

References

[1] Molokken, K. and Jorgensen, M. (2003) A Review of Software Surveys on Software Effort Estimation. 2003 *International Symposium on Empirical Software Engineering*, 30 September-1 October 2003, 223-230.

[2] Song, Q. and Shepperd, M. (2011) Predicting Software Project Effort: A Grey Relational Analysis Based Method. *Expert Systems with Applications*, **38**, 7302-7316. http://dx.doi.org/10.1016/j.eswa.2010.12.005

[3] Khatibi, V. and Jawawi, D.N. (2011) Software Cost Estimation Methods: A Review. *Journal of Emerging Trends in Computing and Information Sciences*, **2**, 21-29.

[4] Afzal, W. and Torkar, R. (2011) On the Application of Genetic Programming for Software Engineering Predictive Modeling: A Systematic Review. *Expert Systems with Applications*, **38**, 11984-11997. http://dx.doi.org/10.1016/j.eswa.2011.03.041

[5] Albrecht, A. and Gaffney, J.E. (1983) Software Function, Source Lines of Code, and Development Effort Prediction: A Software Science Validation. *IEEE Transactions on Software Engineering*, **SE-9**, 639-648. http://dx.doi.org/10.1109/TSE.1983.235271

[6] Bailey, J.W. and Basili, V.R. (1981) A Meta-Model for Software Development Resource Expenditures. *Proceedings of the 5th International Conference on Software Engineering*, Piscataway, 107-116.

[7] Ruchika Malhotra, A.J. (2011) Software Effort Prediction Using Statistical and Machine Learning Methods. *International Journal of Advanced Computer Science and Applications (IJACSA)*, **2**.

[8] Yadav, C.S. and Singh, R. (2014) Tuning of Cocomo ii Model Parameters for Estimating Software Development Effort Using GA for Promise Project Data Set. *International Journal of Computer Applications*, **90**, 37-43. http://dx.doi.org/10.5120/15542-4367

[9] Wang, F.-S. and Chen, L.-H. (2013) Heuristic Optimization. In: Dubitzky, W., Wolkenhauer, O., Cho, K.-H. and Yokota, H., Eds., *Encyclopedia of Systems Biology*, Springer, New York, 885-885.

[10] Uysal, M. (2010) Estimation of the Effort Component of the Software Projects Using Heuristic Algorithms. INTECH Open Access Publisher, Croatia.

[11] Alaa, F. and Al-Afeef, A. (2010) A GP Effort Estimation Model Utilizing Line of Code and Methodology for NASA Software Projects. *IEEE 10th International Conference on Intelligent Systems Design and Applications (ISDA)*, Cairo, 29 November-1 December 2010, 290-295.

[12] Bhattacharya, P., Srivastava, P. and Prasad, B. (2012) Software Test Effort Estimation Using Particle Swarm Optimization. In: Satapathy, S., Avadhani, P. and Abraham, A., Eds., *Proceedings of the International Conference on Information Systems Design and Intelligent Applications* 2012 (*INDIA* 2012), Visakhapatnam, January 2012, Vol. 132 of Advances in Intelligent and Soft Computing, 827-835. Springer, Berlin and Heidelberg.

[13] Maleki, I., Ghaffari, A. and Masdari, M. (2014) A New Approach for Software Cost Estimation with Hybrid Genetic Algorithm and Ant Colony Optimization. *International Journal of Innovation and Applied Studies*, **5**, 72-81.

[14] Yang, X.-S. and Deb, S. (2009) Cuckoo Search via Levy Flights. *World Congress on Nature Biologically Inspired Computing, NaBIC* 2009, Coimbatore, 9-11 December 2009, 210-214.

[15] Kennedy, J. and Eberhart, R. (1995) Particle Swarm Optimization. *IEEE International Conference on Neural Networks*, **4**, 1942-1948.

[16] Yang, X.-S. (2010) A New Metaheuristic Bat-Inspired Algorithm. In: Gonzlez, J., Pelta, D., Cruz, C., Terrazas, G. and Krasnogor, N., Eds., *Nature Inspired Cooperative Strategies for Optimization (NICSO* 2010), Vol. 284 of Studies in Computational Intelligence, 65-74. Springer, Berlin and Heidelberg.

[17] Yang, X.-S. (2009) Firefly Algorithms for Multimodal Optimization. In: Watanabe, O. and Zeugmann, T., Eds., *Sto-*

chastic Algorithms: Foundations and Applications, Vol. 5792 of Lecture Notes in Computer Science, 169-178. Springer, Berlin and Heidelberg.

[18] Sheta, A., Rine, D. and Ayesh, A. (2008) Development of Software Effort and Schedule Estimation Models Using Soft Computing Techniques. *IEEE Congress on Evolutionary Computation, CEC* 2008 (*IEEE World Congress on Computational Intelligence*), Hong Kong, 16 June 2008, 1283-1289.

[19] Oliveira, A.L.I., Braga, P.L., Lima, R.M.F. and Cornélio, M.L. (2010) GA-Based Method for Feature Selection and Parameters Optimization for Machine Learning Regression Applied to Software Effort Estimation. *Information and Software Technology*, **52**, 1155-1166. http://dx.doi.org/10.1016/j.infsof.2010.05.009

[20] Huang, X., Ho, D., Ren, J. and Capretz, L. (2006) A Soft Computing Framework for Software Effort Estimation. *Soft Computing*, **10**, 170-177. http://dx.doi.org/10.1007/s00500-004-0442-z

[21] Dave, V. and Dutta, K. (2014) Neural Network Based Models for Software Effort Estimation: A Review. *Artificial Intelligence Review*, **42**, 295-307. http://dx.doi.org/10.1007/s10462-012-9339-x

[22] Keung, J., Kocaguneli, E. and Menzies, T. (2013) Finding Conclusion Stability for Selecting the Best Effort Predictor in Software Effort Estimation. *Automated Software Engineering*, **20**, 543-567. http://dx.doi.org/10.1007/s10515-012-0108-5

[23] Boehm, B., Abts, C., Clark, B. and Devnani-Chulani, S. (1997) COCOMO II Model Definition Manual. University of Southern California, Los Angeles.

[24] Sheta, A.F. (2006) Estimation of the COCOMO Model Parameters Using Genetic Algorithms for NASA Software Projects. *Journal of Computer Science*, **2**, 118-123. http://dx.doi.org/10.3844/jcssp.2006.118.123

24

Multimedia Internet-Based Platform Project for Saudi Students' English Language Learning

Basim H. Alahmadi

Madinah College of Technology, Madinah, KSA
Email: bassiem@yahoo.com

Abstract

This paper sets out to shed light on the hierarchical stages of producing technology-enhanced learning software designed to promote English language learning of Saudi students at Madinah College of Technology, Saudi Arabia. The aim of the software was to meet the learners' language needs, which defined the learning objective. The paper highlights how suitable language learning theories were implemented by coordinating the interface design theories and principles underpinning the production process. Toward the end of the paper, an evaluation of the strengths and weaknesses of the software is investigated. Finally, the prospects of the software's future work are presented.

Keywords

Technology-Enhanced Educational Material, Design Theories, User-Interface

1. Defining the Aim of This Project: Objectives and Learners' Needs

It is axiomatic that designing and producing any technology-enhanced learning material are a complicated process of two parts: theoretical and technical. By the theoretical part, we mean the design process, e.g., planning and making the blueprints, whereas the technical part means the actual construction, e.g., programming. These two parts must be dealt with equally according to the existing academic background. The theoretical part always dominates the technical part, because the latter is defined by the earlier.

The aim of this software originated from the absence of interaction in Saudi English classrooms, a major deficiency in Saudi English as a foreign language EFL class [1]. Therefore, this project was initiated exclusively to act as a catalyst to fill this gap. The author created a software called "Support Your Football Team!". As the name indicates, the program entices students to practice their language while discussing one of their biggest personal interests, football. Thus, four international football teams were selected according to their high percentage of supporters among Saudi students. Regrettably, the selection of those teams relied on the author's 15-year teaching experience in Saudi EFL classrooms, and not on methodological results. The four teams were: F. C. Barcelona (Spain), Manchester (UK), AC Milan (Italy), and Ajax (Holland). They were from different countries so as to foster more interaction and enthusiasm between the learners.

Next, we need to describe the learning objectives of this software. As discussed above, the football factor was incorporated to augment the students' interaction. This interaction was attained after successfully receiving comprehensible input and producing conceivable output. Accordingly, the object of constructing this software was to produce interaction through comprehensible input and conceivable output among the interlocutors, *i.e.*, the students.

The aims and objectives were built on the learners' needs. Learners' needs can be measured by conducting a Needs Analysis (NA). NA is a relatively new concept to language teaching. Yet, NA has long been conducted unconsciously by teachers and other stakeholders (a group of people who have the right to have input into the curriculum process) at schools to assess their learners' "language competence". Reference [2] defined NA as "techniques and procedures for obtaining information from and about learners to be used in curriculum development".

Many researchers believe that learners' needs are crucial to the design of technology-enhanced educational materials [1] [3] [4]. Reference [5] made "identifying learners' needs" the first step of their seven-step model for the production of educational materials. As for interactive multimedia production, reference [6] proposed that there are two approaches: a technology-driven approach and a learner-based approach. He (*ibid*) posited that designers need to concentrate on learner-based models rather than relying solely on technology-driven models that are created only for aesthetic purposes.

Given this swift outline of the significance of learners' needs in educational software, let us now shed light on Saudi students' needs. The author used Jolly and Bolitho's seven-step model and began the first step (identifying learners' needs) by identifying the targeted learners' needs. These needs were spelled out by [7] as follows:

1) Poor linguistic competence.
2) Negative attitudes toward Language 2 L2.
3) Shyness and inhibition.
4) English is not supported outside the classroom.

This software was designed to address these deficiencies. The first weakness could be improved by increasing the students' language output. The second pitfall was hoped to be addressed by using the students' enthusiasm for their teams as a vehicle to learn language. The third seemed to be avoided by introducing the chat facility, where anonymity was maintained with avatars and aliases. The fourth problem was handled by the technology's mobility factor. It is now clear that this covers Jolly and Bolitho's second step of the model, which is "exploration of the need".

This software has provided a considerable amount of English language text about each of the four teams, including images, text, audio and video, as well as hyperlinks to take the students to those teams' websites and their supporters. It is hoped that all of the four English language skills will be practiced. Moreover, the author has provided a chat facility so that learners can produce comprehensible output with each other. If learners' needs and current pedagogical theories are interrelated, then this is an interesting area to investigate in the next section.

2. English Language Teaching and Design Theories Applied in This Software

2.1. Pedagogical Aspects

The fourth step in Jolly and Bolitho's model is "pedagogical realization". The importance of considering current pedagogical theories in the specific context underpinning educational software production has been repeatedly asserted by many computer-assisted language learning (CALL) software researchers [4] [8] [9]. Pedagogical theories were in harmony with design theories when the author constructed this software. Reference [10], as an expert in educational interactive media and CALL, accentuates that technology must be seen only as a participant in creating interactive educational media, rather than as a pioneering element. It is with regret that many educational institutions concern themselves with the appliances of multimedia and do not focus on learners' needs by producing learner-based design interactive models. This software presents a student-centered design model that can encourage users to have more comprehension utterances. It was achieved by means of providing key linguistic brief chunks. This, coupled with the chat facility, can lead to a facilitative interaction atmosphere among learners [1]. Reference [10], defined seven principles for developing CALL materials: 1) supplying major linguistic quantity, 2) offering modification of the linguistic input, 3) presenting chances for comprehensible output, 4) providing opportunities for noticing errors, 5) providing chances to correct ill-stated output, 6) anchoring friendly interaction between the user and the computer, and 7) playing roles in L2 tasks. The chat facility integrates Chapelle's previously mentioned criteria. A plethora of previous studies conducted in this field have revealed that professionally implemented, interactive educational technology programs (e.g., chat) contributes significantly to fruitful learning experiences [8] [9].

While piloting the first stage of this software, the author noticed that his learners increased their motivation, enhanced their task achievement, and produced greater interaction. Students asked the author to allow them to communicate with other teams' supporters outside the class, but as this was not feasible in this software, the author was unable to fulfill this request. This demonstrates the clear result that students' shyness and inhibitions were minimized. As for the language content, this software focuses on meaning-based learning tasks [8] by providing key dates of the achievements of each of the teams. This was accomplished by supplying a few concise sentences and tables about each of the four teams with visual aids. To tackle the first students' needs of poor linguistic competence, the language was graded from simple to difficult with brief phrases and easy language [8] [9]. Also, the software was targeted to address learners' shyness by designing a user-friendly interface and incorporating easy-to-use navigation, so as to encourage and motivate them to use this software. Reference [1] claimed that computer-assisted class discussion (CACD) is a great equalizer among learners, especially because it targets passive or marginalized students.

In order to deal with students' negative attitudes toward L2, the home page was designed to be engaging and attractive to the students [6]. In an attempt to foster successful language learning, the software utilizes a lot of instructional media, e.g., visuals, sound and videos, so as to be compatible with the learners' preferences and their different learning styles [8]. Reference [3], argues that the more language quantity students are exposed to, the more chances they have to encounter a fruitful language learning environment. Throughout the design process, the idea that this software was created exclusively and privately for Saudi students was heightened. This was achieved by employing a Saudi flag, an avatar of a Saudi boy, and the icon of the institution where they study. Having done this, the third stage of Jolly and Bolitho's model for the production of educational materials was addressed: the "contextualization". According to [6] technology-enhanced designers are strongly encouraged to develop a sense of the cultural awareness of their learners. Failing to do so may cause "learners [to] experience negative feelings in their learning because they think that their entity is put at risk; it distorts their situational and linguistic reality". Concerning the last aspect, of language learning being kept at class, this can be overcome by the issue of mobility. Reference [4], considers this mobility to be CALL's greatest advantage. This software addressed this and the three preceding aspects of language learning. As this sections shed lights on the design theories underpinning the production of this software, the following section will present a concise outline of the nature and features of this software.

2.2. Technical Implications

The application is demonstrated using a *Mediator* 7 *pro*, a multimedia authoring icon-based software program. *MatchWare Corp.* produced this award-winning interactive page-oriented multimedia program that offers a wide range of capabilities such as building pages, adding contents and creating activities. *Mediator* 7 *pro* is compatible with HTML, HTML codes and Flashes. Educational aids such as hypertexts, hotspots, and animations can be easily anchored at this educational tool. This multimedia package also allows for chat facility by means of synchronous computer networks and/or connecting to the Internet. The author has implemented this chat facility where the screen is split into two halves: the top half shows students interlocutors' replies; the bottom half shows the students his massage as he is typing. Additionally, it has the facility to save the complete record of any written transactions. This software was designed for first-term students at Madinah College of Technology (MCT), Madinah, Saudi Arabia, studying in the computer department. These students are secondary school graduates who have studied English for six years or more. Their English level is lower-intermediate; however they are good computer users. This icon-based software, as posed earlier, meet the learners' needs as it focuses on introducing these students to technical English language, namely vocabulary, which they will need in the field of their specialization. Therefore, among the aims of this software is to enable students to comprehend basic technical English in their field as well as preparing them for enrolment in advanced courses of similar nature. As discussed above, while producing this software, Jolly and Bolitho's seven stage model were followed for producing educational material. The next section will resume to illustrate how Jolly and Bolitho's model was applied throughout the production of this software.

In order to meet the fifth step of Jolly and Bolitho's model, which is about the "production of materials". The user-interface is a crucial element that must be taken into consideration when producing interactive educational materials. It can help the user achieve the utmost level of functional competence of the software if applied successfully and efficiently. Reference [11], as a veteran in interactive media, defines the user-interface as the dynamic interaction between the user and the elements that are anchored on the screen. If we recall the objectives of this software, which was receiving and producing comprehensible input, we will find the following quote of [9] worth stating:

The function of the interface system is to assign user-input to internal representations of the application and internal representations of the application to the output that is comprehensible to the user. The type of input and output modes employed by the interface system determines the type of the interface.

Reference [9] (*ibid*) posed that the user-interface can be classified into one of three categories:

1) Computer-interface: where the functionality relies more on how the computer processes information.

2) User-centered: where the functionality concentrates on how the user processes information.

3) Designer-centered: where the focus is on how the designer prefers to lay out the information.

Although it is clear that the second category is more efficient and beneficial, the current software was done with an equal amount of both the second and the third categories. This is attributed to the fact that the software was designed and produced by an individual teacher, who could not afford to cover the huge expense of constructing it solely based on the second category.

Internal representations to which [9] referred to above were deployed. For example, light brown and yellow colors were used for the background, which, according to [12], can reveal liveliness and friendliness, and help the eye to absorb the elements clearly. However, reference [13] contradicts this argument and states that yellow should be used only for short text due to its bright nature. Following this, the author only used yellow text with a beige background and in short bullet points. The text was kept in the same font, because, according to [6]:

Text has a significant invisible effect on the reader in that every font has three basic attributes: first, size, measured in points; second, weight, which is a "relative measurement of the thickness of the strokes that make it up"; and third, style, which is Roman, Bold or Italic. Changing font means changing these three attributes.

Moreover, the layout was also an important parameter. According to [13] "the position of the separate elements in relation to the screen and in relation to each other" must be consistent throughout the whole website. Thus, the author incorporated the same colors and shaped buttons for the comparable tasks. For example, on every team's pages, the user finds the same colored background and can find the navigation buttons anchored at the lower part of the page with the same dark red colors. Finally, pictures, as a vital part of the internal representations, were meant as a visual explanation for the text or labels. Researchers stress the fact that images should not be used for decorative purposes only [11]; Thissen, 2004 [4]. The next section investigates one of the most pivotal stages of computer-aided educational materials: evaluation.

3. Evaluation of the Strong and the Weak Aspects of This Software

As this software adopted Jolly and Bolitho's model for the production of educational materials, the sixth step "students' use of material" was conducted. The student used the software and the author observed them. This authors' observation helped gain a more genuine sense about the "technical considerations, e.g. installation and networking; multimedia design criteria, e.g. aesthetics and help; and pedagogical factors, e.g. integration and fulfillment of learning objectives" [6]. This step paved the way for applying the last step in [5], model which is "evaluation". First, the author needs to highlight the fact that he, as an individual, faced some problems in constructing this software. The economical restrictions, or what has recently been called the "bleeding edge" of the resources, *i.e.*, that some resources are very expensive, and the author was not capable of paying for those resources. If this software was professionally constructed and generously subsidized, it would have fewer inadequacies in both theoretical and technical aspects.

Some of the weak points of this software will be discussed. For example, some very authentic and useful English media for the Barcelona team was available, but due to its relatively high price, this software used some free Internet media instead, whose quality was not very remarkable. Even though it was free, it took the author hours to find due to the cultural sensitivity issues associated with Saudi students. Reference [1] elaborated on this issue further in his article, and this subject is beyond the scope of this paper. The fair skill level in programming yielded some limitations to this software. Had there been some professional help in Flash media, there would have been great software. In particular, editing the video clips was very debilitating and annoying, due to the aforementioned factor of cultural sensitivity. This was not the case with the pictures, because the author was able to edit, crop, and even create his own pictures. Moreover, the sound files are not yet completed as initially planned. Instead, the students can click a hyperlink where they are transferred to a YouTube page to listen to the sound files. Most of these sound files were interviews and official *torhymne*. A *trohymne* is a playable unique sound for a club or a university. Concerning authentic tasks for the software, the previous limitations have minimized the quality and quantity of the tasks. For instance, the author planned to add some games or tasks inside the authentic source, such as recording video of a technical analysis of a match. However, this has not been feasible due to limitations stated earlier.

In spite of these weaknesses, this software has many strong points. First, the students stressed the fact that they were very happy and surprised to see their favorite hobby being practiced in English rather than dull ready-course-materials. In fact, this attitude is very profitable to language learning, and is called "learner-driven curriculum" [3]. They also expressed their smooth ease with the navigation. Furthermore, the readability of the text, the continuity of information, and the consistency of the screen layout was also praised by the students. They found the experience appealing, constructive, and profitable, which pushed them to request to try the software once again. Most significantly, they liked the idea of the chat very much, because it was full of enthusiasm and interesting. This evaluation of the pros and cons of the software led me to think about how the disadvantages could be addressed in the post-production phase, which the next section discusses.

4. Further Development

The prospect of the post-production development of any technology-enhanced material is a great advantage in comparison with paper-based material. In the previous sections, a number of improvements were suggested, some of which are indispensable. To begin with, this software should encompass more teams, because while piloting, the author discovered students who wanted to support more than one international team that were in different countries. So, the author wishes to add Bayern-Munich (Germany), Paris Saint-German (France), F. C. Porto (Portugal), and Galatasaray (Turkey). These teams were nominated by the students, not by the author. In addition, it would be more interesting if the author could provide subtitles with the sound files so that the students could practice both skills of listening and reading. If a visual explanation of the sounds on the screen could be provided, online dictionaries for those words could also be provided. Additionally, some difficult sound files, like the interviews, could be replaced by the author's recorded voice, because the students were more apt to comprehend slower conversations than faster ones. With the cooperation of other supporters from international countries, this software can connect Saudi students to chat with the same team's supporters or advocates from international countries. This would create collaborative learning and scaffolding, especially if they are both non-native speakers and share the same interests [1]. By doing this we can maximize the chances of providing all seven of the criteria posed earlier by [10].

The influence of video games nowadays cannot be ignored; the students are seeing a great demand for adding short clips. By doing this, we can find exactly what we need to show or convey instead of a long and thorough Internet search for a specific bit of information. For example, at one of the texts, there is a scenario where the goalkeeper scores a goal in the other team. The internet search yielded no result. With this video game, we will be able to create the scenario we want. Also, we can organize championships and leagues and divide students into two teams. Each team has players and supporters. This will be an interaction inducing atmosphere.

5. Conclusion

A great deal of potential of this software is missing due to the author's limited skills in programming; with this knowledge from experts in programming, the prototype can be vastly improved. This software failed to record students discourse both verbal and written. With this facility installed in the software, we can monitor the students' improvements by making a discourse analysis for the students' output. In this sense, the software can enter an add-in process, where an unprecedented, professional, and promising piece of technology-enhanced interactive software is created.

References

[1]   Alahmadi, B. (2007) The Viability of Computer-Assisted Class Discussion CACD as a Facilitator of Communicative Interaction. *Jaltcall*, **3**, 3-32.

[2]   Nunan, D. (1994) The Learner Centred Curriculum. Cambridge University Press, Cambridge.

[3]   Beatty, K. (2003) Teaching and Researching Computer-Assisted Language Learning. Longman, London.

[4]   Hubbard, P.L. (1996) Elements of CALL Methodology: Development, Evaluation, and Implementation. In: Pennington, M.C. and Stevens, V., Eds., *The Power of CALL*, Athelstan, Bolsover, Houston, 15-32.

[5]   Jolly, D. and Bolitho, R. (1998) A Framework for Materials Writing. In: Tomlinson, B., Ed., *Materials Development in Language Teaching*, Cambridge University Press, Cambridge, 90-115.

[6]   Alahmadi, B. (2010) Interface Design Theories of Foreign Language Multimedia Software. *ICIMIT IEEE CFP* 10531-PRT, 540-544.

[7]   Abu Ghararah, A. (1998) Teaching English as a Foreign Language: Procedures, Techniques and Activities. Tawbah Library, Riyadh.

[8]   Peterson, M. (2000) Directions for Development in Hypermedia Design. *Computer Assisted Language Learning*, **13**, 253-269. http://dx.doi.org/10.1076/0958-8221(200007)13:3;1-3;FT253

[9]   Plass, J.L. (1998) Design and Evaluation of the User Interface of Foreign Language Multimedia Software: A Cognitive Approach. *Language Learning & Technology*, **2**, 35-45.

[10] Chapelle, C. (1998) Multimedia CALL: Lessons to Be Learned From Research on Instructed SLA. *Language Learning and Technology*, **2**, 22-34.

[11] Elsom-Cook, M. (2001) Principles of Interactive Multimedia. McGraw-Hill, London.

[12] Thissen, F. (2004) Screen Design Manual. Communicating Effectively through Multimedia. Series X, Springer, Berlin.

[13] Barfield, L. (2004) Design for New Media Interaction Design for Multimedia and the Web. Pearson Education Limited, Harlow.

25

Toward Developing a Syllabus-Oriented Computer-Based Question-Banks Software to Support Partially Computerized Exams

Sulieman Bani-Ahmad

Department of Computer Information Systems, Faculty of Information Technology, Al-Balqa Applied University, Salt, Jordan
Email: Sulieman@bau.edu.jo

Abstract

Aims: This study aims at designing and implementing syllabus-oriented question-bank system that is capable of producing paper-based exams with multiple forms along with answer keys. The developed software tool is named X(Chi)-Pro Milestone and supports four types of questions, namely: Multiple-choice, True/False, Short-Answer and Free-Response Essay questions. The study is motivated by the fact that student number in schools and universities is continuously growing at high, non-linear, and uncontrolled rates. This growth, however, is not accompanied by an equivalent growth of educational resources (mainly: instructors, classrooms, and labs). A direct result of this situation is having relatively large number of students in each class-room. It is observed that providing and using online-examining systems could be intractable and expensive. As an alternative, paper-based exams can be used. One main issue is that manually produced paper-based exams are of low quality because of some human factors such as instability and relatively narrow range of topics [1]. Further, it is observed that instructors usually need to spend a lot of time and energy in composing paper-based exams with multiple forms. Therefore, the use of computers for automatic production of paper-based exams from question banks is becoming more and more important. **Methodology:** The design and evaluation of X-Pro Milestone are done by considering a basic set of design principles that are based on a list of identified Functional and Non-Functional Requirements. Deriving those requirements is made possible by developing X-Pro Milestone using the Iterative and Incremental model from software engineering domain. **Results:** We demonstrate that X-Pro Milestone has a number of excellent characteristics compared to the exam-preparation and question banks tools available in market. Some of these characteristics are: ease of use and operation, user-friendly interface and good usability, high security and protection of the question bank-items, high stability, and reliability. Further, X-Pro Milestone makes initiating, maintaining and archiving Question-Banks and produced exams possible. Putting X-Pro Milestone into real use has showed that X-Pro Milestone is easy to be learned and effectively used. We demonstrate that

X-Pro Milestone is a cost-effective alternative to online examining systems with more and richer features and with low infrastructure requirements.

Keywords

Exam Preparation Tools, Syllabus-Oriented Question Banks, Partially Computerized Exams, Iterative and Incremental Software Development Model, X-Pro Milestone

---

1. Introduction

Student numbers in universities are becoming higher every day [2] [3]. Statistics show that this increase in student numbers is not accompanied by an effective and equivalent growth of educational resources such as instructors and computer labs [4] [5]. This makes the usage of fully computerized examination tools (that allows students to set for tests and exams using a computer, usually networked) prohibitively impossible especially in developing countries where proper infrastructure is not available and not affordable [2] [3] [6].

Exams can be [5]: 1) fully computerized, 2) partially computerized, or 3) paper-based (not computerized). In fully computerized tests, each student views and directly responds to test items (or questions) using a computer. Students' responses along with the list of questions are maintained in a computer server. This makes grading exams to be fully automated [4]. In partially computerized tests, computer software is used to prepare printable exam-forms, and the student responds to exam items using a pencil. A computer software can be used later to automatically evaluate student's responses to exam items, this step can also be manual. In pure paper-based tests the student uses a pencil to respond to test items in manually prepared exam-forms. This means that computers are neither required while preparing the exam-forms nor during exam sessions. It is observed that partially computerized exams are the ideal choice when having large number of students setting for exams. In fact, under such circumstances, fully-computerized and pure paper-based tests can be prohibitively expensive [3]-[9].

In this paper we design and implement a personalized and syllabus-oriented question-bank system that is capable of producing paper-based exams with multiple forms along with answer keys. The developed software tool is named X-Pro Milestone and supports four types of questions, namely: Multiple-choice, Short-Answer, True/False and Free-Response Essay questions.

The design and evaluation of X-Pro Milestone is done by considering a basic set of design principles. Those design principles, in turn, are based on a list of identified Functional and Non-Functional Requirements. Deriving those requirements is made possible by developing X-Pro Milestone using the Iterative and Incremental model from software engineering domain.

We demonstrate that X-Pro Milestone is equipped with a number of excellent characteristics and feature that cannot be found in other exam-preparation and question-bank tools available in market. Some of these characteristics are: ease of use and operation, user-friendly Graphical User Interface (GUI) and good usability, high security and protection of the question-bankitems, high stability, and reliability. Further, X-Pro Milestone makes initiating, maintaining and archiving course syllabus question-banks and produced exam instances not only possible but also interesting. Putting X-Pro Milestone into actual use by a number of instructors has showed that X-Pro Milestone is easy to be learned and can be effectively used even by un-experienced computer users. We demonstrate that X-Pro Milestone is a cost-effective alternative to online examining systems with more attracting features.

2. Problem Statement and Requirements Analysis

2.1. Problem Statement

The following is the *problem statement* that we are tackling through the X-Pro Milestone software.

"Given a set of multiple-choice, true-false, short-answer, and free-response questions organized under a set of *sections* where each section contains a set of *question pools*. We would like to design a software tool that 1) randomly selects a set of m question pools $P(m)$ from the set of *preselected sections*, and after that, 2) randomly selects a set of m questions $Q(m)$ from the selected set of *question pools*; *one* question is randomly selected from *each pool*, 3) after that, the software produces a set of *n* different exam-forms out of the set $Q(m)$.

The produced exam-forms must be optimized to minimize the effect performance interference (that is cheating) as cheating negatively affects the evaluation process and, in turn, the educational system [2] [6] [10]. Reducing cheating can be achieved through having many-enough exam-forms produced by randomly permuting 1) choice-list items (for multiple-choice questions), 2) questions, or 3) both [3]-[5]. The randomization should produce uniformly distributed correct-choices over the set of possible positions within choice-lists to reduce the negative effect of randomly responding to multiple-choice question by students."

Producing multiple exam-forms should be done by permuting 1) the list of questions, or items, this is applicable to all types of questions, including multiple-choice questions, 2) or the list of choices of each question, this applies to multiple-choices questions only, or 2) both; that is permuting questions as well as choices. The user should have the option of selecting a *different set* of question for each exam-form produced. Each of the *n* exam-forms is to be produced along with its specific answer-key. The list of choices is to be properly permuted such that the probability of observing the correct answer at one position within the list of choices is equal to the probability of observing it at any other position (the computer uniform random number generator is to be used for that purpose). The goal of this requirement is to minimize the chance that an examiner receives high score solely by clustering his/her answers at one given position, not because of his/her real achievement.

Each question pool includes a set of questions covering a *specific course objective*. It is assumed that the instructor, when preparing his/her course question-bank for a given course, subdivides the syllabus into a set of well-defined course objectives or topics.

Notice that course text-books nowadays are prepared with a set of objectives for each chapter. Text-book publishers usually provide online objective question banks [11]. In fact, text-books are more and more becoming course-oriented which makes the usage of our proposed software ready for this line of book authoring.

The idea in the proposed software is to select exactly one question from each question pool. We argue that this guarantees that the produced exam effectively covers relatively *wide range of topics*.

The importance of the proposed software comes from the fact that exam questions in general, and multiple-choice questions specifically, are difficult to construct as they are relatively very sensitive to construction mistakes and, thus, require much of the instructor's focus [4] [12]. Studies also show that the creation of well-structured multiple-choice questions guarantees a more advanced understanding of the relationships between the concepts of the learning material as presented in the textbook [8] [9]. We believe that helping instructors to establish and maintain course question banks is vitally needed to maintain, refine, improve and reuse high-quality well-constructed exam questions.

2.2. Requirement-Analysis of X-Pro Milestone

In addition to allowing instructors to create, maintain and produce course question banks, the following list represents the functional and non-functional requirements considered when developing the X-Pro Milestone software [13] [14]:

Backup and Recovery: The application should allow for backing up and archiving course question banks for future referencing.

Documentation: The application's user interface should be user-friendly and intuitive and thus require minor documentation. A user should be able to easily learn how to use the software without the need to always refer to a lengthy and difficult-to-memorize documentation.

Efficiency: Defined as resource consumption for given load. The application should be simple and not need more than a normal desktop computer with no specialized hardware, network or software components. The application should also be stand alone and require no other software.

Effectiveness (resulting performance in relation to effort): Producing exams using the software should take minimal effort from the instructor. This, however, should not negatively affect the functionality of the application.

Emotional factors: In addition to having a simple and intuitive user-friendly user interface, the application should give the instructor positive feelings toward the value of the software. In fact, those who used the software already are pleased and feel comfortable as the application saved them long time and efforts. The true value of the application is in the fact that the effort an instructor put when preparing an exam years ago contributes to the success and the quality of the exam the instructor will be producing next. Test items that were added to the course question banks should be available to be included in future exam instances. We refer to this as *test-item reusability*.

Exploitability and Privacy: Course question banks are meant to be private and personal. That's why our application should store and maintain those question banks on the user's local machine which is supposed to be personal and not accessible by *unwanted users*.

Extensibility: In software engineering, software versioning is used to control software versions and updates. The application should be produced in versions such that required updates are deployed to its installations instantly. For that, the application should check for updates each time the instructor runs it. In addition to that, the course question-bank is stored along with the version number of the software. This allows the user to use future versions of the software and migrate his/her course question banks to the newer version and benefit from the added features, and to carry-forward his/her customizations to the next major version upgrade. This is referred to backward compatibility of software. To achieve that, the application should follow *open* and *widely accepted standards*.

Failure Management: the application should help instructor find the location of each question in the produced exam-form and preview it in the question bank. This should help the instructor fix any question that may have typos or to continuously improve the quality and readability of the questions (check next point).

Maintainability, Modifiability and Quality: The application should allow for incremental improvement of course question banks. Specific questions must be properly referenced so that the user can revisit previously saved and archived questions for editing and quality improvement. This should allow for having incremental improvement of test items.

Portability: Course question banks need to be stored in a way that allows the user to copy or move them around (if needed).

Scalability (Horizontal, Vertical): In our context, horizontal scalability refers to the ability to add sections and question pools to a given course bank. Vertical scalability refers to the capability of course question-bank system to allow the user to add questions to a specific question pool (that represents a specific course learning objective). The X-Pro Milestone should provide both features.

Security and Protection: The X-Pro Milestone is meant to be personal and to be installed on the user's personal machine. Thus, the security feature depends solely on how secure the file system of the user's desktop is. The protection feature also depends solely on how the user's account on the host machine is protected.

The above requirements have been obtained through putting two previous versions of similar application into service since year 2001. Some features provided by X-Pro Milestone may be needed by specific type of users. But for completeness, we included every feature we found to be useful to any group of users. Deriving those requirements is made possible by developing X-Pro Milestone using the Iterative and incremental development approach from software engineering domain (**Figure 1**).

The Iterative and incremental development approach involves testing and evaluation while development, this allows for fine modification and early improvement of the initial design of software while implementing it before the deployment step. Many requirements of the software, however, were collected after software deployment by taking feedbacks from real users. Those requirements were collected since 2001 when the first version of the software was put into service [3]-[5].

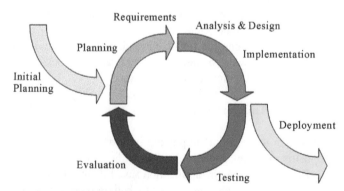

Figure 1. The Iterative and incremental development approach from software engineering domain.

The key idea behind this model is to develop the targeted software through *repeated cycles* (*i.e.*, iterative) and in *smaller portions* at a time (*i.e.*, incremental) as shown in **Figure 1**. This allows software developers to benefit from what they learned so far during development of earlier parts or *revisions* of the software. Learning comes from both 1) the development and 2) practical use of the system.

Historically, X-Pro Milestone has started in 1999 with a simple implementation of the software that simply allows the user to enter multiple-choice question, the software produces printable forms of automatically produced set of exam instances. The software requirements are enriched since then and the software is iteratively enhanced until X-Pro Milestone is implemented with more features [15]. At each iteration, *design modifications* are made and new functional capabilities are added to that simple implementation.

2.3. Functional Requirements of X-Pro Milestone

Next we summarize a set of functional requirements that we considered when developing X-pro Milestone. We also describe how our software meets those requirements.

Management of Course Question Banks: This includes creating and maintaining course question banks. The user is also able to archive and create backup copies of those course question banks.

Support of wide and comprehensive types of questions: The developed application supports wide spectrum of question types: multiple-choice, true/false, short-answer and free-response (essay) questions.

Allowing the User to Include Figures within Questions: X-Pro Milestone allows the user to add figures in the form of 1) images (of any format that is supported by web browsers; e.g., JPG, PNG, and GIF formats), 2) HTML code snippets, and 3) plain text contents. The figures can be inserted within any question directly. Alternatively, the user may include the figure at the end of the exam instance and the application will automatically add an appropriate reference to that figure within the question text. Figures in exam instances are automatically assigned unique ID numbers; the user needs not to be worried about numbering at all.

Next we list some *extra features* added to X-Pro Milestone. Through putting the application into real service, we found that those features prove useful to some users:

- Allowing users to add comment lines within question banks. Those lines are ignored when producing exam instances.
- Properly adding indentation and numbering to the course question-bank sections and to the question pools. This improves the readability of the question bank. It should also allow the user to quickly navigate to any required section or pool.
- Automatic building of a navigation tree with foldable and expandable nodes that should allow the user to preview the structure of the current course question-bank and directly navigate to any section or question pool within the course bank.
- Provide a mechanism for the user to label sections and question pools.
- Allowing the user to add text formatting tags in questions. One possible benefit of this feature is helping the user emphasize certain keywords in the question to bring the attention of the student to them. This also should help adding equations and probably computer code segments within the question text.

3. The Proposed Software

In this section we describe our software, the X-Pro Milestone, and show how we could successfully achieve the requirements listed in the previous section.

3.1. Understanding the X-Pro Milestone Input

X-Pro Milestone Supports a number of question types. Those are, Multiple-Choice, Short-Answer, True-False and Free-Response question types.

Each type of the three questions has the same generic structure. **Figure 2(a)** shows the basic structure of the course question-bank in X-Pro Milestone. That is; a number of sections, each section is composed of a number of question pools. Each question pool, in turn, includes one or more question. A question pool represents a specific and well-defined *course objective* or *subtopic*. This means that questions that belong to the same question pool are somehow topically similar and *cannot be* included in the same exam-form instance. The wisdom behind this course question-bank structuring is to guarantee that produced exams properly cover the course material.

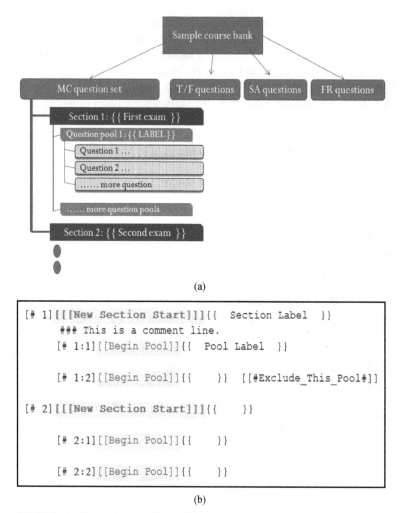

(a)

```
[# 1][[[New Section Start]]]{{  Section Label  }}
        ### This is a comment line.
        [# 1:1][[Begin Pool]]{{  Pool Label  }}

        [# 1:2][[Begin Pool]]{{    }}  [[#Exclude_This_Pool#]]

[# 2][[[New Section Start]]]{{    }}

    [# 2:1][[Begin Pool]]{{    }}

    [# 2:2][[Begin Pool]]{{    }}
```

(b)

Figure 2. (a) X-Pro Milestone course question-bank structure; (b) X-Pro Milestone Sample course question-bank structure.

The following is a list of the basic X-Pro Milestone tags used to indicate sections, question pools and questions.

- The [[New Section Start]] starts a new section.
- The [[Begin Pool]] tag starts a new pool.
- The [[Begin Question]] tag starts a new question.

Figure 2(b) shows a sample of two sections. Each section is composed of two question pools. The section label can be something like {{First Exam Set}} or {{Final Exam Set}}. The pool label describes the specific course objective being measured by the list of questions enclosed within the current pool. As a good practice, we recommend that the instructor subdivides the course objectives into three sections. The first section represents the set of objectives to be covered and evaluated in the first midterm exam. The second section represents the set of objectives to be covered and evaluated in the second midterm exam. And finally the last section represents the set of objectives to be covered and evaluated after the second exam and before the final exam. Later, when producing exam instances, one question is to be randomly selected from each pool of a given section. This way, the instructor guarantees that the same question will not appear twice in the exam and that the list of selected questions covers the set of course objectives properly.

The number of pools inside each section is left to the instructor. However, as a good practice, we recommend that the number of pools in the "First Exam" section be equal to 20 if the weight of the first midterm exam is 20 points. In this case, each question (that will be selected from one of the 20 pools available) will be of one point weight. Same applies to the "Second Exam" section. The "Final Exam" section is quite different. It is known that final exams cover 1) the topics included in the first and the second midterm exams, in addition to 2) the material covered after the second exam and before the final exam date. This means that the set of questions that will appear in the final exam will be selected from the set of pools that are located in the first, the second and the last section of the course question bank. Consequently, the instructor is free to subdivide the "final exam" section into any number of pools he/she prefers.

In X-Pro Milestone, lines that begins with the "Comment line" tag (that is "###") are considered comment lines and will be skipped while processing the user's input (as shown in **Figure 2(b)**).

3.2. X-Pro Milestone Syntax for Supported Question Types

Figure 3 shows a sample multiple-choice question. The figure shows two sections each is of two question pools.

The [[Begin Question]] indicates the beginning of a new multiple-choice question. The [[Begin Choice List]] tag indicates that the lines after are the list of choices of the current question. The set of lines after the [[Begin Question]] and before the [[Begin Choice List]] tags represent the multiple-choice question stem. This means that the question stem may be composed of multiple lines. However, the [[Begin Choice List]] tag is optional. In this case the question stem is assumed to be composed of one single line. The lines that follow that line represent the list of choices.

Each line in the list of choices represents one choice. A choice my not span multiple lines. The "<ca>" next to a choice indicates that this choice is a correct choice (used later by the application to produce the answer key table). The <ca> is referred to as the "correct answer" tag. A multiple-choice question may have one or more correct choice.

Each multiple-choice question can have up to six choices. Those choices will be later permuted to produce exam-forms. To force one specific choice to remain in-place (will *not* be permuted), you put the "do not permute" tag next to that choice; that is the <dnp> tag. This helps the user to have choices like "All above" or "both *A* and *C* are correct" choices.

The [[#Inline_Choices#]]} tag next to the [[Begin Question]] tag indicates that the list of choice in the produced exam-form will be put in-line (next to each other) as shown in **Figure 4**. Otherwise, they will be viewed in a normal vertical list as shown in **Figure 5**.

Figure 6 shows a sample of two true-false questions and two short-answer questions. Each question appears in a single line. Each question is of two parts: 1) the question text, and 2) the correct answer put between the "[[" and "]]" tags (referred to as the short-answer opening and closing tags).

```
[# 1][[[New Section Start]]]{{ Section Label  }}
    [# 1:1][[Begin Pool]]{{  Pool Label  }}
           [[Begin Question]] [[#Inline_Choices#]]
               Your question goes here.
               [[Begin Choice List]]
               First Choice
               Second Choice <ca>
               Third Choice
               Fourth Choice <ca>
               Fifth Choice <dnp>


    [# 1:2][[Begin Pool]]{{      }}
[# 2][[[New Section Start]]]{{      }}
    [# 2:1][[Begin Pool]]{{      }}
    [# 2:1][[Begin Pool]]{{      }}
```

Figure 3. The syntax of a typical multiple-choice question in X-Pro Milestone.

```
1.  Your question goes here.
        A. First Choice  B. Second Choice  C. Third Choice  D. Fourth Choice  E. Fifth Choice
```

Figure 4. A sample multiple-choice question with its choice-list displayed inline.

Figure 7 shows a sample free-response essay question. Each free-response essay question is of two parts: 1) the question text that may span multiple lines. It appears after the [[Begin Question]] tag and before the [[Begin answer]] tag, and 2) the correct answer that will appear after the [[Begin Answer]] tag. Again, the answer may also span multiple lines.

3.3. X-Pro Milestone User's Interface

Figure 8 shows a screen shot for the main user interface of the X-Pro Milestone. It shows five areas; the menu bar, the toolbar, the left pane and the right pane, and finally the Application Flags areas.

The left pane displays the basic functional tab pages of X-Pro Milestone. The key tab pages are:

- The "Multiple-choice questions" tab page: through which the user enters the set of Multiple-Choice (MC) questions.
- The "Short-Answer questions" tab page: through which the user enters the set of Short-Answer (SA) questions.
- The "True-False questions" tab page: through which the user enters the set of True/False (TF) questions.
- The "Free-Response questions" tab page: through which the user enters the set of Free-Response essay (FR) questions.

Figure 9 shows the "Multiple-choice questions" tab page. The pane on the left provides a space in which the user enters the multiple-choice questions. The pane at the middle is the current "Tab Page Explorer" that allows the user to navigate directly to any of the sections and pools available in the current tab page.

Figure 10 shows the "Figures and attachments" tab page through which the user manipulates the set of figures referred to within the exam questions (this includes: importing, removing, previewing, and adding notes to any figure in the course bank). Each figure file must have a unique label of the user's choice (otherwise, the software will automatically assign a unique label to the figure while importing it). This label is included in the filename of the figure file between double square brackets. This label will be later used when inserting figures inside exam questions. This tab page displays information about the selected figure from the list, e.g., its full filename,

```
1.  Your question goes here.
          A. First Choice
          B. Second Choice
          C. Third Choice
          D. Fourth Choice
          E. Fifth Choice
```

Figure 5. A sample multiple-choice question with its choice-list displayed in multiple lines.

```
[[Begin Pool]]{{ Sample TF pool }}
     The three basic light colors are 'Red, Green and Blue'. [[True]]
     The result of 5+6 is 14.[[False]]

[[Begin Pool]]{{ Sample SA pool }}
     33-44 is____ . [[ -11 ]]
     3X=33,  [rArr] x=____ . [[ 11 ]]
```

Figure 6. Sample True-False questions.

```
[[Begin Pool]]{{ Sample FR pool }}
     [[Begin Question]]
          Name the three basic light colors.
     [[Begin Answer]]
     1. Red
     2. Green
     3. Blue
```

Figure 7. Sample Free-Response questions.

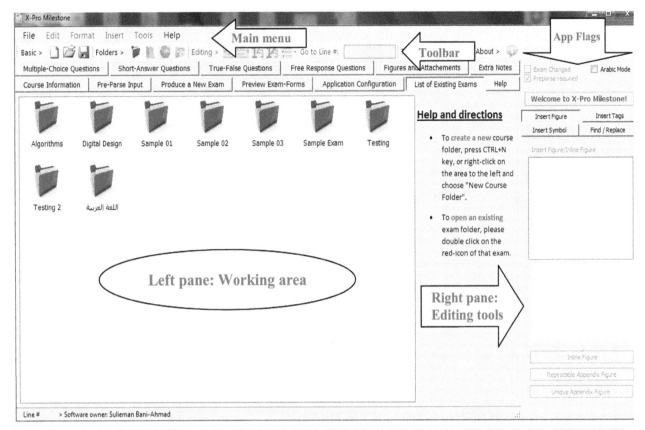

Figure 8. Major parts of the X-Pro Milestone user interface.

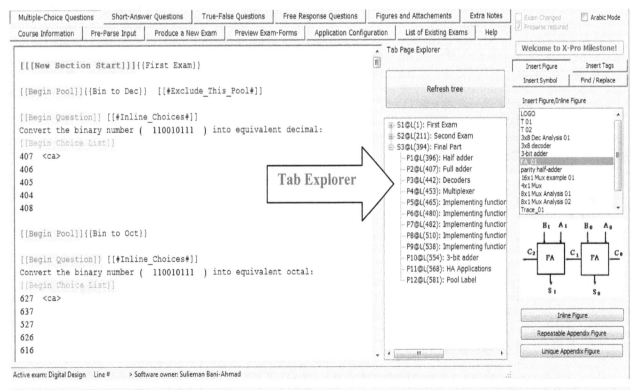

Figure 9. The "Multiple-choice questions" tab page.

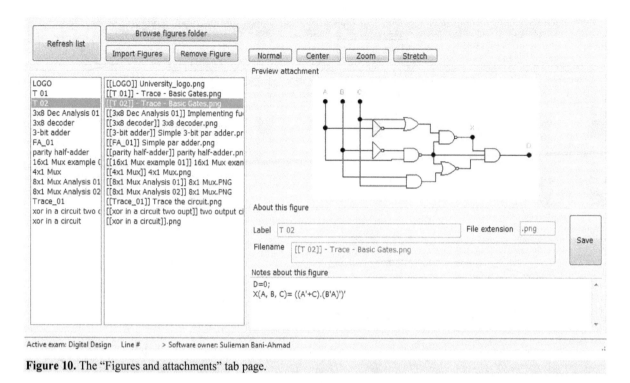

Figure 10. The "Figures and attachments" tab page.

file extension, label, notes about this specific figure, and it shows the user a preview of this figure.

3.4. Producing Exam Instances Using X-Pro Milestone

In order to produce an exam out of an existing course question-bank, the following steps are to be taken:

Step A: Pre-parsing the course question-bank using through the "Pre-Parse" tool located at the "Pre-Parse Input" tab page (Figure 11)

Before the user can produce exam instances from his/her course question bank, he/she needs to pre-parse the course question-bank to check if the course has syntax or structural errors. If the user chooses to check the "Exclude empty pools" check box shown in **Figure 11**, then observing empty pools will be considered as warnings not as errors.

Other errors that the pre-parser may identify are 1) finding empty sections, 2) finding a multiple choice question with no choice list or only one single choice item.

Step B: Producing Exam instances through the "Produce a New Exam" tab page.

After the user pre-pares the course question-bank with no errors, the "Produce a New Exam" tab page will be activated and its content will be refreshed. The user can now produce exam instances. This is done in four steps.

Step B.1: In which the user chooses the set of sections to be included and the number of pools to be randomly selected (**Figure 12**).

Step B.2: Setting exam information: As shown in **Figure 13**. This includes for example the exam date, time and date, the exam class (first, second or final exam), etc.…

Step B.3: Setting exam instructions: as shown in **Figure 14**.

Step B.4: Choosing the form generator settings through the "Produce a New Exam" tab page as shown in **Figure 15**. Those settings include: 1) the number of forms required, 2) the form ID style, 3) wither the user wants to hide the form ID from the student in the produced forms, 4) the permutation options, 5) wither the user wants to have the same set of questions in all produced forms or not, 6) the multiple-choice answer table and answer-key styles.

Step B.5: Previewing produced exam-forms using the "Preview and Export Exam-Forms" tab page (**Figure 16**).

The user can now preview the produced exam-forms. The user can choose to preview the produced exam-form using Microsoft Internet Explorer (recommended) or Google Chrome.

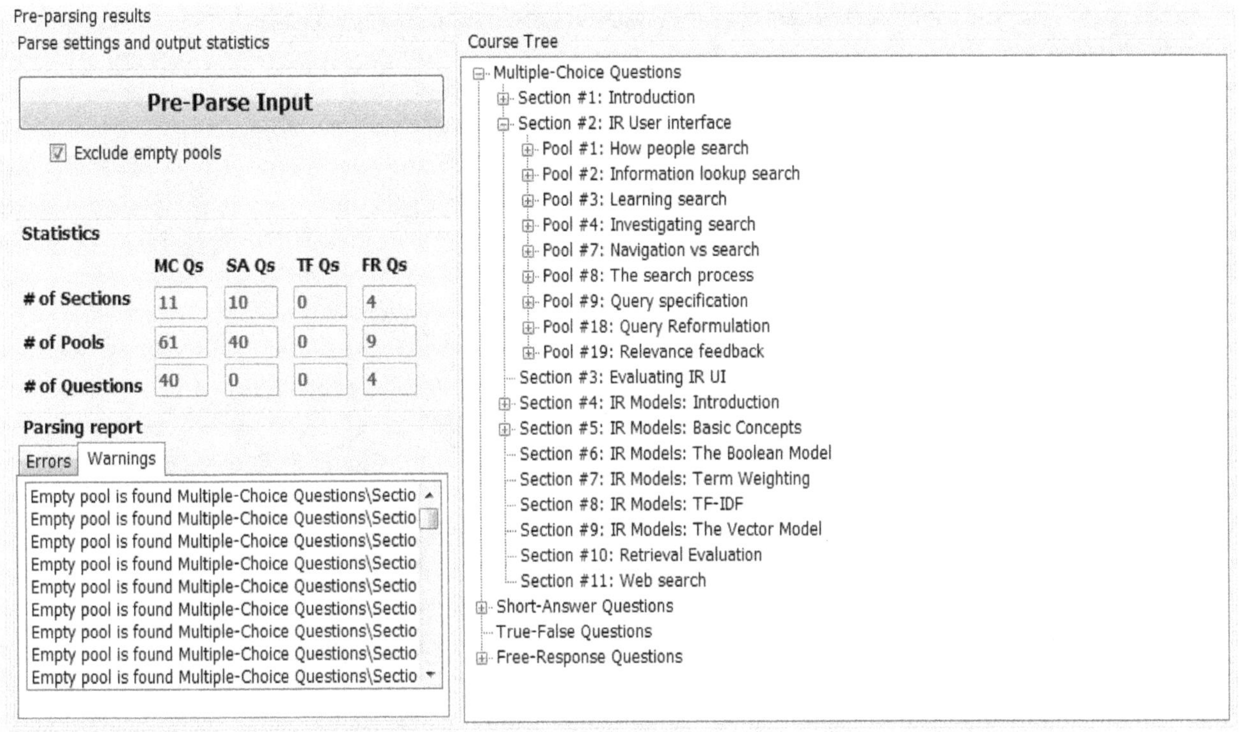

Pre-parsing results
Parse settings and output statistics

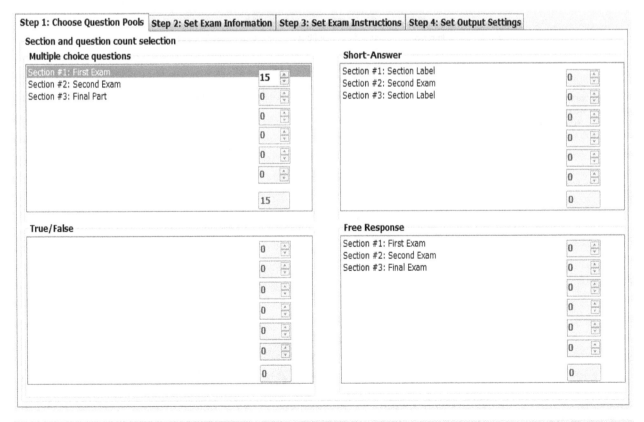

Figure 11. The "Pre-Parse Input" tab page.

Figure 12. Choosing sections and question pools for exam production.

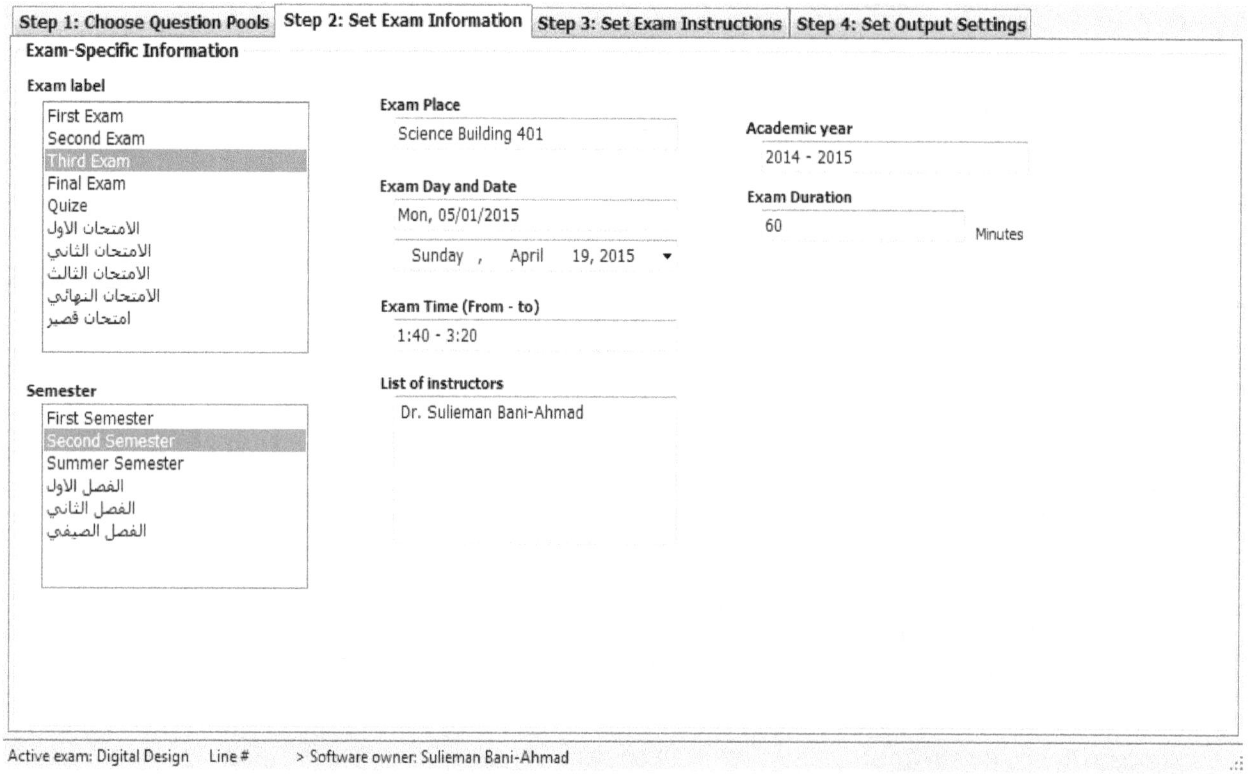

| Step 1: Choose Question Pools | Step 2: Set Exam Information | Step 3: Set Exam Instructions | Step 4: Set Output Settings |

Exam-Specific Information

Exam label

First Exam
Second Exam
Third Exam
Final Exam
Quize
الامتحان الاول
الامتحان الثاني
الامتحان الثالث
الامتحان النهائي
امتحان قصير

Exam Place

Science Building 401

Exam Day and Date

Mon, 05/01/2015

Sunday   ,   April   19, 2015   ▼

Exam Time (From - to)

1:40 - 3:20

List of instructors

Dr. Sulieman Bani-Ahmad

Academic year

2014 - 2015

Exam Duration

60

Minutes

Semester

First Semester
Second Semester
Summer Semester
الفصل الاول
الفصل الثاني
الفصل الصيفي

Active exam: Digital Design   Line #   > Software owner: Sulieman Bani-Ahmad

Figure 13. Setting exam information for exam production.

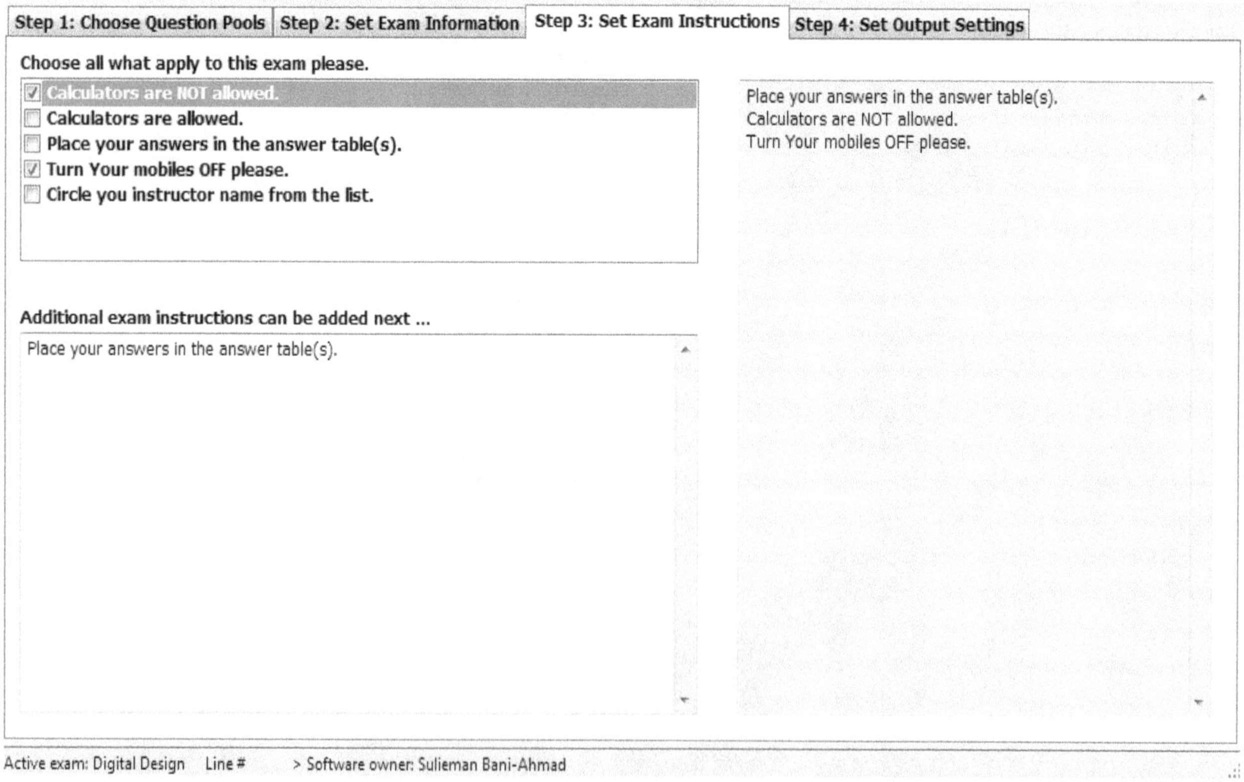

| Step 1: Choose Question Pools | Step 2: Set Exam Information | Step 3: Set Exam Instructions | Step 4: Set Output Settings |

Choose all what apply to this exam please.

☑ Calculators are NOT allowed.
☐ Calculators are allowed.
☐ Place your answers in the answer table(s).
☑ Turn Your mobiles OFF please.
☐ Circle you instructor name from the list.

Place your answers in the answer table(s).
Calculators are NOT allowed.
Turn Your mobiles OFF please.

Additional exam instructions can be added next ...

Place your answers in the answer table(s).

Active exam: Digital Design   Line #   > Software owner: Sulieman Bani-Ahmad

Figure 14. Setting exam instructions for exam production.

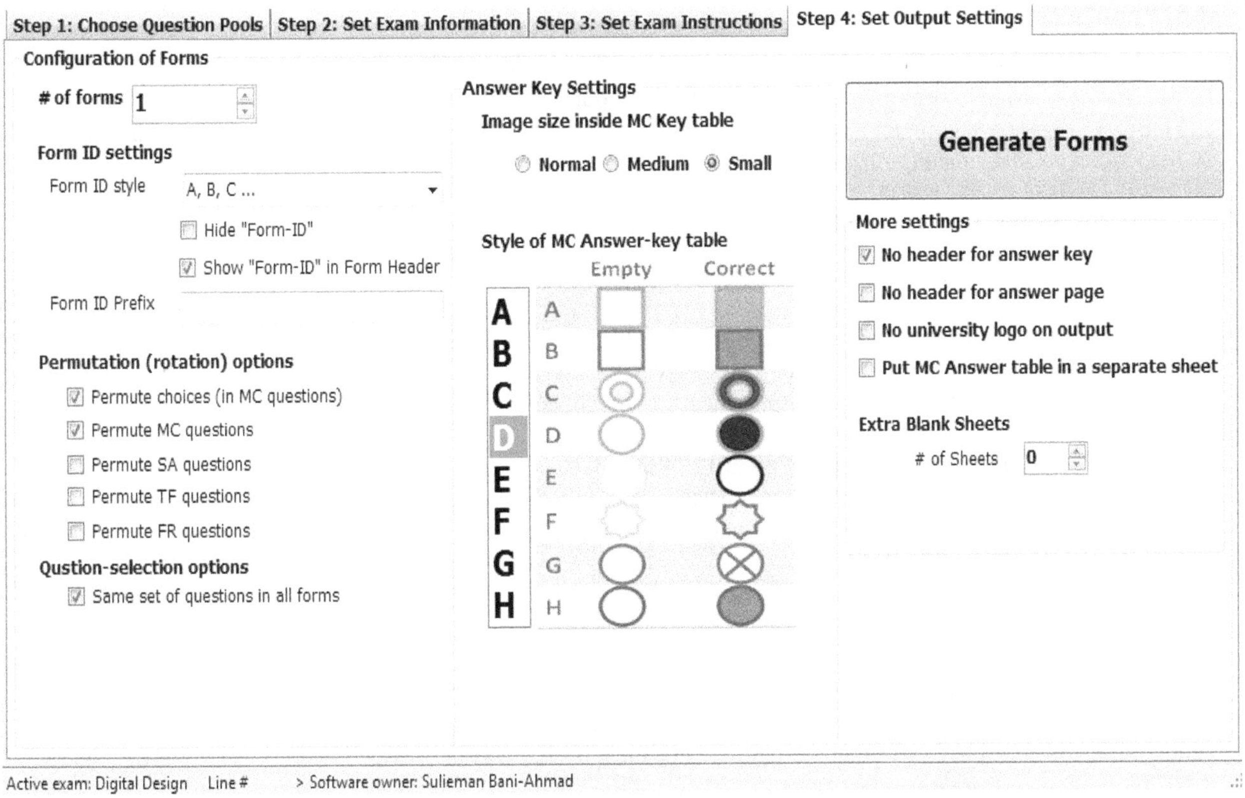

Figure 15. Choosing form-generator setting for exam production.

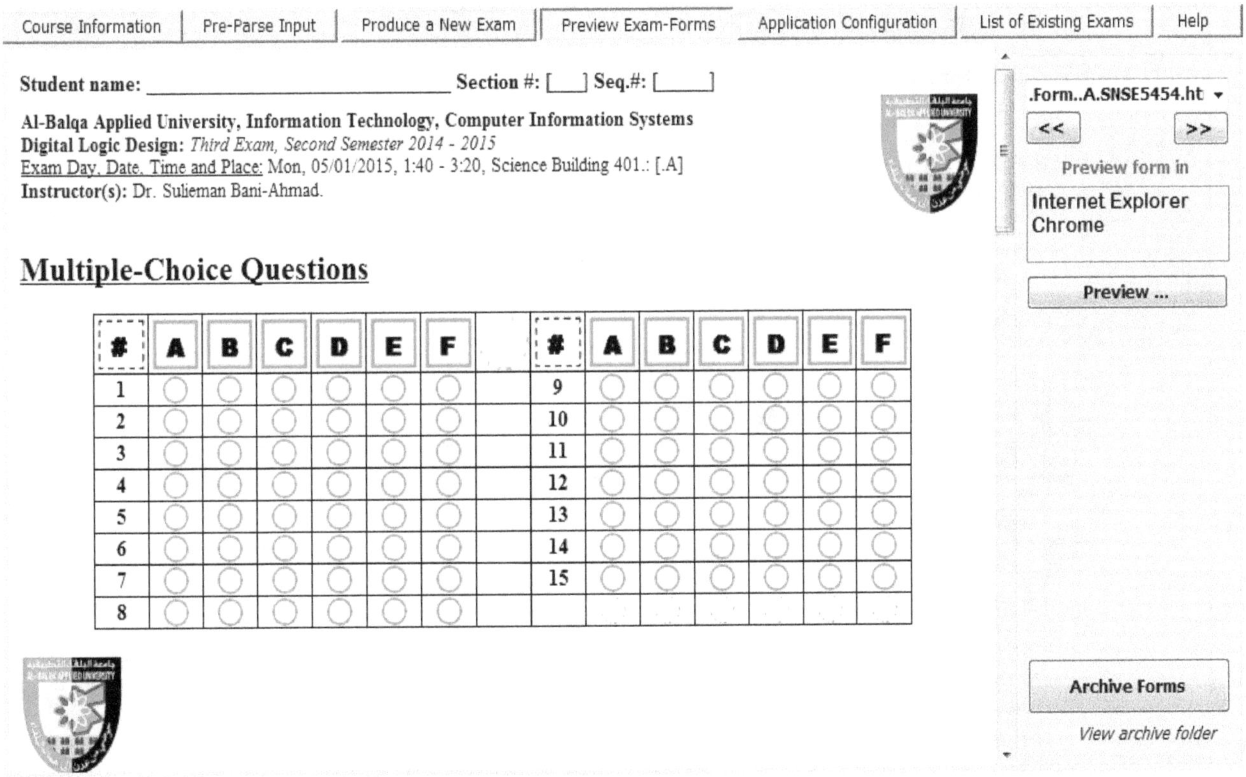

Figure 16. Previewing produced exam-forms.

3.5. Printouts of Exam Instances

In order to have a printed copy of the form, the user needs to preview the exam-form using Microsoft Internet Explorer (or any available up-to-date browser) and print it out through the browser.

Figure 17 shows a sample multiple-choice questions answer key. The user may print this table on a thermal slide to facilitate student answer table grading.

3.6. Extra Features of X-Pro Milestone

Next are some of the extra features that X-Pro Milestone provides.

3.6.1. Manipulation of Course Question Banks

Through the "List of Existing Exams" tab page (**Figure 18**), the user can 1) create a new course-bank, 2) open existing course question banks (for editing), 3) backup or archive an already existing one.

3.6.2. Inserting Figure from the Pre-Fed Set of Figures

Figures can be inserted inside the text of any question (and even in the choice list of a multiple-choice question). Figures inside the course question-bank have one of three settings:

1) Inline Figures

A figure can be inserted **inline**; that is, it will appear with the question in the produced exam-form (*i.e.*, it will not appear at the end of the exam-form as appendix as illustrated in **Figure 19**).

2) Repeatable Appendix Figures

A figure can be inserted as a **repeatable figure** at **the end of the exam-form as appendix**. That is; if the figure is referenced inside *n* questions in the same exam-form, then the same figure will appear *n* time in the appendix of the exam-form. Notice that the figure inside the question will be replaced by a *proper reference* to the

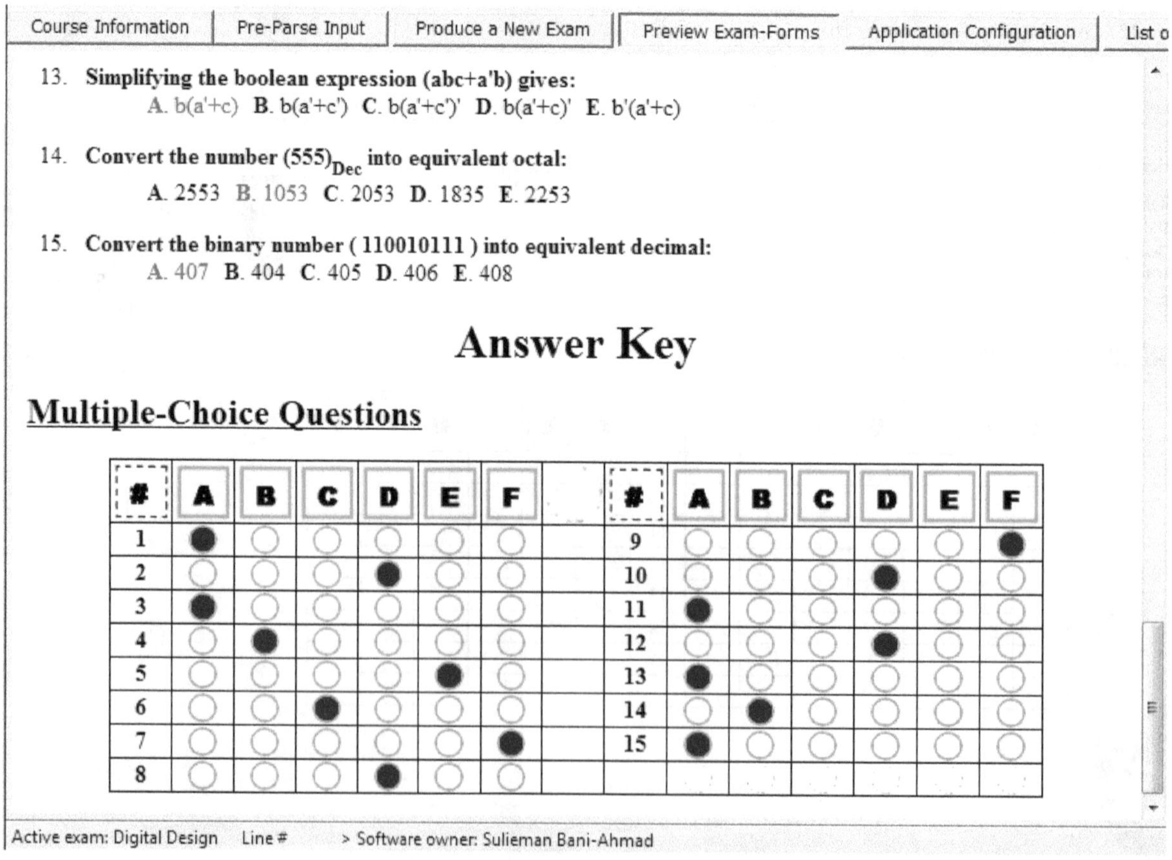

Figure 17. The answer key of the produced exam-form.

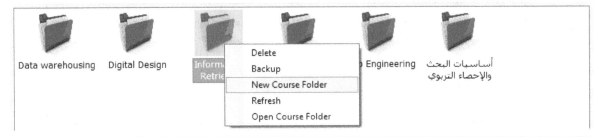

Figure 18. Manipulation of course questions banks.

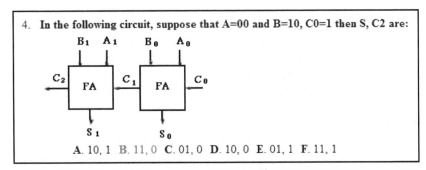

Figure 19. Example multiple-choice question with an inline figure.

figure as it appears in the appendix part of the form. e.g., it will be replaced by "**Figure 5**", or "figure x" in general. The sequence number "x" here is *automatically generated* by the software; the user does not have to worry about this issue.

3) Unique Appendix Figures

A figure can be inserted as a **unique (not repeatable)** figure at **the end of the exam-form as appendix**. That is; if the figure is referenced inside *n* questions in the same exam-form, then this figure will appear *only once* in the appendix of the exam-form. Again, as in Repeatable appendix figures, the figure reference inside the question will be replaced by a proper reference to the figure as it appears in the appendix part of the exam-form. e.g., it will be replaced by "**Figure 5**", or "figure x" in general. The sequence number "x" here is automatically generated by the software. Again, the user does not have to worry about this issue.

4) More Protection Features

To protect already inserted questions (especially multiple-choice questions) from being mistakenly altered by the user, the user may want to *add protection* to that particular question from being edited.

X-Pro Milestone is also equipped with

a) A simple, word-based spell checker.

b) A tool to insert symbols (e.g., Π, $\cap$, $\rightarrow$, ...)

c) A tool to insert formatting tags that allows the user to enter entities such as equations and chemical formulas (such as $E = MC^2$ and H_2O).

3.7. A Word about X-Pro Milestone User Friendliness

Most important of all, X-Pro Milestone is user-friendly. According to [14], the most important features that identify user friendly software are the following. Those features were all considered when developing X-Pro Milestone.

- **Simple to install, easy to remove, and easy to update**: X-Pro Milestone is Windows-based; it can be installed into the system and can be safely removed through the Control Panel of the operating system. The user does not have to be expert to do these tasks. The software can be downloaded from the following link Http://sulieman.net/xpro/get. Updates are automatically detected and the user will be automatically notified of them.
- **Intuitive, Pleasant, easy-to-navigate Graphical User Interface (GUI)**: all functions that the application provides are directly reachable through the application main menu. Controls and components are grouped

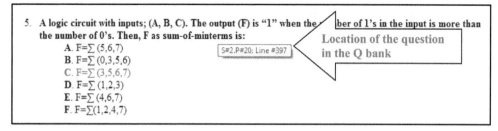

Figure 20. Example multiple-choice question with a popup indicating the location of the question in the question bank.

into tab pages on the same Windows form, which is the main screen of the application. This *flat layout* of the user interface helps the user have immediate and continuous interaction with those components and maximizes the user's benefit of all the functionalities provided by X-Pro Milestone.

- **Doesn't need third-party software**: X-Pro is stand-alone application. The user does not need database management system or any other difficult-to-find third-party software. The only third-party software the application requires is Microsoft's Internet Explorer, which automatically comes with the hosting environment; that is the Windows Operating system.

- **Adheres to standards**: The input of the application follows the Rich Text Format (RTF) standard. The output of the application; that is the exam-forms, is produced in the form of standard *HTML and CSS* formats. Both are well-known and widely-accepted standards.

- **Effective error handling**: If the user finds some typos or mistakes in any of the questions of the produced exam instance, then he/she can locate and directly navigate to the erroneous question. This is achieved by placing the mouse pointer on top of the question in the web browser or in the "Preview and Export Exam-Forms" tab page as shown in **Figure 20**. A balloon will pop up informing the user about the section number, the pool number and the line number where the question is placed within the course question bank.

As indicated in **Figure 20** also, the correct answer of the multiple-choice question is displayed in **red color** (in preview-mode only, when the exam-form is printed out, all the choices will *look and feel similar*). This feature is needed if the user would like to double-check the correctness of the question.

4. Conclusion

In this paper we presented X-Pro milestone, a tool that enables instructors to construct a course-syllabus personalized question-bank of his/her own. X-Pro Milestone supports wide spectrum of question types (multiple-choice, true/false, short-answer essay questions, and free-response questions). The user can also produce exam instances with multiple forms based on a set of randomly selected set of pools. Those pools, in turn, are also randomly selected from within a set of pre-fed set of section. X-Pro Milestone has unique features that make it superior to other available software packages in the market. For instance, X-Pro Milestone question banks are personalized, portable, and highly customizable to fit user's needs. X-Pro Milstone is capable of automatically producing formatted and printable exam-forms along with an answer sheet and an answer key for each form. Putting the software into practice shows that it significantly reduces the effort required by the user to prepare and grade his/her exams. X-Pro Milestone is a cost-effective alternative to computer-based examination systems while maintaining the same level of quality assurance in terms of cheating prevention.

Acknowledgements

I would like to thank Prof. Ahmad Audeh from the faculty of Education at Yarmouk University, Jordan, for his long support and advices during the development of the software. I also would like to thank my colleague Dr. O. Dorgham from Al-Balqa Applied University for his kind support and observations on the software usability.

References

[1] Cen, G., Dong, Y.X., Gao, W.L., Yu, L.N., See, S., Wang, Q., Yang, Y. and Jiang, H.B. (2010) A Implementation of an Automatic Examination Paper Generation System. *Mathematical and Computer Modeling*, **51**, 1339-1342. http://dx.doi.org/10.1016/j.mcm.2009.11.010

[2] Ministry of Higher Education—Jordan (2010) MOHE Statistics. The Ministry of Higher Education and Scientific Research. http://www.mohe.gov.jo

[3] Bani-Ahmad, S. and Audeh, A. (2010) Re-Engineering of Multiple-Choice Exam-Form Production Tools: Cost-Effective and Quality-Assurance Approach. *Proceedings of the* 2010 *International Conference on Education and Information Technology* (*ICEIT*), Chongqing, 17-19 September 2010, v3-260-v3-264. http://dx.doi.org/10.1109/iceit.2010.5608376

[4] Bani-Ahmad, S. (2010) The ExPro: A New Multiple-Choice-Based Exam-Form Production Package. *The 8th Conference of the Faculty of Education, "Education in the Era of Alternatives"*, Yarmouk University, Irbid.

[5] Bani-Ahmad, S. and Audeh, A. (2010) Re-Engineering of Multiple-Choice Exam-Form Production Tools: Cost-Effective and Quality-Assurance Approach. *Journal of Software Engineering*, **4**. [Journal Paper]

[6] Maharey, S. (2011) Higher Education: Challenges for Developing Countries. Commonwealth Education Partnerships. http://www.cedol.org/wp-content/uploads/2012/02/Steve-Maharey-article.pdf

[7] ProProfs Blog (2011) Essential Ways to Prevent Cheating in Online Assessments. http://www.proprofs.com/blog/2011/11/essential-ways-to-prevent-cheating-in-online-assessments/#sthash.QxBAimru.dpufhttp://www.proprofs.com/blog/2011/11/essential-ways-to-prevent-cheating-in-online-assessments/

[8] Hutchinson, D. and Wells, J. (2013) An Inquiry into the Effectiveness of Student Generated MCQs as a Method of Assessment to Improve Teaching and Learning. *Creative Education*, **4**, 117-125. http://dx.doi.org/10.4236/ce.2013.47A2014

[9] Fayyoumi, A., Mohammad, H. and Faris, H. (2013) Mobile Based Learning and Examination: Students and Instructors Perceptions from Different Arab Countries. *Journal of Software Engineering and Applications*, **6**, 662-669. http://dx.doi.org/10.4236/jsea.2013.612079

[10] Fayyoumi, A. and Zarrad, A. (2014) Novel Solution Based on Face Recognition to Address Identity Theft and Cheating in Online Examination Systems. *Advances in Internet of Things*, **4**, 5-12. http://dx.doi.org/10.4236/ait.2014.42002

[11] Johnston, S.P. and Huczynski, A. (2008) Textbook Publishers' Website Objective Question Banks: Does Their Use Improve Students' Examination Performance? *Active Learning in Higher Education Journal*, **7**, 11-22.

[12] Burton, S., Sudweeks, R., Merril, P. and Wood, B. (1991) How to Prepare Better Multiple-Choice Test Items: Guidelines for University Faculty. Brigham Young University Testing Services.

[13] Pressman, R. and Maxim, B. (2014) Software Engineering: A Practitioner's Approach, 8th Edition. McGraw-Hill. Boston.

[14] Wallen, J. (2010) 10 Things That Make Software User-Friendly. TechRepublic. http://www.techrepublic.com/blog/10-things/10-things-that-make-software-user-friendly/

[15] Wikipedia. Iterative and Incremental Development. http://en.wikipedia.org/wiki/Iterative_and_incremental_development

26

Metric Based Testability Estimation Model for Object Oriented Design: Quality Perspective

Mahfuzul Huda[1], Yagya Dutt Sharma Arya[1], Mahmoodul Hasan Khan[2]

[1]Department of Computer Science & Engineering, Invertis University, Bareilly, India
[2]Department of Computer Science and Engineering, IET, Lucknow, India
Email: mahfuzul@iul.ac.in

Abstract

The quality factor of class diagram is critical because it has significant influence on overall quality of the product, delivered finally. Testability has been recognized as a key factor to software quality. Estimating testability at design stage is a criterion of crucial significance for software designers to make the design more testable. Taking view of this fact, this paper identifies testability factors namely effectiveness and reusability and establishes the correlation among testability, effectiveness and reusability and justifies the correlation with the help of statistical measures. Moreover study developed metric based testability estimation model and developed model has been validated using experimental test. Subsequently, research integrates the empirical validation of the developed model for high level acceptance. Finally a hypothesis test performs by the two standards to test the significance of correlation.

Keywords

Testability, Testability Model, Effectiveness, Reusability, Testability Factors, Design Phase

1. Introduction

Building quality software is an important issue considering that software industries are now used in all kind of environments, including some where human life depends on the computer's correct functioning to get better performance and to get competitive advantage [1]. Object orientated technique has rapidly become accepted as the preferred paradigm in industrial software development environments for large-scale system design [2] [3]. Classes in object oriented system provide an excellent structuring mechanism that allows a system to be divided into well designed units which may then be implemented separately [4]. One of the major advantage of having object orientation is its support for software reuse, which may be achieved either through the simple reuse of a class in a library or via inheritance [5]. Object oriented paradigm has created new challenges to testing, which has to deal with new problems introduced by the powerful object oriented features such as encapsulation, inheritance, coupling cohesion, polymorphism, and dynamic binding. Especially dealing with instantiations of classes and their collaboration may be very difficult when testing is performed [6]. Testability suggests the testing intensity, and gives the degree of difficulty which will be sustained during testing of a particular position to identify a fault [7].

It is an inevitable fact that software testability information is a helpful strategy complementary to testing. Higher test coverage may be completed by making a design more testable for the same quantity of effort, which as a result increases the confidence to the system. It is evident from literature review that there is no known complete and comprehensive model or framework available for estimating the testability of object oriented software taking design phase into consideration [8]-[12]. The model proposed in this paper addresses many issues raised by various researchers and practitioners. This model has low-level design metrics well defined in terms of design characteristics. The set of empirically identified and weighted object oriented design properties are used to assess the testability. Rest of the research paper is organized as follows: Section 2 and Section 3 describe software testability and testability at design phase. Section 4 describes testability factors and key contributors. In Section 5, a Metric Based Testability Estimation Model for Object Oriented Design: Quality Perspective has been proposed, design properties have been defined and a brief description of identified metrics has been included. The effectiveness of this model in predicting design testability has been validated against several real world projects in Section 6. It has been concluded that testability predicted by this model shows high correlation with evaluators assessments in Section 7 and a hypothesis test based on 2-sample t-test is being performed and confidence interval is being observed by the difference of two standard mean in Section 8. Finally study concluded with some key findings in Section 9 and Section 10.

2. Software Testability

Software testability study has been an essential research direction since 1990s and becomes more pervasive when entering 21st century [13] [14]. According to IEEE standard, the software testability refers to the degree to which a system or part facilitates the performance of tests and the establishment of test criteria to determine whether those test criteria have been met [15]. In ISO 9126 quality model, testability holds a prominent place as part of the reusability characteristic of software quality [16]. In order to minimize the testing effort, an attempt can be made to predict which class is more testable, by looking at two classes [17]. Testability, comprising of certain characteristics of a software system that makes it easier or harder to test and to analyze the test results, is an important factor to achieve an efficient and effective test process. Designing, verifying and measuring highly testable software becomes an important and challenging task for software designers [10]. Much of the research work reveals that maximum efforts have been dedicated with the source code. The determination of testability for an already written code may be too costly because in latter the changes are introduced the more expensive they are [18]. An extensive survey of literature reveals that processes, guidelines, and tools related to software testability are missing [19]. Thus, there appeared to be need for evaluating the testability of software in early stage of development life cycle without the availability of code. Availability of a suitable and adequate measuring model at the early stage of development enables early prediction of system testability, therefore, enhances the quality of making necessary changes.

3. Software Testability at Design Phase

A design is a process that starts from a study of a domain problem leading to some formal documentation. Software design, in some ways, is an eccentric art [20]. At the first instance, it may result in a model of the domain problem by formally capturing and representing the user's requirements and hence, paving the way for a conceptual relation. During the design stages of software, it is represented in terms of requirement specifications, architectural and detailed design diagrams [11]. These representations capture the structure and behavior of the software before it is implemented. The representations are then transformed into the actual software implementation. The challenge is to study how these representations impact the final implementation of the software, with the aim of identifying characteristics and/or patterns in the representations that may enhance or perhaps impair testability. Identifying such characteristics and/or patterns would enable one to create representations of software that evolve into better testable implementations and thus, improve on the time and effort-efficiency during software testing [12]. Improving software testability is clearly a key objective in order to reduce the number of defects that result from poorly designed software [21]. Testable design is more specific then good design because it is explicitly intended to match a particular test context. One proactive strategy that organizations can adopt is to design their software products with testability as one of the key design criteria. Aspects of testability like design effectiveness and reusability behavior are the primary focus of good design and require special treatment. No doubt, it is a key to the successful development of quality software. It is also the step that will determine the overall structure, nature, and approach of the resulting software.

4. Testability Factors and Major Contributors

Plenty of work has been carried out in describing the need and importance of incorporating software testability since early 90s. A number of methods of measuring testability have been proposed. Unfortunately, significant achievements made by the researchers in the area have not been widely accepted and are not adopted in practice by industry. It has been found that there is a conflict in considering the factors while estimating software testability in general and at design level exclusively. It has been inferred from the literature survey on testability analysis that there is a heavy need of identifying a commonly accepted set of the factors affecting software testability [11] [12] [15] [21]. A significant effort has been prepared to collect a set of software testability factors namely, effectiveness, understandability, simplicity, reusability, self descriptiveness, complexity, traceability and modularity that can affect software testability at design time in development life cycle [3] [5]. Out of these testability factors, some of them have their direct impact in evaluating testability of object oriented software, while other factors have less or negligible impact. An endeavor has been made to identify the testability factors that accurately affect software testability estimation at design phase. "Effectiveness" and "Reusability" are identified the key testability factors that accurately affect software testability Estimation and fulfill the quality criteria, particularly effectiveness quality criteria is traceability, understandability, self descriptiveness and Reusability quality criteria is complexity, simplicity. Therefore, it comes into view realistic to include effectiveness and reusability for testability Estimation at design phase.

5. Software Testability Model Development

Dromey's quality model [22] and Testability Quantification Framework [9] have been considered as a basis to develop the Metric Based Testability Estimation Model for Object Oriented Design. **Figure 1**, shows the correlation establishment among Testability, Testability factors, Design Metrics, and describes the estimation process of testability model. This involves subsequent steps:

1. Identification of Testability Factors that influences testability of software.
2. Identification of Object Oriented Design Metrics.
3. A means of linking them.

The relative significance of individual identified testability factors that have major impact on testability estimation at design phase is weighted proportionally. The values of these design metrics can be identified by class diagram metrics. In order to set up a metric based model for Testability estimation, a multiple regression technique has been used to get the coefficients of regression variables and regression intercept, shown in **Table 1**. Identified testability factors will take part in the role of independent variables while testability will be taken as dependent variable. Estimation of testability is very helpful to get testability index of software design for high

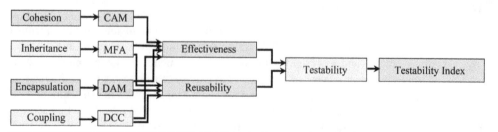

Figure 1. Correlation among testability, testability factors and design metrics.

Table 1. Correlation coefficients[a].

Model		Unstandardized Coefficients		Standardized Coefficients	t	Sig.
		B	Std. Error	Beta		
1	(Constant)	59.524	48.835		1.219	0.347
	Effectiveness	−4.671	3.739	−0.563	−1.249	0.338
	Reuseability	0.806	0.351	1.034	2.294	0.149

a. Dependent Variable: Testability.

quality product. Multivariate regression equation is given in Equation (1) which is as follows

$$Y = a_0 \pm a_1 X_1 \pm a_2 X_2 \pm a_3 X_3 \pm \cdots \pm a_n X_n \tag{1}$$

where

Y is dependent variable

$X_1, X_2, X_3, \cdots X_n$ are independent (regressor) variables.

$a_1, a_2, a_3 \cdots a_n$ are the regression coefficient of the respective independent variable.

a_0 is the regression intercept

It has been broadly reviewed and discussed in Section 4; Effectiveness and Reusability are the major factors affecting software testability estimation at design phase. Therefore, these identified major testability factors were addressed well in advance while incorporating testability at design stage. By applying the regression method, study already developed Effectiveness Model [3] and Reusability Model [5] that is given in Equations (2) and (3) respectively. The model of Effectiveness and Reusability forms the strong basis for development of Testability Estimation Model.

$$\text{Effectiveness} = 8.783 - 1.614 * \text{Encapsulation} + 11.141 * \text{Inheritance} - 0.866 * \text{Coupling} - 6.477 * \text{Cohesion} \tag{2}$$

$$\text{Reusability} = -37.111 + 3.973 * \text{Coupling} + 32.500 * \text{Inheritance} + 20.709 * \text{Encapsulation} \tag{3}$$

It was observed that every Object Oriented Design metrics affect quality factor. Design metrics namely Inheritance (MFA: Measure of Functional Abstraction), Encapsulation (DAM: Data Access Metrics), Cohesion (CAM: Cohesion Among Methods) and Coupling (DCC: Direct Class Coupling) are used to address the key testability factors namely Effectiveness and Reusability. These two identified factors are further used to measure testability index of object oriented software at design stage in development life cycle. **Figure 1**, gives an overview of the main idea. In order to establish a model for software testability estimation, a multiple regression method discussed in Equation (1) has been applied. Consequently considering, the impact of design metrics namely Inheritance, Coupling, Cohesion and Encapsulation on testability contributors "Effectiveness and Reusability", following multiple regression model has been formulated that can be used to develop testability model for object oriented software.

$$\text{Testability} = \alpha 0 \pm \beta 1 \times \text{Effectiveness} \pm \beta 2 \times \text{Reusability} \tag{4}$$

For developing software testability model, the data has been taken from [23], which consist of six commercial software projects with around 10 to 20 number of classes. The values of design metrics namely, Encapsulation Metrics (DAM), Inheritance Metrics (MFA), Coupling Metrics (DCC) and Cohesion Metrics (CAM) and the values of "Effectiveness and Reusability" have been used. Using SPSS, math work software correlation coefficients are calculated and model of testability Estimation is thus formulated as given in Equation (5).

$$\text{Testability} = 59.524 - 4.671 \times \text{Effectiveness} + 0.806 \times \text{Reusability} \tag{5}$$

In **Table 2** the result of Model Summary is most helpful when performing multiple regressions. In this table, "R" is the multiple correlation coefficient that is used to know how strongly multiple independent variables are related to dependent variable. "R square" gives supportive coefficient of determination.

Table 2. Model summary.

Model	R	R Square	Adjusted R Square	Std. Error of the Estimate
1	0.851[a]	0.725	0.450	10.80129

a. Predictors: (Constant), Reusability, Effectiveness.

6. Validating the Developed Testability Estimation Model

The applications for case studies in validation process for the developed testability model (Equation (5)) have been taken from [24]. We labeled the applications as: Case Study A, Case Study B, Case Study C, and Case Study D. All the Case Studies are application software, developed in C++, shown in **Table 3(a)**.

The descriptive statistics of the output **Table 3(b)**, **Table 3(d)**, **Table 3(f)**, **Table 3(h)** for case study A, case study B, case study C, case study D respectively, give the valuable record of statistics that are mean, standard deviation and number of tests including 10 to 20 numbers of classes in each test. The correlation analysis tables namely **Table 3(c)**: Correlations Analysis for Case Study A, **Table 3(e)**: Correlations Analysis for Case Study B, **Table 3(g)**: Correlations Analysis for Case Study C and **Table 3(i)**: Correlations Analysis for Case Study D, give Pearson correlation analysis between testability and key factors. **Table 3(j)** concludes the result of the Pearson correlation analysis for testability estimation model, which shows that for all the projects, both Effectiveness and Reusability are strongly correlated with Testability. The value of Pearson correlation "r" lies between ±1. Positive value of "r" in **Table 3(j)**: shows positive correlation between the Testability and Effectiveness as well as Testability and Reusability. The values of "r" close to 1 specify high degree of correlation between them in **Table 3(j)**.

7. Empirical Validation of Developed Testability Model

Empirical validation of work proves that how significant developed model, where metrics and model are able to quantify the testability index of object oriented design in design stage. This validation is an essential phase of research to estimate the developed model for appropriate execution and high level acceptability. It is also the fine approach and practice for claiming the model acceptance. To justify claiming for acceptance of developed model, an experimental validation of the developed testability model at design phase has been carried out using tryout data [24]. In order to validate developed model, the value of metrics are available by using above data set for following projects in **Table 4**. Through experiment, testability index value of the projects has been computed using the developed model, followed by the computation of testability ranking. These computed rankings are then compared with the known ranking given by experts with Charles Speraman's Rank Coefficient of Correlation method.

Table 4, indicates a very important correlation between the calculated ranking and given ranking of testability estimation model, at the 0.01 for a 99% confidence interval.

- $r_s > 0.4815$ means significant results.
- Testability Estimation model had statistically significant rank correlations with 23 of 23 projects.

Charles Speraman's a Coefficient of Correlation r_s was applied to test the significance of correlation between Calculated Values of Testability model and its "Known Values". The "r_s" was calculated using the formula given by Speraman's Coefficient of Correlation

$$r_s = 1 - \frac{6\sum d^2}{n\left(n^2 - 1\right)} \qquad -1.0 \le r_s \le +1.0 \tag{6}$$

where
r_s is coefficient of Rank Correlation
d is the difference between calculated index values and known values of reusability.
n is the number of software projects for experiment. (In this research n = 23 software projects).
$\sum$ is notification symbol, significance "The Sum"

The correlation index values between testability obtained by developed model and expert ranking are shown in **Table 4**. Pairs of these index values with correlation values r_s [± 0.4815] are checked in correlation values **Table 4**. The correlations are good enough with high degree of confidence, which is up to 99%. Therefore; study

Table 3. (a): Case study group and projects; (b): Descriptive statistics for case study A; (c): Correlations analysis for case study A; (d): Descriptive statistics for case study B; (e): Correlations analysis for case study B; (f): Descriptive statistics for case study C; (g): Correlations analysis for case study C; (h): Descriptive statistics for case study D; (i): Correlations analysis for case study D; (j): Correlations analysis summary.

(a)

Case Study Group	Projects
Case Study A	4
Case Study B	5
Case Study C	4
Case Study D	4

(b)

	Minimum	Maximum	Mean
Testability	50.72	61.39	56.0475
Effectiveness	2.06	4.40	3.1034
Reusability	1.75	27.80	16.9501

(c)

	Testability	Effectiveness	Reusability
Testability	1	0.988	0.872
Effectiveness	0.988	1	0.902
Reusability	0.872	0.902	1

(d)

	Minimum	Maximum	Mean
Testability	22.66	26.10	24.7120
Effectiveness	5.20	19.20	10.9616
Reusability	−13.82	41.60	10.5418

(e)

	Testability	Effectiveness	Reusability
Testability	1	0.835	0.770
Effectiveness	0.835	1	0.994
Reusability	0.770	0.994	1

(f)

	Minimum	Maximum	Mean
Testability	50.72	61.39	56.0475
Effectiveness	2.06	4.40	3.1034
Reusability	12.00	27.80	19.5117

(g)

	Testability	Effectiveness	Reusability
Testability	1	0.988	0.971
Effectiveness	0.988	1	0.993
Reusability	0.971	0.993	1

(h)

	Minimum	Maximum	Mean
Testability	50.72	61.39	56.0475
Effectiveness	2.06	4.40	3.1034
Reusability	1.75	27.80	16.9501

(i)

	Testability	Effectiveness	Reusability
Testability	1	0.782	0.994
Effectiveness	0.782	1	0.820
Reusability	0.994	0.820	1

(j)

	Testability × Effectiveness	Testability × Reusability
Case Study A	0.988	0.872
Case Study B	0.835	0.770
Case Study C	0.988	0.971
Case Study D	0.782	0.994

Table 4. Calculated ranking, known ranking and their relation.

Projects	Testability Value		Testability Ranking		Σd^2	r_s	$r_s > 0.4815$
	Calculated Value	Known Value	Estimated Ranking	Known Ranking			
P1	51.31	5.8787	19	19	0	1.00	√
P2	50.72	7.7159	18	20	4	1.00	√
P3	60.77	9.1878	22	22	0	1.00	√
P4	61.39	9.5653	23	23	0	1.00	√
P5	59.61	9.1742	21	21	0	1.00	√
P6	20.25	2.2678	8	15	49	0.98	√
P7	23.57	2.615	12	16	16	0.99	√
P8	37.54	5.0134	17	17	0	1.00	√
P9	56.61	5.0223	20	18	4	1.00	√
P10	33.65	1.599	16	10	36	0.98	√
P11	16.74	1.176	4	3	1	1.00	√
P12	5.45	0.832	1	2	1	1.00	√
P13	7.13	1.49	2	6	16	0.99	√
P14	17.83	1.294	6	5	1	1.00	√
P15	19.31	1.772	7	11	16	0.99	√
P16	23.28	1.532	11	7	16	0.99	√
P 17	23.22	2.242	10	14	16	0.99	√
P18	17.17	2.242	5	13	64	0.97	√
P 19	16.38	1.577	3	9	36	0.98	√
P 20	26.02	1.547	15	8	49	0.98	√
P 21	24.08	1.243	13	4	81	0.96	√
P 22	22.66	2.041	9	12	9	1.00	√
P 23	24.74	0.5995	14	1	169	0.92	√

can conclude without any loss of generality that Testability Estimation Model, measures are highly reliable and significant at design phase.

8. Hypothesis Testing of Coefficient of Correlation

A practical coefficient of correlation of Effectiveness and Reusability with Testability strongly indicates the higher significance and importance of taking into consideration both the identified key factors (Effectiveness and Reusability) for making an evaluation of software testability at design phase. Moreover to justify the result, a test to compute the statistical importance of the correlation coefficient obtained possibly will be appropriate. A null hypothesis testing is applied to test the significance of Correlation Coefficient (r) using the given Equation (7):

$$t = \frac{r\sqrt{n-2}}{\sqrt{1-r^2}} \tag{7}$$

With $n - 2$ degree of freedom, a coefficient of correlation is evaluated as statistically important when the t value equals or exceeds the t critical value in the t distribution critical values.

H_0 (T^E): Testability and Effectiveness are not highly correlated.

H_0 (T^R): Testability and Reusability are not highly correlated.

Using 2-tailed test at the 0.05 for a 95% confidence interval with different degrees of freedom, it is clear from **Table 5(a)** and **Table 5(b)**, the null hypothesis is rejected (with the exception of, for Case Study "D" of "Testability and Effectiveness" and Case Study "A" of "Testability and Reusability"). As a result, the researcher's claim of correlating Testability with Effectiveness and Reusability at design phase is Statistically justified.

9. Key Contributions and Findings

This Study developed 'Metric Based Testability Estimation Model for Object Oriented Design: Quality Perspective'. The Model has been validated using the same set of try-out data. An empirical validation of the developed model is also performed using try-out data. Some of the major findings are as given below:

- Software testability has been recognized as a key factor to quality software, addressed in design phase of object oriented software development to produce quality software.

Table 5. (a): Correlation coefficient test for testability and effectiveness; (b): Correlation coefficient test for testability and reusability.

(a)

	Case Study A	Case Study B	Case Study C	Case Study D
Testability × Effectiveness	0.988	0.846	0.988	0.782
tr	9.046345	2.628374	9.046345	1.774351
tr-Critical Value	2.776	2.5706	2.776	2.776
tr > tr-Critical Value	√	√	√	×
H_0(T^E)	Reject	Reject	Reject	Accept

(b)

	Case Study A	Case Study B	Case Study C	Case Study D
Testability × Reuseability	0.872	0.770	0.951	0.994
tr	2.519263	2.90	5.743702	12.85178
tr-Critical Value	2.776	2.5706	2.776	2.776
tr > tr-Critical Value	×	√	√	√
H_0(T^R)	Accept	Reject	Reject	Reject

- Low level measures of each of the testability factors may be obtained.
- Software design constructs are most appropriate and power full for controlling software quality factors in design phase.
- There is a feasibility of establishing correlation between testability and other quality factors in the order to address them in design phase.
- Effectiveness and Reusability are identified as two major factors affecting software testability in designing phase.
- Testability indexing (TI) is possible using the model "Metric Based Testability Estimation Model for Object Oriented Design: Quality Perspective" for Industry project ranking.
- The models may be generalized and used by other researcher for making testability leveling of projects undertaken.

10. Conclusion

Software testability key factors namely effectiveness and reusability are identified and their significance on testability Estimation at design phase has been tested and justified. Testability Estimation model for object oriented design has been developed and the statistical inferences are validated for high level model acceptability. The developed model to evaluate testability of object oriented software is extremely consistent and correlated with object oriented design artifacts. Testability Estimation model has been validated theoretically as well as empirically using experimental test. That validation study on this research work proves that developed testability estimation model is highly acceptable, more practical in nature and helps the software industry in project ranking.

Acknowledgements

First and foremost, I would like to express my sincere gratitude to my supervisor Prof. Dr. YDS Arya & Co-supervisor Associate Prof. Dr. M H Khan for the continuous support of my PhD study and research, motivation, enthusiasm. Their guidance helped me in all the time of research. Last but not the least; I would like to thank my parent for their patience, understanding and support that drive me to complete my study.

References

[1]   Amin, A. and Moradi, S. (2013) A Hybrid Evaluation Framework of CMM and COBIT for Improving the Software Development Quality.

[2]   Binder, R.V. (1994) Design for Testability in Object-Oriented Systems. *Communications of the ACM*, **37**, 87-101. http://dx.doi.org/10.1145/182987.184077

[3]   Huda, M., Arya, Y.D.S. and Khan, M.H. (2015) Evaluating Effectiveness Factor of Object Oriented Design: A Testability Perspective. *International Journal of Software Engineering & Applications* (*IJSEA*), **6**, 41-49. http://dx.doi.org/10.5121/ijsea.2015.6104

[4]   Esposito, D. (2008) Design Your Classes for Testability. http://dotnetslackers.com/articles/nnet/Design-Your-Classes-for-Testability.aspx

[5]   Huda, M., Arya, Y.D.S. and Khan, M.H. (2015) Quantifying Reusability of Object Oriented Design: A Testability Perspective. *Journal of Software Engineering and Applications*, **8**, 175-183. http://dx.doi.org/10.4236/jsea.2015.84018

[6]   Zheng, W.Q. and Bundell, G. (2008) Contract-Based Software Component Testing with UML Models. *International Symposium on Computer Science and Its Applications* (*CSA '08*), 978-0-7695, 13-15 October 2008, 83-102.

[7]   Zhao, L. (2006) A New Approach for Software Testability Analysis. *Proceeding of the 28th International Conference on Software Engineering*, Shanghai, 985-988. http://dx.doi.org/10.1145/1134285.1134469

[8]   Huda, M., Arya, Y.D.S. and Khan, M.H. (2014) Measuring Testability of Object Oriented Design: A Systematic Review. *International Journal of Scientific Engineering and Technology* (*IJSET*), **3**, 1313-1319.

[9]   Huda, M., Arya, Y.D.S. and Khan, M.H. (2015) Testability Quantification Framework of Object Oriented Software: A New Perspective. *International Journal of Advanced Research in Computer and Communication Engineering*, **4**, 298-302. http://dx.doi.org/10.17148/IJARCCE.2015.4168

[10]   Gao, J. and Shih, M.-C. (2005) A Component Testability Model for Verification and Measurement. *Proceedings of the 29th Annual International Computer Software and Applications Conference*, Edinburgh, 26-28 July 2005, 211-218. http://dx.doi.org/10.1109/COMPSAC.2005.17

[11]   Lee, M.-C. (2014) Software Quality Factors and Software Quality Metrics to Enhance Software Quality Assurance.

British Journal of Applied Science & Technology, **4**, 3069-3095.

[12] Fu, J.P. and Lu, M.Y. (2009) Request-Oriented Method of Software Testability Measurement. *Proceedings of the ITCS 2009 International Conference on Information Technology and Computer Science*, Kiev, 25-26 July 2009, 77-80.

[13] IEEE Press (1990) IEEE Standard Glossary of Software Engineering Technology. ANSI/IEEE Standard 610.12-1990.

[14] Lo, B.W.N. and Shi, H.F. (1998) A Preliminary Testability Model for Object-Oriented Software. *Proceedings of the International Conference on Software Engineering, Education and Practice*, Dunedin, 29-29 January 1998, 330-337. http://dx.doi.org/10.1109/SEEP.1998.707667

[15] Badri, M. and Toure, F. (2012) Empirical Analysis of Object-Oriented Design Metrics for Predicting Unit Testing Effort of Classes. *Journal of Software Engineering and Applications*, **5**, 513-526. http://dx.doi.org/10.4236/jsea.2012.57060

[16] ISO (2001) ISO/IEC 9126-1: Software Engineering—Product Quality—Part-1: Quality Model. Geneva.

[17] Bach, J. (1999) Heuristics of Software Testability.

[18] Mulo, E. (2007) Design for Testability in Software Systems. Master's Thesis. http://swerl.tudelft.nl/twiki/pub/Main/ResearchAssignment/RA-Emmanuel-Mulo.pdf

[19] Mouchawrab, S., Briand, L.C. and Labiche, Y. (2005) A Measurement Framework for Object-Oriented Software Testability. *Information and Software Technology*, **47**, 979-997. http://dx.doi.org/10.1016/j.infsof.2005.09.003

[20] Jungmayr, S. (2002) Testability during Design, Softwaretechnik-Trends. *Proceedings of the GI Working Group Test, Analysis and Verification of Software*, Potsdam, 20-21 June 2002, 10-11.

[21] Bruntink, M. and Van Deursen, A. (2004) Predicting Class Testability Using Object-Oriented Metrics. *Proceedings of the Fourth IEEE International Workshop on Source Code Analysis and Manipulation*, Chicago, 15-16 September 2004, 136-145.

[22] Dromey, R.G. (1996) Concerning the Chimera (Software Quality). *IEEE Software*, **13**, 33-43. http://dx.doi.org/10.1109/52.476284

[23] Khan, R.A. and Mustafa, K. (2009) Metric Based Testability Model for Object Oriented Design (MTMOOD). *ACM SIGSOFT Software Engineering Notes*, **34**, 1-6.

[24] Bansiya, J. (2002) A Hierarchical Model for Object Oriented Design Quality Assessment. *IEEE Transaction on Software Engineering*, **28**, 4-17. http://dx.doi.org/10.1109/32.979986

Distributed C-Means Algorithm for Big Data Image Segmentation on a Massively Parallel and Distributed Virtual Machine Based on Cooperative Mobile Agents

Fatéma Zahra Benchara[1], Mohamed Youssfi[1], Omar Bouattane[1], Hassan Ouajji[1], Mohammed Ouadi Bensalah[2]

[1]Laboratory SSDIA, ENSET Mohammedia, University Hassan II of Casablanca, Casablanca, Morocco
[2]FSR, University Mohammed V, Rabat, Morocco
Email: benchara.fatemazahra@gmail.com, med@youssfi.net, o.bouattane@gmail.com

Abstract

The aim of this paper is to present a distributed algorithm for big data classification, and its application for Magnetic Resonance Images (MRI) segmentation. We choose the well-known classification method which is the c-means method. The proposed method is introduced in order to perform a cognitive program which is assigned to be implemented on a parallel and distributed machine based on mobile agents. The main idea of the proposed algorithm is to execute the c-means classification procedure by the Mobile Classification Agents (Team Workers) on different nodes on their data at the same time and provide the results to their Mobile Host Agent (Team Leader) which computes the global results and orchestrates the classification until the convergence condition is achieved and the output segmented images will be provided from the Mobile Classification Agents. The data in our case are the big data MRI image of size (m × n) which is splitted into (m × n) elementary images one per mobile classification agent to perform the classification procedure. The experimental results show that the use of the distributed architecture improves significantly the big data segmentation efficiency.

Keywords

Multi-Agent System, Distributed Algorithm, Big Data Image Segmentation, MRI Image, C-Means Algorithm, Mobile Agent

1. Introduction

Multi-agent system is the aim of several researchers and developers in order to design and implement some methods and solutions which improve existing methods and create new ones in order to achieve high performance results, save time and make the work easy in many domains. As examples, in the renewable energy domain [1] the authors proposed a method that parallelizes the procedure for detection of illegal consumers of electricity which can be improved by the use of a distributed architecture based on the multi-agent systems; and in web semantic domain [2] the authors proposed a novel model for automatic construction of business processes based on multi-agent systems. In the high performance computing domain, the authors in [3] proposed the use of this technology in order to improve the management, the flexibility and the reusability of grid like parallel computing architectures.

For each new technology or method, we can distinguish its straightness and weakness. That is the case of the researchers who start by analyzing these two items related to their field in order to propose and argue their ideas. As in [4], we start by analyzing the state of the art about the parallel computing strategies. We can say that the growth of number of data to be processed and the convergence of the applications from the standard to the distributed one make it necessary to use many cores of processors as a supercomputer. Due to the high cost of the supercomputers and the real parallel machines, it is feasible to use the parallel virtual machine as in [5] for specific work and [6] for global needs. It is based on a parallel and distributed grid computing that cooperates with the power of processors from heterogeneous computers by forming a distributed system for parallel computing. So it is possible to split tasks and data between them in order to reach the hoped level of high performance computing. But we do not need to forward the main component which is responsible of creating and managing the grid computing and also which supports the computing performance keys (load balancing, fault tolerance and communication cost) in the distributed system. As in [7] we propose a middleware for parallel and distributed computing which manipulates virtual processors (VPU objects) in different nodes of the grid. It is an innovated idea that was developed using the power of the multi-agent system.

In this paper, we propose a new method for big data classification which is a distributed c-means algorithm. It is based on different previous works and applied to MRI cerebral segmentation images in order to be implemented on a mobile agents' parallel and distributed virtual machine. In this case we use the power of multi-agent system especially the mobile agents to answer to the parallel computing challenges where some of them are presented in [8] with a critical way. So we need to use applications that can run the scalable parallel algorithms and ensure a high performance computing for different cases. As in [9] the authors showed the improvement of the time efficiency of a medical reasoning system using multi-agent architecture. In [10] the authors proposed a parallel and distributed model based on mobile agent for high performance computing where we implemented the distributed c-means algorithm for MRI cerebral images segmentation.

Big data image segmentation is an analyzing image strategy which is emerged especially in the medicine domain using different algorithm specifications where the execution of the programs is based especially on the parallel computing strategy in order to achieve effective results. In this case we choose to test by the c-means classification algorithm to implement it on different parallel architectures. In [11], the authors proposed a method that subdivided the c-means program into several elementary operations which were organized in pipeline structure. In [12], the authors have proposed an optimal clustering solution based on a reconfigurable array of processors, while in [13] the authors proposed a SIMD parallel segmentation c-means algorithm.

The proposed method in this paper is a distributed c-means algorithm for big data classification; it is assigned to be implemented on a parallel and distributed virtual machine based on mobile agents. The corresponding distributed program is validated on a multi-agent system platform using the JADE middleware and an extensible and flexible smart grid computing of the same size as the input image. This paper is organized as follows: the second section makes an overview of the distributed computational model. Section 3 presents the distributed c-means algorithm while Section 4 is focused on the results concluded by implementing this distributed c-means algorithm. The last section presents some interesting obtained results and the effectiveness, and some perspectives of this work.

2. Distributed Computational Model

2.1. Model Overview

A cooperative multi-agent platform is a massively parallel and distributed virtual machine where the mobile agents which represent the Processing Elements (PEs) are involved in the execution of the parallel programs on different structures (SIMD, SPMD, MIMD…) and topologies (2D Mesh, 3D Mesh, hierarchical…) according to the parallel problem to resolve.

In this work we implement the well known algorithm for big data image segmentation which is the c-means algorithm as a distributed program on this model by using SPMD structure. The main components which are engaged to perform the execution of this program are the host agent and the team worker agents that are designed to play the roles introduced in **Figure 1**.

2.2. Intelligent Mobile Agents Grid Computing

This model is based on an intelligent grid computing organized as a bidimensional 2D mesh topology (**Figure 2**) of size m × n, in which each mobile agent MPE (Mobile Processing Element) is localized in row *i* and column *j* and has an AID (Agent Identifier). **Figure 2** shows an example of (2 × 2) workers machines hosted by M0. All the agents (*i*, *j*) in the mesh execute their tasks autonomously and maintain asynchronous communication by exchanging ACL (Agent Communication Language) Messages between each other over the grid computing. In order to achieve a high performance computing of the big data image segmentation, it is important to deploy the large amount of skills of these agents, as:

1) Autonomy: each mobile agent can perform, image classification autonomously. It can extend its activities to make the diagnostic on images and generates reports and data for eventual decisions.

2) Adaptability: it can execute its tasks in different environments with the same performance as in the environment where it was created.

3) Mobility: it can move from one machine to another and resume its tasks if some parallel computing challenges happen.

4) Asynchronous communication ability: it can exchange data, tasks and knowledge using ACL message in remote or local communication.

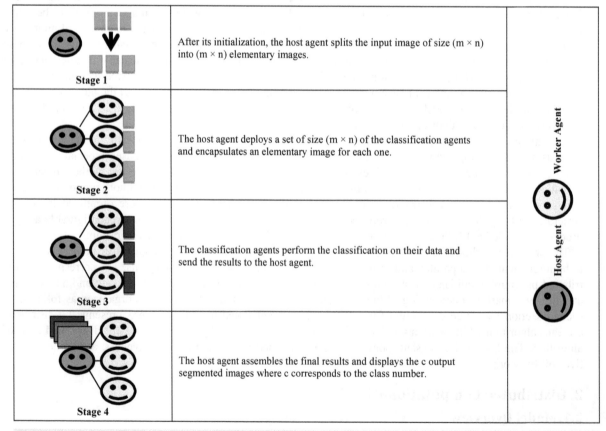

Figure 1. Overview of the main goal of the model.

3. Distributed Segmentation Algorithm

3.1. Standard C-Means Algorithm

The c-means algorithm as defined in [13], is an image segmentation algorithm which consists on a partitioned groups of set S of n attribute vectors into c classes (clusters C_i $i = 1, \cdots, c$). In this algorithm [13] authors used the pixel gray level as the main classification attribute. The finale goal is to find the class centers (centroïd) that minimize the cost function J defined by the following equation: $J = \sum_{i=1}^{c} J_i = \sum_{i=1}^{c} \sum_{k \in Ci} d(x_k, c_i)$. To do so, we have to execute the different equations, given in **Table 1**.

The c-means classification is achieved using the following algorithm stages which are summarized in **Figure 3**.

3.2. Distributed C-Means Algorithm

In this section, we present our distributed implementation of the c-means algorithm on a cooperative multi-agent platform using the 2D mesh architecture of the same size as the input image (MRI cerebral image of 256 gray levels). MRI images are stored on a cooperative multi-agent platform one pixel per agent. In order to perform the distributed c-means classification of the image in this model we need to perform the following three global stages as shown in **Figure 4**.

1) Host agent initialization: when our segmentation platform goes on. The host agent is the first one created, and initialized by the size of the data image which is in our case (m × n).

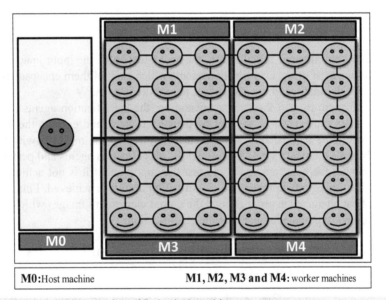

| **M0:** Host machine | **M1, M2, M3 and M4:** worker machines |

Figure 2. 2D mesh mobile agent grid computing of 5 physical machines.

Table 1. The different equations needed for the classification c-means.

Equation number	Equation	Description
1	$J = \sum_{i=1}^{c} J_i = \sum_{i=1}^{c} \left(\sum_{k \in Ci} \|x_k - c_i\|^2 \right)$	The objective function defined by the Euclidean distance (distance between i^{th} center c_i and the kth data of S).
2	$u_{ij} = \begin{cases} 1 \ if \ \|x_k - c_i\|^2 \leq \|x_k - c_k\|^2, \forall k \neq i, \\ 0 \ Otherwise \end{cases}$	The membership matrix element where $i = 1$ to c, $j = 1$ to n, for a total number n of points in S. It has two properties: $\sum_{i=1}^{c} u_{ij=1}, \forall j = 1, \cdots, n$ $\sum_{i=1}^{c} \sum_{j=1}^{n} u_{ij} = n$
3	$c_i = \frac{1}{|C_i|} \sum_{k, (x_k \in C_i)} x_k$	The class center where $i = 1$ to c by the average of all its attribute vectors and $|C_i|$ is the cardinal of C_i.

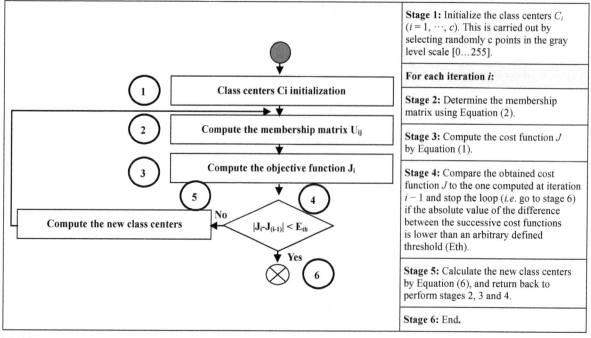

The flowchart and stage descriptions shown include:

1 — Class centers Ci initialization	**Stage 1:** Initialize the class centers C_i ($i = 1, \cdots, c$). This is carried out by selecting randomly c points in the gray level scale $[0\ldots255]$.
2 — Compute the membership matrix U_{ij}	**For each iteration i:**
	Stage 2: Determine the membership matrix using Equation (2).
3 — Compute the objective function J_i	**Stage 3:** Compute the cost function J by Equation (1).
4 — $\|J_i\text{-}J_{(i\text{-}1)}\| < E_{th}$	**Stage 4:** Compare the obtained cost function J to the one computed at iteration $i - 1$ and stop the loop (*i.e.* go to stage 6) if the absolute value of the difference between the successive cost functions is lower than an arbitrary defined threshold (Eth).
5 — Compute the new class centers (No)	**Stage 5:** Calculate the new class centers by Equation (6), and return back to perform stages 2, 3 and 4.
6 — ⊗ (Yes)	**Stage 6:** End.

Figure 3. Standard classification c-means stages.

2) Grid construction: just after the initialization, the host agent splits the input image into (m × n) elementary images and then deploys a list of the classification agents which each of them encapsulates an elementary image and moves to a specific destination where it supposes to execute it tasks.

3) C-means classification: to start the data segmentation, the classification agents process, the classification tasks and the initial class centers which are sent by their host agent, and execute the local class determination task in order to compute the membership matrix. Then they replay the message with the results to their host agent which assembles the elementary results from all the classification agents and performs the global class determination and computes the cost function J and test the condition. If it is not achieved, it sends a new class centers to the classification agents to repeat the classification until it is achieved. Finally the host agent sends a request to the classification agents in order to send the output elementary images which will be assembled in order to display the c output segmented images for the classification.

4. Distributed C-Means Algorithm Implementation and Results

4.1. Multi-Agent System Middleware

This cooperative and intelligent platform is a distributed and parallel virtual machine on which we implemented the image segmentation algorithm according to the model of **Figure 5**. It is based especially on the JADE middleware [14] and on the mobile agent skills.

Thanks to the JADE middleware, we prepare the platform where we run the parallel and distributed c-means program. The main components of this model are:

- The main container: it is the first container which starts in the platform and which is different from the others by its two special agents (the AMS agent and the DF agent). It connects all the performed containers in the platform.
- The host container: is the second container that is started in the platform where the host agent is created in order to manage the required infrastructure and computational inside in the physical grid computing.
- The agent containers: the free containers are started in the platform to receive groups of the classification agents so that each group can execute its classification tasks.

In a multi-agent system, we distinguish the mobile agents that have interesting and additional skill from the other agents which is the ability to migrate between nodes. It is considered the one key of the high performance computing and it fit well with our main goal.

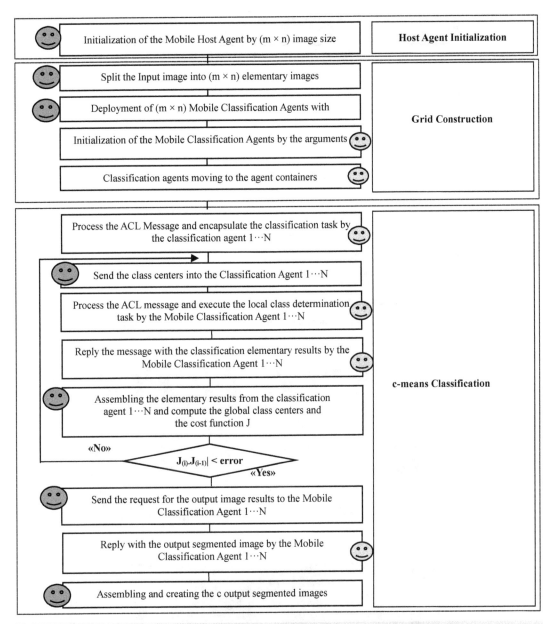

Figure 4. Distributed c-means program execution organization chart.

The mobile agents are considered as Processing Elements (PEs) which encapsulate tasks and data in order to achieve the parallel programs execution. So they are independent inside their containers, where they are deployed, in order to stay or move to the most suitable environment to achieve perfectly their tasks. They have the ability to communicate between each other asynchronously by exchanging ACL messages. Thanks to the high performance of the mobile agent we can take strong control about all the parallel computing challenges: load balancing, fault tolerance and communication cost. This allows us to constitute a cooperative and intelligent grid for high performance computing.

4.2. Implementation and Results

This part presents the implementation of the proposed distributed c-means program in our cooperative platform according to the organization chart presented in **Figure 4** using the MRI cerebral image. We obtain the following results: the **Figure 6(a)** corresponds to a human cerebral cut; it is the original input image of the program which is split into (m × n) elementary images as in **Figure 6(b)**. And the **Figures 6(c)-(e)**, are the segmented

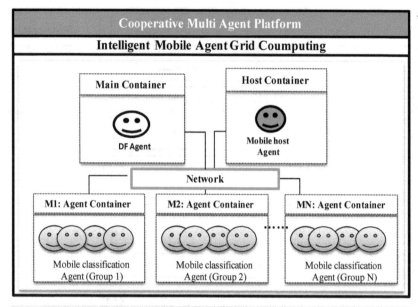

Figure 5. Distributed computational model architecture for c-means classification.

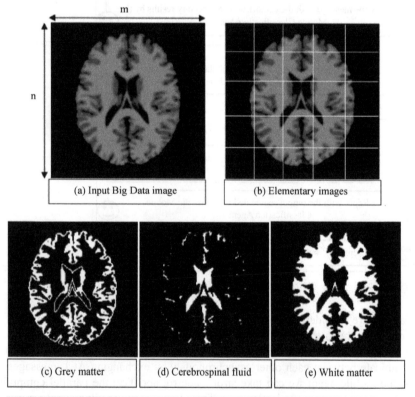

Figure 6. Segmentation results by the elaborated distributed program.

output images where each of them corresponds to a specific class: the gray matter, the cerebrospinal fluid and the white matter.

The effectiveness features of this distributed method for data image classification is shown under these three cases of studies for dynamic convergence analysis and time classification analysis under the fourth case.

1) $(c_1, c_2, c_3) = (1, 2, 3)$ where we see clearly in **Table 2** the convergence of the algorithm after 15 iterations to the final class centers $(c_1, c_2, c_3) = (28.60, 101.60, 146.03)$ and which are illustrated in **Figure 7**.

Table 2. Different states of the classification algorithm starting from class centers $(c_1, c_2, c_3) = (1, 2, 3)$.

Iteration	Value of each class center			Absolute value of the error
	c_1	c_2	c_3	$\left| J_n - J_{n-1} \right|$
1	1.00	2.00	3.00	4.96E+06
2	1.00	2.00	120.14	4.42E+06
3	1.00	33.86	129.57	3.26E+06
4	4.38	51.91	132.04	1.33E+06
5	6.15	58.40	133.23	1.50E+05
6	7.14	60.05	133.43	5.36E+04
7	7.14	65.14	134.44	2.34E+05
8	16.70	72.44	134.64	9.02E+05
9	21.49	90.47	141.16	2.76E+06
10	24.68	93.37	142.41	1.24E+05
11	28.60	95.44	142.42	7.92E+04
12	28.60	96.71	142.98	1.02E+05
13	28.60	100.94	145.51	2.41E+05
14	28.60	101.60	146.03	5.64E+03
15	28.60	101.60	146.03	0.00E+00

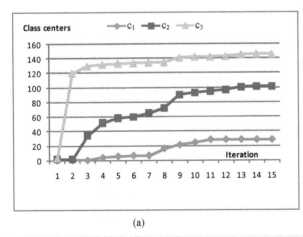

(a)

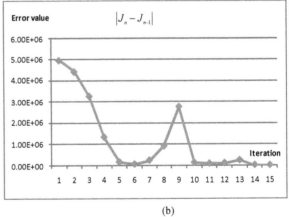

(b)

Figure 7. Dynamic changes of the class centers starting from $(c_1, c_2, c_3) = (1, 2, 3)$. (a) Class centers; (b) Error of the objective function.

2) $(c_1, c_2, c_3) = (1, 30, 255)$ where the algorithm converges to the same final class centers of the case 1 $(c_1, c_2, c_3) = (28.60, 101.60, 146.03)$ after 5 iterations as shown in **Table 3** and which are illustrated in **Figure 8**.

3) $(c_1, c_2, c_3) = (140, 149, 255)$ where the algorithm converges to the final class centers $(c_1, c_2, c_3) = (33.37, 103.50, 146.03)$ after 10 iterations as shown in **Table 4** which are illustrated in **Figure 9**.

In **Figure 10**, we present the variation of the classification time according to the number of agents involved in the computing using the initial class centers $(1, 2, 3)$.

In this experience, the used distributed system is composed by 8 CPUs. We notice that the execution time is decreasing according to the number of classification agents. From 8 agents, the classification time saved become very small. This is due to the fact that the distributed system is composed of 8 CPUs.

Table 3. Different states of the classification algorithm starting from class centers $(c_1, c_2, c_3) = (1, 30, 255)$.

Iteration	Value of each class center			Absolute value of the Error
	c_1	c_2	c_3	$\left| J_n - J_{n-1} \right|$
1	1.00	30.00	255.00	1.47E+08
2	4.32	102.35	151.79	1.43E+08
3	24.68	100.37	146.29	1.42E+06
4	28.60	101.60	146.03	4.53E+04
5	28.60	101.60	146.03	0.00E+00

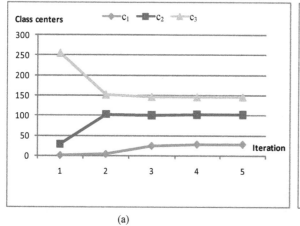
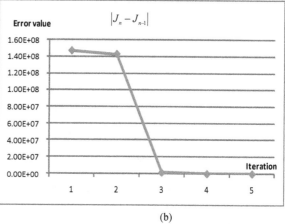

(a)   (b)

Figure 8. Dynamic changes of the class centers starting from $(c_1, c_2, c_3) = (1, 30, 255)$. (a) Class centers; (b) Error of the objective function.

Table 4. Different states of the classification algorithm starting from class centers $(c_1, c_2, c_3) = (140, 149, 150)$.

Iteration	Value of each class center			Absolute value of the error
	c_1	c_2	c_3	$\left| J_n - J_{n-1} \right|$
1	140.00	149.00	150.00	4.01E+07
2	95.62	148.99	151.95	2.65E+07
3	82.13	140.26	152.83	3.72E+06
4	73.36	127.72	151.79	1.81E+06
5	51.98	117.99	151.79	3.41E+06
6	40.07	114.55	151.15	7.80E+05
7	34.22	107.44	147.88	6.90E+05
8	33.37	104.04	146.29	1.21E+05
9	33.37	103.50	146.03	2.45E+03
10	33.37	103.50	146.03	0.00E+00

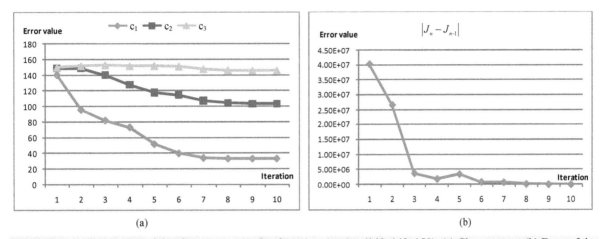

(a) (b)

Figure 9. Dynamic changes of the class centers starting from $(c_1, c_2, c_3) = (140, 149, 150)$. (a) Class centers; (b) Error of the objective function.

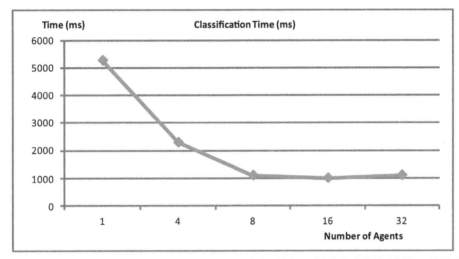

Figure 10. Time of classification (Tc) depending on the number of agents and with initial class centers $(c_1, c_2, c_3) = (1, 2, 3)$.

5. Conclusion

In this paper, we have presented the distributed c-means classification algorithm and its implementation on a cooperative platform based on mobile agents. We considered a new method that allows us to distribute the c-means algorithm and encapsulate its program in mobile agents. In order to execute the parallel programs in our grid computing, the data are splitted and the program instructions are shared between the mobile agents. We considered a segmentation application algorithm on MRI cerebral image which is performed on this new cooperative multi-agent platform. The obtained results show that we can reduce the complexity of the parallel programs thanks to the benefits of mobile agents. Moreover, it contributes to overcoming the big data challenges and offers a high-performance computing tool using multi-agent system. This cooperative agent platform is flexible and extensible for parallel algorithms trends.

References

[1]   Depuru, S.S.S.R., Wang, L.F., Devabhaktuni, V. and Green, R.C. (2013) High Performance Computing for Detection of Electricity Theft. *International Journal of Electrical Power & Energy Systems*, **47**, 21-30.
      http://dx.doi.org/10.1016/j.ijepes.2012.10.031

[2]   Coria, J.A.G., Castellanos-Garzón, J.A. and Corchado, J.M. (2014) Intelligent Business Processes Composition Based on Multi-Agent Systems. *Expert Systems with Applications*, **41**, 1189-1205.
      http://dx.doi.org/10.1016/j.eswa.2013.08.003

[3]   Sánchez, D., Isern, D., Rodríguez-Rozas, Á. and Moreno, A. (2011) Agent-Based Platform to Support the Execution of Parallel Tasks. *Expert Systems with Applications*, **38**, 6644-6656. http://dx.doi.org/10.1016/j.eswa.2010.11.073

[4]   El-Rewini, H. and Abd-El-Barr, M. (2005) Advanced Computer Architecture and Parallel Processing. Wiley, Hoboken.

[5]   Migliardi, M., Baglietto, P. and Maresca, M. (1998) Virtual Parallelism Allows Relaxing the Synchronization Constraints of SIMD Computing Paradigm. *High-Performance Computing and Networking Lecture Notes in Computer Science*, **1401**, 784-793. http://dx.doi.org/10.1007/BFb0037206

[6]   Youssfi, M., Bouattane, O. and Bensalah, M.O. (2010) On the Object Modelling of the Massively Parallel Architecture Computers. *IASTED International Conference on Software Engineering*, Innsbruck, 71-78.

[7]   Youssfi, M., Bouattane, O., Benchara, F.Z. and Bensalah, M.O. (2014) A Fast Middleware for Massively Parallel and Distributed Computing. *International Journal of Research in Computer and Communication Technology*, **3**, 429-435.

[8]   Hwu, W.-M. (2014) What Is Ahead for Parallel Computing. *Journal of Parallel and Distributed Computing*, **74**, 2574-2581. http://dx.doi.org/10.1007/BFb0037206

[9]   Rodríguez-González, A., Torres-Niño, J., Hernández-Chan, G., Jiménez-Domingo, E. and Alvarez-Rodríguez, J.M. (2012) Using Agents to Parallelize a Medical Reasoning System Based on Ontologies and Description Logics as an Application Case. *Expert Systems with Applications*, **39**, 13085-13092. http://dx.doi.org/10.1016/j.eswa.2012.05.093

[10] Benchara, F.Z., Youssfi, M., Bouattane, O., Ouajji, H. and Bakkoury, J. (2014) A Fast Middleware of Parallel and Distributed Virtual Machine Based on Mobile Agents for High Performance Computing. *Proceedings of CMT*14, Morocco, 260-263.

[11] Ni, L.M. and Jain, A.K. (1985) A VLSI Systolic Architecture for Pattern Clustering. *IEEE Transaction on Pattern Analysis and Machine Intelligence*, **PAMI-7**, 80-89. http://dx.doi.org/10.1109/TPAMI.1985.4767620

[12] Tsai, H.R. and Horng, S.J. (1999) Optimal Parallel Clustering Algorithms on a Reconfigurable Array of Processors with Wider Bus Networks. *Image and Vision Computing*, **17**, 925-936. http://dx.doi.org/10.1016/S0262-8856(98)00167-X

[13] Bouattane, O., Cherradi, B., Youssfi, M. and Bensalah, M.O. (2011) Parallel Cmeans Algorithm for Image Segmentation on a Reconfigurable Mesh Computer. *Parallel Computing*, **37**, 230-243. http://dx.doi.org/10.1016/j.parco.2011.03.001

[14] Padgham, L. and Winikoff, M. (2004) Developing Intelligent Agent Systems. Wiley, Hoboken. http://dx.doi.org/10.1002/0470861223

Permissions

All chapters in this book were first published in JSEA, by Scientific Research Publishing; hereby published with permission under the Creative Commons Attribution License or equivalent. Every chapter published in this book has been scrutinized by our experts. Their significance has been extensively debated. The topics covered herein carry significant findings which will fuel the growth of the discipline. They may even be implemented as practical applications or may be referred to as a beginning point for another development.

The contributors of this book come from diverse backgrounds, making this book a truly international effort. This book will bring forth new frontiers with its revolutionizing research information and detailed analysis of the nascent developments around the world.

We would like to thank all the contributing authors for lending their expertise to make the book truly unique. They have played a crucial role in the development of this book. Without their invaluable contributions this book wouldn't have been possible. They have made vital efforts to compile up to date information on the varied aspects of this subject to make this book a valuable addition to the collection of many professionals and students.

This book was conceptualized with the vision of imparting up-to-date information and advanced data in this field. To ensure the same, a matchless editorial board was set up. Every individual on the board went through rigorous rounds of assessment to prove their worth. After which they invested a large part of their time researching and compiling the most relevant data for our readers.

The editorial board has been involved in producing this book since its inception. They have spent rigorous hours researching and exploring the diverse topics which have resulted in the successful publishing of this book. They have passed on their knowledge of decades through this book. To expedite this challenging task, the publisher supported the team at every step. A small team of assistant editors was also appointed to further simplify the editing procedure and attain best results for the readers.

Apart from the editorial board, the designing team has also invested a significant amount of their time in understanding the subject and creating the most relevant covers. They scrutinized every image to scout for the most suitable representation of the subject and create an appropriate cover for the book.

The publishing team has been an ardent support to the editorial, designing and production team. Their endless efforts to recruit the best for this project, has resulted in the accomplishment of this book. They are a veteran in the field of academics and their pool of knowledge is as vast as their experience in printing. Their expertise and guidance has proved useful at every step. Their uncompromising quality standards have made this book an exceptional effort. Their encouragement from time to time has been an inspiration for everyone.

The publisher and the editorial board hope that this book will prove to be a valuable piece of knowledge for researchers, students, practitioners and scholars across the globe.

List of Contributors

Ziyue Liu and Fuzhong Wang
Department of Physics, Tianjin Polytechnic University, Tianjin, China

Mohamed Sayed
Faculty of Computer Studies, Arab Open University, Kuwait City, Kuwait
On Leave from Faculty of Engineering, Alexandria University, Alexandria, Egypt

Faris Baker
Faculty of Computer Studies, Arab Open University, Kuwait City, Kuwait

Wilhelm Hasselbring
Software Engineering Group, Department of Computer Science, Kiel University, Kiel, Germany

Fadi M. Al-Ghawanmeh
Music Department, University of Jordan, Amman, Jordan

Zaid R. Shannak
SRS International, Amman, Jordan

Mihai-Octavian Dima
Institute for Physics and Nuclear Engineering, Bucharest, Romania

Dima Suleiman and Mariam Itriq
Department of Business Information Technology, King Abdullah II School for Information Technology, The University of Jordan, Amman, Jordan

Aseel Al-Anani, Rola Al-Khalid and Amjad Hudaib
Department of Computer Information Systems, King Abdullah II School for Information Technology, The University of Jordan, Amman, Jordan

Junjie Zhou, Xingdong Zhang and Chunxiao Xiu
Key Laboratory of Geo-Detection (China University of Geosciences, Beijing), Ministry of Education, Beijing, China
School of Geophysics and Information Technology, China University of Geosciences, Beijing, China

Lama Rajab, Heba Z. Al-Lahham and Fatima Obaidat
The University of Jordan, Amman, Jordan

Raja S. Alomari and Vipin Chaudhary
The University at Buffalo, Buffalo, USA

Mahfuzul Huda and Yagya Dutt Sharma Arya
Department of Computer Science & Engineering, Invertis University, Bareilly, India

Mahmoodul Hasan Khan
Department of Computer Science and Engineering, IET, Lucknow, India

Amjad Hudaib, Rola Al-Khalid and Aseel Al-Anani
Department of Computer Information Systems, King Abdullah II School for Information Technology, The University of Jordan, Amman, Jordan

Mariam Itriq and Dima Suleiman
Department of Business Information Technology, King Abdullah II School for Information Technology, The University of Jordan, Amman, Jordan

Doha Malki and Mohamed Bahaj
Department of Mathematics and Computer Science, University Hassan 1st, Settat, Morocco

Yousef Kh. Majdalawi, Tamara Almarabeh, Hiba Mohammad and Wala Quteshate
Department of Computer Information Systems, King Abdullah II School for Information Technology, The University of Jordan, Amman, Jordan

Moupojou Matango Emmanuel
Department of Computer Science, University of Yaounde 1, Yaounde, Cameroon

Moukouop Nguena Ibrahim
National Advanced School of Engineering, Department of Computer Science, University of Yaounde 1, Yaounde, Cameroon

Dan Zhao, Li Miao and Dafang Zhang
College of Information Science and Engineering, Changsha, China

Amjad Hudaib, Fawaz Al-Zaghoul, Maha Saadeh and Huda Saadeh
Department of Computer Information Systems, King Abdullah II for Information Technology Department, The University of Jordan, Amman, Jordan

Yunfeng Hou, Chaoli Wang and Yunfeng Ji
Department of Control Science and Engineering, University of Shanghai for Science and Technology, Shanghai, China

Thair Hamtini, Shahd Albasha and Marwa Varoca
Department of Computer Information Systems, University of Jordan, Amman, Jordan

Ammar Huneiti and Maisa Daoud
Department of Computer Information Systems, the University of Jordan, Amman, Jordan

Naseer Ahmad, Muhammad Waqas Boota and Abdul Hye Masoom
Department of Computer Science, Virtual University of Pakistan, Lahore, Pakistan

Nadeem Akhtar and Muhammad Nauman
Department of Computer Science and IT, The Islamia University of Bahawalpur, Baghdad-ul-Jadeed Campus, Bahawalpur, Pakistan

Deepa Gangwani
Research Scholar, Banasthali University, Rajasthan, India

Saurabh Mukherjee
Department of Computer Science, Banasthali University, Rajasthan, India

Lama Rajab and Tahani Al-Khatib
Computer Information Systems, The University of Jordan, Amman, Jordan

Ali Al-Haj
Princess Sumaya University for Technology, Amman, Jordan

Nazeeh Ghatasheh
Department of Business Information Technology, The University of Jordan, Aqaba, Jordan

Hossam Faris, Ibrahim Aljarah and Rizik M. H. Al-Sayyed
Department of Business Information Technology, The University of Jordan, Amman, Jordan

Basim H. Alahmadi
Madinah College of Technology, Madinah, KSA

Sulieman Bani-Ahmad
Department of Computer Information Systems, Faculty of Information Technology, Al-Balqa Applied University, Salt, Jordan

Mahfuzul Huda and Yagya Dutt Sharma Arya
Department of Computer Science & Engineering, Invertis University, Bareilly, India

Mahmoodul Hasan Khan
Department of Computer Science and Engineering, IET, Lucknow, India

Fatéma Zahra Benchara, Mohamed Youssfi, Omar Bouattane and Hassan Ouajji
Laboratory SSDIA, ENSET Mohammedia, University Hassan II of Casablanca, Casablanca, Morocco

Mohammed Ouadi Bensalah
FSR, University Mohammed V, Rabat, Morocco

CPSIA information can be obtained
at www.ICGtesting.com
Printed in the USA
LVHW011031070523
746328LV00005B/564